Canadian

INTERNATIONAL

Relations

Canadian
INTERNATIONAL
Relations

DANIEL MADAR

BROCK UNIVERSITY

Prentice Hall Allyn and Bacon Canada
Scarborough, Ontario

Canadian Cataloguing in Publication Data

Madar, Daniel R., 1941–
    Canadian international relations

Includes index.
ISBN 0-13-080030-9

1. International relations. 2. Canada—Foreign relations. I. Title.

JZ1305.M32 2000   327   C99-930227-2

Prentice-Hall, Inc., Upper Saddle River, New Jersey
Prentice-Hall International (UK) Limited, London
Prentice-Hall of Australia, Pty. Limited, Sydney
Prentice-Hall Hispanoamericana, S.A., Mexico City
Prentice-Hall of India Private Limited, New Delhi
Prentice-Hall of Japan, Inc., Tokyo
Simon & Schuster Asia Private Limited, Singapore
Editora Prentice-Hall do Brasil, Ltda., Rio de Janeiro

ISBN 0-13-080030-9

Vice President, Editorial Director: Laura Pearson
Acquisitions Editor: Dawn Lee
Art Director: Mary Opper
Developmental Editor: Laura Paterson Forbes
Production Editor: Matthew Christian
Copy Editor: Donna Lubin Goldman
Production Coordinator: Wendy Moran
Marketing Manager: Christine Cozens
Cover Design: Julia Hall
Cover Image: David Rigg/Tony Stone Images

1 2 3 4 5 WEB 04 03 02 01 00

Printed and bound in Canada.

Visit the Prentice Hall Canada Web site! Send us your comments, browse our catalogues, and
more. **www.phcanada.com** Or reach us through e-mail at **phabinfo_pubcanada@prenhall.com**

To Dori, Heather, Andrew and James

Table *of* Contents

Preface

One of the most appealing qualities of International Relations (IR) is that it is open to new concepts. Some of that open-mindedness is due to the breadth of concerns of IR, concerns that range across the full expanse of human organization. Some is also due to the changing nature of international phenomena. Conceptual understandings of IR were tested by the end of the cold war. The profession's response has been adaptive and occasionally ingenious. For people wanting to keep up with the rapid and significant changes in IR, conceptual sophistication has been almost unavoidable. For people who enjoy variety and contention, these have been unusually good times.

The primary aims of this text are to be conceptually sophisticated, contemporary and Canadian. Conceptual sophistication can be learned. It is a lasting asset for students who include introductory IR courses in a broader program of undergraduate arts and social science, and it is a valuable preparation for students who continue with IR at the senior undergraduate and graduate levels. Concepts must be presented in full for these benefits to appear. Textbooks that provide only brief introductions and sporadic references leave incomplete impressions and little understanding of concepts at work. By focusing on the main theories of IR at the outset and by applying them throughout, the author aims for a more comprehensive understanding of the material presented.

With 1990s scholarship animating some static and cheerless topics—sovereignty, for one—being current has its appeal as well, and the Canadian experience has the attraction of immediacy. How immediate that experience can be is shown by Ontario's transformed position in North America's economy—a highlight in the chapter on globalization.

Conceptual sophistication, currency and a Canadian focus have a more general purpose: to make textbooks engaging to read. The nature of IR itself performs much of that task. In fact, it allows us to devote the first section to theory where assumptions and implications are interesting in their own right.

Features of this Book

This text is divided into four major sections. The individual chapters in the four sections are self-contained and stand independently. They can be arranged in sequences to suit particular course designs. Canadian examples are featured in every chapter. A few examples are: Trudeau's peace initiative, the Turbot War, dependency analysis and Canadian political economy and a security audit of Canada. No single conceptual approach is favoured. Instead, theories are presented in light of the phenomena they emphasize and the assumptions they make. These juxtapositions invite students to compare and consider what the theories show.

Section One, Theory, puts the main theories of IR in the forefront. Chapter 1, Neorealism and Institutionalism, presented in Chapter 2, frame much of the IR literature and are the clearest efforts to apply rationalist approaches. Chapter 3, Liberal IR Theory, addresses states and societies. Chapter 4, Constructivism, seeks to incorporate subjective elements in a coherent way. Chapter 5, Critical Theory, Postmodernism and Feminism, discusses how these approaches employ divergent epistemologies toward separate ends. Emphasis in this section is placed on origins, main tenets and views of the international world. Each chapter contains tables that summarize and compare the main tenets. The chapters are substantial enough to deliver adequate background and explanation but concise enough to retain momentum. To apply each theory while it is still fresh, the chapters in Section One conclude with a brief Canadian Reality Check, which shows how the theory just presented treats Canada's decision to enter a free trade agreement with the United States—arguably one of this country's most pivotal episodes.

The chapters following Section One address specific issues. In these chapters, the theories are highlighted in text boxes to keep them continually in view and to show how they address the issues at hand. Theories are featured when they have distinctive things to show. For example:

➤ Neorealism frames some of the book's discussion of threats and safety, but it also addresses mercantilist trade policies and the security dilemmas created by civil conflict.

➤ Constructivism speaks to the effectiveness of international norms but also to European integration and the coherence of member states.

➤ Critical Theory provides a frame of reference for dependency analysis but also applies a global perspective to armaments in the developing world.

➤ Postmodernism and Feminism illuminate national identity.

➤ Postmodernism also addresses international norms, and Feminism treats hospitality to foreign investment as a personal metaphor.

Section Two, Territoriality and Identity, contains individual chapters on sovereignty, identity and nationhood (Chapter 6), ethnic identity (Chapter 7), globalization (Chapter 8) and government and foreign policy (Chapter 9). Sovereignty is discussed in light of its historical evolution and current practice, highlighting the origins of Canada's boundaries, de Gaulle's Centennial visit to Canada and the development of Canadian sovereignty. Ethnicity and national unity are treated in light of theories of national mobilization, political modernization and civil conflict. Globalization's origins are also explained, and the nature of transnational economic activity and implications for governance are emphasized. Government and foreign policy are discussed in light of state structure, the reconciliation of preferences, the role of institutions and public sentiment.

Section Three, Security, contains individual chapters on sources of peril (Chapter 10) and sources of safety (Chapter 11). Threats are examined in reference to the security dilemma, offensive and defensive postures, and intentions. Safety is framed as location, the ability to affect preferences and collective measures.

Section Four, Wealth, Human Rights and the Environment, discusses sources of wealth presented in mercantilist, dependency and liberal perspectives as well as critiques of these perspectives (Chapter 12). Human rights and the environment are discussed within the framework of international law (Chapter 13).

A Note to the Instructor

To those who have been involved in IR for a while, the outpouring of new literature in the 1990s was particularly impressive. It brought together insights from the broader social sciences, philosophical awareness and a cogent understanding of method and proof. One reads this literature with an appreciation of the personal repertoires it reflects. Some of the most original work has been from younger scholars. This literature can also be seen as a maturing of long efforts in the field to extend conceptual reach and sharpen logical structure. The results are not complete, but the progress is remarkable. This book was written from that appreciative standpoint.

To people who have recently begun teaching a course in introductory IR, this is a chance to share a fresh experience with students who are just forming their impressions of the field. For those instructors in particular, this book makes continuous reference to the conceptual literature of IR, almost always to work that has appeared since 1993. The direct quotations and endnotes are instrumental: they show what the recent literature *does*.

IR instructors in Canada have long understood the need for a textbook that takes Canada as its point of reference. When a Canadian example is particularly important for students to know or when it is particularly illustrative, it is highlighted. Discussing theory in terms of examples and experiences familiar to Canadian students cannot help but be useful. For example: the chapter on trade and economic relations highlights John A. Macdonald's National Policy, and the chapter on sovereignty highlights the early Hudson's Bay Company.

Other examples reflect the universal nature of IR: France granting overnight independence to the Republic of Guinea; Bosnia and the collective uses of force; the decision of the British House of Lords to extradite former Chilean president Augusto Pinochet to Spain.

For more detailed guidelines on teaching the material in this text, an Instructor's Manual is available.

Acknowledgements

Prentice Hall Allyn & Bacon Canada amply deserves its reputation for the highest standards of professionalism. At every stage of writing and production, this book benefited from the talent, judgement and enthusiasm of the people involved. To the two acquisitions editors, Cliff Newman and Dawn Lee, go my appreciation for their confidence in the book's concept. The quiet encouragement of Jennifer Schenkel, the developmental editor, kept the chapters coming in. Matthew Christian, the production editor, handled multifarious tasks and pressures with poise, dispatch and unfailing good cheer. Karen Elliott, associate editor, gracefully elicited an instructor's manual. Donna Lubin Goldman, the copy editor, wielded her pen with deftness, understanding, and a respect for style. Altogether, one couldn't ask for better talent, support, and collegiality.

The five reviewers engaged by Prentice Hall, George MacLean of the University of Manitoba, Denis Stairs of Dalhousie, Tom Keating of the University of Alberta, Alistair Edgar of Wilfrid Laurier University, Andrew Moravcsik of Harvard and Alex Wendt of Dartmouth, helped shape the book's coverage and balance. Special thanks go to Andrew Moravcsik of Harvard University for his comments on a draft of Chapter 3, and to Alexander Wendt of Dartmouth College for his comments on a draft of Chapter 4. Their encouragement was especially welcome. Responsibility for interpretations of their work, of course, is mine. Thanks also go to Moira Russell, Brock University's Social Science Reference Librarian, and to the Map Librarian, Colleen Beard.

More general appreciation goes to my colleagues in the Politics Department at Brock University. The interests shared and the ideas exchanged over the years find points of reflection throughout this book.

Chapter (1)

Introduction

Approaching IR

The international world is a fascinating drama. To observe it, we follow the newspapers and television news. To understand it, we study international relations. Observed reality is a series of discrete events. Understood reality is a set of connected events. The difference between observing and understanding is theoretical knowledge: being able to identify structures, patterns and relationships. It is **theory** that transforms events into understood phenomena. The premise of this book is that theory is primary to understanding. Mastery of a subject is essentially a mastery of its theory. In keeping with the primacy of theory, this book is organized to present IR's four main theories right at the outset. The rest of the book applies them to IR's principal topics.

What are the payoffs of this approach? First, theories do not have to be extracted from illustrations and narrative. Their origins, central tenets and views of the international world are laid out at the beginning. The topics that follow in the book are framed directly in reference to them and show how they apply to Canada. Second, having the theories in mind as you proceed keeps the topics directly connected to a larger scheme. A coherent sense of development is the reward. That is particularly important in IR because its topical breadth can easily make it appear sprawling and disorganized. Keeping the topics centrally connected keeps them manageable. Theory is the connector.

Finally, IR theories are appealing in their own right. They represent ingenious efforts to explain a complex and changeable reality. They have emerged in a reactive pattern with each theory intended to supply a previously missing dimension, and each stage has been accompanied by debate and contention. Because IR's phenomena are so diverse, IR has drawn widely from the social sciences. The four theories covered in this textbook apply ideas of rationality from microeconomics, ideas of individual interests and collective action from political science and ideas of identity and structuration from sociology. Recent critiques of IR theory draw even more widely from Critical Theory, Postmodernism and Feminism, and their challenges to IR have been pitched at the fundamental level of knowledge, inquiry and experience.

Each theory works differently, and there is no single master theory. With each one emphasizing different aspects of the international world, much of the challenge, controversy and satisfaction in IR is determining which one is best for the question at hand. Critical Theory, Postmodernism and Feminism leaven the question with their own perspectives. The plan of the book is to put the theories to use, topic by topic, and see what they show. The final benefit is a sophisticated initial understanding of a compelling and diverse field. That sophistication again comes from theory.

IR as a Field of Study

What does IR study? A useful way of approaching this question is to see IR as politics. Together with political science, IR is basically occupied with strategic human interaction. The participants are affected by what the others do, making them interdependent. Because their purposes differ and because they know that each one's behaviour can influence the outcome, they calculate their actions. These considerations give us the basic ingredients of politics: interdependence (each participant is affected by the others), differing purposes (the participants do not seek the same things), **strategic behaviour** (others' purposes and actions are taken into account) and shared interest in the results (what transpires makes a difference).[1]

The interactions are affected by several conditions: how much value the participants attach to their purposes, how important the outcome is to them, how similar or contradictory their purposes are, how they understand the process of interaction—particularly whether they see it as just or unjust—and how much power they have to affect the outcome. Variations in these conditions affect the nature of politics. The more that purposes are in conflict, the more participants may seek to use power. Whether participants use power depends partly on whether they see the process as legitimate and fair and partly on whether they see their involvement in the process as a one-time event or as a longer continuous engagement. When they perceive the process as fair and when they expect it to continue, they may be more interested in securing its legitimacy than in using their leverage for one-time gains.[2]

One way of ensuring such fairness and legitimacy and of ensuring workable politics over a long period is to construct rules and institutions to regulate interactions. To political philosophers, that is a basic way of characterizing the conditions that produce social contracts and governments. A social contract is formed when a group of people agrees to submit to a constituted authority in exchange for a secure and legitimate political process. The popular success and legitimacy of that process are two of the foundations supporting democratic government.

IR's Separate Path

It is here that IR and political science part company. Political science studies interactions that occur *within* states under the rules and institutions of government. IR studies interactions that occur *among* states in the absence of any governing structure. That division has been a fundamental one since efforts began after World War II to define IR as a field of study. The crucial division is between domestic and international order with a governed domain within state boundaries and an ungoverned realm outside. States are the most effective and consequential actors, making them central to IR. Their behaviour determines what that external realm is like.

The effects work in both directions. The behaviour of states collectively constitutes the international system. Conditions in that system in turn mediate states' behaviour. This two-way relationship sounds straightforward, but one of IR's biggest challenges has been explaining it. As we will see, it is the basic question in the textbook's four theories. To get an immediate sense of what is involved, consider your relationship to society and society's relationship to you. To what extent do individuals, including yourself, create society? To what extent are individuals, including yourself, created by society? IR scholars ask the same questions about states and the **international system**.[3]

Order and Anarchy

Order, and the lack of order, are fundamental. Order is possible within states because of governments, but outside states there is no government. Without such an authority, the international realm is anarchic. All of the four theories regard **anarchy** as a basic condition. Although anarchy has been central to IR's definition as a field and has been its main point of difference with political science, the nature and implications of anarchy pose a challenge. A basic problem has been conceptualizing something that has no authoritative structure. Martin Wight, a British scholar who was one of the first to seek to define IR after World War II and whose work has received renewed attention in recent years, doubted that such conceptualization was possible within the usual tradition of political philosophy. Wight saw a sharp disjuncture between political philosophy's rich antecedents in understanding authority domestically and its mostly incidental observations about the lack of authority internationally, reflecting a basic appreciation that conditions within states are fundamentally different from those among states. This distinction was made even though much of European political philosophy was based upon a postulated state of nature, a condition in which political order or authority is absent.

One political philosopher who considered the domestic/international divide was Thomas Hobbes (1588–1679). Equal and solitary human individuals, facing a state of nature, could choose security by submitting to a powerful governing authority. Looking abroad, however, Hobbes saw states unable to form the same kind of authority among themselves. Individuals could find protection within states because a government could pool its resources for common defence against other states. For states themselves, self-help was necessary because there was no international authority to protect them. States were still better off than individuals because their ability to organize defence gave them much more robust protection. Individuals, solitary and equal, were on their own. Protection within a state was their safest course. The result was a divided system: collective order and security domestically but separation and exposure internationally.[4]

Because of that basic divide at national boundaries, any successful theory of IR, Wight maintained, could not be an extension of theory about states. Political science could not simply move its concepts into IR. Instead, IR theory would have to be a theory of an interstate *system*. Although writings about international law addressed that system as early as the 17th century, international anarchy, by undermining the basis of any legal enforcement and making compliance voluntary, limited how much law-based theories could explain, particularly when states pursue conflicting purposes. A theory of IR would have to be political. This view set a challenge that IR theorists have been seeking to meet ever since. One consequence, as we will see, is IR's focus at the international system level and its reluctance until recently to look very deeply into individual states in explaining the system.

Is anarchy inevitable and permanent? Again, the contrast between domestic and international order has been regarded as fundamental. Setting the tone of much subsequent IR scholarship, Wight was not optimistic that there could ever be historical progress away from anarchy to some more stable and equitable international order. Historical progress has been possible within states because of legitimate and effective rule, as the advent of social programs and civil rights in the world's democratic and industrial countries shows. In a vivid image, Wight considers what Sir Thomas More and Henry IV would see if they returned to England or France in the mid-20th century. Domestically, they would find an impressive evolution of public services and protections. Internationally, it is more likely that they would be struck by resemblances to what they remembered:

a state-system apportioned between two Great Powers each with its associates and satellites, smaller powers improving their position by playing off one side against another, universal doctrines contending against local patriotism, the duty of intervention overriding the right of independence, the empty professions of peaceful purpose and common interest... the play would be the same old melodrama.[5]

Order, Anarchy and IR

Anarchy and order are central to the four theories presented in this textbook: Neorealism, Institutionalism, Liberal IR theory and Constructivism. A pessimistic and static view of international anarchy is Neorealism's touchstone. Anarchy is also Institutionalism's point of reference, but its view emphasizes the possibilities of cooperation and progress. Neorealism and Institutionalism are both explained in Chapter 2. Liberal IR theory accepts the international system as anarchic but emphasizes that its condition depends on the actions of states. These in turn are shaped by domestic interests. Liberal IR theory is presented in Chapter 3. Constructivism emphasizes the transformations of anarchic situations that occur when convergent understandings develop among states. Constructivism is presented in Chapter 4.

Critical theorists, postmodernists and feminists object to IR's occupation with anarchy. All regard the sharply drawn division between states and the international system as part of a more generally arbitrary and oppressive political order that blocks progress and emancipation. IR theories emphasizing that division provide ideological support for an unjust international order. We will see these critiques in Chapter 5.

How wide *is* the separation between domestic and international politics? Does "chaos, lack of order and constant threat" really characterize the international system? Is Canada's security, for example, in continuous peril? The answer depends on how starkly one conceives of anarchy. Strong notions of anarchy depict an international system that is uncertain and dangerous, affecting states so powerfully that they either cope or fail. That, as we will see, is the essential perspective of Neorealism. Adopting less drastic notions of anarchy, as other scholars do, one can envisage a rather orderly international system.[6] One fixture of such a system is common international rules and institutions, which cushion anarchy's effects and allow cooperation and progress. Institutionalists emphasize the international system's network of rules and institutions and see considerable order and predictability.[7] From their separate perspectives, both Liberal IR theory and Constructivism emphasize that the degree of anarchy depends on what states themselves actually do.

A final perspective takes account of the last decade's record of collapsed statehood and rule. The situations in Somalia, Bosnia and Rwanda, when conflicts there were at their height, were frightfully and immediately anarchic thereby eroding the comfortable distinction between domestic safety and international peril.[8] As we will see in Chapter 6, which treats state sovereignty as variable and contingent, and in Chapter 7, which considers national unity, one effect of the recent experiences of civic breakdown has been to reconsider IR's tidy state/system dichotomy. Globalization has raised questions of its own as we will see in Chapter 8. Reconsiderations are nothing new. With the experience of England's civil war in mind, Hobbes's prime concern was personal security in a domestic political order.

As we will see throughout this book, debate at this fundamental level characterizes IR as a field. Few scholars believe that a thorough and adequate conceptualization of the international world has yet been achieved. That is one reason for IR's openness to approaches from other disciplines.

Four Focuses

IR's main concerns can be seen in these four points:

> **Theory.** The international system's structure and dynamics and its relationship to the behaviour of states require connection.

> **Territory and Identity.** Powerfully affected by conceptions of national identity, states continue to the main source of international interests and action. Sovereignty, the pivot of the international system, is a variable and changing practice.

➤ **Security.** Security questions inhere in anarchy whatever its degree. Security is most easily seen in military terms, but states increasingly consider other sources of threat such as economic instability and ecological disasters.

➤ **Wealth, Human Rights and the Environment.** The ability to produce wealth resides in individual states' economic organization, resources and their connections through trade and investment. The international economy increasingly impinges on the welfare of states and perhaps ultimately on their structure. Although authority lies within individual state jurisdictions, human rights and environmental responsibility are increasingly regarded as universal and obligatory.

These focuses organize the textbook into four sections.

Section I: Theory

We will see the development, central tenets and perspectives of IR's four main theories: Neorealism, Institutionalism, Liberal IR theory and Constructivism. Although these four theories emphasize different aspects of IR, together they provide a comprehensive basis for understanding the field. Presentation will emphasize their particular views of the international world and compare their central tenets. The three critical perspectives, Critical Theory, Postmodernism and Feminism, have influenced IR's recent conceptual development. In the subsequent sections, the four theories will be applied and their points of emphasis shown. The views of the three critiques will also be displayed.

Section II: Territory and Identity

Beginning with the evolution of sovereignty, the second section looks at statehood and national identity. Sovereignty and statehood are not uniform and uncontested. Some of the world's states are so weakly constituted that their sovereignty is more official than actual. Sovereignty also varies with international agreements and commitments. National identity, which has begun to receive attention from IR theorists, is both a support and a threat to modern statehood. We will look at the ways in which conflicting understandings of identity can threaten states' unity and legitimacy and, at the extreme, cause civil war. The other source of threat, economic integration among states, will be considered for its impact on the ability to govern and on the meaning of sovereign boundaries. Finally, we will consider the effects of government on international behaviour.

Section III: Security

The end of the cold war has largely removed the threat of nuclear or massive conventional war. At the same time, the international system has no effective and consistent means of providing for individual states' security. In addition, states are beginning to define their security in more than military ways: the environment, migration, international organized crime, terrorism and economic crises. We will examine sources of peril. We will also examine security cooperation, norms and institutions as sources of safety.

Power, as we saw at the beginning, may enter political relationships when conflicting purposes are present. Multiple purposes accentuated by anarchy have made power one of IR's traditional concerns. The conventional meaning of power in IR has been military, but there are other ways of influencing outcomes. One of those ways, particularly useful to moderately sized states such as Canada, is working through international institutions and utilizing international norms and opinion. At the same time, sophisticated military weapons are available to most states, and co-production arrangements are increasingly common. We will consider the question of weapons proliferation and its implications for both individual states' security and the international order. Finally, we will look at the role of formal international law and informal norms as sources of order and security, at the role of formal organizations such as the United Nations (UN) and the North Atlantic Treaty Organization (NATO) and at institutions such as non-proliferation and chemical weapons agreements.

Section IV: Wealth, Human Rights and the Environment

For a number of reasons, economic activity is unevenly developed around the world. A half century of trade reform under the General Agreement on Tariffs and Trade (GATT) and the World Trade Organization (WTO), together with liberalization of the world's financial system, have drastically lowered barriers to commerce and investment. At the same time, states intervene in their economies and affect the terms of trade. This ability varies among states and among sectors, producing a system that remains irregular and contentious. We will look at doctrines of mercantilism and dependency that emphasize inequality and the protective role of the state and at the doctrine of liberalism that emphasizes collective benefits and openness.

Human rights and the environment are two increasingly universal issues. We will examine how human rights came to be seen as an international obligation and explore both the limitations facing states wishing to safeguard or improve them as well as the ways they are promoted beyond the areas of state activity. The environment is also regarded as a global issue. We will examine how this view reached the international level and came to influence governments, and we will look as well at the sources of effective and equitable action.

Understanding First Principles

A helpful way of approaching any theory is to look first to its basic principles or ideas. British IR scholar David Sanders provides a useful way of considering first principles. All theories, he argues, "have both (1) a largely non-negotiable and non-falsifiable 'core' and (2) a set of testable propositions that are to a greater or lesser degree derived from that core."[9] This statement is helpful. First, it shows that even complex-sounding theories have a foundation of elementary ideas or first principles. Approaching theories on that basis makes them less intimidating. The presentations of the theories in the next three chapters highlight their main tenets. Second, Sanders' statement shows why there is controversy in fields such as IR. "**Non-falsifiable**" means not capable of being disproved. There are objective and subjective aspects.

Objectively, a theory is non-falsifiable if it is stated in such general terms that it can explain any occurrence and hence can never be proved wrong by contrary evidence. The issue is not just empirical. A theory also reflects an intuitive understanding of the world. Neorealism's core idea of stark anarchy and danger reflects a very different understanding than does Institutionalism's core idea of underlying cooperation. Subjectively, a theory is non-falsifiable to people who personally and intuitively prefer its understanding of the world. Controversy can indicate objective disagreement, but it may also show clashing subjective preferences. Among the four theories, Neorealism has been particularly contentious. Adherents of the other three theories, along with critical theorists, postmodernists and feminists, object to Neorealism for various reasons, but all strongly disagree with its severe and unpleasant view of anarchy. "Non-negotiable and non-falsifiable" is a way of indicating that people may espouse theories both on their objective merits and on their intuitive plausibility or appeal.

This is not at all to say that by acknowledging preferences we abandon empirical methods and mental discipline and that IR can be whatever we want it to be. For empirical social scientists, subjective preferences are all the more reason to be very attentive to method and to be honest and careful in gathering and presenting evidence. Reliable knowledge requires a willingness to modify or abandon theories in the face of discrepant or contradictory evidence although partially disconfirmed theories can still be useful in directing our attention and shaping our questions.[10] Acknowledging preferences does help us understand why some people are attracted to questions of cooperation and others to conflict and why some people focus on trade and others on terrorism. Preferences may be more general. The three critical perspectives, Critical Theory, Postmodernism and Feminism, all focus on oppression.

The three chapters of Section I present Neorealism and Institutionalism, Liberal IR theory and Constructivism. Section I concludes with a chapter on the three critical perspectives. As you read through the theories' and critical perspectives' origins and basic ideas, be aware of your own reactions. Do *you* find some more appealing or plausible than others? What accounts for your preferences?

A Canadian Reality Check: IR Theory and Free Trade

Since the theories and critical perspectives presented in Section I are based on different core ideas and emphasize different aspects of international behaviour, it is helpful to get an immediate practical sense of them before going on to their application in the following sections. At the end of each chapter in Section I, a Reality Check will briefly apply that theory or perspective to show its viewpoint in concrete terms. The application is Canada's decision to enter a free trade agreement with the United States, arguably one of Canada's most pivotal choices of this century (see Canadian Reality Check 1.1). The theories and critical perspectives take quite different views not so much on the merits of the decision as on what factors are important.

Canadian Reality Check 1.1

Free Trade: The Pivotal Choice

Free trade with the United States represented Canada's final turn away from the legacy of John A. Macdonald's National Policy. In the minds of many, Canada's identity as a nation depended on a distinctive and separate national economy, and proposing free trade placed both economy and identity at a crossroads. Proponents argued that Canada, an export-dependent country without secure access to any major market, could not afford to stay out of agreements particularly when large blocs such as the European Community were already in place, when similar ones might form elsewhere and when protectionist politics in the United States put Canadian exports at risk. Opponents argued that Canada would lose its economy, its culture and its independence. Public sentiment was sharply divided, and a sense of irreversibility pervaded the debate.

Uncertainty heightened the stakes. Arguments in favour of free trade are ultimately prospective and theoretical. In exchange for surrendering protections for domestic producers, states will benefit from larger markets abroad, more efficient industries and more competitively priced goods. That was the case in theory. In the mid-1980s, there were few concrete examples to assess. The European Community was successful but multilateral. In North America, there were only two candidates and one had a very large economy. The only analogously bilateral case was Australia and New Zealand, but the countries' differences from the United States and Canada did not provide much comparison. What was clear was that the decision was historic.

The Reality Checks take up the free trade decision from the perspective of each theory. The next Reality Check at the end of Chapter 2 applies neorealist and institutionalist views. The purpose is to provide a short and immediate application while the theory's major points are still fresh.

IR as an International Field

How international is IR? Scholars in IR speak of an Anglo-American tradition, referring to the fact that IR as a separate discipline with a distinctive body of theory developed and advanced primarily in Britain and the United States. Closely associated were Canada and Australia. IR has been taken up in parts of Europe since then, but in many countries such as Spain, Italy and Greece it is quite new. Beyond Britain, IR in Europe is best established in Scandinavia, Germany and the

Netherlands. One factor favouring these three states' ties to British and North American IR is the fact that most of their scholars publish in English, and a number, particularly in Germany, were trained in North America. French universities locate IR in legal studies, making for a less theoretically based profession. Because of France's academic traditions and the fact that most French IR scholars do not publish in English, its practice also has been more insular.[11] In Asia, IR is best established in Japan, South Korea, Taiwan and Singapore.

What accounts for the Anglo-American predominance? On the American side, a long tradition of belief in science provided a hospitable environment for theoretical and empirical social science including IR. Some major developments had quite local origins. IR's close association with political science can be traced to the University of Chicago in the 1920s and 1930s where major early figures in both disciplines sought to transform them into modern social sciences. The results had lasting effects on both political science and IR.[12] Leavening the development was the arrival of prominent and theoretically minded scholars fleeing Naziism. In Canada, the work of Harold Adams Innis placed Canadian political economy in an international perspective. Another factor favouring IR was a receptive North American outlook. Compared to Europe, both the United States and Canada had protected and peaceful histories and have been credited with an open-minded attitude toward the study of international affairs and diplomacy, matters about which Europeans had more jaded and fatalistic views.

After World War II, the cold war heightened concern in both Canada and the United States about their international roles and made the governments, particularly the American, interested in policy-relevant social science.[13] Both the United States and Canada expanded their university systems in the 1960s, multiplying the opportunities for IR research and teaching and enlarging the population of IR scholars.

In Britain, momentum toward a discipline of IR was given an important start by the scholar E.H. Carr whose now-classic book, *The Twenty Years' Crisis*, helped to set the direction of IR's development after the war. We will see more about Carr's influence in Chapter 2. Several other scholars, including Martin Wight, were important early conceptualizers. Joined later by the Australian scholar Hedley Bull, they were instrumental in forming the "**English School**," an approach to IR that emphasizes structures of order and stability. IR in Britain has expanded since then. As a discipline, it closely observes and draws from North American IR but regards itself as somewhat independent, particularly of heavily formal and mathematical methods, which it treats as parochially North American.

For Canada and the United States, the growth of IR after World War II represented a broader shift in outlook. Both countries had been strongly isolationist in the interwar period. World War II forced both to recognize that detachment from the international world had allowed enemies to become increasingly more dangerous. Recognizing the failure to appreciate the true threat of Naziism and Fascism until war had become inevitable led to a drastic transformation of government and public outlooks. For Canada, historian J.L. Granatstein characterizes the change from isolationism to internationalism as unprecedented in its speed and completeness.[14]

Materially, the end of World War II left both the United States and Canada in predominant positions. With all of Europe's former great powers exhausted, the United States had the largest economic capability, and the task of postwar leadership settled in Washington. The same exhaustion gave Canada an enhanced international position as a middle power. The onset of the cold war confronted both countries with new international obligations. Both abandoned their earlier refusal to join military alliances with Europe and supported the economic cooperation that produced such postwar institutions as the General Agreement on Tariffs and Trade.

These differing roles and positions in the postwar world affected the way IR was addressed in Canada and the United States in those years. The differences are evident in writings on foreign policy. Because foreign policy writing addresses specific issues and problems from a national perspective, it reflects differences between states more clearly than do IR's more comprehensive efforts. American writing, particularly about the cold war, radiated **superpower** responsibilities and outlooks such as nuclear deterrence, the structural workings of bipolar international systems and questions of economic hegemony. During the early cold war decades of the 1950s and 1960s, Canadian writing was occupied with Canada's position as a middle power. Later, as concerns about levels of American investment in Canada became an issue in the mid-1960s, much of the attention shifted to Canada's position as the neighbour of the United States. In both cases, Canada's situation relative to other countries was the central issue.

In the view of two scholars, Maureen Appel Molot and Denis Stairs, Canada's position has been overly emphasized as the determining factor of its foreign policy, placing too much emphasis on external conditions and too little on national choice and purpose.[15] Much of the middle-power writing was concerned with cooperation in multilateral structures and emphasized Canada's role more than its interests. In writings about Canada's relationship with the United States, the positional perspective focused on the disparity of power, emphasizing again the determining effects of Canada's position.[16] In IR's basic system/state dichotomy, the system predominated in this writing, not the Canadian state. In contrast, much of the cold war writing on American foreign policy focused very specifically on its state interests. *Canadian Foreign Policy*, launched in 1993, reflects a more state-focused orientation in Canada.

Compared to foreign policy writing, IR is more specifically based in theory and tends to focus on general structures and processes. IR scholars also tend to work with the same theories and methods, which strongly affect the questions that are addressed and the conclusions that are reached. These factors dilute distinctively Canadian and American characteristics. They also show why theory can be such a source of contention. It strongly affects what the IR profession does. In the same way, critiques that are made by one country's IR scholars often occur to those in the other. Canadian scholars have often regarded Neorealism as embodying an American great-power perspective, but that observation has been made by Europeans and Americans as well. At the general and often abstract level of IR theory, distinctively national perspectives become indistinct, and it is often difficult to distinguish particular origins and outlooks.

There has been recent interest in IR's historical development as a profession. When professionalization occurs, members take on perspectives that are shaped in considerable degree by theory, advanced training and prevailing conceptions. North American IR has become highly professionalized with graduate programs in nearly all universities, major journals, large conventions and a highly interactive community. American and Canadian IR scholars take their advanced degrees in many of the same universities, read the same journals, attend conferences together and co-author works. These conditions support a community that shares basic understandings and terms of reference. That professionalization, together with the cohesive effects of IR's theory and methods, make it difficult to identify a singularly Canadian school of IR thought. In contrast, scholarship on Canadian foreign policy, because of its more particular focus, is clearly distinctive in outlook.

How to Read This Book

The design of this book is to begin with the four theories and the three critical perspectives. Following that, the remaining four sections examine IR's major topics of territory and identity, security, wealth and human rights and the environment. Treatment of each topic will show how the theories and critical perspectives apply. This design works best when Section I is read as a basic grounding. It can serve as a reference and reminder in the subsequent sections. The tabulation of the theories' main tenets in each of Section I's chapters provides these at a glance. At the end, this design should yield a well-integrated theoretical and topical understanding of IR.

This book takes the view that Neorealism, Institutionalism, Liberal IR theory and Constructivism are useful in their own ways. Neorealism, for example, can be a powerful and cogent way of understanding conflict and insecurity particularly when armed force is a factor. Constructivism can show how states define their identities and respond to changes both within themselves and in other states. The three critical approaches continue to affect IR. One result is a reflective self-awareness in recent writing, a change from a more categorically assertive emphasis in earlier work. Postmodernism has deliberately placed itself "outside" in a position of dissidence, but one of its influences in IR has been a greater interest in exploring ideas that previously had been taken for granted. One example, as we will see in Chapter 6, is sovereign statehood. Long regarded as a static and dry legal topic, it has come to be seen as a variable and historically contingent practice.[17]

As you proceed, it is important to remember that none of the four theories is comprehensive and that all emphasize some areas more than others. Neorealism, for example, is not interested in the ways states define their interests and make decisions because it assumes that all states respond rationally to the same set of external conditions. In contrast, Constructivism and Liberal IR theory are very interested in the ways states perform those tasks. Showing those differences is one reason for presenting the theories side by side, topic by topic.

Summary

International Relations is the newest social science. It studies political behaviour, but unlike political science it focuses on an ungoverned structure—the international system. IR's continuing task has been dealing with the fact of anarchy. Conceptualizing a structure that has no authority as well as understanding its connection to the behaviour of states has been a monumental challenge. After 50 years of work and ingenuity, there is still no single IR theory. What we have instead is a plurality of them. The textbook focuses on the most important current theories. Each is based on different core ideas, and each emphasizes different aspects of the relationship between system and states. IR's receptivity to ideas and debate has provided audience for a number of critical approaches. Three of the most recently influential critiques—Critical Theory, Postmodernism and Feminism—are considered.

IR's diverse concerns can be condensed into four basic concentrations: territory and identity, security, wealth and human rights and the environment. The theories and critical perspectives illuminate these topics in different lights. No theory has a comprehensive explanation, and one of IR's challenges is deciding which is best for the topic at hand.

Making those choices is also one of IR's satisfactions.

ENDNOTES

1   Alan Lamborn, "Theory and the Politics in World Politics," *International Studies Quarterly* 41 (June 1997) 190

2   *ibid.,* pp. 191, 193.

3   Alexander Wendt, "The Agent-Structure Problem in International Relations Theory," *International Organization* 41 (Summer 1987) 335–70; David Dessler, "What's at Stake in the Agent-Structure Debate," *International Organization* 43 (Summer 1989) 441–74; and Martin Hollis and Steve Smith, "Beware of Gurus: Structure and Action in International Relations," *Review of International Studies* 17 (October 1991) 393–410.

4   Martin Wight, "Why Is There No International Theory?" in James Der Derian, ed., *International Theory: Critical Investigations*, New York: New York University Press, 1995, p. 30; R.B.J. Walker, "Gender and Critique in the Theory of International Relations," in V. Spike Peterson, ed., *Gendered States: Feminist (Re)Visions of International Relations Theory*, Boulder, CO: Lynne Rienner, 1992, p. 189.

5   Wight, "Why Is There No International Theory?" p. 25

6   Barry Buzan, "From International System to International Society: Structural Realism and Regime Theory Meet the English School," *International Organization* 47 (Summer 1993) 327–352.

7   Helen Milner, "The Assumption of Anarchy in International Relations: A Critique," in David Baldwin, ed., *Neoliberalism and Neorealism: The Contemporary Debate*, New York: Columbia University Press, 1993, pp. 143–146, 162–166.

8   Miles Kahler, "Inventing International Relations: International Relations Theory after 1945," in Michael W. Doyle and G. John Ikenberry, eds., *New Thinking in International Relations Theory*, Boulder: Westview, 1997, p. 43.

9   David Sanders, "International Relations: Neo-Realism and Neo-Liberalism," in Robert Goodin and Hans-Dieter Klingemann, eds., *A New Handbook of Political Science*, Oxford: Oxford University Press, 1996, p. 435.

10   Gary King, Robert O. Keohane, Sidney Verba, *Designing Social Inquiry: Scientific Inference in Qualitative Research*, Princeton: Princeton University Press, 1994, p. 101.

11   A.J.R. Groom, "The World Beyond: The European Dimension," in Margot Light and A.J.R. Groom, eds., *Contemporary International Relations: A Guide to Theory,* London: Pinter, 1994, p. 220–230.

12   Kahler, "Inventing International Relations," p. 26.

13   Stanley Hoffmann, "An American Social Science: International Relations," *Daedalus* 106 (Summer 1977) 44–51.

14   J.L. Granatstein, "Looking Backwards: The Journal's First Year," *International Journal* 33 (Winter 1978) 115–17.

15   Maureen Appel Molot, "Where Do We, Should We, or Can We Sit? A Review of Canadian Foreign Policy Literature," *International Journal of Canadian Studies* 1–2 (Spring-Fall 1990) 79–81; Denis Stairs, "The Postwar Study of Canada's Foreign Policy," *International Journal* 50 (Winter 1994-1995) 12–19.

16   Stairs, "The Postwar Study of Canada's Foreign Policy," 19–32.

17   Janice Thomson, *Mercenaries, Pirates, and Sovereigns,* Princeton: Princeton University Press, 1994. Her comments on the influence of postmodernism are on pp. 14, 160–161.

WEBLINKS

Daily newspapers are a good source of current information on IR.

The Toronto Globe and Mail's site is:
www.globeandmail.com

The New York Times has a registered site at:
www.nytimes.com

General research information on IR can be found on the University of British Columbia Library site:
www.library.ubc.ca/poli/international

The University of Wales at Aberystwyth has a comprehensive online database of IR resources:
www.aber.ac.uk/~inpwww/resour.html

Two interesting regional sites are:
www.Arab.net/   and   www.africanews.org/

ONLINE DATABASES

University libraries contain three online databases that are excellent IR resources. They can be accessed through the libraries' computer terminals.

Political Science Abstracts
This is an index of journal literature. Its advantages are quick online access and brief descriptions of each article, which quickly indicate whether the material is pertinent.

EBSCO
This database not only includes full texts of peer-refereed articles from the professional literature, but also provides current news information. Users can e-mail some of the articles to themselves. Topics can be searched by subject and name.

Canadian Business and Current Affairs (CBCA)
An excellent source for current news. Many of the items indexed are from specialized and trade publications for which it is difficult to find other comprehensive listings. CBCA is a good index for the Globe and Mail, and most university libraries have back issues on microfilm.

Chapter 2

Neorealism and Institutionalism

Origins in War and Dismay

The first university IR department was established after World War I in Wales at the University of Aberystwyth. It was part of a broader interest in understanding the Great War's causes and in preventing another catastrophe in the future. The IR research of the interwar period, in keeping with the policies of governments in Europe and North America, was focused on applications of international law and on the design and operation of international organizations such as the League of Nations. The purpose was promoting cooperation and peace. When war came again in 1939, governments were blamed for having failed to prevent it, and IR was blamed for having failed to anticipate it.

One of the foundation works of modern IR theory, *The Twenty Years' Crisis,* was written in 1939 by British scholar Edward Hallett Carr as a diagnosis of what had gone so drastically wrong. Carr argued that both allied governments and IR scholars had assumed that states had an inherent interest in cooperation and peace and had assumed that the modern international order's natural condition was harmony. The possibility that some states might want to overturn the system did not fit that mental scheme. Such thinking, in light of what actually happened, was idealistic and wishful, Carr argued. IR should concentrate instead on understanding the international world as it actually is. Doing so requires a focus on states' intentions and their power to act on them. For the cogency and elegance of its argument, *The Twenty Years' Crisis* remains one of IR's classic statements.[1] One of its consequences was to associate traditional liberalism, one of the mainline approaches in political science's study of domestic politics, with a discredited impracticality in IR.[2] That was an unfair caricature, in the view of recent scholarship, but in the 1940s and 1950s liberalism was an almost unheard voice in IR.[3] It has only recently re-emerged in its full traditional form as we will see in Chapter 3.

Focusing on intentions and power gained currency as World War II ended and the cold war began. In 1948, a refugee from Nazi Germany, Hans Morgenthau, wrote a textbook, *Politics Among Nations: The Struggle for Power and Peace.*[4] Intending his book for both students and govern-ments, Morgenthau drew on European history to formulate a set of principles for understanding IR and guiding states. The principles' core assumption was that politics is a struggle for power. The power and intentions of states and the balances of power among them should be IR's concerns. To preserve peace, Morgenthau held, national leaders must be vigilant over other states' intentions and over changing configurations of power. Balances preserve stability, and imbalances invite war. Termed **Realism**, this view of IR can be seen as a response to the lesson of World War II and as a reflection of the cold war's positional rivalry and anxiety. Note its Hobbesian view of the conditions of security: there are no protections beyond the resources and calculations of the state. *Politics Among Nations* was widely used in Canadian and American universities, and had you been taking Introductory International Relations 40 years ago, it most likely would have been your textbook. Reading it today evokes a sense of those years. Since the end of the cold war, debate about the role

Canadian Press/CP photo/Moe Doiron

Over a half century later, the horrific memories of Dieppe still haunt Ronald Beal. The Second World War veteran was among Canadians who fought in the battle at the French town August 19, 1942, Canada's bloodiest day of the war. IR realists were deeply affected by World War II and the failures to prevent it.

of history and philosophy in IR has revived interest in Morgenthau. As we will see in Chapter 5's treatment of critical approaches, broader considerations such as these have animated much recent debate over IR's methods and outlooks.

Challenge

The realist view of the international world was not without controversy even during the worst years of the cold war and was criticized from a number of directions. One early criticism was that its theory was too loosely specified: power and balances of power—Morgenthau's main ideas—were stated so generally that they could mean a number of things, producing ambiguous and contradictory theory and policy guidance.[5] A more qualitative criticism was that his emphasis on power and conflict discouraged any search for cooperation and progress. In recent years, Morgenthau has been given credit by some IR scholars for a broader philosophical appreciation of human nature than was previously acknowledged and for his hope that power politics could eventually be transcended by world government.

The source of Realism's most important challenge was empirical observation. Looking at the actual international world, a number of scholars saw that Realism had no provision for the growing connections of trade and finance and for the susceptibility of states to non-military developments. Focusing on them produced a strikingly different view of the world. Instead of simple balances of state power, "networks... appeared to be the appropriate metaphor for an international system increasingly dominated by transnational relations, economic concerns and an expanding web of international norms, rules and institutions."[6] Economic relations and non-state actors populated Robert O. Keohane's and Joseph Nye's widely influential *Power and Interdependence*, which challenged Realism's central emphasis on military balances of power.[7] Instead, the focus was on international economic ties and on the ways they make states vulnerable to each other's actions.

Looking at all the ways states could affect one another showed that military power was present in only some areas of international conflict and influence and that non-military issues, particularly economic ones, could significantly affect states' interests and welfare. Although they might be less dire than the ones occupying realists, the international ties transmitting them were pervasive and undeniable. Military power was also not the key factor in many kinds of conflicts. Nye, surveying conflicts between Canada and the United States, found that Canada prevailed more often than not.

Besides expanding the understanding of influence and vulnerability, these sorts of findings broadened IR's notion of conflict. Economic issues, which previously had interested mostly international lawyers and trade specialists, entered IR's main agenda. As an even more fundamental challenge, scholars adopting the interdependence perspective questioned the centrality of the state—the anchorage of Realism. Transnational corporations in particular were seen as important international actors.

In Britain, meanwhile, Oxford scholar Hedley Bull advanced a view of the international world that emphasized an underlying order based in common expectations and practices and resembling features of domestic societies.[8] Bull did accept anarchy as a structural description of the international system, but he was interested in why it seemed so orderly and stable. One constraining influence on states' raw exercise of power, Bull believed, is the patterns of expectations and the norms of behaviour that states establish as they interact with each other, much in the same way that individuals and organizations in domestic societies do as they interact. Although Bull and others at the time had difficulty specifying how those norms and patterns actually work as constraints and limitations, the view of the international world as an emerging form of society squarely challenged the power politics of Realism. These fundamental challenges did not go unanswered.

Response: Neorealism

The reaction was to bring states, anarchy and power back to the fore.[9] The result was *Theory of International Politics* by Kenneth Waltz.[10] In terms of the number of commentaries, debates and critiques his book has provoked since its appearance in 1979, it is arguably IR's most broadly influential work. One index of its impact is the name it has earned: **Neorealism**. Waltz sought to rescue Realism by boiling it down to a deductive and tight system-level theory. He did so by applying

microeconomic reasoning. States in the international system, he asserts, are like firms in a market. In both, individual actions create an interactive setting in which "an actor's optimal strategy depends on the other actors' strategies."[11] Like markets, Waltz argues, the international system arises from the behaviour of individual actors pursuing their own interests. Contrary to each individual's self-interest, however, the collective structure they create—a market or an international system—constrains their pursuit.[12] Like markets, the international system may impose unsought-after conditions that individual members must heed but cannot control, an ironic collective result of self-interested individual action.

Using this reasoning, Waltz explained the international system as a result of states pursuing their interests amidst anarchy and explained state behaviour as responses to conditions generated by the system. The structure of the system itself is determined by arrangements of military power. Coercion, or the threat of it, is the driving force of state calculations, and security is the prime concern. States determine the status of their security by evaluating their capabilities against those of other states. Unfavourable balances are cause for concern. Because the system is anarchic, there is nothing to stop states with superior capabilities from exploiting them.

Note what Waltz achieves. As we saw earlier, Wight believed that theories of states could not explain IR. A proper IR theory would be *systemic*. By focusing on states' external conditions as defined by coercive power, Waltz explains their actions at the system level; their domestic structures or politics are not necessary to know. We should note that Waltz can be read in two ways. One reading emphasizes the role of states: the system is the result of what states do. The other reading emphasizes the role of the system: what states do is a result of the system. Waltz himself is ambiguous on that point but seems to emphasize system over states.[13]

A system-level explanation provides important advantages. One is economy of data. If it is possible to explain the behaviour of states in reference only to their external conditions, the effort and complexity of assessing domestic factors is eliminated. Another advantage is transparency. Conditions at the international level can be readily observed and analyzed. The inner workings of states are a much more daunting proposition. A third advantage is simplified assumptions about behaviour. States, like firms in microeconomics, seek to maximize their gains and behave rationally. If all states seek gain and if all are rational, their behaviour can be logically calculated in the same way that economists can calculate firms' behaviour in a market. Again, no domestic information is necessary: under these assumptions, states respond to external conditions in the same way.

Positing self-interested actors in a competitive system makes the neorealists' international world inherently positional and competitive. The currency of states' interactions is power, and their prime concern is gains—to advance them where possible and to protect them where necessary. Since states can be expected to exploit advantages, each state's minimal objective is to prevent others from making gains at its expense. Differences matter. Losses and defeat are real possibilities.

Together, these are powerful ingredients: an explicitly system-level theory, a field of inquiry that neatly omits domestic politics and a concise assumption of rationality. Waltz and his advocates believe Neorealism to be a major step forward in constructing a formal and coherent IR. One reason for Neorealism's influence is that it *does* provide an explanation at the system level. An index of the power of this theory is the 20 years of debate it has provoked in IR. At issue is Neorealism's thoroughness and accuracy of explanation and its view of the international world.

Counter-Response: Institutionalism

Reactions came rapidly. As we saw earlier, scholars criticized Morgenthau's pessimism about cooperation and progress and his overemphasis of military power. In the 1980s, scholars criticized Waltz for the same things: competition as IR's enduring condition and security as its prime concern. This time, however, some of his most sophisticated critics *adopted* Neorealism's key features: a competitive and anarchic system, the pursuit of self-interest and rational behaviour. Their objective was to escape the stigma heaped on liberalism after World War II by retaining the liberal view that states seek cooperation *but also* incorporating the neorealist assumption that states act rationally to secure gains. This time there could be no accusation of wooly idealism. These liberals were originally known as *neoliberals* to designate their adoption of Neorealism's rationalist approach. Where they differed from Neorealism is over the nature of the gains that states seek. That difference has led to a broader disagreement about the possibilities of cooperation.

As their approach developed, neoliberals came to be known as neoliberal institutionalists, or simply **institutionalists**. *That* label designated their belief that dependable cooperation among states requires constructing sets of rules and procedures to assure compliance and prevent cheating. Worry about cheating comes from taking on the assumption that all states rationally pursue gains for themselves. If that is true, states require protection against cheating before they are willing to risk cooperation. Institution is the social science term for constructed rules and procedures—hence the label institutionalist.

Neorealists, as we saw, believe that security is states' prime concern. That being so, states will try to prevent any gains that provide other states with exploitable advantages. Fear of unequal outcomes hinders cooperation. Playing safe is the prudent strategy, and states enter negotiations warily. Since few agreements yield *exactly* equal gains, the basis of cooperation is infrequent and narrow. Institutionalists take a more relaxed view. States, they believe, are satisfied with gains that provide advantages to all and do not worry if some states get more than others. What is important is that all end up better off. Because differences in gains are not crucial, institutionalists believe, states find it possible to reach agreements and to cooperate in a number of areas—even though the international system is anarchic and even though states rationally seek gains for themselves.

Cooperation is possible, in the institutionalist view, because states share common interests in stability, particularly in economic and financial relationships, and in taking joint action to address collective problems. They need common institutions of rules and procedures to achieve the needed collective action and coordination. In contrast, seeking the same results individually is much more expensive in terms of transaction costs—the effort of reaching agreements and understandings on a state-by-state basis. Institutions pool those costs by bringing all the participants together and enabling them to share information and expertise and to formulate common policies.[14] In that way, institutions facilitate cooperation by making it more direct and convenient. Constructing rules alleviates concerns that some states may cheat. Altogether, in the institutionalist view of the world, pragmatic cooperation moderates the effects of anarchy, making international progress possible. Institutions can be formal organizations such as the International Monetary Fund (IMF), or they can be based more loosely on a set of rules such as the North Atlantic Fisheries Organization (NAFO).[15] We will see more about the North Atlantic Fisheries Organization when we examine the Canada-European Union Turbot War in the next chapter.

Neorealism's and Institutionalism's Core Tenets

To show the two theories' similarities and differences, we will look at them side by side in table 2.1.[16]

TABLE 2.1   Similarities and Differences

Similarities	
Neorealism	*Institutionalism*
The international system is anarchic	The international system is anarchic
States must rely on their own resources	States must rely on their own resources
States rationally seek to maximize their own interests	States rationally seek to maximize their own interests
The preferences and actions of other states are the primary factors accounting for individual states' behaviour; external conditions are paramount	The preferences and actions of other states are the primary factors accounting for individual states' behaviour; external conditions are paramount

Differences	
Neorealism	*Institutionalism*
The international system is inherently competitive, and states must be vigilant about other states' gaining advantages—particularly the ability to use force. The gains that matter most are the **relative gains** that give one side an advantage—even a small one. It's the edge that counts.	The international system's anarchic condition can be moderated because states are interdependent economically and share unwelcome exposure to major wars and ecological disasters. The gains that matter most are the absolute ones that make all states better off or that help them all avoid common threats. It's the collective benefit that counts.

TABLE 2.1   continued

Increasing one's own military power decreases the chances that other states will make threats or use force	Awareness of mutual interests gives states the ability to cooperate to achieve joint gains or protections
Because the ability to threaten and coerce is always present among states, they must always be prepared to use offensive or defensive armed force	The collective benefits from initial and low-level cooperation set the stage for more widespread cooperation in the future

The Neorealist and Institutionalist Views of the World

Both Neorealism and Institutionalism share a large common ground. Both regard states as the principal actors in IR, anarchy as the condition of the international system and rational self-interest as each state's motivation. They differ over the dangers and opportunities states face.

Neorealists worry about small differences because in the absence of any international governing order, those gains could provide others with advantages to exploit. As self-interested actors, states always have that potential. Unequal gains, in the words of one neorealist, might make states "more domineering friends or even more powerful adversaries."[17] Does this mean that prudent states should be suspicious of *all* other states? A literal application of Neorealism's tenets would answer yes: One never knows what others might do if given the opportunity or capability.

A more qualitative application would take account of the history of particular relationships. Taking this view, we should note, relaxes one of Waltz's key assumptions that all states are alike in the way they respond to external conditions. As we proceed, it is possible to see an ascending scale of sensitivity to other states' relative gains (see table 2.2), beginning at the low end with long-term relationships of peace, trust and cooperation and finishing at the high end with long-term relationships of warfare, deception and fear. We can also see the low end as indicating nominal consequences and the high end as indicating severe ones. Thus, another state's not living up to the letter of an agreement would be a relative gain, but only a nominally consequential one, while a major advance in another state's ability to mount a military attack would be severely consequential.[18]

States in relationships at the low end are less worried about relative gains by the other side because their experience makes them confident that gains will not be exploited and trust will not be violated. Applied to military power and defence, this confidence characterizes a "**security community**" in which states, from their experience with each other, have virtually ruled out the possibility of war and believe that any disputes will be settled peacefully. Members of security communities are not frightened when other members increase their military power. In 1957,

TABLE 2.2   Tabulation of Sensitivity

Sensitivity to Relative Gains

Low	Moderate	High
Solid basis of confidence	Mixed expectations	Apprehension
History of cooperation	Chequered experience	History of conflict
Nominal consequences	Noticeable consequences	Severe consequences

when the security community idea was put forward, Scandinavia, along with Canada and the United States, were cited as exemplars of that kind of relationship.[19] The community has grown since then. A recent census lists these members:

- **Europe**: the Scandinavian countries, Ireland, the United Kingdom, Portugal, Spain, France, Belgium, Luxembourg, Netherlands, Germany, Switzerland and Austria
- **North America**: Canada, the United States and Mexico
- **Asia-Pacific**: Japan, South Korea, Philippines, Taiwan, Singapore, Australia and New Zealand [20]

We will see more about the basis of security communities in Chapter 11 when we examine sources of safety.

Some neorealists agree that states dealing with trusted partners need not be as cautious as when dealing with adversaries.[21] Sombre perceptions, however, are appropriate at the other end of the scale. States that have a history of conflict and regard each other as threats have very good reasons to fear any gains.[22] That wariness describes the two superpowers during the cold war. Despite the fact that both states' military power was massive, each was minutely concerned with force levels and balances.

Who the other state is does make a difference. In one scholar's words, "It cannot be stressed enough that states discriminate in the ways that they relate to other states...And precisely because states discriminate, they make different sorts of calculations about the costs and benefits of cooperation depending upon whom they are dealing with."[23]

Where does this leave Neorealism and Institutionalism? Both sides can indicate persuasive cases to support their views. Neorealists can point to the majority of the world's states that are outside the security community as proof that concern with safety and small gains is still widespread. The international community's embargo of weapons to Iran and Iraq shows a consensus that neither state should gain military capability. Several pairs of states show the legacy of war and conflict: India and Pakistan, North and South Korea, Greece and Turkey, Israel and Syria. India's and Pakistan's calculation of threats includes the fact that both have tested nuclear weapons and have been at war three times since independence in

1947. Institutionalists can point to an equally impressive record of cooperation: the rapid negotiation of an international agreement to limit gases that destroy the ozone layer, a widespread ban (sponsored by Canada) on the use of anti-personnel mines and an International Monetary Fund that rushed billions of dollars in emergency loans to Asian states facing financial panics. (We will see more about the Asian economic crisis in Chapter 12.)

Neorealism and Institutionalism might join at the low-threat end of the scale. A neorealist would take a calm view of gains, and an institutionalist could argue that states in such confident relationships have a good basis for cooperation and the pursuit of mutual benefits. The two views diverge over passive composure (Neorealism) and active cooperation (Institutionalism). For neorealists, the prospects are limited: being calm is not the same as being optimistic. For institutionalists, the prospects are potentially expansive: cooperation over time builds confidence for increasingly far-reaching endeavours. The point of divergence is the frequency and expectability of cooperation. Neorealists would see fewer opportunities for trust and more reasons to be vigilant. Even so, the differences in outlook may be small. Some scholars see those differences as increasingly negotiable and anticipate an eventual merger.[24] Remember the two theories' common elements: an anarchic, self-help international system, individual pursuit of gains and rational behaviour.

For now, it is probably the most useful to see Neorealism and Institutionalism as using the same basic assumptions to address two different areas. For areas of military conflict and insecurity, Neorealism's cautious assumptions emphasize exploitable gains and vigilance. For economic and environmental issues, Institutionalism's more expansive assumptions emphasize common interests in the face of interdependence, mutual benefits and common hazards. More philosophically, neorealists see anarchy and uncertainty as profound dimensions of the human condition, and institutionalists see cooperation as a moral virtue.[25]

Rational Trust

As we have seen, both Neorealism and Institutionalism make strict **assumptions of rational behaviour** and self-interested seeking of gains. No other theories make those assumptions with such consistency and discipline. What follows from them?

For both neorealists and institutionalists, the key question is how much states can trust each other. Trust centres on reciprocity. In interpersonal relations, returning a favour is an act of **reciprocity**. Not returning a favour is taking advantage of the giver. In IR, neorealists' suspicion reflects a fear of non-reciprocity: concessions will not be returned. The institutionalists' more relaxed view reflects a confidence in reciprocity: even though states are self-interested, it is possible to construct arrangements in which they exchange concessions for mutual benefits. Still we can ask: when is it rational to cooperate? Game theorists are very interested in that question. Here is a version of one of the most famous games of cooperation, **Prisoner's Dilemma**:

The Situation

You and a friend have submitted identical essays and have been accused of academic dishonesty. Your department chair and the dean do not know which one of you wrote the essay and which one of you copied it. The only evidence they have is that both essays are exactly the same. You are being interviewed in separate rooms. Since the chair and dean have to prove dishonesty, they are counting on one of you to confess. They remind you that honesty is the best policy and promise that confession and contrition will be rewarded. You figure that your friend is being told the same thing. Should you confess or stonewall?

Four Possible Outcomes

➤ **Both stonewall:** Despite the offer of leniency, you deny any wrongdoing and insist that the situation is a fluke. Your friend does likewise. Your mutual denials leave the chair and the dean without proof and force them to let the matter drop. You are both let off with a warning.

➤ **Both confess:** Figuring that you will only compound your problems by lying, you confess to having lent your friend the essay. Your friend, figuring the same thing, confesses to having copied it. Lending and copying are equally serious violations, but because you both come clean the penalty is lenient: F—but not zero—on the assignment and no further action.

➤ **Stonewall/Confess:** You stonewall resolutely, but your friend, hoping for leniency, confesses and blames you saying that you had promised only to look at the essay. The chair and the dean assume that your friend is telling the truth. You, by stonewalling, appear to be lying. The chair and dean are not amused. You get zero on the assignment and a note in your university file, assuring expulsion if you commit a second offence. Rewarded for help in resolving the matter, your friend walks.

➤ **Confess/Stonewall:** You confess and your friend stonewalls. You walk and your friend gets zero and a note in his or her file.

Table 2.3 shows the possible moves. The numbers show the weightings of the outcomes for you and your friend.

Two of the outcomes are mutual (3/3, 1/1) and two are divided (0/5, 5/0). The best mutual outcome is a warning (3/3) that you get by both refusing to confess, and the worst mutual outcome is a lenient penalty (1/1) that you get by both confessing. The divided outcomes are the drastic ones (0/5, 5/0) in which the confessor goes free while the stonewaller gets the full penalty. To get the best mutual outcome (3/3), you each have to rely on the other's refusing the offer of leniency. By both accepting the offer (1/1), you get the worst mutual outcome. That is still preferable to taking the full penalty while your friend walks (0/5). What is your best move?

It depends on how much you trust your friend not to confess. If you are highly confident, your best move is to cooperate, which will get you both off with a warning. If you do not trust your friend, your best move is to defect. If your friend de-

TABLE 2.3   Matrix of the Prisoner's Dilemma

		You	
		Cooperate	Defect
Your Friend	Cooperate	You = 3 Friend = 3 Both stonewall	You = 5 Friend = 0 Friend stonewalls You confess
	Defect	You = 0 Friend = 5 You stonewall Friend confesses	You = 1 Friend = 1 Both confess

fects also, you will get a lenient penalty, but that is preferable to your friend's defecting while you cooperate. Your friend is making the same calculations: if your friend misplaces trust and cooperates while you defect, you walk instead. If your friend does not trust you, his or her best move is to defect.

It makes a difference whether Prisoner's Dilemma has only one play or a series of plays. For a serial game, you must visualize a situation different from the one just seen, which is inherently single-play. Instead, there are a number of rounds, and in each one players have the choice of cooperating or defecting. The stakes in the serial game are the same, but because there is more than one round the gains are cumulative. Because there are a number of rounds, however, the strategy is different. In a serial game, your best initial move is to assume trust and cooperate. If your partner does the same, you share the best mutual outcome. If your partner defects, you retaliate in the next round but in subsequent rounds resume cooperating as soon as your partner does. If your partner defects again, you follow the same procedure. This strategy is called **Tit-for-Tat**.[26]

Serial play does not always produce mutually beneficial outcomes. The players may not have complete information or may not be able to make optimal calculations. Tit-for-Tat is merely the most promising strategy for achieving positive outcomes and limiting defections. Inferring from the different logic of once-only and serial play, we can see how Prisoner's Dilemma could support both neorealist and institutionalist views. Neorealist suspicion is supported by the one-play version: the rational incentive to defect is very strong, and there is no second chance. Institutionalist confidence is supported by the serial-play version: extended games allow cooperation to develop through shared benefits and punished defections (see Figure 2.4).

If you are thinking that there is more to the development of cooperation than rational game-playing, you are right, as we will see in Chapter 4 when we consider Constructivism. Prisoner's Dilemma and other models of rational calculation posit fixed preferences.[27] The players' beliefs about each other are limited to gain and loss.

If the players' ideas and understandings of each other are acknowledged at all in rational models, they are minor considerations, and there is no provision for their being transformed as the game progresses. Transformation through interaction and experience is the main point of Constructivism.

FIGURE 2.4   Prisoner's Dilemma: The View from Inside

How would the logic of Prisoner's Dilemma look to real prisoners? IR scholar James Der Derian found out when he taught a world politics course to inmates in a medium-security facility.[28] What was the reaction? At first, he relates, they were "flattered that a discipline of higher learning would find so much of value in a predicament with which they had intimate experience." As they considered that experience, they began questioning Prisoner's Dilemma: "Why would supposedly rational actors like states not do what they had learned to do early in their careers: figure out before the crime who is likely to snitch, which stories would stick, which situations called for collective as opposed to individual action and when tacitly accepted norms (like loyalty and honour) should apply in the absence of formal ones (like the law)."

Convinced that the theory did not fit the real world as they knew it, they conducted simulations of Prisoner's Dilemma interrogation using other inmates as subjects. What were the results? "These students," Der Derian observed, "relying on reputation, perception and intuition, proved adept at regularly predicting outcomes that defied the conventional strategic logic of the game. In subsequent reviews, they explained how traditional codes of silence, pre-scripted stories and other intersubjective rituals of honour—all specific to their prison society—defied generalization into timeless, reductionist, instrumentalist (i.e. rationalist) principles." What did Der Derian conclude? "Situated, constructed identities rather than permanent, unitary interests were at work." What did the conclusion show? The prisoners had "effectively deconstructed the realist premise of the Prisoner's Dilemma as well as the behaviouralist assumption of evolutionary tit-for-tat learning." By experience, the inmates were constructivists, not neorealists or institutionalists.

Rational Behaviour and IR

What does Prisoner's Dilemma have to do with IR? We have seen that the central question in anarchy is confidence and trust. Where there is confidence, both sides will get the best mutual outcomes (3/3). Where there is none, the temptation to defect leaves both worse off (1/1). That outcome is still preferable to cooperating while the other defects (0/5). Is there a way to solve this dilemma? Moving from voluntary cooperation to a system of rules and enforcement would. In domestic political orders, law—particularly the law of contracts—penalizes partners who defect. Those who fail to keep contracts can be taken to court.

In the international world, contracts cannot be enforced, and cheating or exploiting advantages are always a possibility. A state that has agreed to a fishing treaty designed to limit catches and preserve stocks can gain by violating it. Other states have the choice of violating it as well, defeating the purpose of preservation and leaving them all worse off, or accepting one of their number's getting unfair benefits. If we accept that international cooperation is always preferable to selfish state actions and if we also accept that states pursue their own gains, we need to know when cooperation is rational.

Prisoner's Dilemma is an elegant and stylized model of rational calculation. As we saw, it enumerates the players' possible moves, their preferences (represented by the weight of the numbers in the matrix) and all of the combinations that follow. Waltz extended an invitation to game theory when he postulated rational and gain-seeking states and an anarchic environment. In those settings, there is nothing to prevent defection and cheating—the very point of the neorealist view of the world. Invoking the analogy of microeconomics, where **game theory** is used to model the behaviour of firms in markets, attracted that discipline's formal and axiomatic methods.[29] The international system, as we saw, can produce outcomes that none of the actors wants. That resonates tantalizingly with Prisoner's Dilemma in which rational but untrusting players end up with mutual defection and mutual loss. More generally, assuming rational behaviour is necessary for building coherent and deductive theory. Thus neorealists and institutionalists had available a powerful tool for analyzing their most pressing question: when is it rational to cooperate?

Game theory joined the two schools in the 1980s.[30] Setting the trend of matching Prisoner's Dilemma to theory was Robert Axelrod's *The Evolution of Cooperation*. Robert Keohane applied the same reasoning to international cooperation, and Axelrod and Keohane collaborated on a more specific application, "Achieving Cooperation Under Anarchy."[31] Their view is that, under specified conditions, cooperation is rational. On the neorealist side, Joseph Grieco has used game theory to show that those conditions are limited.[32] At issue is whether game theory better supports neorealist views or institutionalist ones. The question has sponsored active debate and has produced highly deductive, carefully constructed contributions to each side. For its part, game theory provides a precisely delimited arena of debate by reducing complex situations and motives to a concise and specified set of preferences and outcomes. This work, which now constitutes a much-cited core of literature, is impressive as carefully applied logic.

Critiques of Deductive Rationality

Can this formal and deductive approach be criticized? There are several important avenues. Noting them provides a glimpse of the basic trade-off that is made in conceptualizing a complex reality: Reducing and condensing factors to construct a workably coherent and concise theory may distort the theory by leaving important things out or assuming them to be constant.

Within the strictly delimited terms of game theory itself, both neorealists and institutionalists have been criticized for employing a contradictory definition of anarchy, for treating state interests as given and for using a contradictory definition of absolute and relative gains.[33] The same kind of criticisms have been lodged more generally. By reducing preferences to simple functions, formal models eliminate personal and situational factors that may decide what actors really do. Game theory says nothing about the sources of preferences and interests or how and when these change. It also assumes that the preference weightings assigned in the game are the same as those of real-world actors. Game theory can demonstrate which behaviour will be rational according to the assigned preferences but cannot tell whether people in the real world, people who may weight their preferences differently, will be rational in the same way.[34]

A related but much broader critique is that rational analysis has no historical dimension. Instead of incorporating the kinds of experience between states that produce, as was seen earlier, both security communities and sharp enmities and that carry with them legacies of trust and suspicion, deductive theory depicts IR as a "permanent game, which can appear to have followed more or less the same rules for time immemorial."[35] A feminist variant criticizes the postulated rational actor as "disembodied, ageless, sexless, transcendent of historic particularity" and as being collectivized all too easily as the state.[36] We will see much more about feminist critiques in Chapter 5.

A more complex question follows: How much can a formal model, regardless of how carefully it condenses real-world factors, ever accommodate all of the conditions bearing upon national leaders' choices: how factions within their own and other countries will react, how much information the participants have, what kind of advice they are receiving, whether they see the decision as setting precedents, what effects the decision will have on third countries and the effect of the decision on the leaders' domestic political positions.[37] This problem is not limited to IR. Political science studies of electoral behaviour make use of powerful deductive models, also inspired by microeconomics, to analyze voter choice. The question for political scientists is reconciling "the expectations that are generated by the political economy models and the empirical reality as we know it."[38]

Neorealism and Institutionalism: The Major Test

Empirical criticism concerns a theory's fit with the facts. Neither Neorealism nor Institutionalism, empirical critics point out, can account for the end of the cold war, one of the most sweeping changes in modern history. The reason, the critics assert, is that neither theory has provision for drastic and fundamental changes of national interest. (To see Neorealist and Institutionalist perspectives on free trade read Canadian Reality Checks 2.5, 2.6, and 2.7.)

Neorealism's emphasis on suspicion and relative gains makes it particularly vulnerable. The cold war ended when Mikhail Gorbachev committed his Soviet government to "new thinking" and decided to seek accommodations with the West. For neorealists, that would be irrational behaviour because acting on "new thinking" would mean giving unbalanced concessions on important security matters. No prudent leader would provide such openings to an adversary.

Neorealists would also expect the West to exploit such signs of weakness. Instead, the West reciprocated.

Institutionalists came to the end of the cold war somewhat better equipped. By stretching notions of self-interest enough, an institutionalist might imagine a rapid spiral of cooperation in which one successful episode leads to another. Even so, such leaps of faith and action are difficult to encompass within assumptions of mutual gain-seeking behaviour, which dictate limited and incremental moves. Instead, the cold war's end was a sea change.[39] A broader theoretical scope is needed precisely to account for the transformation of states' interests and attitudes.[40] It was that change, not incremental transactions, that ended the cold war.

What is missing is a way of addressing the understandings and preferences that national leaders draw from their own states and from their interaction with other states. Liberal IR theory examines the domestic interplay of ideas and interests in shaping states' international behaviour. Constructivism focuses on the origins and transformative potential of mutual understandings between states. We will see these two theories in the next two chapters.

There are more fundamental objections to Neorealism and Institutionalism. Critical theorists, postmodernists and feminists focus their criticism on knowledge, beliefs and political purpose, and their arguments have framed almost 20 years of debate in IR. For now, having just seen an empirical criticism, bear in mind that there are more basic points of dissidence. These we will see in Chapter 5.

Canadian Reality Check 2.5

Neorealism and Free Trade

Neorealism's view on Canada's entering free trade negotiations with the United States is straightforward: Beware when dealing with more powerful states, even friendly ones (remember the statement about "more domineering friends"). They will concentrate on pursuing their own interests and can be expected to seek gains for themselves. Complex trade negotiations are risky because of the number of various elements involved—treatment of particular commodities and industries, investment rules, subsidies and taxation, for example.

Because each side brings different sets of elements to the table and because a common agreement must be reached, the elements must be combined and traded off to reach a deal. Even when the two sides cooperate and achieve mutual gains, there are still many ways to divide them up. The larger state may use its advantages to push for combinations that favour its interests. Both may end up with **absolute gains** and be better off, but the final distribution may favour the stronger power.[41] A neorealist would also be concerned about unequal incentives and would caution that the side which enters negotiations with greater interest in a deal is at a disadvantage.

That is exactly what Canadian nationalists warned: Canada will be taken to the cleaners. "You're selling out the country," charged Liberal leader John Turner in his 1988 election debate with Prime Minister Brian Mulroney. There was also worry about unequal incentives: Canada initiated the negotiations and appeared to want them more, giving the US the option of proceeding at leisure and extracting concessions.

Note the connection between economic nationalism and Neorealism: both views of the world emphasize power and competition and the prudence of keeping safeguards.[42] For economic nationalists those safeguards are trade protections. Free trade agreements lower them. We will see more about economic nationalism in Chapter 12.

Canadian Reality Check 2.6

Institutionalism and Free Trade

Institutionalism's view is also straightforward: Precisely because trade with the United States is so vitally important to Canada, it is crucial to place the relationship under a set of rules. That was the view taken by the Mulroney government and other free trade advocates. Acting on the same principle, the Trudeau government broached the idea of sectoral trade agreements with the United States in 1983. There the purpose was to bring particular industries such as urban transit vehicles under trade rules.

An institutionalist would point out that the cooperation necessary to reach and maintain a trade accord does not require *complete* harmony. Instead, states that are interdependent in important areas have enough interest in order and stability to negotiate their differences.[43] The positive motivation for setting rules is the prospect that both sides will be better off. Advocates of free trade pointed to a formidable body of liberal trade theory to make the case for mutual gain. We will see more about free trade, rules and global economic interdependence in Chapter 12. The institutionalist's final case is this: When states have incentives to cooperate, when the terms of cooperation are complex and when divided interests are mixed with mutual purposes, constructing an institution is the most durable approach. A comprehensive free trade agreement augmented by a dispute resolution panel is a good example of such an institution.

Canadian Reality Check 2.7

Neorealism's and Institutionalism's Common Point

State power and self-interest are central. The question is whether mutual gains and sufficient safeguards are possible through cooperation and whether Canada's interests can be adequately secured.

Summary

Realism became IR's dominant theory following World War II. Neorealism, a condensed and more formalized version, appeared in 1979 and has been a focus of criticism and debate in IR since then. Neorealism's tenets are straightforward—a reflection of its conciseness: states are unitary and rational actors, and they seek gains in an international condition of anarchy. That being so, states must be vigilant about the gains of other states because these may be exploited. Security is states' prime concern, and cooperation is problematic.

Institutionalism emerged as a reaction to Neorealism's emphasis on conflict. Instead, Institutionalism assumes that states prefer cooperation but require safeguards against cheating.

Such safeguards are necessary because states are assumed, just as in Neorealism, to be unitary and rational and to pursue gains. The gains important in Institutionalism, however, are absolute ones that make all participants better off. The prospect of achieving absolute gains motivates cooperation.

Because the two theories share so many assumptions in common, some scholars believe that they will eventually be merged into a single theory. In their present form, some scholars believe, Neorealism is better suited to situations of conflict and insecurity, and Institutionalism is better suited to situations of common interest.

Because both theories are predicated on rational state behaviour, both have been hospitable to formalized logical models of conflict and cooperation. The exemplar of those models is Prisoner's Dilemma. Their advantage is showing the logical consequences of particular kinds of structures and behaviour. Logical models have been criticized for leaving out factors that could affect behaviour in the real world.

ENDNOTES

1   Edward Hallett Carr, The Twenty Years' Crisis, 1919–1939: An Introduction to the Study of International Relations. New York: Harper and Row, 1939.

2   Richard Little, "The Growing Relevance of Pluralism," in Steve Smith, Ken Booth and Marysia Zalewski, eds., International Theory: Positivism and Beyond? Cambridge: Cambridge University Press, 1996, pp. 73–74, 83.

3   Miles Kahler, "Inventing International Relations: International Relations Theory after 1945," in Michael W. Doyle and G. John Ikenberry, eds., New Thinking in International Relations Theory, Boulder, CO: Westview, 1997, 23–30.

4   Hans J. Morgenthau, Politics Among Nations: The Struggle for Power and Peace, New York: Alfred A. Knopf, 1948.

5   Ernst B. Haas, "The Balance of Power: Prescription, Concept, or Propaganda?" World Politics 5 (July 1953) 442–47.

6   Barry Buzan, "The Timeless Wisdom of Realism?" in Smith, Booth and Zalewski, International Theory: Positivism and Beyond? p. 49.

7   Robert O. Keohane and Joseph Nye, Power and Interdependence, Boston: Little Brown, 1977.

8   Hedley Bull, The Anarchical Society, London: Macmillan, 1977

9   Robert O. Keohane, "Problematic Lucidity: Stephen Krasner's 'State Power and the Structure of International Trade,'" World Politics 50 (October 1997) 151–53.

10 Kenneth Waltz, Theory of International Politics, Reading, MA: Addison-Wesley, 1979

11 Robert Powell, "Anarchy in International Relations Theory: The Neorealist-Neoliberal Debate," International Organization 48 (Spring 1994) 315.

12 John Gerard Ruggie, "Continuity and Transformation in the World Polity: Toward a Neorealist Synthesis," in Robert O. Keohane, ed., Neorealism and its Critics, New York: Columbia University Press, 1986, pp. 134–135.

13 Martin Hollis and Steve Smith, "Beware of Gurus: Structure and Action in International Relations," Review of International Studies 17 (October 1991) 399–403.

14 Robert O. Keohane, "Institutional Theory and the Realist Challenge After the Cold War," in David Baldwin, ed., Neorealism and Neoliberalism: The Contemporary Debate, New York: Columbia University Press, 1993, p. 274.

15 Robert O. Keohane, "International Institutions: Two Approaches," International Studies Quarterly 32 (December 1988) 383.

16 This list is condensed from David Sanders, "International Relations: Neo-Realism and Neo-Liberalism," in Robert Goodin and Hans-Dieter Klingemann, eds., A New Handbook of Political Science, Oxford: Oxford University Press, 1996, pp. 441–44.

17 Joseph Grieco, "Understanding the Problem of International Cooperation: The Limits of Neoliberal Institutionalism and the Future of Realist Theory," in Baldwin, ed., Neorealism and Neoliberalism, p. 303.

18 Ted Hopf, "The Promise of Constructivism in International Relations Theory," International Security 23 (Summer 1998) 174.

19 Karl W. Deutsch, et al., Political Community and the North Atlantic Area, Princeton: Princeton University Press, 1957, pp. 5–6.

20 Richard Ned Lebow, "The Long Peace, The End of the Cold War, and the Failure of Realism," International Organization 48 (Spring 1994) 269.

21 Grieco, "Understanding the Problem of International Cooperation," p. 323.

22 Sanders, "International Relations: Neo-Realism and Neo-Liberalism," p. 437

23 ibid., p. 438.

24 Ole Waever, "The Rise and Fall of the Inter-Paradigm Debate," in Smith, Booth and Zalewski, eds, International Theory: Positivism and Beyond, pp. 163–64

25 Buzan, "The Timeless Wisdom of Realism?" p.50.

26 Robert Axelrod, The Evolution of Cooperation, Princeton: Princeton University Press, 1984.

27 Judith Goldstein and Robert O. Keohane, "Ideas and Foreign Policy: An Analytical Framework," in Judith Goldstein and Robert O. Keohane, eds., Ideas and Foreign Policy: Beliefs, Institutions, and Political Change, Ithaca: Cornell University Press, 1993, p. 4.

28 James Der Derian, "The Scriptures of Security," Mershon International Studies Review 42 (May 1998) 117.

29 George W. Downs, "The Rational Deterrence Debate," World Politics 41 (January 1989) 225.

30   Earlier applications of game theory in IR tended to focus on the more limited area of nuclear strategy.

31   Robert Keohane, After Hegemony, Princeton: Princeton University Press, 1984; Robert Axelrod and Robert Keohane, "Achieving Cooperation under Anarchy," World Politics 38 (October 1988) 226–54.

32   Grieco, "Anarchy and the Limits of Cooperation," in Baldwin, Neorealism and Neoliberalism.

33   Powell, "Anarchy in International Relations Theory," 329–38.

34   Richard Ned Lebow and Janice Gross Stein, "Rational Deterrence Theory: I Think, Therefore I Deter," World Politics 41 (January 1989) 208–09, 214–15.

35   R.B.J. Walker, "History and Structure in the Theory of International Relations," in Der Derian, ed., International Theory, p. 321.

36   Jean Bethke Elshtain, "Feminist Themes and International Relations," in Der Derian, ed., International Theory, p. 351.

37   Sanders, "Neo-Realism and Neo-Liberalism," p. 434

38   Edward Carmines and Robert Huckfeldt, "Political Behavior: An Overview," in Goodin and Klingemann, eds., The New Handbook of Political Science, p. 226.

39   Rey Koslowski and Friedrich V. Kratochwil, "Understanding Change in International Politics: The Soviet Empire's Demise and the International System," International Organization 48 (Spring 1994) 215–47.

40   Joseph Nye, "Neorealism and Neoliberalism," World Politics 40 (April 1988) 246.

41   Stephen Krasner, "Global Communication and National Power: Life on the Pareto Frontier," World Politics 43 (April 1991) 362–64.

42   Robert Gilpin, The Political Economy of International Relations, Princeton: Princeton University Press, 1987, 31–35, 183–90.

43   Keohane, "International Institutions: Two Approaches" 380.

Chapter ③

Liberal IR Theory

The State: Filling in the Blank

One of the primary criticisms of Neorealism is that it defines state interests as exogenous.[1] What states seek to achieve or protect is determined in an international setting in which all states pursue gains. As we saw in the last chapter, Neorealism emphasizes the insecurities that inhere in that condition, and institutionalists emphasize the potential benefits of cooperation. Neither incorporates the domestic source of state interests other than to assume that all states behave rationally. Excluding domestic factors was, as we saw, no oversight. Waltz wanted to construct a theory of the international *system*, not of individual states. Explaining the nature of the international system from the behaviour of its member states was, in his view, to commit the fallacy of reductionism, which accounts for a whole as a simple sum of its parts. His purpose was to treat the international system as a political system of interacting states. Assuming that states behave rationally subsumes societies and preferences. For Neorealism and Institutionalism that is enough. But what is lost by leaving out the sources of preferences and factoring out societies?

Neither Neorealism nor Institutionalism can explain why some interests are more important than others—why, for example, a state would put a higher foreign policy priority on trade in steel than on international investment banking. Instead, factoring out the origins of interests within states leaves Neorealism and Institutionalism to explain priorities and state behaviour simply as a reaction to what other states do. From there, it is logical to say that the system shapes state actions and that the possibilities available to states depend on the actions and capabilities of others. States' efforts succeed or fail according to those conditions. That result is consistent with system-level theory's emphasis on interaction and outcome. The source of interaction, what states seek to achieve or defend, is simply assumed to be gain.

Neorealism and Institutionalism are partial theories of politics because they exclude the domestic half of the equation: the ways interest groups and governments assess events in the international system define their preferences and shape national policy.[2] By assuming unitary rationality, these theories block out that entire political dimension. What is needed, critics have argued, is a theory of the state. Such a theory would work "from the bottom up" by identifying the domestic sources of interests and action.[3] Preferences form within different domestic societies, and interdependence transmits their effects across national boundaries. States mediate the process both domestically and internationally. This view extends to the international system a long-standing and familiar view of statehood.

The Political Science Legacy

Political science has a rich history of developing theories of the state, and liberal theory forms a particularly long tradition. Liberal theory holds that groups are the basis of political life. People form groups with others who share their interests, and together they seek to influence policies and decisions that affect them. Policies are not proclaimed by government but result from government's effort to balance and reconcile contending interests. The interests of groups may conflict strongly, but their political power motivates government to take them all into account and come up with policies that do not alienate important blocs of support. Because policy is made by compromise, it is generally moderate. Extreme policies and radical decisions are a sign either of strong alignment among a number of groups favouring the same thing or of one group having determinate influence. For individual people, the same principle applies; people have more than one interest and may belong to more than one group. These personal interests and group memberships tend to offset one another, making for moderation at the individual level.

There is room in pluralist politics for radical change, but for that to occur it must have broad public support. Governments instituting such change without public support or continuing radical policies after public support has declined, risk losing their political base. Publics and groups that are fundamentally divided on important issues but that possess equal political influence make for difficult and unstable compromises and, when these conditions are acute, for turbulent government. Publics and groups that share a broad consensus produce more harmonious politics. For that reason, liberals believe, government action must always be understood in reference to its political settings.[4] Demands for government action arise from people's interests. The essence of politics is the articulation and reconciliation of those interests.

These liberal views have two important implications. First, the state is not supreme and is not detached from society. Instead, states are "embedded" in their societies and are directly affected by popular preferences and organized pressures.[5] To stay in power, governments must be attentive to the preferences of groups. Policies represent not singular state initiatives but the outcome of contests among groups to influence the state and shape policy. The role of the state is to mediate and find common ground. Politics is supreme. Second, liberalism contradicts the notion of a single national interest.[6] The national interest, in a liberal view, represents not a singular definition but a group consensus. The state does not proclaim the national interest; people and groups seek to shape it. States do not pursue fixed interests because people's interests are not fixed. They change when conditions and ideas change. Interests are not only selfish ones. Liberalism believes that people are quite capable of being generous and of cooperating to pursue common benefits. One of the sources of generosity emphasized by Liberalism is an individual sense of duty and obligation to others. Together these ingredients produce a view of state interests as "multiple and changing and both self-interested and other-regarding."[7] If these ideas sound familiar it is because liberal pluralism is one of political science's basic concepts and is one of the core topics in introductory courses in the discipline.

Liberalism has had an interrupted career in IR. We saw earlier that realists after World War II blamed a myopic interwar idealism for failure to act earlier against Naziism and Fascism. The occupation of IR scholars and many governments with the perfection of international law and the League of Nations was based, it was charged, on an unrealistic assumption that states' interests could be reconciled. The illusion of enlightenment and harmony was shattered by the war. Blame was directed at liberals.

The charge of naiveté, in the view of recent commentaries, was unfair. Although interwar liberals were interested in international law and the League, they were also beginning to focus on economic interdependence that crystallized much later in IR in the 1970s. Nonetheless, the charge of impractical idealism stuck. Feeling discredited, liberal pluralists after the war concentrated on domestic politics where they developed an elaborate scholarship in the 1950s and 1960s, leaving international politics to the developing field of IR where realists held sway.[8]

Interest in international economic interdependence in the 1970s marked the re-emergence of liberalism in IR. As we saw in Chapter 2, liberal scholars disagreed strongly with neorealists about the primacy of conflict. True to their liberal heritage, their preference was cooperation. To engage the debate on an equal footing, some liberals *accepted* Neorealism's premises of self-interest and gain-seeking.[9] The purpose was to show that those premises could also support cooperation and, less obviously, to show that liberals too could be rationalistic and pragmatic. This approach has come to be called Institutionalism. As we saw earlier, Institutionalism shares Neorealism's basic assumptions that the state is the primary actor, that states are self-interested and that states behave rationally. The main difference between the two theories, as we also saw, is when it makes sense for states to cooperate.

In adopting Neorealism's premises, liberals abandoned the domestic political life of the state.[10] Instead, they worked at the system level: interests are defined by gain-seeking behaviour among states in the condition of anarchy. To the system level, institutionalists brought the view that states prefer to cooperate but fear cheating. About the source of state interests themselves, however, institutionalists had nothing further to say. Some way was needed to focus internationally while treating preferences domestically. A very new liberal theory melds the two dimensions. For liberals it has been a long journey home.

The Theory

Andrew Moravcsik has fashioned a number of liberal themes into a theory of IR.[11] The pivots of the theory are preferences and interdependence. The preferences are those of individual groups within states and of states themselves. Those preferences motivate political action domestically as groups seek to have them adopted as policy, and they shape state strategies internationally as states seek to achieve their purposes with other states. Interdependence, as we saw in Chapter 2, transmits the effects of actions and constitutes the international milieu within which states must function. A policy or decision taken by one state is felt by another state and by groups within it. They, in turn, may respond by modifying their preferences and strategies. In emphasizing preferences and interdependence, **Liberal IR theory** intends to fill two requirements. First, by accounting for the sources of preferences within a state, it opens the dimension that Neorealism and Institutionalism, by arbitrarily assuming state interests, close off. Second, by recognizing interdependence among states, it operates within the framework of IR.

States form strategies for realizing their preferences abroad.[12] The greater the degree of interdependence, the more likely it is that one state's strategy will affect others, both states and groups within states. The stronger the preferences involved, the more important are the consequences. Depending on the way one state's strategy aligns with that of another, the effects may be welcome or resisted, incidental or central. Whether a state's strategy results in conflict or cooperation depends on the other state's preferences and its strategy for advancing them.[13] Because it is preferences and strategies themselves that produce conflict or cooperation, Liberal IR theory accommodates both. Conflict or cooperation is the result of harmonious or opposing preferences and strategies and neither is an inherent property of the international system. The condition of the international system at any particular time is simply the result of what states, acting on their preferences, choose to do.

Because other states' responses vary, Liberal IR theory envisages a range of situations. The emphasis is on understanding the way states advance and accommodate their preferences with particular strategies in particular situations.[14] Because preferences are diverse, because they are spread across a multitude of issues and because a number of states form strategies in light of them, international relations can be visualized as a disparate and changing array of situations in which preferences are engaged and state strategies are acted upon. For each state, the result is a mixture of strategies across a range of issues. For the international system, the result is a variable field on which cooperation and conflict occur according to states, preferences and issues. In each instance the outcomes depend on the strategies pursued by states and the ways other states resist or accommodate them. By allowing for fluid combinations of cooperation and conflict, Liberal IR theory surmounts the limits of Neorealism, which is predicated on conflict, and those of Institutionalism, which is predicated on cooperation. Together with Constructivism, presented in the next chapter, Liberalism expands IR's range of explanation.

Preferences

Preferences originate within groups in society and are formed of both interests and ideas. Interests are material. Individuals and groups seek to protect their existing goods and benefits and will act to increase them if doing so does not put their existing holdings at risk.[15] They organize to enlist government support when their own abilities to pursue their interests are inadequate. Ideas are just as important. Although they are not material and immediate, they represent desired conditions: justice, security, identity.

Ideas of identity and justice address the proper territory of the state, who should govern and which people should be enclosed within the boundaries. Preferences arising from these ideas become demands when the real situation is discrepant: boundaries not matching nations or a desired form of government not being the one that exists.[16] As we will see in Chapter 7, which examines statehood and nationality, demands involving boundaries and national identities contain potent ingredients of conflict. Preferences can also arise over the proper form of government itself. Democratic states tend to regard authoritarian ones as less legitimate. That difference may become important in times of conflict with

Canadian Press/CP photo/Fred Chartrand

Brian Robertson of the Canadian Recording Industry Association listens as David Baskin of the Canadian Music Publishers Association talks to reporters as they, along with other representatives of cultural groups, hold a news conference over the Canadian Copyright Act. Representatives of economic interests seek to have government policy reflect their preferences.

authoritarian states attracting suspicion and hostility because of the way they deal with domestic dissent. Human rights are closely bound with these ideas and become demands when they address conditions at home or in other states, as we will see in Chapter 13. Public policies can evoke conflicting preferences about government's proper role. One example is social welfare. Debates and influence easily cross national boundaries and affect preferences elsewhere.

International commerce generates a host of demands. Sectors of the economy that are unable to survive foreign competition may seek to use their political resources to pressure the government for protection.[17] The list of affected preferences expands with interdependence. High levels of international trade may create both winners and losers in a state and varying preferences for state action. Reconciling them domestically is difficult because people are affected differently. Reconciling them internationally is difficult because they disturb relations with trading partners.[18]

It is accurate to say that the more diverse and complex a society is, the greater array of preferences it will generate. How governments reconcile them into external strategies depends partly on the groups' respective political influence, partly on other states' preferences and strategies and partly, as we will see next, on the government's own preferences.

Institutions

By institutions, Liberal IR theory means government organizations and laws. The organizations include not only Parliament but also federal agencies. The Department of Foreign Affairs and International Trade is the most important one for Canada's dealings with other states. Others are involved because of particular policy responsibilities. For Canadian airlines, Transport Canada is a key agency because of its responsibility for domestic and international civil aviation. Officials within those institutions who have professional expertise in their policy area have ideas and interests as well, and they can form policy preferences although as civil servants they are required to be nonpartisan. Together with the preferences of the elected government, which can be held quite openly, the preferences of domestic agencies form a context in which some demands from domestic groups resonate more strongly than others.

In Canada's federal state, provincial governments have their own ideas and interests and form their own preferences. Laws, including the constitution, regulate what federal and provincial governments may do. Together, institutions and laws affect how governments respond to group demands.

Government, in the liberal view, is a "transmission belt" of domestic ideas and interests.[19] Because governments must balance and reconcile various interests to stay in power, they cannot afford to ignore important groups. To enhance their influence, groups may ally on particular issues. Although government institutions may influence the outcome, liberal theory sees government policies resulting primarily from attending to group preferences and pressures.

This process need not be democratic. Authoritarian governments also attend to group interests, but the difference between them and democratic governments is the breadth of representation. Authoritarian governments may be very attentive to a few powerful groups and exclude or suppress many others. Because authoritarian governments do not depend as directly on popular support as do democratic ones, they have a broader latitude of action. Liberal IR theory recognizes that representative institutions and practices vary among governments and that they, as well as their society's demands, determine what states seek to achieve. Whether broadly or narrowly representative, government policy-making is "constrained by the underlying identities, interests and power of individuals and groups."[20]

Governments differ in their ability to meld demands into consistent policy. Policies that are consistent reflect stable sets of demands and the ability of the government to harmonize them. Policies that shift or that are contradictory reflect difficulty in reconciling conflicting interests or beliefs or in maintaining a stable balance of support. Interests themselves change in response to new domestic or international conditions, requiring new political accommodations.

The International Dimension

States and their domestic groups do not exist in isolation. **Interdependence** among states makes them sensitive to others' actions across a range of issues. States pursue their preferences in light of the opportunities and constraints created by others, and realizing those preferences depends on what the others do. Whether there is conflict or cooperation depends upon group aims, the way they are translated into state strategy and the way that strategy meshes with other states' strategies.[21] Because interaction occurs issue by issue and state by state, there is no automatic harmony of interests, but neither is there inherent conflict. International conflict and harmony are aggregates of the particular issues at hand. Whatever condition prevails is a reflection of state strategies and the political force behind them. The international system does not determine conflict or harmony. The preferences and strategies of states do.

Conflict does become more likely both domestically and internationally when important benefits and goods are scarce or threatened. That increases the willingness of groups and states to take risks to protect what they have. When resources are abundant, conflict is less likely because demand is less keen. The same is true of beliefs and practices. Conflicts over state borders, culture and basic forms of government can be severe because they address fundamental values and beliefs. Agreement on basic values and beliefs promotes harmony.[22] In the same way, frequent clashes between states produce difficult relations while frequent agreement produces easier ones. Although long patterns of conflict or accord can come to typify states' relationships, a liberal would argue that it is important to think issue by issue. Conflict in one issue area does not rule out cooperation in another, nor do broad and long-standing areas of opposed interests preclude some areas of common interest. Which areas those are depends on preferences and the way states reconcile them into strategy.

Canadian Preferences and Strategies

Canadian wheat farmers prefer open world markets. Like American and Australian wheat farmers, Canadians can employ efficiently extensive cultivation and have a strong export advantage. Some of the wheat farmers' interests are historically based. Unlike Canadian industrial producers who enjoyed tariff protection from the time of John A. Macdonald's National Policy until recently, Canadian wheat farmers have always sold onto the world market. Their interest is that the market be open and fair, and one of their preferences has been to reduce import barriers to major markets such as the European Union. Transforming these preferences into a state strategy, the Canadian government was one of the major members of the Cairns Group. Formed by agricultural exporting states during the Uruguay Round of the General Agreement on Tariffs and Trade negotiations in the 1980s, the Cairns

Group pushed for freer access for their products. More recently, some Canadian wheat farmers have sought direct access to the international market by bypassing the Canadian Wheat Board and thereby putting them in conflict with the government's preference to continue regulating grain sales.

The Canadian Manufacturers Association was strongly in favour of protected markets and tariffs until it changed its view in the early 1980s. Its preferences were also formed by the National Policy, which had encouraged Canadian industrialization by creating a domestic market sheltered by tariffs against competing imports. Those preferences generally agreed with the government's until the early 1980s when a severe recession and the rising threat of protectionism against Canadian exports prompted the government to re-examine its trade and industrial policy. The most important outcome was a state strategy of free trade with the United States. Persuaded that exporting had become a promising and attractive proposition, most Canadian manufacturers have shifted their preferences to freer trade particularly in emerging markets such as Asia and Latin America. These preferences accord with the government's, which has expanded its strategy to promote trade in those same areas. Team Canada trade missions to Asia and Latin America, with delegations composed of national political and business leaders, symbolize the fusion.

Liberal IR Theory in Sum:

State preferences are shaped by societal ideas, preferences and institutions. States may have preferences of their own, but because states are representative institutions their preferences are shaped by domestic politics. Domestic preferences and ideas may be affected by international influences. Strategies are states' means of pursuing preferences abroad, and strategic interactions among states produce a diverse field of activity. Cooperation or conflict depends on the strategies that states pursue.

Differences with Neorealism and Institutionalism

According to Neorealism and Institutionalism, states create opportunities and constraints for each other, and international politics is the process of rationally defending interests. The interests themselves arise from the actions of others. The only thing to know about states themselves is that they are rational and seek gain. The stakes of gain and loss are defined in light of other states' actions, and the task is to respond rationally to the circumstances created. Liberals argue that this view of states leaves out the reasons for action that arise from their own societies and narrows relations among states to eliminate the interdependent connections between states and their societies. Neorealists and institutionalists might object that Liberalism is nothing more than a new way of presenting studies of foreign policy. Foreign policy has been a distinct field from IR because it focuses on individual states and explains their behaviour. Foreign policy studies remain fixed on individual states and do not address the international system as a whole. The system has been IR's domain. Liberal IR theory, its advocates respond, *is* IR-level because it "can explain not only the 'foreign policy' goals of individual states but the 'systemic' outcomes of interstate interactions."[23]

The international system's condition is another basic point of disagreement. International conflict and harmony, according to Liberal IR theory, arise from the states pursuing their preferences. When the interests converge there is harmony, and when they diverge there is conflict. Neither is an inherent property of the international system. Its condition depends on what states choose to pursue, making the system variable over time. Neorealists, as we saw, believe that conflict resides in international anarchy. Institutionalists believe that states will cooperate if they can construct proper safeguards within international institutions and rules.

Core Tenets: Liberal IR Theory and Neorealism/Institutionalism Compared

In Chapter 2, we saw Neorealism and Institutionalism's differences and similarities. Their main point of difference is when it is rational for states to cooperate. Their points of similarity are their assumptions of states as unitary and rational actors, their emphasis on gain as the motive of state action and their belief in anarchy as the international condition. To facilitate tabulation of their similarities and differences with Liberal IR theory, we will merge them in table 3.1.

TABLE 3.1   Similarities and Differences

Similarities	
Liberal IR theory	*Neorealism/Institutionalism*
States are the prime international actors	States are the prime international actors
Rational behaviour is assumed	Rational behaviour is assumed.

Differences	
Liberal IR theory	*Neorealism/Institutionalism*
Rational behaviour includes groups as well as governments	The rational actor is a unitary state
Ideas and interests of groups, mediated by government institutions, are the source of national strategies	National interests originate in the state's desire to pursue fixed gains and avoid losses

TABLE 3.1   continued

State interests can be known by looking at the position of the state in domestic and transnational society	State interests can be known by looking at the structure of the international political system, defined as the distribution of resources or information
Conflict and cooperation depend on the interests that states pursue	Conflict is assumed (Neorealism) Preference for cooperation is assumed (Institutionalism)[24]

Deduction and Induction

We saw in Chapter 2 that one of the criticisms of Neorealism and Neoliberalism is their deductive emphasis. State interests and rational actions are derived from the actions of other states. The explanatory emphasis of Liberal IR theory is reversed: state interests and actions arise from preferences. Applying Liberal theory we proceed inductively. We add up the various influences, factor in the role of the government and discover the policy. Proceeding further to the level of the international system, we find states pursuing their preferences with one another. The condition of the international system is the product of the various states' strategies for realizing those preferences. This reverses the pattern of inference of Neorealism and Institutionalism. They begin with the international system's condition and derive rational state policies. Liberal IR theory begins with state policies and derives the international system's condition.

What are the advantages and disadvantages? On the side of Liberal IR theory, one could say that it does not assume either state interests or a particular international system. It waits for them to appear and analyzes them. Nothing is categorically excluded. The task is simply to be sure that all of the interests have been identified and analyzed. One could object that such a procedure, while it may explain state interests and actions after the fact, is not predictive. A liberal could respond that states may establish track records of backing particular kinds of policies, reflecting stable patterns of group interests and government mediation. Such patterns provide a basis for assumptions about future behaviour.

Is there a disadvantage? Analysis of groups and preferences is inherently more complex because of the number of actors it accommodates, including the state itself. The multiple and interactive sources of state behaviour make analysis an extensive task. That is precisely the purpose of constructing a powerful theory. Powerful theories, we saw, are ones that have few terms but explain a range of phenomena. If a powerful theory can deliver the same explanations with a fraction of the complexity, it clearly is preferable. Using a powerful theory depends on whether the factors it assumes away or holds constant are important to the question at hand.[25] If they are, they should be accommodated. Liberal IR theory provides one means of doing so.

There is also the question of explanatory bias. A liberal could argue that Neorealism and Institutionalism, by assuming either conflict or cooperation to be the international system's inherent condition, may be biased towards conclusions that show conflict or cooperation. By excluding domestic factors, Neorealism and Neoliberalism may be incapable of accommodating factors that would provide balance. We saw that criticism in the last chapter with Neorealism's failure to anticipate the end of the cold war.

As a final point, a more modest liberal could claim that the theory's primary use is in supplying an explanation of the state. Comprehensive coverage can be added by explaining the behaviours of groups of states and the ways they interact. In the end, however, a liberal would maintain that groups are the basis of politics. State actions and interactions proceed from there.

The Liberal View of the World

Liberal IR theory is so new that there have not yet been major applications of it. Nonetheless, some of its basic assumptions and outlooks are familiar enough that applications come readily to mind. As an illustration, we can see how a liberal would tackle the Turbot War between Canada and Spain in 1995 (see Figure 3.2).

FIGURE 3.2 The Turbot War: Quotas and Quarrel

In 1992, the federal government, alarmed at the sharp drop in fish stocks in the waters off Atlantic Canada, imposed a moratorium on catching northern cod. In 1994, further bans and cutbacks were set for other groundfish. Canada could enforce these measures within its 200-mile economic zone, but beyond that limit fishing is under the jurisdiction of an international body, the Northwest Atlantic Fisheries Organization (NAFO). Composed of 15 member states including Canada, NAFO regulates fishing by assigning annual quotas to each country. Throughout the 1980s, NAFO, also concerned about fish stocks, set moderate limits.

That changed when Spain and Portugal joined the European Union (EU). They immediately began pressing the EU, which represents its members at NAFO, to use its influence to get higher quotas. NAFO continued with its moderate approach as Canada imposed the moratorium in 1992. In 1994, NAFO halved the international quota for turbot. Canada agreed to the measure but worried that neither NAFO nor the EU could adequately monitor individual fishing vessel's compliance.[26] Ottawa worried that overfishing beyond the 200-mile limit could badly harm the stocks.

Spain and Portugal continued to push the EU for higher quotas and eventually got them. NAFO procedures allow states that disagree with their quota to set an independent one. The EU used that expedient and declared that vessels of its member states would take three times their allotment. Most of the new portion the EU gave to Portugal and Spain, both of which were already taking 3/4 of the total turbot catch.[27] That behaviour supported Ottawa's and the Atlantic provinces' view that Spain and Portugal were the major problem.

Soon after, Canada's parliament passed amendments to the Coastal Fisheries Protection Act that authorized Canada to arrest foreign fishermen taking endangered stocks beyond the 200-mile limit and exempting those waters from jurisdiction of the International Court of Justice, which hears cases involving the high seas.[28] The EU strongly protested that Canada has no jurisdiction in international waters and that any interference would violate international law. In March 1995, Canada seized a Spanish fishing boat just outside the limit and towed it to port. The boat was found to have much smaller fish aboard than were allowed and to have used illegal nets. A false compartment was discovered that contained additional tons of fish well over the boat's limit. Also found was a double set of logbooks showing the officially permitted catch and the actual one. The boat and captain were detained and a large fine was levied. Two weeks later, Canadian fisheries officers cut the nets of a second Spanish trawler fishing just beyond the Canadian limit. Charging Canada with piracy, Spain sent two warships to the area with orders to fire if Canadian officials boarded Spanish trawlers fishing in the international zone. Canada sent out a frigate. The EU threatened economic retaliation.[29]

With tensions rising, Canada and the EU negotiated a redivided quota. Although the total catch was increased, Canada came away satisfied that enforcement would be stricter. The EU was relieved to see a settlement although it was chided by the Spanish government for insufficient support. The British government, whose waters are also frequented by Spanish trawlers, was sympathetic to Canada throughout the affair. The EU was not sympathetic, and its relations with Canada remained irritable for some time.

Looking to the domestic as well as the international sources of the conflict, a liberal IR theorist would ask these two questions:

➤ What preferences made the Spanish government push for higher quotas?
➤ What preferences made the Canadian government take such strong action?

Remember the guiding liberal principle: to understand states' behaviour, take their domestic politics into account. States have no built-in inclination to either conflict or cooperation. What they do depends on the issue, the demands of domestic groups and the mediating effects of institutions and laws. Those demands and actions in turn may be responses to actions by other states.

What about Spain? A liberal would look first to domestic interests. Half of Spain's fishing fleet and all of its turbot boats have their home ports in the province of Galicia. Located in the relatively poor and undeveloped northwestern part of Spain, the province relies on fishing as a mainstay of employment. Both the Spanish and Portuguese have fished off Atlantic Canada for centuries and regard the area as a historical domain. By the 1980s, Spanish fleet owners were facing depleted stocks in other waters and believed that Canada was using the quotas to give itself an unfair share. The Spanish fleet owners were determined to push hard for better access. Their preference was more fish.

On their side was unemployment. Lower quotas, they argued, would increase joblessness in an already poor region. A bonus was very strong support in Spanish public opinion, which saw Canada as the offending side. The mediating effects of Spanish institutions were also favourable. The government of Prime Minister Felipe Gonzalez, aware of its appearance of inconstancy in the eyes of the public, could not afford to be seen backing down on such an emotionally charged issue. The fleet owners calculated that the government could be pushed to take a tough line.[30] Spain's strategy was to push for higher quotas in NAFO and to challenge any new restrictions set by Canada.

High unemployment and dependence on the fishery also beset Atlantic Canada. In Newfoundland, the fishery provides one-quarter of the province's jobs and supports some 700 coastal communities. The 1990s were particularly hard for the Maritimes because Ottawa had already cut back quotas on Canadian catches. The 1992 and 1994 moratoriums devastated employment, putting some 40,000 fishery employees out of work. The mediating effects of Canadian institutions favoured the fishery whose owners and workers are located in many communities across the Maritimes and are well represented in both provincial and federal politics. With John Crosbie and Brian Tobin, the Conservative government of Brian Mulroney and the Liberal government of Jean Chretien had strong fisheries advocates in the Cabinet. In the election campaign of 1993, Jean Chretien had promised direct measures against offending foreign trawlers. Once the conflict began in 1994, Ottawa enjoyed strong support in Canadian public opinion.[31] Its preference was to protect existing fish stocks.

On both sides, a liberal could point to substantial domestic elements in the dispute and their effect on the government's strategy of confrontation. They raise an interesting question. Without regional unemployment and effective political pressure, would either the Spanish or Canadian governments have escalated the issue as much as they did or would they have kept to the more normal pattern of negotiation, the means by which the matter was eventually settled? What if public opinion in Canada had strongly opposed armed confrontation as it has done in other instances? What if environmental groups in Europe, which are very concerned to protect Canadian seals, had mobilized to protect Atlantic fish? And what if an opposing coalition of powerful domestic interests had gotten involved? On the Canadian side there indeed was concern that the Turbot War was jeopardizing relations with the EU just when efforts were underway to increase trade. If the crisis had dragged on and the EU had begun carrying out its threats of economic retaliation, would Canadian exporters and banks have weighed in?

As we have seen, Liberal IR theory's distinction is including domestic political factors. How would a neorealist approach the episode? We saw a preview in Chapter 2's discussion of Prisoner's Dilemma. Overfishing would be a classic application. By violating the agreement while others complied, Spain could score unilateral gains. Without an international way of enforcing the agreement and penalizing Spain, Canada's alternatives are to do nothing or overfish too. International anarchy makes direct action against the fishing vessels necessary. In the absence of an effective international authority, force is the ultimate instrument for resolving disputes and protecting interests. In the Turbot War, no one else would stop the vessels from fishing.

And what would be the institutionalist explanation? The North Atlantic Fishing Organization's rules did not prevent Spain from cheating, nor was NAFO effective enough to prevent the European Union's decision to set its own quota. A stronger institution is needed although the drastic scarcity of fish and the win/lose outlooks of the participants make the prospect difficult.

The three explanations emphasize different aspects. For extracting political information at the state level, the liberal pluralist approach asks appropriate questions. For generalizing about force and cooperation at the system level, Neorealism and Neoliberalism provide spare but sufficient information.

Critiques of Liberal IR Theory

Beyond Liberalism's appetite for domestic political information, are there other critiques that could be made? An important one regards the autonomy of the state from domestic politics. Liberalism, as we saw, treats governments as seeking to reconcile domestic group pressures into policy. What if, however, the government defines national interest in a way that either opposes important domestic interests or simply acts independently of them? IR scholarship in the 1980s emphasized the autonomous role of the state. In that characterization, the institutions of government such as ministries and departments not only form their own views on issues but also hold broader outlooks of the state's position and role. Because these officials are not elected, their outlooks can persist over time forming an element of continuity in state policy.[32] Their views come to bear when they advise governments and when they implement government policies and rules. How autonomous a particular ministry is depends on its legal authority, on whether its jurisdiction is shared or exclusive and on the level of political support from the government.[33]

When they are carrying out existing laws and policies, government agencies that have high levels of autonomy are able to act against the interests of important groups. Because the officials in those agencies are not elected, their policy advice can be independent. Governments that make laws and policies do depend on groups and the general public for support but on particular issues may decide to defy them for the good of the state. In response, a liberal would maintain that governments cannot defy or ignore their constituencies for very long. A liberal would also regard the long-term professional views from ministries and agencies as ingredients that would be factored into the more general process of accommodating demands.

How much latitude governments actually have depends partly on the level of public attention. Public opinion tends to focus on immediate bread-and-butter questions and to become interested in foreign policy in response to dramatic events abroad, to immediate threats to the state or to threats to personal welfare, particularly job security. In broad areas of international affairs, the public's lack of consistent attention or strong preferences gives the government room to define particular national interests and policies. Groups, on the other hand, remain quite attentive to issues that affect their interests. (To see a liberal perspective on free trade, read Canadian Reality Check 3.3.)

Canadian Reality Check 3.3

Liberal IR theory and Free Trade

Canada's decision to seek a free trade agreement with the United States would fascinate a liberal. The implications of free trade affected almost every significant group in Canada, and persuasive economic and nationalist ideas were prominent. Groups and the public were divided, and central institutions of the government had clear preferences.

There were several major blocs. Canadian manufacturers who had been historically protectionist revised their views in the 1980s. By 1985 when the Mulroney government announced its intention to seek an agreement with the United States, manufacturers were solidly in support. Many westerners who historically had resented having to sell at open world prices and buy at protected domestic ones were also in support. Many Quebecers saw free trade as an economic opportunity. The largest bloc of opposition existed with the labour unions in central Canada that feared that open competition with American firms would hurt jobs and wages. Also strongly opposed was the influential Toronto arts community, which expected Canadian culture to be engulfed.

The political parties were divided with the Progressive Conservatives supporting the initiative and the New Democratic and Liberal parties opposing it. The 1988 federal election was fought over free trade with the Conservatives pledged to implement the draft agreement completed in 1987 and the other two parties pledged to abandon it. The Liberals and New Democrats received more of the vote, but the allocation of seats gave a majority to the Conservatives who implemented the agreement.

The electoral results reflected a divided but very attentive public. The stakes combined national identity and economic self-interest, and two contending ideas were freely in play. On the pro-free trade side was an impressive body of economic theory that demonstrated absolute gains even when states have economies of different sizes. The Canadian economy would benefit from opportunities to sell into the world's largest national market. The deal, its supporters claimed, was "win-win" for Canada. The nationalist idea was equally pronounced. Canada's survival had always depended on resisting integration with the United States. Free trade would be an irreversible first step to that end. As well, free trade would end tariff and other protections to Canada's industries. The effects would hit people directly.

Federal ministries, particularly those responsible for foreign affairs and trade, had come to support free trade. That was the result of an initiative launched during the 1980-82 recession by the Trudeau government. Worried at the severity of the recession and its toll on Canadian manufacturing, the government ordered a comprehensive review of Canada's trade and economic policies. One part of that initiative was the Macdonald Royal Commission, which conducted an exhaustive study and recommended free trade. In the process of the review, many officials in the Department of Foreign Affairs and International Trade came to support the idea of free trade. They broached it to the new government of Brian Mulroney in 1984.[34] Initially opposed, Mulroney adopted the idea and initiated talks with the United States.

A liberal pluralist would focus on the domestic sources of free trade and the political alignments among important groups and regions. The political parties would be considered for their role in focusing public opinion and in helping to decide the outcome. The attitudes in the relevant parts of the government would be considered for their power to influence thinking about the issue particularly in senior political quarters. Public opinion, always significant, would be more important because free trade was a politicized election issue. Because of the ways these ingredients could interact, a liberal pluralist would emphasize the element of contingency: free trade was by no means inevitable. What if there had been no major recession in 1980 and no resulting doubts about basic economic and trade policies? What if the Macdonald Royal Commission, instead of lending its support to free trade, had recommended statist industrial policies and continuing trade protection? What if the Liberal Party had gotten more votes?

The international side of Liberal IR theory would focus attention on American motives. The United States was interested but regarded a pact with Canada as an alternative to getting comprehensive new rules written into the General Agreement on Tariffs and Trade, which was undergoing complex and difficult negotiations in the Uruguay Round. On two important issues, trade in services and agriculture, America was opposed to both European and developing states. An agreement with Canada, America's prime trading partner, would provide a safeguard should the Uruguay Round fail and demonstrate that the United States was quite capable of negotiating bilateral agreements. On trade questions generally, public opinion and Congress were concerned about American competitiveness and about partners taking unfair advantage, but neither set of concerns focused on Canada. Japan was seen as the major threat.

Again, a liberal would be interested in contingency. What if GATT were not a collateral factor? What if Congress had been as suspicious of broad trade agreements then as it is now?

Summary

Compared to Liberal IR theory, Neorealism and Institutionalism can be seen as outside-in theories. They focus on conditions in the international system and account for state behaviour as rational responses to them. Liberalism, in contrast, is an inside-out theory. It focuses on the domestic sources of state behaviour and treats conditions in the international system as the interactive result. We will see more about outside-in and inside-out approaches when we look at government and foreign policy in Chapter 9.

Liberalism brings to IR a long-standing and highly developed approach to domestic politics. We saw that this approach went into an eclipse in IR at the end of World War II and began to re-emerge only in the 1970s. Institutionalism, although it shares a long liberal interest in cooperation, was framed in Neorealism's terms. Liberal IR theory returns to the domestic roots of politics. Compared to Neorealism and Institutionalism, its advantage is being able to account for state behaviour without depending on deductive methods and external causes. Its disadvantage is the greater amount of information it requires.

ENDNOTES

1   Robert Powell, "Anarchy in International Relations Theory: The Neorealist-Neoliberal Debate," *International Organization* 48 (Spring 1994) 317–20.

2   Robert O. Keohane, "Institutional Theory and the Realist Challenge after the Cold War," in David Baldwin, ed., *Neorealism and Neoliberalism: The Contemporary Debate*, New York: Columbia University Press, 1993, pp. 294–95.

3   David Sanders, "International Relations: Neo-Realism and Neo-Liberalism," in Robert Goodin and Hans-Dieter Klingemann, eds., *A New Handbook of Political Science*, Oxford: Oxford University Press, 1996, pp. 432–33.

4   Mark W. Zacher and Richard A. Matthew, "Liberal International Theory: Common Threads, Divergent Strands," in Charles W. Kegley, Jr., ed., *Controversies in International Relations Theory: Realism and the Neoliberal Challenge,* New York: St. Martin's Press, 1995, pp. 118–19.

5   *ibid*, p. 118.

6   Richard Little, "The Growing Relevance of Pluralism?" in Smith, Booth and Zalewski, eds., *International Theory: Positivsm and Beyond?* Cambridge: Cambridge University Press, 1996, pp. 70–71.

7   Zacher and Matthew, "Liberal International Theory," p. 118.

8   Little, "The Growing Relevance of Pluralism?" p. 74; Miles Kahler, "Inventing International Relations: International Relations Theory after 1945," in Michael W. Doyle and G. John Ikenberry, eds., *New Thinking in International Relations Theory*, Boulder: CO: Westview, 1997, pp. 23–28.

9   Keohane, "Institutional Theory and the Realist Challenge after the Cold War," p. 271.

10   Kahler, "Inventing International Relations," pp. 39–44.

11   Andrew Moravcsik, "Taking Preferences Seriously: A Liberal Theory of International Politics," *International Organization* 51 (Autumn 1997) 513–53.

12   *ibid.,* 519.

13   *ibid.,* 521.

14   *ibid.,* 545.

15   *ibid.,* p. 517

16   *ibid.*, p. 527

17   *ibid.*, p. 528

18   *ibid.*, p. 529

19   *ibid.*, p. 518

20   *ibid.*

21   *ibid.*

22   *ibid.*, p. 517.

23   *ibid.*, p. 523.

24   My appreciation to Andrew Moravcsik for clarification on several of these points. Any errors or mis-interpretations that remain are mine.

25   Powell, "Anarchy in International Relations Theory," 317–25.

26   Donald Barry, "The Canada-European Union Turbot War: Internal Politics and Transatlantic Bargaining," *International Journal* 53 (Spring 1998) 256.

27   *ibid.*, p. 258.

28   *ibid.*, p. 251.

29   *ibid.*, pp. 267–68

30   *ibid.*, p. 281

31   *ibid.*, p. 256.

32   Kim Richard Nossal, "Analyzing the Domestic Sources of Canadian Foreign Policy," *International Journal* 39 (Winter 1983–84) 1–22; Stephen Krasner, "U.S. Commercial and Monetary Policy: Unravelling the Paradox of External Strength and Internal Weakness," *International Organization* 31 (Autumn 1977) 635–72.

33   Michael Atkinson and William Coleman, "Strong States and Weak States: Sectoral Policy Networks in Advanced Capitalist Economies," *British Journal of Political Science* 19 (January 1989) 47–67.

34   G. Bruce Doern and Brian W. Tomlin, *Faith and Fear: The Free Trade Story*, Toronto: Stoddart, 1991, pp. 17–19.

Chapter 4

Constructivism

Interests, Interaction and Transformation

Is something missing in Neorealism and Institutionalism besides a theory of the state? To get a sense of what that might be, recall the observation that concluded Chapter 2's discussion of serial-play Prisoner's Dilemma: "If you think that there is more to the development of cooperation than rational game-playing, you are right." That additional element is the shared understandings that emerge between people as they interact. Cooperation develops not just because people choose a succession of rational moves, but because in doing so they become cognizant of each other and the common nature of their situation.[1] As those understandings expand with experience, they affect what each side expects from the other. Those expectations in turn influence each side's own understandings of its role and its interests. These new understandings modify the relationship. Theorists speak of these as intersubjective understandings. If interaction continues long enough these understandings crystallize into specific expectations and implicit rules.

Returning to serial-play Prisoner's Dilemma (see pp. 25–26), imagine that the two players know nothing about each other, have had no previous dealings and have no idea what to expect. In Prisoner's Dilemma, players cannot communicate or observe each other's deliberations. Each other's moves are all they can see. In situations in which each partner has only one move, the rational incentive to defect is very strong because there is no second chance. Situations that involve a series of moves are different because each one provides the players an opportunity to evaluate the other's behaviour and to plan their next move. A cooperate move in this setting signals a willingness to cooperate further. If the other side defects, retaliating with defect shows a refusal to be taken advantage of but a willingness to continue playing. Because the game continues, serial-play Prisoner's Dilemma is a process of sequential learning with each side making inferences and conclusions about the other.[2] We examine three scenarios.

In the first scenario both you and your partner cooperate on the first move. What would you surmise about your partner? Some of the absolute uncertainty would be removed. A person who begins by cooperating is probably not completely hostile or greedy. You assume that your partner is making the same initial estimate about you. Since cooperate/cooperate provides the best mutual outcomes, you feel encouraged. What should your second move be? Unless you have some motive other than playing for mutual gains, cooperate is again the best choice. You would make it on the basis, still provisional, of your partner's intitial display of trust and good faith.

You both continue to play cooperate/cooperate. In addition to seeing mutual gains accumulate, you are beginning to develop a fair measure of confidence in your partner. You assume that your partner, seeing exactly the same outcomes, is developing the same confidence in you. How does that shape your expectations? Contemplating a lengthening track record of cooperative moves, you begin ascribing more general degrees of trust. As a social person you begin envisaging what your partner is like and inferring positive characteristics. Your understanding of your situation shifts accordingly. You begin to sense that you both have a stake in the game's success. Knowing that your partner's winnings are exactly the same as yours, you believe that your role is cooperative and that your interest is helping your partner play successfully. You believe that your partner is defining his or her role and interest the same way. Because there is no communication or contact between you, the inferences you make are based only on moves. The important thing is that you have developed a *feeling* of complementary roles and shared interests.

We turn to the second scenario. You begin with cooperate as your first move, but your partner defects. What does that tell you? Within the parameters of Prisoner's Dilemma, the implications are not pretty. One implication is that your partner, in the absence of any experience, does not trust you at all. Even before seeing your first move, your partner has played defensively. A more worrisome implication is that your partner has used the first opportunity to take advantage of you, defecting while you cooperate and thereby scoring the highest possible gain. In that light the first move is aggressive and unsettling. A third possibility is that your partner's move is a gambit to intimidate you and seize the initiative.

For your second move, you retaliate by playing defect and showing that you are not a patsy. What are your expectations about your partner now? It is probably accurate to say that you are doubtful and wary. Your partner responds in the next several moves with cooperate, but you remain uneasy. You lack confidence that your partner is committed to cooperation and wonder if more surprises are in store. What kind of understanding are you developing about your role and interests? Cautious and protective would be a reasonable surmise. What about your situation? Uncertain and risky probably describes it. Despite a series of cooperate moves, you feel unable to assume that your partner is dependable. A broader sense of shared interests has even less support.

We examine the last scenario. You cautiously play defect as your first move. Your partner defects too, setting off an unpleasant sequence. With no basis for assuming trust, you are unwilling to risk a cooperate move because doing so would leave you with zero and your partner with five if your partner again defects. Your partner appears to share that estimation. Each move is defect/defect. As the moves accumulate and the scores remain stuck at 1/1, you wonder what your partner must be like. Is he or she following a self-protective role and wishing for some positive sign of common interests to begin cooperating? Does your partner for some indiscernible reason prefer these minimal results? Does your partner believe that his or her self-protective behaviour is merely a rational reflection of what appears to be your own? From your position it is almost impossible to infer anything hopeful. You begin to define your situation as boxed in and wonder how to end it.

In each of these scenarios you were guided by your partner's moves, but you may also have been guided by your understandings of how you *should* play. Is it proper, for example, to try to get the best of your partner even before seeing any indication of what he or she is going to do? Is seeking a basis of cooperation the right approach or does doing so make you a dupe? These notions are not stated in the rules, which are limited to cooperate and defect. They reflect the understandings you bring to the game. As should-statements (you shouldn't be a sucker; you should be open and above-board; you shouldn't take unfair advantage) they reflect norms of proper behaviour that you have absorbed. In each of the three scenarios, these notions could have affected your moves as much as the situation itself. You may have played cooperate in the first two scenarios not because it is a good opening move in serial-play situations but because you believe it is the proper thing to do.

This is rational game-playing with something extra. That extra element is the way interactive experience, shaped by the understandings you bring to it, affects your definition of the situation. Differing definitions produce different roles. In the first scenario, an unbroken series of cooperate moves supported your taking the role of ally. In the second scenario, a defect move by your partner justified your becoming a suspicious defender, and in the third a dismal and hopeless series of defect moves made you take the role of withdrawer. Interests followed accordingly: helping your partner win, cooperating guardedly and disengaging.

These roles and interests followed from the experience of playing, and the moves shaped and elaborated your understanding as you proceeded. What we have seen in the three scenarios is the way different experiences produce divergent understandings and expectations and how these support similarly distinct roles and interests.

Prisoner's Dilemma is a limited and austere interactive setting. Compare it to a much richer real-world situation in which you could observe your partner's behaviour directly by conversing, bargaining, perhaps socializing and making inferences on that information. Assume an even richer setting in which the two partners are actually two groups of people who operate as diplomatic representatives of their two governments and deal not with a single issue but with several. Part of their understanding of proper behaviour towards each other comes from their governments. Expectations about dealing with representatives of the other side reflect accumulated experience and express roles and interests. Added to these norms of proper behaviour are the representatives' own experiences of dealing with each other, forming understandings and defining their own roles and interests in the situation. Their direct experience feeds back to their governments. The experience that is accumulated from many such encounters may either reinforce or modify each respective government's notions of its role and interests vis-a-vis the other.

The dealings need not be positive. Just as directly experienced cooperation supports premises of trust and reinforces cooperative roles and interests, directly experienced negative interactions support premises of hostility. For Constructivism the important element is interaction itself. Relationships are formed on the basis of experience and are changed or sustained by it. For partners in an interaction, whether they are players in Prisoner's Dilemma or in governments, roles and interests are flexible and depend in part on the other side's behaviour.[3] Because the relationship is interactive, the two sides can be said to constitute each other. What one side believes and does depends in part on the behaviour of the other. Its behaviour in turn is affected by what the first side believes and does.

This dynamic element addresses a major critique of Neorealim and Institutionalism. As we saw in Chapter 1, both Neorealism and Institutionalism posit fixed interests. Both assumed that individuals seek gain whenever possible. Some scholars saw the limits of that assumption in the behaviour of states at the end of the cold war. As we also saw, a rational neorealist actor would not concede openings to an adversary, but that is what the government of Mikhail Gorbachev did in offering flexibility and concessions on long-standing issues that divided the two blocs. Such radical departures are hard for neorealists to explain because prudent behaviour requires incremental moves and step-by-step cautious assessments. Large conciliatory offerings tempt the other side to exploit them.

Institutionalism is not able to envisage radical departures. Its focus also is incremental, constructing agreements and rules step by step. This is prudent because Institutionalism, in assuming that all states seek gains, regards protection against cheating as a major concern. Major departures are risky if they run ahead of constructing dependable agreements and procedures. Because of their prudent incremental approach, neither Neorealism nor Institutionalism has a strong explanation for the end of the cold war. Their commitment to immediate self-interest and rational calculation leaves them unable to encompass radical departures.

The changes that ended the cold war were not incremental. They began when one side reconsidered the positional logic of superpower competition. Reconsideration on one side prompted reconsideration on the other. Changed behaviour followed producing cooperative interactions. In a constructivist perspective, these prompted each side to redefine its role from enemy to cooperator. The result was a fundamentally changed understanding of the relationship between Russia and the West. Revised national interests soon followed. Because these changes involved not only the superpowers but other major states particularly in Europe, they transformed the international system. We will see more about the constructivist view of the cold war later in the chapter. For now, drastic departures are the point at hand. Constructivists believe that an ability to account for them is required in IR theory. They maintain that seeing behaviour interactively gets beyond arbitrary assumptions about state interests.

Origins: Rationalism and Sociology

Including experience and understandings in IR goes squarely against the rationalist emphasis of Neorealism and Institutionalism by introducing interpretative methods. As we saw in the three scenarios, the dynamics were not just those of rational calculation but also of subjective estimates: What must your partner be like? How does that estimate affect your interests and the way you see your common situation? Because of Neorealism's and Institutionalism's strong rationalism, intersubjective factors were not initially welcome in IR theory but entered gradually. They still are contentious as we will see at the end of the chapter.

The need for something more than rationalism was first voiced in 1986 as a critique of Institutionalism. States cooperate not only because international institutions establish rules to follow. The institutions themselves embody "principled and shared understandings of desirable and acceptable forms of social behaviour."[4] Among states belonging to international institutions, those shared and principled understandings evolve through their experience as members. In successful institutions, the participants' expectations converge around agreed forms of behaviour. It is the convergent expectations and the ways they shape the participants' interests and understandings of one another that are the effective basis of cooperation. To the extent those interests and understandings arise from experience, they can be regarded as a form of social learning. This also includes our understandings of proper behaviour in situations like Prisoner's Dilemma. That crucial dimension will not be found in studying formal institutional rules and structure.

Another scholar pointed to a long tradition in liberal political thought of selfishness transforming into cooperation.[5] That occurs when individuals or states deal with one another on common issues and come to recognize common interests. It was argued that by relaxing its rationalistic assumptions, Institutionalism could embrace that broader political tradition. Traditional liberalism also acknowledges the role of ideas. By enriching and broadening the motives for action, ideas reach beyond narrow and self-interested rationalism.[6] We saw in the last chapter that Liberal IR theory treats ideas as potentially important domestic sources of state action. Envisaging ideas at work in a broader international arena expands the possibilities of influence and change. Considerations such as these prepared the ground for **Constructivism**'s more interpretive approach.

Some scholars believe that gauging the effects of ideas and understandings, particularly in complex international settings, is a problematic proposition.[7] Ideas and understandings are intangible and cannot be observed separately. Their role is to influence the thought that shapes observable behaviour. Explaining the role of ideas and understandings therefore requires inferring what the thought process must be.[8] Since the thought process itself is invisible, it is difficult to separate inference from the observer's speculation. For that reason, some scholars have argued, interpretive approaches leave too much latitude for subjectivity to produce reliable knowledge.[9] Defending their approach, constructivists have replied that their work uses evidence and constructs explanations within the regular practice of social science.[10]

We have now seen that the basis of Neorealism and Institutionalism is microeconomic reasoning. We have also seen that the basis of Liberal IR theory is a traditional form of political science. Constructivism's basis is sociology. Sociology contributes two main elements. The first is viewing the relationship between individuals and society as a two-way street. Society's values, rules and roles shape individuals as they engage in society. Individuals, through their actions, shape society. The equivalent relationship in IR is states and the international system. Sociology's second contribution is the perspective of the participant. Because social roles or expectations cannot be observed, a sociological technique called *Verstehen* adopts the participant's perspective to see how he or she understands them. For constructivists in IR, the roles and expectations of interest are the ones that affect states.

We should note that states are not the only focus of constructivist interest in IR. The same emphasis on interaction, experience and understandings can just as easily be applied to domestic politics within states. Externally, Constructivism can focus on Non-Governmental Organizations and their orientations to particular issues such as human rights. In that way, Constructivism is a method with various applications.[11] For our purposes it is best to limit Constructivism to states.

We cannot know for certain how the world looks to someone else. Seeking to infer someone else's perspective moves a considerable distance from merely observing facts. The payoff is deeper understanding. That is particularly useful if the purpose is to find how individuals assess and accommodate norms, expectations and the actions of others. Extending the inquiry from individuals to interacting groups of individuals makes it possible to address the broader field of intersubjective understandings—simply how people see and respond to each other in light of their shared circumstances, knowledge and constraints. In that analysis is the promise of explaining events that transcend immediate self-interest and rational calculation. It is that promise that attracts constructivists in IR.

Thinking Sociologically

This sociological outlook is probably less familiar than the rationalist outlook of Neorealism and Institutionalism and the traditional political science outlook of Liberalism. A way of getting a more immediate sense of it is to recall the question asked at the beginning of this textbook's Introduction: To what extent do individuals including yourself create society? To what extent are individuals including yourself created by society? This question was posed then simply to introduce IR's central occupation of explaining systems and actions. Returning to it now helps to understand the circular connection between individuals and society. Constructivism is interested in the same circular connection between states and the international system.

The basic idea drawn from sociology's theory of **structuration** is that individuals and society are inseparable. Society, for its part, is an aggregation of individuals, and their behaviour collectively determines what society is like. If large numbers of people behave violently, we accurately speak of a violent society. If large numbers are thrifty and frugal, we accurately speak of a delayed-gratification society. At the same time, individuals interact with society, and society's limits and expectations affect what they do. Individuals living in a violent society think and act differently in matters of personal safety than do individuals living in a peaceful society. Individuals living in a delayed-gratification society regard money differently from the way it is regarded by individuals living in a society in which carrying large credit card balances is normal. This refers to discretionary spending, not student debt.

Adding the ingredient of identity makes this perspective more interesting. The source of individuals' actions is their identity. Where identity originates is a complex question, but in the structurationist view it is an interactive product of individuals and societies. People bring to society their identities—a composite of outlooks, values, behaviours and experience. As they engage in society they find that some of these attributes are successful and rewarded and some are not. As socially aware beings, individuals absorb values and outlooks they encounter.

This does not imply that individuals have no autonomy and are simply molded creations of their surroundings. The structurationist view is more sophisticated. Individuals' identities are an amalgam of the internal and the external, of the personal and the social. Through repeated interaction with society this amalgam changes. The same is true of society. Its identity is a complex product of the values, experience and expectations it carries forward from the past and of the continuous effects of individuals' behaviour. Neither individual nor society can be understood apart from the other because neither exists *prior* to the other. Instead, individuals and societies are a mutual product, each constituted by the other. The process is interactive with individuals affecting societies and societies affecting individuals. Both change in response to one another, and over time these changes can be substantial.[12] A quick way of testing these statements personally is to recall the comparisons your parents and grandparents make between what society's expectations are now and what they were when they were your age. Your parents' and grandparents' expectations, a structurationist would add, also changed society.

The Theory

States and the international system constitute each other. What states regard as their roles and interests derives from their relationships with other states. Together, states determine the condition of the international system and, most importantly, produce the system's **norms**, expectations and requirements. These norms define proper behaviour. In return, these norms affect what states do by shaping their roles and interests. In defining what those are, states are also affected by their own inner characteristics—being wealthy or poor, secular or religious, African or European. States' behaviour then either reinforces the system's norms and expectations or changes them. If those norms and expectations change, states' roles and interests again are affected. The relationship is circular and reinforcing. States shape the system / The System shapes states / States shape the system. . . .[13]

We begin with states. According to constructivists, states have no inherent international roles. Instead, they acquire understandings about their roles and their positions through "collective meanings." These are constructed among states *in relation* to one another. In that way, a state's role resides in a particular context.[14] In other words, what states understand themselves to be depends on the way they fit into a broader set of interactions with other states. If states interact in consistent patterns, their relationships form the basis of the system's norms and expectations.

In the constructivist view, norms and expectations are simply entrenched understandings that emerge from consistent behaviour. Those norms and expectations in turn affect the way states define their roles. State roles are thus not autonomous and absolute but are formed in reference to others. Other states' roles are formed in the same way. Relationships are the key. To understand a state, one needs to examine its connections with other states and the common understandings that result. The norms and expectations that affect states arise from those understandings.

We can see this relationship in Canada's international role of peacekeeper. Liberal IR theory, as we saw in the last chapter, places much emphasis on ideas, and the idea of peacekeeping has enjoyed consistent support with the Canadian public. Constructivists are interested in the interactive dimension. In behaving as a peacekeeper, Canada responds not only to an international norm against violent conflict but also to international expectations of what Canada's role should be. Because Canada has functioned as a peacekeeper for so many years, that role is well established and states respond positively. Their response reinforces Canada's international role as a peacekeeper. Some constructivists would go further and argue that playing the role of peacekeeper also helps to constitute Canada's domestic identity by defining Canadians to themselves.[15]

This may be a disorienting way of considering identities and roles. We are used to thinking of states as having particular indigenous characteristics. Constructivists look at identity more comprehensively. It is the way a state understands its international role. That understanding does not form in isolation but emerges from dealings with other states. Role identities are the basis of states' interests. How states conceive of themselves and their roles amongst other states shapes their interests.[16]

Next we look at the international system. It too is understood interactively. Its form and characteristics result from the actions of its members. "Any given international system does not exist because of immutable structures, but rather the very structures are dependent for their reproduction on the practices of the actors."[17] When those practices change, the system changes. State roles and interests, following the circle of cause and effect, change in response. If the member states adopt congruent roles and interests, their behaviour reinforces the new system. If they adopt different roles and interests instead, they change the system again. States and the system mutually constitute each other in a continuous and circular process.[18]

Constructivists are very interested in the effects of norms. As we just saw these are common understandings of proper behaviour. When they are sufficiently well established and strong, states not only adhere to them but construct their roles and interests in reference to them. Strong norms are important internationally because they can regulate and constrain state behaviour, contributing to international order and stability. (Norms can also be destructive: An international norm of predatory imperialism, which authorizes states to take what they want from other states by force, would produce a very disorderly and unstable system.) These norms emerge not from rational self-interest, as Institutionalism depicts the process, but from important values. These values generally arise from the behaviour of states, but they can also have more widespread sources. General abhorrence of chemical weapons is one example as we will see later in the chapter. Values become formal when they are inscribed in international conventions or treaties. Informally, they are effective to the degree that they affect states' behaviour.

Constructivists maintain that rational self-interest, the vehicle of cooperation in Institutionalism, is insufficient to explain how norms actually develop. Norms emerge interactively as states become committed to cooperation in particular areas. In undertaking cooperation, states begin with a common purpose, but it may be provisional and reversible. Once they begin cooperating, their understandings of one another change, and they begin to see their interests in reference to the common norms that emerge. That in turn prompts them to "internaliz[e] new understandings of self and other [and acquire] new role identities..."[19] As the process continues, states come increasingly to identify their interests in light of the norms. Collectively, they will come to see shared interests in the norms' effective operation. To the extent such commitment develops, norms will be durable.

Because the world is becoming increasingly interdependent and because states act in many instances on the basis of shared understandings and expectations, both formal and informal, norms are an important aspect of IR. They underwrite the webs of cooperation and coordination that a complex international system requires. For a constructivist, the international system is anarchic, but norms provide for commitment, predictability and stability. To the degree that norms are prevalent and effective, the absolute degree of flux and change in the system is constrained. At the same time, radical redefinitions of identity and interest can quickly undo elaborate edifices of commitments and understandings.

Differences with Neorealism/Institutionalism

Constructivists share several important points in common with neorealists and institutionalists. As we saw earlier, Constructivism is a theory that can focus on various kinds of actors. The form of Constructivism we have been discussing emphasizes the state as the prime actor in IR. The comparisons that follow are based on that emphasis.

Neorealists, institutitonalists and constructivists all agree that the state is the prime actor, that the international system is anarchic and that states act rationally.[20] The main points of difference are the sources and consequences of state action. Neorealists, assuming that all states seek gains and that states with advantages will exploit them, worry about imbalances and unequal capabilities. Since the international world is anarchic, the capabilities of greatest concern are those that affect security. States rationally define their security position in respect to other states' capabilities. When those capabilities are superior or when the other state is enhancing them, neorealists are always concerned about the underlying intention. For constructivists, in contrast, it is the relationship that matters. Material capabilities such as military forces have meaning only within particular understandings. The armed forces of the United States, for example, has a different meaning for Canada than for Cuba.[21] For both, the material capabilities in question are the same, but the understandings differ sharply. If pairs of states have common role identities as enemies, military forces will be very important. If that identity is not present, military forces are of concern only if the identity changes. As we saw with the end of the cold war, role identities can indeed change. For that reason, a constructivist would argue, weaponry does not create enmity—it reflects it.

Institutionalists treat the process of cooperation as a rational effort to secure collective benefits and prevent cheating. States do so by creating institutions that reduce each one's cost of securing cooperation unilaterally and facilitate information-sharing and compliance. Constructivists regard cooperation as emerging from particular sets of understandings among states. States inherently seek neither cooperation nor conflict. Cooperation follows instead from the way they define their roles and interests vis-a-vis one another. Major shifts of states' understandings of one another may produce striking transformations from relations of conflict to cooperation and vice versa.

Core Tenets: Constructivism and Neorealism Compared

Because Constructivism addresses both conflict and cooperation, it is helpful to compare its tenets to Neorealism's and Institutionalism's separately (see Table 4.1).

TABLE 4.1   Similarities and Differences

Similarities

Constructivism	Neorealism
States are the principal actors	States are the principal actors
The international system is anarchic	The international system is anarchic
The international system is constituted by the actions of states	The international system is constituted by the actions of states
The international system shapes and constrains states' interests	The international system shapes and constrains states' interests
States behave rationally	States behave rationally
States are quite capable of generating security threats	States are quite capable of generating security threats

Differences

Constructivism	Neorealism
States' interests are based on the way they understand their relations with other states	States' interests are based on gain
The most important international structures are the understandings that arise from state interactions	The most important international structures are material
These understandings shape states' roles and interests	These material structures shape states' threats and interests
The significance of material resources, such as military power, depends on the inter-subjective context.	The significance of material resources, such as military power, is determinate [22]

Core Tenets: Constructivism and Institutionalism Compared

We now compare Constructivism and Institutionalism (Table 4.2).

TABLE 4.2   Similarities and Differences

Similarities	
Constructivism	*Institutionalism*
States are the principal actors	States are the principal actors
The international system is anarchic	The international system is anarchic
States behave rationally	States behave rationally
Effective norms bring order and predictability to the relationships of states	Effective norms bring order and predictability to the relationships of states
Differences	
Constructivism	*Institutionalism*
States' interests are based on the way they understand their relationships with other states	States' interests are based on gain
What states expect from other states depends on their relationships with them	States prefer cooperation but fear cheating
Norms emerge from the convergence of values and common understandings.	Norms are contained in formal and informal institutions

The Constructivist View of the World

Constructivists argue that their approach's prime advantage is accounting for dramatic changes. By looking at interactions they can see the effects of states' behaviour on their understandings of one another. Changes in those understandings support more general changes in the states' role identities. Changed identities, in turn, support broader changes in state behaviour. The end of the cold war is a dramatic example (see Figure 4.3).

FIGURE 4.3 The End of the Cold War: From Rigidity to Fluidity

The cold war international system's structure was bipolar with one centre in Washington and the other in Moscow, and the prevailing dynamic was rivalry. National interests, particularly for the superpowers, placed a premium on armaments and defence. Fearing gains by the other, each side was vigilant about military force levels and political encroachments. At the nuclear level, military power was organized in massive American and Soviet arsenals. Regionally, nuclear and conventional forces were organized in two large military alliances, NATO and the Warsaw Pact. Continuous political and military positioning maintained a threat of war.

The end of the cold war transformed the international system from a bipolar configuration to a more traditional system of states. That loosened the constraining requirements on state behaviour. For both the superpowers and their allies, it was now possible to interact across the previously forbidding bipolar divide. The system change allowed the United States and Russia to relax their postures of military confrontation and return to more normal patterns of interstate relations. These include both conflict and cooperation. The two states have not agreed about the treatment of Iraq since the Gulf War of 1991, but they have worked together to scale back their nuclear forces. On any particular issue the two states' alignments are shaped not by the adversarial logic of superpower rivalry but by their common position as principal states. The transformed international system allows a much freer play for influences from other states than was possible under bipolarity, and these also affect the two powers' identities and interests.

NATO and Warsaw Pact states, which had previously confronted one another in Europe with immense military forces, have become trading partners and regard themselves as fellow members of a single Europe. In the most telling manifestation of a new order, Poland, Hungary and the Czech Republic, previously of the Warsaw Pact, became members of NATO.

How would a constructivist approach that historic transformation? The starting point is role identities. The roles of the superpowers, developing out of a long record of hostile interactions, were those of enemies. Antagonistic and suspicious behaviour supported intersubjective understandings of mistrust and conflict, which reinforced the more general opposing interests. The change began when one side, the Soviet Union, redefined its role. President Mikhail Gorbachev, convinced that the Soviet economy could no longer bear the costs of military competition, decided that saving the economy required easing relations with the West. Doing so required revisioning the Soviet Union's identity of cold war opponent. Gorbachev began making known to the Western powers his interest in exploring ways of lowering tensions including reducing nuclear arms levels. When Western states decided that his interest was genuine, their understandings began to shift away from expectations of hostility. That confidence supported return gestures. Those gestures continued the cycle, encouraging the Soviet Union to explore further relaxation. The crucial move in the process was the Soviet Union's abandoning the policy of treating its international sphere of influence as irreversible. Loosened Soviet controls in Eastern Europe followed thereby removing a major element of conflict and hostility with the West and providing convincing evidence that the new Soviet role identity was authentic.[23]

From a constructivist perspective, the initiating event was the Soviet Union's redefining of its role from adversary to potential cooperator. Through conciliatory gestures, it communicated that new role to the West, altering the previous understanding. By reciprocating, the West encouraged further cooperation. As the process continued, the role identities of the West began changing from enemies to cooperators. Because of the two superpowers' central positions, their new roles transformed the international system.

We can see the same process with state interests in the cold war. During the cold war, a major interest of the participants was high military preparedness, reflecting their adversarial roles. High preparedness, constructivists emphasize, is not inevitable but depends instead on the understandings that emerge from relationships. During the cold war, adversarial relationships led the superpowers to put a premium on armed forces, but roles and relationships have changed. Force levels that were once regarded as expensive but necessary have now become expensive and redundant.

The same principle also works the other way around. If hard-line nationalists were to come to power in Russia and redefine its role from frequent cooperator to expansionist adversary, its interests would again emphasize armed force. That change would affect the understandings of other states and redefine their roles from cooperators to defensive adversaries. Their interests, accordingly, would re-emphasize military elements.

FIGURE 4.4   Chemical and Nuclear Weapons: The Importance of Revulsion

There are many weapons that kill and maim populations, but chemical and nuclear weapons have earned special opprobrium. The norms against chemical and nuclear weapons are contained in international conventions. The norms are powerful enough to have supported a United Nations inspection and verification regime for Iraq to ensure that all of its weapons of mass destruction, particularly its chemical and nuclear ones, have been located and destroyed. What distinguishes these weapons? Others also kill in large number and have been used against civilian targets. Firebombing of cities is an equally horrible use of armed force. Much smaller weapons can produce their own atrocity. Firing mortars into marketplaces, as the Bosnian war showed, is barbarous, but mortars are not outlawed. Why do chemical and nuclear weapons have their unique status?

A recent study traces the origins to values and experience. Gas warfare in World War I left a legacy of revulsion that was soon recorded in an international convention. Nuclear weapons came to be regarded, first by scientists in the West and then by the general public, as grossly disproportional to any human purpose.[24] Treaties to limit their testing and proliferation followed.

Constructivists point to the social force of values. If values are shared widely, they can be transformed into international norms as treaties and agreements. On many issues that do not affect the public at large, the underlying consensus may exist only among governments. Other issues may engage the public at large. Weapons of mass destruction and memories of their use spread their implications widely.

Critiques of Constructivism

Constructivism is still a new theory and has not yet attracted systematic critical evaluation. The criticisms raised so far are interesting to note as an index of what theorizing about a complex subject involves.

The first addresses the relationship between states and system. The idea that states and the international system constitute each other sounds simple enough intuitively, but it is a process to be explained. Explanation would look for causal connections. "To constitute" implies some causal influence, but what is it and how does it work? How is it related to **intersubjective understandings**, both in origin and in effect?[25] Constructivists reply by maintaining that identifying and evaluating the effect of intersubjective understandings requires both empirical observation (what states actually do) and interpretation (what states seem to gather from each other's actions). Together, the two kinds of evidence can show the effects in question. The critics' response takes up the issue we saw at the beginning of the chapter about empirical observation and personal interpretation. The two are *not* interchangeable. Empirical and subjective analysis produce very different kinds of results. They cannot simply be blended together like ingredients in a cake.[26] For their part, constructivists maintain that their use of evidence is within the bounds of regular social science. Finally, Constructivism has been criticized as melding states, system and behaviour together, forming a seamless entity that affords no theoretical points of entry. Everything is simply related to everything else.[27] These last critiques get quickly into the philosophy of science, but they are worth noting as an index of what can be involved in making apparently simple connections.

A different line of criticism challenges the constructivist notion that state identities and interests are flexible and situational and that selfishness can be transcended through convergent understandings. Self-interest, according to this criticism, is not an arbitrary neorealist and neoliberal assumption but is firmly fixed in human behaviour in groups. People in groups look to themselves and their interests first, a result of the dynamics that bond them together. As people become members of a group, they increasingly identify with it. As that happens, they develop loyalty, perceive common interests and distinguish their group from others. The stronger their degree of solidarity with their group, the more likely they are to disregard the interests of other groups and see them as inferior. Because an "us versus them" outlook is rooted in loyalty and affiliation, it does not change. One's own group always comes first. That view, drawn from social psychology, squarely challenges Constructivism's notion that interests can be transformed from conflict to cooperation. Group solidarity, the criticism holds, is the more powerful force. It is the reason "...why strong in-groups are the most likely to have strong out-groups; why ethnocentrism is ubiquitous; and why group egoism, self-help and relative gains are ever present in international politics."[28] A constructivist might reply that what is true of groups may be quite different for states, which are larger, more structurally diverse and generate more complex processes of action.

A final criticism from neorealists is that existing deployments of arms may make it too dangerous for a state to make the first move in initiating cooperation.

Whether that is so depends on the motives of the other state. If its motives are defensive and non-expansionist, it may welcome an initial gesture of goodwill and peaceful intentions and reciprocate, just as a constructivist would expect. That would begin a positive sequence of changed relationships and identities as happened at the end of the cold war, but if the other state's motives are greedy and acquisitive, it may read a gesture of goodwill as a sign of weakness. Instead of cooperating, it may believe that now is the time to score some gains. Instead of beginning a process of beneficial reciprocity, the initiating state may end up with a more confident and aggressive adversary. What actually occurs depends on the other state's motives. When those motives are not clear, conciliatory moves are risky.[29] That conclusion is different from the spirit of Constructivism, which holds that states can change intersubjective understandings by changing their behaviour.

Material factors such as weapons may indeed have inherent significance. In the face of high mistrust or greedy motives, a neorealist would argue, existing weapons constrain cooperative gestures either because they support a stable balance that may be dangerous to disturb or because they are capabilities that a newly confident adversary can convert from passive defence into active offence. By focusing on understandings instead of forces, constructivists may be too optimistic about the possibilities of changing behaviour. Such change, a neorealist would caution, depends also on motives and material constraints.

This difference can be boiled down to a question of priorities. Neorealists argue that the material structure, comprised of elements such as arms levels, is so often the main influence on states' behaviour that focusing on it first simply makes sense. Constructivists argue that those structures are often indeterminate; it is not clear what their influence is. In those situations, it is better to focus on other factors such as intersubjective understandings and common norms. Bypassing the fixed approaches of Neorealism has been one of Constructivism's touted advantages. Some neorealists claim to be flexible. When the material structure is not clearly influential, neorealists "ought to have little trouble" in giving greater attention to other factors including intersubjective ones.[30] (To see a constructivist viewpoint on free trade, read Canadian Reality Check 4.5.)

Canadian Reality Check 4.5

Constructivism and Free Trade

Constructivism emphasizes transformation of identities and relationships. Canada's decision to seek a free trade agreement with the United States represented such a drastic shift of a historic identity that one might see it as a virtual reversal. Even more strikingly, it came on the heels of the National Energy Program, which took direct measures to *increase* Canada's control of its petroleum industry. The free trade initiative followed as well the government's revival of the Foreign Investment Review Agency's role in screening new foreign investments. These policies were in keeping with a long tradition of treating the economy as a mainstay of Canada's identity and regarding American ownership and influence as threats to that identity.

That tradition was shaken by the recession of 1981. Unlike previous recessions, this one severely harmed Canada's industrial sector. The Trudeau government, deeply concerned that the recession was beyond its ability to contain, ordered a review of Canada's economic and trade policies. A Department of External Affairs-led task force came to a cautious view in favour of free trade with the United States, and in 1983 Cabinet authorized seeking a series of sectoral agreements with the United States.[31] That initiative faltered because Canada and the United States were unable to agree on which industrial sectors to include. One year later, senior officials in External Affairs recommended free trade to the new Mulroney government. Meanwhile, the Macdonald Royal Commission, convened to examine Canada's situation and prospects, conducted an exhaustive study. In 1985, it too recommended free trade, and in the same year the Mulroney government formally launched the initiative.

Because economic relations with the United States were such a deeply rooted part of Canada's national identity, the initiative provoked controversy and division. The matter was decided in the rancorous 1988 election, which returned the Conservatives who were pledged to implement the agreement. Another major recession occurred in 1990 just as the free trade agreement was taking effect. Critics of the agreement blamed lay-offs and closings on free trade. Supporters argued that the recession would be worse without access to a large export market.

Subsequently, a new Liberal government expanded the agreement to include Mexico, creating the North American Free Trade Agreement, and signed a bilateral free trade agreement with Chile. Canada's policy now actively supports free trade for the hemisphere. The government's dealings with the United States have emphasized ways of expediting the flow of bilateral commerce, which amounts to $1.4 billion per day. The government has also taken part in multilateral negotiations to reduce remaining barriers to foreign investment, an exact reversal of the purpose of the Foreign Investment Review Agency.

Because Constructivism deals with transformations *between* countries, we need to note the American side. There, identity is divided and uncertain. On the one side is the identity of the United States as a bulwark of global free trade. Originating in efforts after World War II to promote economic recovery, that identity has sustained continuous American support for global trade liberalization. On the other side is an identity of vulnerability that originated in the 1960s when competitors began regaining their advantages and the United States began running trade deficits.

Protectionism has become a political force supported by both labour-backed liberals and isolationist conservatives. Congress approved NAFTA by a narrow margin and in 1997 refused to give the president "fast-track" authority to negotiate wider trading agreements with Latin America. Without fast-track authority, draft agreements could be amended in Congress, giving opponents the latitude to gut key provisions. A constructivist might see a contested and unstable identity. To the benefit of the bilateral relationship, the American public does not see Canada as part of America's trade problems.

On Canada's side, a constructivist might see a historic identity transformed. The depth and contention of the free trade debate is an index of how deep that identity was. Although the agreement has been in place only since 1989, the abatement of controversy and the public's equanimity about new trade agreements with Latin America, closer ties with Asia and efforts to expedite movement across the American border might be seen as evidence of significant change.[32] Supporting that transformation has been a steady record of trade surpluses. A constructivist would be even more interested in the evolution of shared understandings among Canada, the United States and Mexico. Both Canada and Mexico, for different reasons, have histories of wariness of the United States. The trade agreements, a constructivist would argue, could not have been concluded without some initial transformation. Whether the changing relationships under NAFTA support further transformation remains to be seen. Of equal interest is the influence of the three states' identities on the evolution of the NAFTA relationship.

Is this change irreversible? A constructivist would emphasize that any identity and set of interests depends upon intersubjective understandings. As long as those understandings among Canada and its trading partners provide positive results and as long as they are mutually supported, the orientation is likely to be stable. At the same time, a constructivist would caution, changes in those understandings could produce equally significant transformations. In the same way that nobody foresaw the end of the cold war's apparently enduring understandings, the same is true now about the ones supporting regional trade and expanding agreements

Summary

Constructivism approaches IR from the perspective of two-way relationships. This perspective derives from sociology, which regards individuals and societies as mutually constitutive. Constructivism in IR promises an interactive way of accounting for changed interests and transformed relationships. Its advantage is that it does not depend on arbitrary assumptions of state interests nor does it ascribe categorical importance to material factors. The importance of such factors as military force emerges as a result of states' relationships and understandings; it does not cause or explain those relationships. Instead, relationships reflect states' identities and interests. The emphasis is interactive and reciprocal.

Norms arise when interaction generates shared and common understandings and expectations among states. The norm of non-proliferation reflects a widespread opposition to chemical and nuclear weapons. The norms' effectiveness in regulating states' behaviour depends on the strength of the understandings supporting them.

ENDNOTES

1 Alexander Wendt, "Collective Identity Formation and the International State," *American Political Science Review* 88 (June 1994) 390.

2 Alexander Wendt, "Anarchy Is What States Make of It: The Social Construction of Power Politics," *International Organization* 46 (Spring 1992) 416.

3 Jeffrey T. Checkel, "The Constructivist Turn in International Relations Theory," *World Politics* 50 (January 1998) 326.

4 Fredrich Kratochwil and John Gerard Ruggie, "International Organization: A State of the Art on the Art of the State," *International Organization* 40 (Autumn 1986) 764.

5 Joseph Nye, "Neorealism and Neoliberalism," *World Politics* 40 (April 1988) 246.

6 Judith Goldstein and Robert O. Keohane, "Ideas and Foreign Policy: An Analytical Framework," in Judith Goldstein and Robert O. Keohane, eds., *Ideas and Foreign Policy: Beliefs, Institutions, and Political Change,* Ithaca: Cornell University Press, 1993, pp. 4–6.

7 *ibid.*

8 Steve Smith, "Positivism and Beyond," in Steve Smith, Ken Booth and Marysia Zalewski, eds., *International Theory: Positivism and Beyond,* Cambridge: Cambridge University Press, 1996, p. 23.

9 Robert O. Keohane, "International Institutions: Two Approaches," *International Studies Quarterly* 32 (December 1988) 390–91.

10 Alexander Wendt, "Constructing International Relations," *International Security* 20 (Summer 1995) 75.

11 My appreciation to Alexander Wendt for clarifying this point.

12 Alexander Wendt, "The Agent-Structure Problem in International Relations Theory," *International Organization* 41 (Summer 1987) 360.

13 David Dessler, "What's At Stake in the Agent-Structure Debate," *International Organization* 43 (Summer 1989) 452–53.

14 Alexander Wendt, "Anarchy Is What States Make of It: The Social Construction of Power Politics," *International Organization* 46 (Spring 1993) 397.

15 Ted Hopf, "The Promise of Constructivism in International Relations Theory," *International Security* 23 (Summer 1998) 173.

16 Wendt, "The Agent-Structure Problem," p. 398.

17 Rey Koslowski and Friedrich Kratochwil, "Understanding Change in International Politics: The Soviet Empire's Demise and the International System," *International Organization* 48 (Spring 1994) 216.

18 Ronald Jepperson, Alexander Wendt, Peter Katzenstein, "Norms, Identity, and Culture in National Security," in Peter Katzenstein, ed., *The Culture of National Security: Norms and Identity in World Politics*, New York: Columbia University Press, 1996, pp. 52–53, 63–64.

19 Wendt, "Anarchy Is What States Make of It," p. 417.

20 Wendt, "Constructing International Relations," 72.

21 Wendt, "Anarchy Is What States Make of It," p. 397.

22 List derived from Wendt, "Collective Identity Formation and the International State," 385.

23 Koslowski and Kratochwil, "Understanding Change in International Politics," pp. 233–34.

24 Richard Price and Nina Tannenwald, "Norms and Deterrence: The Nuclear and Chemical Weapons Taboos," in Katzenstein, ed., *The Culture of National Security*, p. 122–23.

25 Martin Hollis and Steve Smith, "Beware of Gurus: Structure and Action in International Relations," *Review of International Studies* 17 (October 1991) 405–08.

26 *ibid.*

27 James Caporaso, "Across the Great Divide: Integrating Comparative and International Politics," *International Studies Quarterly* 41 (December 1997) 566.

28 Jonathan Mercer, "Anarchy and Identity," *International Organization* 49 (Spring 1995) 251.

29 Charles L. Glaser, "The Security Dilemma Revisited," *World Politics* 50 (October 1997) 198.

30 Michael C. Desch, "Culture Clash: Assessing the Importance of Ideas in Security Studies," *International Security* 23 (Summer 1998) 168–69.

31 G. Bruce Doern and Brian W. Tomlin, *Faith and Fear: The Free Trade Story,* Toronto: Stoddart, 1991, pp. 17–19.

32 Joseph Jockel, "Canada and the United States: Still Calm in the 'Remarkable Relationship,'" in Fen Osler Hampson and Maureen Appel Molot, eds., *Canada Among Nations 1996: Big Enough to Be Heard*, Ottawa: Carleton University Press, 1996, p. 113.

Chapter 5

Critical Approaches: Critical Theory, Postmodernism, Feminism

Action, Reaction and Debate in IR

International Relations has developed in a reactive cycle. As we saw in Chapter 2, Realism was a reaction to the Idealism of the 1920s and 1930s. In turn, Realism's narrow focus on states and power induced scholars in the 1970s to emphasize economic interdependence and non-state actors. That produced the reaction of Neorealism, which brought the state back to the centre. Neorealism's occupation with conflict prompted Institutionalism, which emphasized cooperation. Since both assumed states to operate as unitary entities responding to external conditions, neither had a theory of the state itself. To fill that vacancy, as we saw in Chapter 3, Liberal IR theory was put forward. Neorealism and Institutionalism also did not provide for ways in which state interests could be transformed nor for ways in which states, through their interaction, could generate effective common norms. Supplying those missing elements was Constructivism's contribution. There we left the issue in Chapter 4.

For the last 20 years, IR has been engaged in a serious debate about more fundamental questions. Particularly important challenges have been levelled by critical theorists, postmodernists and feminists. The debate has had a significant impact on the way IR is understood, researched and taught. To have a full sense of IR as a field it is important to know not only the basic theories presented in the preceding three chapters but also the controversy and debate. Seeing the theories and controversy side by side provides a good initial understanding of IR's current condition. This chapter will examine **Critical Theory**, **Postmodernism** and **Feminism** and then assess their impact on IR. As a clash of ideas, the debate is interesting to consider. The stakes have been the basic ones of knowledge, values and inclusion, and the terms have been frank. At the end of the chapter we will see how the theories and critiques reconcile.

This has been called IR's Third Debate. What were the first two? We saw the First Debate in the postwar disillusionment with Idealism and the rise of Realism. The core text of that debate, we noted, was E.H. Carr's *The Twenty Years' Crisis*. The Second Debate followed in the 1960s as a reaction to Realism's historical and philosophical emphasis. The challengers were statistically trained scholars who argued that IR, along with other branches of political science, was not scientific and needed the discipline of quantitative methods. Their opponents who supported historical and philosophical methods countered that statistics without a broader understanding produces meaningless data collection. There was some accommodation. Statistical methods are used in several subfields of IR, particularly the formal study of conflict. The best places to look for quantitative scholarship are the *Journal of Conflict Resolution* and the *Journal of Peace Research*. A less direct effect of the Second Debate was Neorealism's and Institutionalism's quest for scientific rigour through formal and deductive method and their adoption of logical models based in game theory. We saw the use of Prisoner's Dilemma in Chapter 2. Reaction to that tight rationalism sparked the Third Debate in the early 1980s.

Method and the Critical Challenge

The core of the challenge was that IR, with Neorealism and Institutionalism in particular, is too uncritical about its basic assumptions. By positing a spare and lean rationality epitomized by Prisoner's Dilemma, neorealists and institutionalists either assumed away or suppressed important political values and implications. Particular objection has been made to the stark and unreflective assumption of self-interest and the focal concern with power and position, a result we saw in Chapter 2 of emphasizing the international system's anarchic nature. To people in various quarters, those assumptions embody not the essential nature of the international world but an unacknowledged point of view. By their values, these are theories of a privileged status quo which many believe unjust. By their focus on stability, these theories contain an unstated conservative ideology.

In this chapter, we will see the particular objections of critical theorists, postmodernists and feminists. Together, they argue that IR is not reflective enough about the way it theorizes and about the basic assumptions it employs. What is needed is philosophical self-awareness. That is achieved at the level of **metatheory**-theory about the process of theorizing. For people regarding IR from critical perspectives, metatheory provides "the capacity of a perspective to reflect on its own origins and conditions of existence."[1] Because the Third Debate has been pitched at the level of metatheory, much of its literature is abstract. The basic issue, however, is straightforward: Equally important to *what* is being theorized is *how* it is being theorized.

Observers, Objects and Neutrality

That concern leads to fundamental questions of epistemology and ontology, which have figured centrally in the Third Debate. The first two debates were waged at less elevated philosophical levels. To understand the critical theorists', postmodernists' and feminists' objections to IR theory we need to see briefly what epistemology and ontology involve. We should note that philosophers themselves regard the nature of knowledge and understanding as complex questions. Here the issue is being introduced just enough to view the stakes of the Third Debate.

Epistemology is the way we know things. Particular methods of inquiry are guided by an epistemology. You learn methods and their epistemology in courses on research methodology, which many university departments require their students to take. **Ontology** is what is to be known. We can see the connection between epistemology and ontology by considering our common-sense understanding of them. We apprehend the real world (its ontology) by observing it. The notion that we can know something by direct observation is the basis of an epistemology called Empiricism. In philosophical terms, it poses the separability of subject (the observer) and object (what is observed). A person, in other words, can stand apart from an object and know it by looking at it.

This view generally fits our everyday understanding of ourselves and the real world; we know what we see. From observation we build more comprehensive knowledge by inferring general explanations and theories of cause and effect. Empirical epistemology has two important implications. First, it holds that the world exists apart from us, providing us an independent perspective of observation. Second, it holds that we are capable of observing the real world as it actually is, identifying appropriate evidence and inferring accurate explanations.

There are other epistemologies. Critical scholars, as they are often referred to collectively, embrace epistemologies that deny an independent perspective. It is not possible to separate our observations from ourselves and our relationship with the real world. Instead, what we see depends on who we are and where we are situated. What we report back and the explanations we infer are inextricably tied to our identities and beliefs. There is no neutral, independent inquiry. When we proceed further and construct theories from our observations and inferences, critical scholars argue, our identities and beliefs become embedded in them.

This is an important concern because theories provide general explanations, guide further observation and form basic questions. If observation is inherently subjective so then is the resulting theory and the reality it depicts: "Theorizing about 'empirical reality' helps to construct that very reality."[2] Rejection of empirical epistemology is the common ground for critical theorists, postmodernists and feminists although they proceed differently from that basic position, as we will see shortly. The term critical scholars generally use for empirical methods is positivism. Because that term connotes logical positivism, a particularly rigid and extreme position, some scholars believe that Empiricism is a more accurate philosophical label for the way such work is actually done.[3]

For their part, empiricists freely acknowledge the role of values in framing hypotheses to investigate and in evaluating conclusions afterwards. They believe that by conscientiously following formal methods and particularly by carefully framing testable hypotheses and applying logical and statistical tests to variables, data and inferences, scholars can keep their personal values and biases out of the process and produce dependable results. Ideologically framed hypotheses are not a problem because using formal methods can show whether they are true or false. Empiricists also maintain that following formal methods allows others to evaluate the evidence and conclusions gained from the research and to conduct the same research to see whether the results can be replicated. For empiricists, method and its visible and conscientious application is the key to knowledge.

Here we have the lines of formidable conflict. The Third Debate's stakes have been the fundamental ones of the nature of inquiry, knowledge and theory. On the one side, empiricists maintain that dependable knowledge can be discovered and accumulated. On the other side, critical scholars argue that inquiry and theory are inherently value-laden and subjective and that maintaining otherwise, as empiricists do, is being either naive or dishonest. We turn now to the three most important groups of critics: critical theorists, postmodernists and feminists. (We should note that not all feminists reject Empiricism. Empirical feminists believe that it is possible to use regular methodology to investigate feminist concerns.) Beyond denying neutral and unbiased investigation, the three groups' epistemologies differ among themselves. Because of their differing epistemologies and political purposes these three groups do not yet constitute a single alternative approach to IR. Writers speak instead of a "critical project."[4]

Critical Theory

This is not as large a literature as Postmodernism and Feminism, but it embodies beliefs that have long circulated in the social sciences and advances a clear point of view. Its core principles are an amalgam of the thought of the German social theorist Juergen Habermas (1929–)and of the Italian Marxist theoretician Antonio Gramsci (1891–1937).

From Habermas is drawn the idea that knowledge is of three sorts: empirical-analytical, historical-hermeneutic and critical. Each kind of knowledge differs in its method and application. The method and application of empirical-analytical knowledge are the natural sciences. The method and application of historical-hermeneutic knowledge are interpretation and meaning. Critical knowledge's method and application is emancipation. Each kind of knowledge, according to Habermas, has its own "cognitive interest"—an accompanying purpose. In that way, no knowledge is politically neutral. For empirical-analytical knowledge, that interest is "control and prediction." For historical-hermeneutic knowledge, the cognitive interest is subjective interpretation. For critical knowledge, it is freedom.

For Habermas, critical knowledge and its use in emancipation must be achieved with cognitive interests in view. Empirical-analytical knowledge provides concrete understanding, but its cognitive interest of control and prediction binds it to management and the status quo. For that reason, empirical-analytical knowledge is not emancipatory, nor is historical-hermeneutic knowledge. It does provide interpretive insight and understanding, but its cognitive interest makes it too subjective to support action. For Habermas, achieving the critical knowledge needed for emancipation requires seeking "to avoid the simple objectivism of positivism whilst at the same time stopping short of embracing the kind of relativism implicit in traditional hermeneutics."[5]

Achieving that kind of synthesis makes demands on theory itself. Because cognitive interests may contain or conceal unstated purposes such as management and control, there must be some dependable basis for identifying the knowledge needed for emancipation and for detecting opposed rationales and purposes. Identifying purposes and assembling necessary knowledge requires a way of standing apart from conventional forms of thought. At the conceptual level, doing so requires an independent and critical approach to theorizing itself. That posture, to critical theorists, is reflexivity. It performs the theoretical and ethical roles of criticism.[6]

Habermas is not a relativist. Instead, he emphasizes "the existence of foundations for making judgments between knowledge claims." [7] Habermas, in other words, believes that a dependable basis of knowledge is possible to achieve and that it can be integrated with consciously understood and chosen values. Such critical knowledge makes proper and purposive action possible. Postmodernists, as we will see, deny any such foundation.

From these ideas of Habermas, critical theorists in IR have drawn two basic implications. The first is the entanglement of empirical knowledge with control and management. As we saw at the beginning of the chapter, critical theorists, postmodernists and feminists all reject empiricism's basic assumption of the separation of observer and object and thus deny the possibility of independent and value-free theory and inquiry. Because the values of the researcher are present but perhaps not visible, inquiry is inherently political, and knowledge is never neutral.[8] Critical theorists apply Habermas's notion of cognitive interest to identify two political forms of IR theory: "problem-solving" and "critical." Both are tied to political agendas.

Problem-solving IR theory is based on the cognitive interest of management and control and is focused in the present. By beginning with the fact of the international system as it is, problem-solving theories "implicitly accept the prevailing order as [their] own framework" thereby serving the interests of states or classes who "are comfortable with the given order."[9] Critical IR theory, in contrast, is concerned with historical evolution and seeks to identify the conditions and opportunities of change. That purpose derives from Habermas's critical theory of emancipation and is "directed toward an appraisal of the very framework for action."[10]

Realism and Neorealism, in this view, are problem-solving theories. E.H. Carr's original Realism was historically informed and had possibilities for a broader critical awareness, but it was converted by Morgenthau and Waltz into a more instrumentally austere problem-solving theory to guide American policymakers during the cold war. Neorealism, in the view of critical theorists, is not politically neutral. In depicting the international system as a power contest and in depicting states as rationally defending existing positions, Neorealism's cognitive interest is management, control and preservation. Its political agenda is conservative.

Not all scholars, we should note, have agreed with the problem-solving label: "I have always been puzzled why some critical theorists...refer to the conventional structural [neorealist] approach as 'problem solving.' How would any policymaker solve problems with it? What would he or she do? Alter the international configuration of power? Modify anarchy? Tell the weak to get stronger, the poor richer?"[11]

For critical theorists, there are more directly ideological grounds for objecting to Neorealism. Its "latent normative element...performs a proselytizing function" that supports a competitive and static world outlook. That outlook overshadows others—which may arise in liberal societies such as the United States and Canada—which reject such vigilance and domination and hold more "optimistic and moralistic" views of humankind.[12]

The second implication drawn from Habermas defines the task of critical theorists. That task is to construct a theory that shows the political interests behind other theories, embraces human emancipation and joins that purpose to empirical research. In contrast to theories like Neorealism that are held to conceal political purposes, Critical Theory is *honestly* political. Its agenda is to "promote a process of education and 'conscientization' among those poorly served by present social and political arrangements through which the disadvantaged can empower themselves to effect radical social change."[13] Habermas, we should note, did not believe in imposing critical knowledge arbitrarily. Instead, he wrote of an "ideal speech situation" in which people could evaluate alternative claims calmly, truthfully and objectively.[14]

The Gramscian elements are the notions of **hegemony** and the political role of intellectuals. Hegemony is Gramsci's notion of preponderance. Domestically, hegemony is political rule based on a blend of persuasion and coercion. Displacing an existing hegemony with a revolutionary one requires forming a rival hegemony by incorporating allied classes and sectors. The revolutionary party's task is to promote the solidarity and mass necessary to eventually displace the existing order. In that task, "intellectuals play a key role... They perform the function of developing and sustaining the mental images, technologies and organizations which bind together the members of a class and of a historic bloc [the rival hegemony] into a common identity."[15]

FIGURE 5.1   Antonio Gramsci

Antonio Gramsci (1891-1937) helped found the Italian Communist Party (PCI) in 1921 and was an important interpreter of Marxism. He worked for several years as an influential journalist in Italian socialist newspapers one of which, *L'Ordine nuovo* (The New Order), he founded in 1919. His most important work is *Lettere dal carcere*, a set of notebooks written during his 11 years of imprisonment by the fascist government of Mussolini. Published in 1947, the notebooks, together with his journalism, represent important modifications of traditional Marxist thought.

Although his ideas were influential, his first years as an Italian Communist Party official were not. Following the party's founding in 1921, Gramsci's interpretive approach to Marxism clashed with the more doctrinaire position of the party's leader, marginalizing his practical influence. In 1922, he was sent to Moscow as an Italian delegate to the Comintern, the coordinative body of the world communist movement, perhaps to get him out of the way. While in Moscow, Gramsci became concerned by the growing climate of authoritarianism in the Soviet Union. Convinced that revolutions cannot be the work of an authoritarian state, in 1926 he wrote a personal letter to the Soviet Communist party's leaders protesting Stalin's efforts to eliminate his opponents although it is not known whether the PCI's delegate ever delivered it.[16]

After returning to Italy, Gramsci became head of the PCI in 1924 and was elected to the Italian parliament. In 1926, Gramsci was arrested by Mussolini's government, which had come to power four years earlier and had taken increasingly violent action against its opponents. In prison, Gramsci recorded his reflections on political thought and action in a set of handwritten notebooks. His health began to fail, and he became unable to write. Afflicted with tuberculosis and arteriosclerosis, he was eventually released. He died in a Rome hospital shortly afterwards.

Gramsci's ideas, which represented important modifications to Marxism, seem surprisingly contemporary. **Marginalization** is one of those ideas. Like Marx, Gramsci believed that class struggle is central to politics and that overturning the ruling order is necessary to end oppression. Instead of seeing an upper and lower class as Marx did, Gramsci saw a more general separation between centre and periphery. That view casts oppression in much broader terms for it is not only economic exploitation, as traditional Marxism holds, but also a more comprehensive exclusion. At the centre is society's small and powerful elite exercising not just the economic and political power emphasized by Marx but social and cultural power as well. The rest of society is marginalized at the periphery. The purpose of politics, Gramsci believed, is to eliminate privilege and remove the barriers that keep people from the centre.[17] Doing so requires overpowering it.

In the same way, Gramsci's central notion of hegemony expands the Marxist idea of class power. The ruling hegemony, in Gramsci's view, is based not only on coercion but also on intellectual and moral leadership. Control is exercised not only by force but also by popular acquiescence. The instruments of control are not only the state's police but also civil society and all its institutions "ranging from education, religion and the family to the microstructures of the practices of everyday life." They maintain "spontaneous" consent to the existing order.[18] For that reason, in Gramsci's view, capitalist liberal democracy is a façade that masks a powerful centre and disguises its influence as popular approval. Unmasking that hegemony and cultivating people's awareness of their marginalization is the revolutionary intellectual's task.

The notion of hegemony helped explain Marxism's crisis in the 1920s and 1930s. Marx predicted that economic contradictions in the advanced industrial states would produce revolution as the masses realized their exploitation and rose up. When that did not happen in Europe—Russia in 1917 did not fit the profile of an advanced industrial state—Marxists were confronted with the fact that the working classes were not revolutionary. That was so, in Gramsci's view, because hegemonic power clad in liberal democracy was so pervasive and consensual. In more recent years, Gramsci has provided one way of explaining the continuing resilience of liberal democracy and capitalism. Overturning their hegemony, Gramsci cautioned, will not be easy because people's beliefs must be changed. The sites of struggle are all of society's institutions.[19]

Following Gramsci, critical IR theorists envisage international hegemony as an encompassing system of military, economic and cultural relations that is supported, as are domestic hegemonies, by a combination of force and persuasion. As in domestic hegemonies as well, the predominant powers include corporations as well as states. The persuasive element is contained in "intellectual, moral and political leadership clustered around an ideologically instilled consensus."

Hegemony is thus ideological as well as material. Its ideology "acts to define the common-sense view of reality in a way biased towards the interests of [a] ruling class," thereby augmenting material power and force as the ruling order's basis of support.[20]

IR theories that implicitly support a status quo, in the view of critical theorists, perform the ideological function of maintaining hegemony. Critical theorists see Institutionalism's cooperative assumptions as not progressive. Instead, the economic cooperation embraced by Institutionalism occurs among *hegemonic* powers. Neorealism, for its part, embraces the underlying availability of force. Together, the two theories' unstated ideology justifies hegemonic states and corporations in their protection of interests and their maintenance of unequal global relationships. Cooperation, instead of being a progressive force, merely supports the adjustments and compromises that are needed to maintain hegemony. Institutionalism's and Neorealism's central assumptions of rationality and self-interest furnish the necessary pragmatism. To critical theorists, Institutionalism and Neorealism underwrite the hegemonic management of dominant states and transnational corporations.

The task of critical IR theorists, following Gramsci's role for intellectuals, is to support the theoretical and ideological construction of an international counter-hegemony. The opportunity for building a counter-hegemony is presented by economic globalization, which is altering existing relationships of production and creating the kinds of social and political dislocation that could support radical change.[21] We will see more about the causes and effects of globalization in Chapter 8. Not all scholars agree that Gramsci's ideas can be transported from 1930s Italy to 1990s IR. On a number of key points, Gramsci is open to several different readings, making his relevance and meaning at least debatable.[22]

Canadian Reality Check 5.2

Critical Theory and Free Trade

Canada's initiative to seek a free trade agreement with the United States reflects the hegemony of business interests and government. They in turn are part of a broader American-based hegemony whose interests are increased access for investment capital abroad, cooperative foreign governments, harmonious economic policies, freely available natural resources and international coordination. The Canadian elite identifies its interests with the American one. Economic theory supporting free trade contains an unstated capitalist ideological element, and its political use is to persuade people to identify their interests with the hegemonic order. The critical theorist's task is to display the purposes behind free trade and support the building of a popular counter-hegemony.

Postmodernism

Postmodernism has replaced Marxism as IR's most radical writing.[23] It shares with Critical Theory and Feminism the denial of neutral empirical knowledge but goes much farther. Postmodernism's object is to complete the demolition of modern thought begun by Friedrich Nietzsche (1844-1900) and Martin Heidegger (1889-1976), who levelled fundamental challenges at the Enlightenment's belief that knowledge has a firm foundation that can be discovered. For postmodernists, denying foundational knowledge has profound implications: "...once it becomes clear that the foundations upon which [Western thought rests] are, ultimately, radically insecure...intellectual life cannot simply proceed in the old ways."[24] No meanings are fixed. Every statement of knowledge may be questioned or, to use the postmodernist term, interrogated. The implications are drastic. Critical Theory, as we just saw, denies that knowledge is politically neutral. Postmodernism denies that knowledge has a base.

Following this view of knowledge, postmodernists deny that any text including this one has inherent meaning. Efforts to ascribe meaning are arbitrary and oppressive acts of power because they seek to manipulate understanding. Particularly oppressive are efforts to classify and categorize because they violate the identities of the things they address.[25] If a postmodernist were with you right now as you read this, he or she would advise you to regard its meaning as indeterminate and to be wary of my motives. There are two reasons to take that attitude. The first is to resist any effort on my part to ascribe meaning because by doing so I am exercising power. The second is to avoid the problem of trying to determine what I intend to say because that cannot be known for certain. The same idea applies to your friends' reading of this text; your reading is as valid as theirs. (The idea applies also to my reading of Postmodernism.) The important thing is to construct your own meaning and resist the imposition of others.

These statements show why Postmodernism, in the literal sense of going to the roots, is so radical; it goes to the roots of meaning and finds nothing constant. The statements also show why Postmodernism is inherently political: shared and accepted meanings exist only because power has imposed them. Postmodernism "looks for no distinction between 'truth' and power, for it expects none."[26] Truth is simply the privileged view of those in power. Without power, meanings are individual and indeterminate. Because those meanings shape our conceptions of ourselves, discovering our own meanings is progress along the road to discovering our identities. To make progress requires being aware of the power behind accepted meanings and resisting them. For postmodernists, the critical task is to disrupt accepted meanings and transgress normal classifications and categories.

Instead of finding evidence of power and imposition in material relationships as critical theorists do, postmodernists find that evidence in language. Far more than being simply a vehicle for transmitting meaning, language represents and enforces patterns of power and inequality. The postmodernist term for that social dimension of language is discourse. Drawing on French philosopher Michel Foucault (1926-1984), postmodernists see discourse as involving "not simply a group of signs or symbols [the content of language] but the overall social practices that systematically form social subjects and the objects of which they speak."[27] What this means is that language not only describes human relationships, it *constructs* them. This occurs because language constructs individuals' identities and defines their relations with others. For Foucault, these relationships evolve historically, and it is important to include that dimension in any analysis. Foucault's term for that work is genealogy.

Drawing on the ideas of French philosopher Jacques Derrida (1930–), postmodernists believe that modern thought as well as language construct identities as arbitrary opposites. A thing's quality is defined by contrasting it to something else. An object or a person is whatever some other object or person is not. Domestic, for example, is known as not international. Female is known as not male. Real is known as not ideological. Core is known as not peripheral.[28] This practice is the "consolidation of identity through the constitution of difference."[29] Note that difference is *constituted* not *natural*. Constituting difference is objectionable to postmodernists because doing so imposes arbitrary identities and because the pairs—subject and other—are not balanced and equal. The subject is privileged by positive attributes while the other receives the negative ones. These attributes, postmodernists emphasize, are people's identities. By treating these attributes as natural, language maintains unequal pairings between privileged and other.

This view has two important implications. If people know their identities only because they have been depicted in reference to something else, their genuine identities exist apart from that arbitrary opposition and remain to be discovered. Finding that autonomous and true identity is emancipation particularly for those who have been marginalized and subordinated by the imposition of unfavourable attributes and who know themselves and their situations only in reference to a positive and privileged opposite.

Second, because these pairings are unequal, constructing identities through language and meaning creates **hierarchies** in which those with favourable attributes are privileged. The unfavourable and opposite ones are projected to the other "as a complication, a negation, a manifestation, an effect, a disruption, a parasitic (mis)representation or a fall from the graceful presence of the first."[30] In these pairings the position of the other is at the margins. Being marginalized is a denial of authentic identity and voice. In that way, control of discourse is an exercise of political power as it designates meanings and identities and creates hierarchies of privilege and marginality. The authority of language, which constructs meanings and oppositions, is the vehicle of political power. Meanings and oppositions are contained, and hidden, in texts. A text is any authoritative statement: a description, a classification, a story—a theory!

The task of postmodernists is to unmask the hidden and oppressive power relationships contained in texts. The tool of deconstruction does so by inverting the unequal pairs so that the other is privileged. Inverting does two things: it shows the arbitrariness of the attributed qualities and allows those who have been marginalized to break free of them and find their own identities. Second, it undercuts the meaning and authority of the text itself and removes it as a source of oppression. Deconstruction is an elaborate technique, and deconstructed texts are quite dense. The purpose is straightforward: to cut away at the foundations of authority and privilege.

As we saw, postmodernists also deny the inherent meaning of any text. The conventional notion of meaning is stated in this formulation: I (the subject) am writing a text (this page) that represents an object (Postmodernism in IR).[31] This common-sense statement is vulnerable on a number of grounds. Philosophers since David Hume (1711-1776) have doubted that any text actually does represent an object. At best, a text can be a "useful way of approaching the object."[32] Postmodernists go much farther. Not only is the object in doubt (because we cannot be sure of any text's description) but so too is the subject (the author). Postmodernists speak of this as the disappearance of the subject. That makes both sides of the common-sense statement problematic: our ability to know an object through a text is doubtful but so too is the subject's own ability to know and transmit it. A subject cannot be certain about what he or she meant when writing the text or that what he or she writes captures it. Time compounds the doubt: what an author intended and understood today may be different tomorrow.[33] That leaves any connection between authorship and text murky and indeterminate. We cannot know what was meant.

For postmodernists, the disappearing subject has a profound implication. We are used to regarding ourselves as sovereign, in charge of ourselves and of what we say. That view, to postmodernists, is false—one of the Enlightenment's misguided notions. Instead, postmodernists speak of "writing under erasure," which is their way of saying that our ability to record meaning is completely open to question. We are not sovereign in the basic area of self-expression. For texts, writing under erasure removes authority as well as meaning: we cannot understand texts as either descriptions of an object or as recordings of an author. If texts have no reference to either authors or objects, we can understand them only in reference to other texts.[34] Postmodernists call that condition intertextuality—the absence of any grounded meaning or clear intention and the need to search for meaning in the reflections between texts. Finding meaning becomes an endless regression among endless texts, each reflecting back on the other. A chamber of mirrors is one visualization. Such a view of texts completely destabilizes any notion of authority and removes any fixed point of reference.

These ideas have had considerable impact on the humanities and social sciences. To what do they connect in IR? Postmodernists in IR are very interested in identities, both individual and collective, in hierarchies and marginalization, in master narratives and silences and in genuine experience. Individual and collective identities must be discovered apart from those that are imposed. People marginalized by hierarchical orders must be heard and their experiences acknowledged.

Postmodernists take special exception to statehood, which they regard as a peculiarly modern and powerful instrument of privilege, marginalization and oppression.[35] Statehood, in their view, is a creation of the Enlightenment and has its first justifications in the master narratives of Enlightenment political philosophers such as Hobbes. As we saw in the first chapter, Hobbes's notions of sovereignty and anarchy have underpinned basic understandings of the nature of IR.

Domestically, in the view of postmodernists, sovereign statehood is a hierarchy of power and rule that privileges some and subordinates others. Internationally, sovereign statehood creates boundaries between self and other and creates identities by opposition, attributing positive ones to the state/self and negative ones to the foreign/other.[36] Postmodernists see the same pairing in IR's basic divide between order within states and anarchy among them. Order enjoys privileged attributes such as peace and safety. Anarchy, the condition of the other, receives negative attributes such as violence and danger. States form hierarchies among themselves with the privileged ones marginalizing the others. Again, the terms are unequally paired: advanced/developing.

To postmodernists, statehood is the source of master narratives that justify arbitrary practices and maintain hierarchies. Master narratives include IR theories. They justify hierarchy and domination by portraying the prevailing state-based order as normal particularly to those whom the order marginalizes. Neorealism, IR's most explicitly state-centred theory, has been a magnet to postmodernists. In their view, Neorealism is a social use of language, a discourse, that maintains hierarchy and domination. Another magnet is national security writing, which justifies defence of the state against the other. To the postmodernist, national defence "bifurcate[s] between 'the self' and 'the Other' in the production of domestic consensus against the overseas enemy."[37] One of the major postmodernist writings in IR is a deconstruction of Waltz's *Theory of International Politics*, the core text, as we saw in chapter 2, of Neorealism. In a long and complex treatment, Richard Ashley finds a hidden depiction of the state and human action that justifies repressive hierarchies at home and a constant practice of conflict abroad to maintain the state's bounded social identity.[38] An earlier and more complex postmodern treatment also by Ashley found Neorealism beset by contradictions and ambiguous meanings.[39]

Postmodernists blame much of the world's problems on the outlook of modern science—another legacy of the Enlightenment. In addition to supporting the fiction of a value-free empiricism, modern science coupled with the political power of the state has been the agency for oppressing women, nature, other races and the poor.[40] One scholar summarizes the view of modernity "as a cultural construction that attempts to extend one particular mode of thinking—rationality—to all corners of the world destroying diversity in the name of progress." Rationality itself is an "ideological construction that is a form of power."[41]

For these reasons, postmodernists are interested in silences and voices. The silences are the areas that IR theory leaves unexplored, and the voices are those of the marginalized whose concerns and identities are left out. Those are not natural omissions but constitute "boundaries that are used to silence and exclude 'others' who are labelled insane, primitive, criminal, terrorist or the like."[42] To remove boundaries and give voice, postmodernists look forward to decomposed meanings and seek common cause with others in resistance. "What dissident scholarship opts for...is a sense of disciplinary crisis [in IR] that resonates with the effects of marginal and dissident movements in all sorts of other localities."[43] (For a postmodernist view of free trade, read Canadian Reality Check 5.3.)

Canadian Reality Check 5.3

Postmodernism and Free Trade

Arguments in favour of free trade are a privileged discourse of political and economic power. Instead of depicting the other as foreign and dangerous, the free trade discourse attributes to the American other cooperative and beneficial qualities. The important other is domestic. Critics of free trade are depicted as short-sighted, uninformed or fearful and are posed as opposites to free trade supporters who are depicted as forward-looking, expert and confident. Canada's identity, always multiple and contested, becomes moreso. Hierarchies abound. Domestically, privileged discourses marginalize workers, minorities and women. Internationally, privileged discourses accept subordination to the United States. Opposition to free trade gives voice to the marginalized and subordinate.

Feminism

Feminism is more broad and eclectic than either Critical Theory or Postmodernism, and it is accurate to speak of many Feminisms: liberal, socialist, Marxist, postmodern and empirical. Feminists taking these and other positions hold different views, and the ones presented here have been the most prominent in the recent IR literature. Feminism does share one common starting point: "Most contemporary feminist scholarship," according to a recent review, "takes gender—which embodies relationships of power inequality—as its central category of analysis."[44] The fact of gender, in other words, precedes all others. This view does not imply that gender determines what women actually do as scholars. "A majority of IR women scholars," according to the same review, "do not work with feminist approaches."[45] Treating gender as primary, however, does bring IR's enterprise into question. "For most feminist IR scholars, I dare say, *all* pre-feminist international relations theory is suspect if not hopeless altogether because of its systematic 'gender bias.'" [emphasis in original][46]

That view squarely addresses epistemology—the way we know things. As we saw at the beginning of the chapter, feminists (except empirical feminists), critical theorists and postmodernists all reject the idea of a detached and objective observer. Constructions of reality are inherently subjective and reflect the observer's beliefs and identity. Critical theorists, as we saw, emphasize the observer's political values and purposes. Feminists emphasize gender: it makes a big difference whether the observer is male or female. The notion of detached objectivity, in their view, is simply a male way of observing the world: "the knowing mind of traditional epistemology is axiomatically a male mind." Asserting that gender affects observation follows directly from the belief that "women's lives differ structurally from those of men."[47] The attitude of the observer, in turn, affects the nature of discovered knowledge.

That makes the question not "what knowledge?" but "whose knowledge?" Critical theorists ask the same question but emphasize the interests of dominant classes and states. Feminists emphasize gender. Skewed observation produces skewed generalizations and skewed theory: "...international theories which claim to offer objective and universal explanations of state behaviour have been constructed out of the behaviour of men."[48]

Accounting for gender differences is one of the prime occupations of feminist theory. One explanation derives from traditional developmental psychology, which depicts boys' separation from their mothers as an important stage in their progress to adulthood. As they achieve autonomy, men come to value independence in all forms and to see it ultimately as a defence against others. That view of male-female difference is drawn from one of Feminism's core texts, *In a Different Voice*, by Carol Gilligan.[49] An autonomous outlook, to feminists, is not an innate human attribute but is rooted in a particular kind of experience based on gender. The kind of impersonal and detached calculation that underpins more general assumptions about rational behaviour is not universal but male.

What IR theory most embodies these outlooks? To feminists, that view of independence looks similar to IR theory's depictions of sovereign states. Sovereign autonomy, self-protection and impersonal calculation, as we saw in Chapter 2, are the main planks of Realism and Neorealism. To feminists, Realism and Neorealism depict "states as primitive 'individuals' separated from history and others by loner rights of sovereignty—backed up, for good measure, by military hardware—and involved in international conventions and institutions only on a voluntary basis."[50] Depicting states as "abstract unitary actors," systemic laws of behaviour "as independent of human agency" and using "rational choice and game theoretic models," Neorealism generalizes from "behaviour that in the modern West has been more typical of men than women. Feminists suggest that these partial models tend to prioritize certain aspects of state behaviour associated with conflict and draw our attention away from other activities in which states are also engaged..."[51] For these reasons, feminists argue, Realism and Neorealism depict not international behaviour but male behaviour.

Females, in contrast, grow up to see themselves as individuals who are still connected with others and who "find their identity within the context of relationships rather than in opposition to them."[52] Such development disposes women to understand IR in terms of cooperation and continuous interaction. That does not make feminists institutionalists. The main objection is that Institutionalism, although it does emphasize cooperation, is still based on sovereign states, rational calculation and self-interest all of which are male outlooks.

Not all feminists believe that such stark female/male categorizations are helpful. One disadvantage is that strong dichotomies—impersonal and rational men vs. connected and empathetic women—reinforce gender stereotypes and make it easy to dismiss women as too idealistic for the real world of international politics.[53]

Another objection is that the supporting feminist epistemology, standpoint Feminism, generalizes not only between men and women but also from the perspective of white, middle-class women in the developed world.[54] Such categorical generalizations not only impose that perspective on poor women in developing states but also transport values such as non-violence. Women who have fought in insurgencies and wars in developing states may take a very different view of combat and defence.[55] Because there is not one single female identity but a multitude, the "unified notion of women's experience" is problematic. Since there are multiple female identities, some scholars suggest that Feminism is an "intrinsically postmodern discourse."[56] We will see more about Postmodern Feminism in a moment.

Another reason for resisting the "privileged epistemic ground" of strongly categorized gender is that it is easy to take the next step and assume that being female makes one a member of a bias-free "universal category" that has a "specific, non-replicable insight into any given culture that is unavailable to a male researcher." Assuming such insight makes it possible to imagine that one shares a "naturally grounded congruity" with people in other cultures and situations. Experiencing female oppression in Canada, it would follow, provides a special understanding of oppression in Guatemala. That congruity may not in fact exist but may colour the observations of those who expect it. Worse assuming such insight privileges female observations over male ones, committing the same fault that feminists criticize.[57]

One proposal for resolving epistemological differences is to adopt a "conversational" approach to knowledge. This approach reflects feminist theory's distrust of empirical approaches and its preference for acquiring knowledge and understanding through narratives and storytelling focused on individual experiences.[58] Of particular interest are the experiences of those who are marginalized in the international world and ignored by conventional IR theory.

Interest in marginalization, narratives and experience suggests that feminists might find a congenial approach in Postmodernism. There are indeed points of connection. Postmodernism's interest in identity and experience matches Feminism's interest in gender identity and experience. Postmodernism's notion that identities are constructed as arbitrary and opposite pairs resonates with Feminism's concern with gender categories such as objectivity/subjectivity, reason/emotion, mind/body, knowing/being.[59] "Importantly for feminist theories of identity," writes one prominent theorist, "woman as 'other' is a relational concept that depends on and is derived from the identity of the male as the universal subject."[60] Postmodernism's view of power as the ability to assign meanings and shape identities agrees with Feminism's view that IR theory upholds gender meanings and identities. In addition, both agree that the pairing is part of the "legacy of Western political and economic thought."[61] In that way, postmodernists and feminists share the same objection to the Enlightenment's fundamental notions of rationality and individuality. For feminists, the consequence is that our common understandings of these two foundations of thinking and identity are gendered.

Viewing the international world as a privileged hierarchy is another point of connection. Postmodernism's interest in marginalization agrees with the feminist view of women as subordinate and silent and links women to marginalized people everywhere. The result is a global composite of paired attributes, hierarchies and silenced voices. "Feminist analysis," in the words of one scholar, "allows us to see how often these unfavourable images are constructed through an association with a devalued 'femininity' when characteristics such as irrational or emotional, often associated with women, are used to portray those on the outside of the state." [62] Sharing marginalization and silence, in that view, makes women the most understanding students of poverty and exploitation. Envisaging a comprehensive hierarchy makes it possible to identify with the experience of all the world's marginalized and silenced, providing an expansive but compelling project of emancipation.

Postmodernism's view that readings can be found in all sorts of texts agrees with the feminist interest in personal narratives. Those narratives, particularly from silenced voices, illuminate the nature of hierarchy and subordination. A recent feminist writing on the oppression of Mexican women uses a novel about a domestic servant in a wealthy Mexico City family as a text to depict a chain of economic oppression and patriarchy. The hierarchy stretches from international capitalism through the Mexican government to peasants in the Mexican state of Chiapas to the peasant women in Chiapas. The writing focuses on the experiences and perceptions of the people involved and uses the novel to support broader generalizations about social relations and inequality. The purpose is to show oppression, relate experience through personal narratives and connect levels in a hierarchy.[63]

Finally, many feminists share Postmodernism's hostility to sovereign statehood, which is regarded as a repressive and hierarchical instrument. Feminists, along with postmodernists, have given much attention to political philosophers who wrote about sovereignty, particularly Hobbes. At issue is the evolution and character of statehood itself. Postmodernists and many feminists regard sovereignty as a formal and regimented order that replaced a much looser, less hierarchical and more interconnected feudal system. The political philosophers who advocated liberation from feudalism through individual autonomy and sovereign rule did not, feminists emphasize, include women. Equality was advocated, but patriarchy was retained.[64] For some, that exclusion of women in the major works of political philosophy discredits any discussion of statehood, even modern and cooperative views of it.[65] Statehood itself is the problematic issue.

Liberal feminists take a more optimistic view. Pointing to the evolution since Hobbes's time of modern democratic states that respond to organized political interests, liberal feminists argue that the state can be useful: "The very fact that the state creates, condenses and focuses political power may make it the best friend and not the enemy of feminists—because the availability of real *political* power is essential to real democratic control."[66] Indeed, in a turbulent and interdependent international world, the modern democratic state provides helpful stability and protection. The feminist task is to organize effective influence.

Not all IR feminists support Postmodernism. One sympathetic scholar sees Postmodernism as a "diversionary association" that risks Feminism's "self-marginalization." The problem is Postmodernism's "conceit...that it alone provides a means of examining structures of domination and giving voice to the oppressed."[67] Postmodernists themselves have been critical. As we saw, postmodernists deny that knowledge has any secure foundation. If that is so, male and female attributes, like other attributes, are free-floating and indefinite. Writing in definite terms about states, sovereignty, identity and "cultural otherness" assumes that they actually exist in some knowable way and that the writer has an idea of their true nature.[68] Such writing is not really postmodern.

Although there have been efforts to resolve the deficiencies of Postmodernism and standpoint Feminism, Postmodernism still contains a basic problem: Arguing, in a postmodern mode, that all experiences and narratives are equally valid does not square with arguing, in a feminist mode, that women's views and narratives "have special authority."[69]

Canadian Reality Check 5.4

Feminism and Free Trade

In free trade, women workers and breadwinners lose out. They occupy lower-end jobs in the economy, are frequently seasonal, part-time and non-union and will bear the first effects of inevitable readjustment. Women's subordinate position in the Canadian labour force is shared by women around the world. Trade-minded governments in Canada and elsewhere will not be sympathetic to maintaining the social programs in which women have the largest stake. The political debate pays insufficient attention to women's concerns.

As we saw earlier, postmodern ideas have had a considerable impact on the social sciences and IR. Marxist ideas, some of which are embodied in Critical Theory, have circulated in IR for decades. Many feminists, however, believe that their ideas are being quietly ignored, and that situation itself has been the subject of debate and analysis. Postmodernism and Critical Theory claim to take Feminism seriously, but they are not always regarded as trustworthy allies as we will see next.

Critical Approaches: The Internal Debate

We can begin with Postmodernism. Those who wish to formulate programs of political action approve of Postmodernism's relish for attacking cherished ideas but argue that it goes too far. Political action depends ultimately on firm knowledge and purpose, but Postmodernism "paralyzes itself into non-action" by holding everything up to question and regarding nothing as certain.[70] The practical effect makes Postmodernism a status-quo doctrine. Some feminists also detect an underlying conservatism because Postmodernism has not "included gender in its catalog of hierarchical dualisms at the core of Western discourses that oppress people and silence their voices."[71] Gender had to be brought in by feminists.

Postmodernism's free-swinging relativism can also make critical theorists wary.[72] *Any* text, given Postmodernism's view of power and discourse, can be read as an instrument of arbitrary and imposed meanings. What is read is up to the individual postmodernist. That makes Postmodernism's most powerful tool, deconstruction, a loose ca(n)non. The same technique that reduced Neorealism's core text, as we saw earlier, to a muddle of contradictions, multiple meanings and hidden messages could just as easily demolish, say, Gramsci. The fact that postmodernists so far have addressed many of the same concerns as critical theorists does not mean that their alignment is predictable. The difference is in Postmodernism's celebration of subjectivity and paralyzed authority, which makes postmodernists (free) radicals and supports a potentially wide selection of texts. *Some* secure ground must be preserved.

FIGURE 5.5   Marx, Lenin and Postmodernism

Associated Press/AP photo/CP Archive

Karl Marx   Vladimir Lenin

How would some of these ideas have looked to Karl Marx (1818-1883) and V.I. Lenin (1870-1924)? The editor of the journal *Partisan Review* put together this brief checklist:[73]

Relativism: Marx and Lenin did not believe in any kind of relativism. Their thinking was founded in absolutes.

Cultural diversity: Neither Marx nor Lenin was interested in any kind of cultural diversity. Lenin supported various nationalisms in Russia, but that was mainly a part of his revolutionary strategy.

Feminism: Neither Marx nor Lenin was especially concerned with Feminism although neither directly opposed it. What they actually believed was that none of these questions could be adequately solved under capitalism and that only under socialism could people be free of prejudice and bigotry.

Liberation movements: In general neither Marx nor Lenin believed in any liberation movements other than the ultimate revolutionary one of introducing socialism. They thought of them as soporifics, as pie-in-the-sky.

Populism: Marx and Lenin did not care for populism in any form. It will be recalled that Marx went so far as to speak of "the idiocy of the village."

Elitism: Neither Marx nor Lenin appears ever to have used the term "elite" or "elitism," but clearly they supported the idea of intellectual quality and an intellectual vanguard.

Third World: Marx had little interest in underdeveloped countries, and Lenin was concerned with them only as part of his revolutionary strategy.

Mainstream scholars have also been critical. One refers to Postmodernism as "negative theory" that produces no outcomes beyond rejection and "wrecking operations."[74] Others tackle Postmodernism on its own grounds. A systematic analysis of several major postmodern IR writings found them guilty of some of the same oppressive practices they criticize, most notably of constructing arbitrary good/bad pairings to cast their opponents in unfairly extreme positions.[75] In one scholar's words, applying Postmodernism has resulted in "bad IR *and* bad philosophy."[76]

Perhaps the ultimate critique is that in the arts where it was once a potent force, Postmodernism is already over. Postmodernism began in postwar Europe as a reaction to the same sense of profound dislocation and loss that produced Existentialism. That sense was sustained by the cold war's horrifying nuclear polarity. Postmodernism expressed dislocation as a "nostalgic eclecticism in architectural forms, [a] prevalence of pastiche and abrupt juxtapositions of imagery in art, and [a] deconstructionist impulse in literature."[77] The sustaining momentum ended in 1989 when, symbolically, the Berlin Wall came down. There has been no new artistic style to replace Postmodernism, and in the words of one commentator, the present "feels like the latter days of a cultural moment, a *fin de siecle*." The loose impulses of the present "will presumably transform themselves, before too long, into the form of new and strong artistic achievements that do, indeed, feel like a new age of style."[78] At the same time, it may be a mistake to ignore Postmodernism. As we will see in boxes throughout the book, it provides a point of view that is available from no other source. We will consider Postmodernism's prospects in IR momentarily. Before doing so, we need to note a final point about Critical Theory and Feminism.

The endeavour in IR that comes closest to Critical Theory's ideal theoretical posture of reflexivity—being able to look critically at the process of theorizing and being aware of the role of political interests—is Feminism.[79] Some feminists, however, are not sure that Critical Theory is sufficiently reflexive itself: "Male scholars concerned with reflexivity in international relations have largely ignored the relevance of philosophical debates within contemporary feminisms."[80] Marxism is not necessarily dependable. It, along with Critical Theory, shares "unacknowledged androcentric metatheoretical presuppositions, which serve to render invisible the unequal power relations between men and women and the accompanying symbolic discourses that sustain them."[81] In the real world, socialism in the former Soviet Union did not eliminate women's inequality. Finally, there is a concern that Critical Theory is too "academic" and detached from political struggle, an "institutionalization" that feminists should avoid.[82]

Detached scholasticism underpins another scholar's counsel about focusing too much on language and not enough on the international world. Commenting on the occupation with sovereign statehood's oppressive discourses, Janice Thomson warns against losing sight of real power: "States are now massive, physical, bureaucratic and coercive institutions that have been developing for some six centuries... I am not convinced that the state might be fundamentally altered if the discourse on the state changed or that it would vanish if we stopped talking about it."[83]

International Relations Theory: Fusion and Accommodation?

Where does this controversy leave IR? As we saw in Chapter 2, Neorealism and Institutionalism have been criticized on conventional grounds as being too arbitrarily deductive, as containing no theory of the state and as being unable to envisage fundamental transformations. As we saw in Chapters 3 and 4, there have been efforts to address those deficiencies. Liberal IR theory has been proposed as a theory of state behaviour that accounts for the political alignments and the definitions of interest and identities that shape state action. Constructivism has been advanced to address transformation. What joins these theories is their empirical epistemology: they practice standard social science. That, as was seen in this chapter, has been precisely the objection of critical theorists, postmodernists and many feminists. Rejecting empirical epistemology separates them from the main body of IR—or does it? Are the differences irreconcilable?

The most interesting perspective on this question is provided by Danish IR scholar Ole Waever. He proposes the continuum shown in Figure 5.6:[84]

FIGURE 5.6   Tabulation of Theories

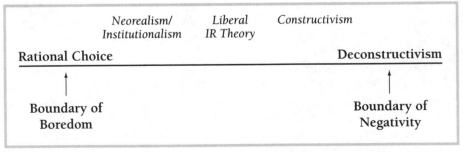

The continuum sets deductive rationality, reflected in game theory and formal economic models of choice, against subjectivity and relativism, reflected in the three critical approaches just seen. Rational Choice is at one end of Waever's continuum, and Deconstructivism is at the other end. The convergence area is in the middle. The Boundary of Boredom is Waever's whimsical way of characterizing the highly formal and deductive nature of much neorealist/institutionalist scholarship, which lies within the boundary but not far from it. Outside the Boundary of Boredom, work becomes so abstract that it loses connection to the real world. At the other end of the continuum, the Boundary of Negativity is Waever's demarcation of the constructive limits of debate. Postmodernism, with its emphasis on demolition, lies beyond the boundary. Between the two boundaries, we can locate Neorealism/Institutionalism, Liberal IR theory and Constructivism.

Neorealism and Institutionalism with their emphasis on rational calculation are at the left end of the continuum. They are shown together because, as we saw in the last chapter, they are very close in assuming rational choice, an anarchic international system and self-interested behaviour and in differing only on trust and cooperation. Many scholars see that difference as narrowing into a single theory. Liberal IR theory is located in towards the middle because of its emphasis on individual and collective values and the mediating role of governmental institutions and laws. Constructivism is the closest to the subjective end of the continuum because of its emphasis on identities and its view of them as interactive and transforming forces. Also warranting Constructivism's placement, there is its view of norms and beliefs as important regulators and agents of change.

This continuum shows an emerging effect of the Third Debate's philosophical occupation with theorizing and method. At the rationalist end of the continuum, Neorealism/Institutionalism have reached their formalistic limits and must allow more qualitative and subjective elements into consideration to avoid becoming arid and marginal. There is now acknowledgement that ideas and not merely rational calculation do indeed matter and that their involvement with international change should be studied.[85] From the rationalist side, there is also acknowledgement that Neorealism and Institutionalism, by factoring out the interactive shaping of interests—the central process in Constructivism—may be eliminating important elements. It is the task of theorists to identify the situations when those interactive elements need to be considered.[86] The effect of these acknowledgements is to open the door to more qualitative applications of Neorealism and Institutionalism—a move toward the centre of the continuum.

From the deconstructive side of the continuum, the central importance of subjectivity and values in Constructivism recognizes much of the critical approaches' objection. Postmodernism's relativistic view of knowledge still keeps it on the far side of the Boundary of Negativity, but some scholars see room for further accommodation. Although constructivists do maintain that their methods are standard empiricism, which is alienating to critical scholars, Constructivism's central notion of identity is promisingly broad and openly acknowledges subjective meanings.[87] More generally, Waever asserts, "more 'philosophical' issues are increasingly welcome in the mainstream," reflecting the impact of the debate about the process of theorizing.[88]

From a Critical Theory perspective as well, Constructivism's explicit accommodation of subjective meanings and interpretive analysis are steps toward the ideal posture of reflexivity. By treating states as the primary actors, Constructivism still falls short of Critical Theory's standard of "radical, emancipatory transformation of the global order."[89] At the same time, Constructivism's interest in international norms is an explicit acknowledgement of the importance of values. Another positive consideration is that effective norms, by restricting the actions of states, can benefit the newer and less powerful ones and thus represent progress toward transformation.[90] One feminist commentator also sees promise in Constructivism's treatment of meaning as a social practice, an outlook congenial to a broader view of gender as a social construction.[91] Liberal IR theory's views of the domestic sources of state interests are directly compatible with Liberal Feminism's views of political action.

As a final index of reconciliation, postmodernists have frequently noted that the original realist formulations of E.H. Carr and Hans Morgenthau (unlike later Neorealism) based much of their analysis on history and philosophical speculation about human nature. Postmodernism's interest in the historical development of accepted conventions and discourses has prompted recent research into the origins and evolution of sovereign statehood, the pillar of Realism and Neorealism. We will see some of that research in the next chapter. One realist scholar also believes that there is ample room in that tradition for both Marxism and Postmodernism. Marxism and Realism are compatible because both are interested in power and struggle. Postmodernism, particularly in its Foucaultian interest in the historical evolution of discourse, fits well with Realism's notion of language and persuasion as one form of power. Compatible as well is Postmodernism's interest in hierarchy and domination.[92] For empiricists, these kinds of questions are amenable to standard-method research. Empiricists term such efforts qualitative research because of their "softer" content.[93]

Where is IR headed? It seems reasonable to expect some further convergence along these lines. One benefit is that the older mainline approaches, Neorealism and Institutionalism, will be broadened and enriched by the philosophical reflections raised in the Third Debate. Another is the addition of two dimensions of analysis: Liberal IR theory's contribution of the inner political workings of the state and Constructivism's contribution of the interactive play of values and identities. Will there be a further fusion of these three theories into one grand synthesis? Probably not. First, it is important to remember IR's inherent complexity. Ranging the levels of analysis from interest group politics in single states to transformation in a whole system of states, such as the end of the cold war, covers too many phenomena to be encompassed in any feasibly limited set of theoretical categories. Second, the theories all work differently and have no single unifying logic. Instead, what is likely to remain is a set of theories that work at different levels: Liberal IR theory for the state, Neorealism/Institutionalism for rivalry and cooperation and Constructivism for the origins and effects of international norms and for the mutual effects of change.

Summary

We have seen the Third Debate's origins in epistemology and ontology. If empirical epistemology is denied, the possibility of value-free inquiry and knowledge becomes problematic. Critical theorists, postmodernists and feminists share that view, but they approach IR from different directions.

Critical theorists, drawing on the ideas of Habermas, emphasize the purposes underlying knowledge and theory and distinguish between preservation of the status quo and emancipation. Drawing from the ideas of Gramsci, they emphasize material and ideological hegemony. The task in the face of hegemony is to detect underlying purposes in theory and knowledge and to construct theory that supports basic transformations.

Postmodernists, drawing on the ideas of Foucault and Derrida, see language as a vehicle of political power and see identities and relationships as embedded in discourses and texts. Identities are constructed as paired and arbitrary opposites, and the attributes are unbalanced between privileged and other. That reflects and supports hierarchies that marginalize others and silences them. The task is to destabilize power and authority by showing the way they are contained in language, texts and attributed identities.

Feminists, although they differ on epistemological and programmatic issues, share the view that gender is primary. Social and political relationships in both domestic and international relations subordinate women and overlook their views and concerns. The experience of their own subordination gives women a special interest in the subordination of others. That interest provides points of commonality with Postmodernism although views differ on the suitability of such an alliance. Feminists agree that IR theory, particularly Neorealism, reflects male experience and concerns and supports gendered inquiry and knowledge.

These fundamental critiques have prompted broader reflection in IR. Although these critiques reject IR's common ground of empirical epistemology, there are points of connection and agreement. IR theory itself is evolving in response to the Third Debate, providing flexible and attentive circumstances.

The remaining chapters in this textbook apply the three theories (Neorealism/ Institutionalism, Liberal IR theory and Constructivism) and the three critiques (Critical Theory, Postmodernism and Feminism) to IR's main topics. We will see their different points of illumination and emphasis. A useful perspective is to regard all the theories as offering distinctive insights. IR is sufficiently complex that no single theory is likely to encompass it entirely. One of the tasks in IR for students and professionals alike is to apply and evaluate the theories in light of what they show. That varies from application to application.

ENDNOTES

1   Wayne S. Cox and Claire Turenne Sjolander, "Critical Reflections on International Relations," in Claire Turenne Sjolander and Wayne S. Cox, eds., *Beyond Positivism: Critical Reflections on International Relations*, Boulder: Lynne Rienner, 1994, pp. 4–5.

2   *ibid.*, p. 5.

3   Michael Nicholson, "The Continued Significance of Positivism," in Steve Smith, Ken Booth and Marysia Zalewski, eds., *International Theory: Positivism and Beyond*, Cambridge: Cambridge University Press, 1996, pp.129, 131.

4   Cox and Sjolander, "Critical Reflections on International Relations," p. 5.

5   Steve Smith, "Positivism and Beyond," in Smith, Booth and Zalewski, eds., *International Theory: Positivism and Beyond*, pp. 27–28.

6   Mark Neufeld, *The Restructuring of International Relations Theory*, Cambridge: Cambridge University Press, 1995, p. 20.

7   Smith, "Positivism and Beyond," p. 28.

8   Neufeld, *The Restructuring of International Relations Theory*, pp. 42–43.

9   Robert W. Cox, "Social Forces, States and World Orders: Beyond International Relations Theory," in Robert O. Keohane, ed., *Neorealism and Its Critics*, New York: Columbia University Press, 1986, p. 209.

10 *ibid.*, p. 208.

11 John Gerard Ruggie, "International Structure and International Transformation: Space, Time, and Method," in Ernst-Otto Czempiel and James N. Rosenau, eds., *Global Changes and Theoretical Challenges: Approaches to World Politics for the 1990s,* Lexington, MA: Lexington Books, 1989, p. 34.

12 Cox, "Social Forces," pp. 212–13.

13 Neufeld, *The Restructuring of International Relations Theory*, p. 20.

14 Smith, "Positivism and Beyond," pp. 27–28.

15 Robert W. Cox, "Gramsci, Hegemony, and International Relations: An Essay on Method," *Millennium* 12 (Summer 1983) 168.

16 Dante Germino, *Antonio Gramsci: Architect of a New Politics*, Baton Rouge: Louisiana State University Press, 1990, p. 183.

17 *ibid.* pp. 56–58.

18 Renate Holub, *Antonio Gramsci: Beyond Marxism and Postmodernism*, London: Routlege, 1992, p. 6.

19 Chantal Mouffe, "Gramsci Today," in Chantal Mouffe, ed., *Gramsci and Marxist Theory*, London: Routledge and Kegan Paul, 1979, p. 11.

20 Gregg J. Legare, "Neorealism or Hegemony? The Seven Sisters' Energy Regime," in Sjolander and Cox, eds., *Beyond Positivism: Critical Reflections on International Relations,* pp. 82–83.

21 Robert W. Cox, *Production, Power and World Order: Social Forces in the Making of History,* New York: Columbia University Press, 1987, pp. 393–403.

22 Randall D. Germain and Michael Kenny, "Engaging Gramsci: International Relations Theory and the New Gramscians," *Review of International Studies* 24 (January 1998) 3–21.

23 Ole Waever, "The Rise and Fall of the Inter-Paradigm Debate," in Smith, Booth and Zalewski, eds., *International Theory: Positivism and Beyond*, p. 166.

24 Chris Brown, *International Relations Theory: New Normative Approaches*, New York: Columbia University Press, 1992, p. 198.

25 William E. Connolly, *Identity\Difference: Democratic Negotiations of Political Paradox,* Ithaca: Cornell University Press, 1991, p. 11.

26 Jim George and David Campbell, "Patterns of Dissent and the Celebration of Difference: Critical Social Theory and International Relations," *International Studies Quarterly* 34 (September 1990) 281.

27 *ibid.*, 285.

28 Richard Ashley, "Living on Border Lines: Man, Poststructuralism, and War," in James Der Derian and Michael Shapiro, eds., *International/Intertextual Relations: Postmodern Readings of World Politics*, Lexington, MA: Lexington Books, 1989, p. 261.

29 Connolly, *Identity\Difference*, p. 9.

30 Ashley, "Living on the Border Lines," p. 261.

31 Brown, *International Relations Theory*, p. 214.

32 *ibid.*

33   *ibid.*, p. 215

34   *ibid.,* p. 213.

35   R.B.J. Walker, "Genealogy, Geopolitics and Political Community: Richard K. Ashley and the Critical Social Theory of International Politics," *Alternatives* 13 (January 1988) 84–86.

36   Richard Ashley, "The Geopolitics of Geopolitical Space: Toward a Critical Theory of International Politics," *Alternatives* 12 (October 1987) 403–34.

37   Bradley Klein, "After Strategy: The Search for a Post-Modern Politics of Peace," *Alternatives* 13 (July 1988) 295.

38   Ashley, "Living on the Border Lines," pp. 290–309.

39   Richard Ashley, "The Poverty of Neorealism," *International Organization* 38 (Spring 1984) 225–86.

40   Anne Sisson Runyan, "The 'State' of Nature: A Garden Unfit for Women and Other Living Things," in V. Spike Peterson, ed., *Gendered States: Feminist (Re)Visions of International Relations Theory*, Boulder: Lynne Rienner, 1992, pp. 123–140.

41   Tony Porter, "Postmodern Political Realism and International Relations Theory's Third Debate," in Cox and Sjolander, eds., *Beyond Positivism*, p. 108.

42   *ibid.*

43   Anna Agathangelou and L.H.M. Ling, "Postcolonial Dissidence within Dissident IR: Transforming Master Narratives of Sovereignty in Greco-Turkish Cyprus," *Studies in Political Economy* 54 (Fall 1997) 8.

44   J. Ann Tickner, "You Just Don't Understand: Troubled Engagements between Feminists and IR Theorists," *International Studies Quarterly* 47 (December 1997) 614.

45   *ibid.* p. 613.

46   Jean Bethke Elshtain, "Feminist Themes and International Relations," in Der Derian, ed., *International Theory: Critical Investigations*, p. 343.

47   Smith, "Positivism and Beyond," p. 29.

48   J. Ann Tickner, "International Relations: Post-Positivist and Feminist Perspectives," in Robert E. Goodin and Hans-Dieter Klingemann, eds , *A New Handbook of Political Science*, Oxford: Oxford University Press, 1996, p. 457.

49   Carol Gilligan, *In A Different Voice: Psychological Theory and Women's Development,* Cambridge, MA: Harvard University Press, 1982.

50   Christine Sylvester, "Feminists and Realists View Autonomy and Obligation in International Relations," in Peterson, ed., *Gendered States*, p. 157.

51   Tickner, "International Relations," p. 457

52   Sylvester, "Feminists and Realists," p. 157.

53   Tickner, "You Just Don't Understand," p. 621.

54   Radha Jhappan, "Post-Modern Race and Gender Essentialism or a Post-Mortem of Scholarship," *Studies in Political Economy* 51 (Fall 1996) 22–28.

55   Susan Judith Ship, "And What About Gender? Feminism and International Relations Theory's Third Debate," in Sjolander and Cox, eds., *Beyond Positivism*, p. 148.

56   Terrell Carver, Molly Cochran and Judith Squires, "Gendering Jones: Feminisms, IRs, Masculinities," *Review of International Studies* 24 (April 1998) 285–86.

57   Elshtain, "Feminist Themes and International Relations," p. 344.

58   Tickner, "You Just Don't Understand," 615.

59   J. Ann Tickner, "Hans Morgenthau's Principles of Political Realism: A Feminist Reformulation," in James Der Derian, ed., *International Theory: Critical Investigations*, New York: New York University Press, 1995, p. 57.

60   J. Ann Tickner, "Identity in International Relations Theory: Feminist Perspectives," in Yosef Lapid and Friedrich Kratochwil, eds., *The Return of Culture and Identity in IR Theory*, Boulder, CO: Lynner Rienner, 1996, p. 150.

61   *ibid.*

62 Tickner, "International Relations," p. 458.

63 Cynthia Enloe, "Margins, Silences and Bottom Rungs: How to Overcome the Underestimation of Power in the Study of International Relations," in Smith, Booth and Zalewski, eds., *International Theory: Positivism and Beyond,* pp. 186–202.

64 R.B.J. Walker, "Gender and Critique in the Theory of International Relations," in Peterson, ed., *Gendered States,* p. 186.

65 Tickner, "You Just Don't Understand," 617.

66 Mona Harrington, "What Exactly Is Wrong with the Liberal State as an Agent of Change?" in Peterson, ed., *Gendered States,* p. 66.

67 Fred Halliday, "The Future of International Relations," in Smith, Booth, and Zalewski, eds., *International Theory*, p. 323.

68 That is one reading of Walker, "Gender and Critique in the Theory of International Relations," p. 197.

69 Margot Light and Fred Halliday, "Gender and International Relations," in A.J.R. Groom and Margot Light, eds., *Contemporary International Relations: A Guide to Theory*, London: Pinter, 1994, p. 51.

70 Agathangelou and Ling, "Postcolonial Dissidence within Dissident IR," p. 8

71 Ship, "And What About Gender?" p.146.

72 Neufeld, *The Restructuring of International Relations Theory*, p. 62.

73 William Phillips, "On the Ideas of Today's Left," *Partisan Review* 75 (Spring 1998) 185–86.

74 Kjell Goldmann, "International Relations: An Overview," in Goodin and Klingemann, eds. *A New Handbook of Political Science*, pp. 413.

75 Roger Spegele, "Richard Ashley's Discourse for International Relations," *Millennium* 21 (Summer 1992) 150–56.

76 Halliday, "The Future of International Relations," p. 320.

77 John Gerard Ruggie, "Territoriality and Beyond: Problematizing Modernity in International Relations," *International Organization* 47 (Winter 1993) 144.

78 Malcolm Bradbury, "What Was Postmodernism? The Arts after the Cold War," *International Affairs* 71 (October 1995) 774.

79 Neufeld, *The Restructuring of International Relations Theory,* p. 68.

80 Ship, "And What about Gender?" p. 131.

81 *ibid.*, p. 132.

82 *ibid.*, p. 148

83 Janice Thomson, *Mercenaries, Pirates and Sovereigns,* Princeton: Princeton University Press, 1994, p. 161.

84 Waever, "Rise and Fall of the Inter-Paradigm Debate," p. 169

85 Judith Goldstein and Robert O. Keohane, "Ideas and Foreign Policy: An Analytical Framework," in Judith Goldstein and Robert O. Keohane, eds., *Ideas and Foreign Policy: Beliefs, Institutions, and Political Change,* Ithaca: Cornell University Press, 1993, pp. 24–26.

86 Robert Powell, "Anarchy in International Relations Theory: The Neorealist-Neoliberal Debate," *International Organization* 48 (Spring 1994) 321–24.

87 Alexander Wendt, "Constructing International Relations," *International Security* 20 (Summer 1995) 72, 75.

88 Waever, "The Rise and Fall of the Inter-Paradigm Debate," p. 168.

89 Neufeld, *The Restructuring of International Relations Theory,"* p. 94.

90 Porter, "Postmodern Political Realism," pp. 123–24.

91 Ship, "And What about Gender?" p. 147.

92 Buzan, "The Timeless Wisdom of Realism?" in Smith, Booth and Zalewski, *International Theory: Positivism and Beyond,* pp. 58–59.

93 Gary King, Robert O. Keohane, Sidney Verba, *Designing Social Inquiry: Scientific Inference in Qualitative Research*, Princeton: Princeton University Press, 1994.

Chapter ⑥

Territoriality, Sovereignty and Statehood

A **state** occupies a given territory, has a population and a government and is recognized by other states. Neatly defined territorial political units, the product of statehood, are the foundation of the international system shaping its spatial order and organizing humankind into formal subdivisions. In the words of one scholar, "the world may be imagined as divided into states by frontiers rather as a farm is divided into fields by fences and walls."[1] In the international system at present, there are 221 states and territorial entities.[2] The current membership of the United Nations, which admits all full-fledged states, is 185. States are the highest level of political authority. Beyond the level of the state, all order is voluntary with states making the decisions. There is no sovereign international authority and no equivalent of a world state.

For that reason, as we saw in Section I, IR theorists have held the demarcation between states and system to be the fundamental one of political authority and anarchy. The boundary between domestic and international politics represents the frontier of sovereign jurisdiction. Within the boundary is the realm of state authority. Beyond the boundary are other states and other jurisdictions. This is not to say that the sovereign state is a permanent and immutable fixture. As we will see in the following two chapters, unified sovereign statehood is under challenge from ethnic consciousness at home and from economic globalization abroad. The European Union and the rise of economic regions represent alternative forms of organization. In addition, as we will see later in this chapter, many developing countries only nominally meet the qualifications of statehood.

As you read this chapter's discussion of statehood and sovereignty, bear two things in mind: First, statehood is the focal centre of all of IR's theories (Postmodernism excepted). Brief boxes in the chapter will show what each theory has to say. Second, statehood itself may not be permanent. Treat this chapter as the state's evolution and current condition. The following two chapters will consider statehood's challenges and prospects.

Sovereignty and Government

Sovereignty—government's "exclusive right to make rules"— is the essence of statehood.[3] States jealously guard their authority to govern within their borders without foreign interference and resist encroachments on their internal rule even when doing so imposes significant costs. A recent example is the government of Colombia, which has struggled to control wealthy and violent drug cartels. The cartels' willingness to bribe and assassinate officials has had "devastating" effects on the Colombian government's authority and independence and on the state's democratic institutions themselves.[4] Even so, Colombia refused an American offer of military personnel to help find and arrest cartel members because that would involve a foreign authority in domestic law enforcement. Severe as the trafficker's threat was, the government feared that agreeing to outside assistance would be even worse because Colombians would see it as an impairment of sovereignty.[5]

Sovereignty is both a legal concept and a collective practice. In law, sovereign states are entitled to exclusive authority within their jurisdictions. In practice, that entitlement depends on reciprocity among states with each recognizing the others' exclusive jurisdiction and expecting the same recognition in return. That collective practice is necessary because there is no world government to enforce legal sovereignty in the way a state government (exercising *its* sovereignty) would enforce its laws. The legal concept of sovereignty is thus a rule that states expect to follow in their dealings with one another.[6] This rule is crucial as it maintains the patchwork of formal state jurisdictions that forms the international system. Because the rule is based on reciprocal practice, however, the international system's most basic level of organization—a set of states—is cooperative and voluntary. When reciprocity fails, states are responsible for defending their sovereignty. The most serious violation of sovereignty is armed incursion across another state's border.

The two dimensions of sovereign authority are territoriality and autonomy. Territorial authority refers to a defined geographic space. It is difficult to imagine other bases of authority. One form is over a particular group of people. If the people move, so does the authority. Gang leaders or heads of nomadic bands would be examples. Autonomy refers to exclusive authority: the government's jurisdiction is supreme.[7] Again, it is difficult to imagine any other kind. Contested or divided authority arises in times of civil war or insurrections and when a foreign government, often after a war, takes up parts of rule and administration.

There is a difference between sovereignty as a collective practice and sovereignty as actual domestic control. Under the rule of sovereignty, states have final authority in deciding what actions to take within their jurisdictions. How much they do is up to them. As exercises of state capacity, the totalitarianism of Hitler's Germany and Stalin's Soviet Union can be seen as domestic control on steroids— the state's level of involvement in those two societies was nightmarishly pervasive. Not all states have that level of capacity. In weak states, effective action in some or many areas is not possible, and in extreme cases control may be limited to the capital city and daylight hours. We will see more about weak states later.

Government is the organized means of exercising authoritative control. Some definitions blur the distinction between government and state while others emphasize the autonomy of the state from both government and domestic society. For our purposes, it is easiest to understand government as directing and managing

FIGURE 6.1   Territoriality and Postmodernism

Postmodernists, as we saw in the last chapter, are very concerned about individual identity and resist anything that arbitrarily constrains or deforms it. Individual identities are realized in interaction with other people and their identities. We all have multiple points of connection. Our natural spirit, in one postmodernist's words, is nomadic, and our identities inhabit "multiple sites and issues."[8] Identity is potential and indeterminate. To secure our identities, we must be free to engage every point of connection. Fixed definitions and categories arbitrarily limit that quest and stifle our potential. How would a postmodernist regard state boundaries and exclusive control?

Drawing boundaries is a violation of human mobility, both physical and spiritual. "Societies territorialize when they delimit the earth, when they fragment land and pretend that those boundaries—between states and between people—are in some way natural or true."[9] Any territory contains a "plurality of possibilities" whose realization is hampered by political enclosure. The exercise of state power that defines and maintains exclusive territories is a form of "masked violence" against human mobility and complete identity.

the state. That view is especially congenial to parliamentary systems such as Canada's in which an elected House of Commons and Cabinet are the government, and the bureaucracy is the administrative instrument of the state. The role of the government is to direct and manage and be accountable for the bureaucracy. Other ways of locating sovereignty are possible. In the European political tradition, sovereignty is located in the permanent state administrative apparatus; in the United States, sovereignty resides not in governments or bureaucracies but in the constitution.[10]

Sovereignty: The Legal and Institutional Views

Sovereignty traditionally was regarded in primarily legal terms: states are entities with particular privileges and obligations among other states. Sovereignty in the legal view is established in conventions and rules. That view of the international system emphasizes regularity because all states are legally the same and continuity because conventions and rules maintain the same forms.

More recently, IR scholars have come to regard sovereignty as an institution: states are constituted by a set of internationally recognized ideas and practices. These practices vary and they can evolve and change. Because sovereignty is based on reciprocity, the actual content of sovereign practice—what uses of authority other states will recognize—can be highly contentious.[11] At issue is the latitude of states to act in particular ways. That latitude varies not because of changes in the law of sovereignty but because of its collective practice.

FIGURE 6.2   Constructivism and Sovereignty

Arising out of the historical conditions of feudalism, sovereignty was a fundamental change in the "mental equipment that people drew upon in imagining and symbolizing forms of political community" representing a "profound" impact on the way people understand community, physical space and political life.[12] Although sovereignty defines a state's rights and obligations respective to other states, it does not define a state's identity nor what it seeks to achieve or protect. Those are rooted more deeply in collective values, principles and laws. Sovereignty itself does not justify any particular state action. What is regarded as proper depends on shared understandings. Those generally reflect the domestic values and norms of the dominant states.[13] When such values are widely shared, they can be powerful. Decolonization occurred when the dominant states redefined the rights and status of colonial territories.

Anarchy exists because of decentralized sovereign authority in the international system, but its effects are socially constructed. Statehood in the condition of anarchy explains neither cooperation nor conflict. The security concerns that worry neorealists arise from particular understandings among states. Cooperation arises from particular understandings as well. Those understandings are the products of particular state identities and their interactive effects. States can change the conditions of anarchy in the direction of either conflict or cooperation by changing their behaviour. In so doing, they change their state identities and the basis of interaction.[14]

Legally, states have the right to make and enforce their own laws. What states recognize as the proper content of laws and enforcement, however, can change. Enforcing laws by torturing people in government custody and by taking people into custody for political offences have increasingly come to be regarded as illegitimate exercises of sovereignty. To the extent that human rights such as these have come to be accepted internationally as standards of government conduct, they represent a rule parallel to the rule of sovereignty. Just as there is no world government to enforce sovereignty, there is also no world government to enforce human rights. The consequences depend on collective practice among states. Increasingly, governments that violate human rights face pressure from other governments. To the extent that pressure is effective, sovereignty is constrained. We will see more about human rights and sovereignty later in the chapter.

States agree to surrender sovereignty when they sign international agreements to limit or control particular activities such as producing chemical weapons or applying tariffs. Signing treaties is voluntary. Under the legal doctrine of sovereignty, the only way to compel a state to sign is to defeat it in war, to abrogate its sovereignty by force. Otherwise, states *choose* to adhere to agreements. Although such action is legally voluntary, it may not be unconstrained. The globalization of trade and finance makes it increasingly self-defeating for states to stay out of international trade and monetary agreements. In signing them, states surrender some of their sovereign right to regulate their economies, but the alternative is exclusion from a rapidly developing international network of investment and production. How much economic sovereignty can states surrender and still function as states? Chapter 8 takes up that question.

It is always natural to regard a prevailing order as the only possible form of organization. Sovereignty, as historical sociologists have shown, has had an irregular development. The European states were not immediately transformed from feudal conditions, and the extension of sovereign practices to overseas territories including Canada was surprisingly circumstantial.

As former colonies gained independence and inherited colonial boundaries and administrations, sovereign statehood did become the world's standard form of political organization. That transition still does not explain the persistence of sovereign statehood nor its ideal for peoples seeking their independence. As an explanation, many IR scholars regard sovereign statehood as an institution that originated in particular historical circumstances in Europe, has been reproduced throughout the world and has become the unquestioned modal form.[15]

If sovereign statehood is relatively recent and if it emerged from a particular set of historical circumstances, will it be remembered as a transitional form of human organization? Until recently, that question would have been hypothetical, but events are moving fast. The European Union is rapidly constructing institutions, including a common currency, that supersede normal state functions. At the local and regional level, cities such as Lyon and Barcelona are developing ties with cities in neighbouring states that outweigh those with their own central governments. Ontario, in the view of a Queen's University economist, is undergoing a transition from Canada's heartland province to a North American economic region state. For their part, central governments throughout the developed world are devolving responsibilities to regions and municipalities. We will see these developments in Chapter 8. For now, the implication is that territorial political organization, once seemingly fixed in the legal view of sovereignty, may be a variable and eventually transitory practice. We see next how the current practice developed.

1648: Rule and Territoriality

The Peace of Westphalia has been regarded as the advent of the modern state system because it put into place sovereignty's central principle: the right of rulers to act authoritatively within their jurisdictions. The Peace of Westphalia of 1648 ended the Thirty Years' War, one of Europe's most disastrous conflicts. Religion was the main issue with Protestantism challenging the unity of what had been regarded as a single Christian community under the nominal rule of the Holy Roman Empire and the guidance of the Papacy. The Peace settled the religious conflict by acknowledging the religion of princes who had become Calvinist (Lutherans had been recognized in 1555 in the Peace of Augsburg) and by granting freedom of worship in most parts of the Empire. More importantly for the development of statehood, the Peace of Westphalia also granted princes in the Empire the right to sign treaties.

For both sides, the Peace represented a second-best outcome to religious victory. With neither Catholics nor Protestants able to extirpate the other and with both exhausted after decades of war, the solution was to prevent future conflicts by removing religion as an issue. That was done not only by restricting it to rulers' discretion, establishing the foundation of sovereignty, but also by establishing a common expectation that religion would no longer be recognized as grounds for war. In that way, Westphalia created a basic norm of international behaviour. Because the Thirty Years' War had been so destructive, states had a common interest in cooperating.[16] The broader implication of these provisions was the triumph of individual rulers over both the Church and the Holy Roman Empire because the provisions removed the princes' obligation to obey. That basic principle set the basis for modern statehood: the right of rulers to exercise jurisdiction over their territories. In that principle was the essential point of transition from medieval to modern international relations

The Peace of Westphalia has long been treated in IR as the pivotal and decisive event in Europe's emergence from feudalism with its overlapping and diffuse arrangements of territory and rule to the modern state system with its defined boundaries, governments and authority. Recent scholarship has shown that statehood's advent was gradual and circumstantial. That same view, we will see later, informs recent scholarship on sovereignty, which has also come to be regarded as circumstantial.

The year 1648 was not a watershed of territorial organization. England already existed as a distinct and bounded political unit as did the city states in northern Italy.[17] The treaty also did not mark a clear transition from medieval to modern forms of authority. The Holy Roman Empire whose authority was reduced by the Peace of Westphalia's allocation of treaty-making power to princes—the equivalent of municipal rulers in the previous order—continued until 1806. The Papacy, another institution, continues still although its political power over Europe began to diminish as rulers began elaborating their new power of sovereignty and collecting taxes. Finally, the Peace of Westphalia was not a watershed between medieval and modern thought. The part of the treaty that has been seen as the major departure, giving rulers the right to sign their own treaties, was only one provision in a 40-page document.[18] The rest was a blend of medieval and modern notions. That fact supports a broader view that the transition from medieval to modern political forms was not sudden but gradual.

The Medieval International World

The medieval system provides a very different view of political rule and makes a good contrast to today's universal institution of sovereign statehood. The two major points of difference are political authority and territory. Authority in the medieval system arose not within particular places but was attached to rulers. That meant that rulers could take their authority with them and claim rule somewhere else. That practice, along with the fact that particular tracts of property could have more than one title, made it possible for more than one ruler to have authority over the same place. Adding to the ambiguity was the lack of clear territorial distinctions between public and private lands.[19] Politically, feudal territories were simply local units of a Christian community.[20]

Notions of rule were bound together with religion and custom. The nominal political authority of the Holy Roman Emperor was blended with the spiritual authority of the Papacy.[21] Together, authority in medieval Europe was plural, not firmly fixed to territory and variable. That in turn made for an ambiguous differentiation between the national and international—the prime demarcation in modern state-based IR. At the popular level, mass identification with a sovereign state—the phenomenon we know today as nationalism—was five centuries in the future.

Rule was also not consistently organized. Instead, it tended to be the effective radius of a ruler's political power. Since that radius could vary ruler to ruler and could be claimed by other rulers, territorial authority was not fixed. In contrast to today's uniform fabric of separate political units, medieval Europe was a crazy quilt of "plural allegiances, asymmetrical suzerainties and anomalous enclaves."[22] Patterns of authority were not constant; again they shifted according to individual rulers' power at any particular time and according to the overlap of one ruler's authority with another's. Compared to the modern state system, the medieval system's ambiguous differentiations of territory and rule represented a very different way of organizing political space. If the modern system of sovereign states is one of clearly demarcated and exclusive units, the medieval one was a "form of segmented territorial rule [that] ...represented a heteronomous organization of territorial rights and claims."[23]

From our historical perspective, such a system might look amusing and irrational. Postmodernists and some feminists take a different view. As we saw in the last chapter, they regard the modern state as a hierarchy of oppression geared for exploitation and warfare. Medieval Europe, in their view, was a more attractively loose and interconnected system of multiple loyalties and ambiguous controls. This system existed within a larger Christian community spiritually dedicated to peace. That image may be too idealized. Medieval Europe was subject to almost continuous violence. That condition resulted from the fact that the individual political units were small and vulnerable, there were no large states to impose order and individual rulers sought to increase their holdings at others' expense.[24]

Sovereignty Evolving

Once the basic principle was granted that rulers had dominion over their subjects and were answerable to no external authority, the elaboration of their own authority was slow and irregular as they experimented with taxation, raising military forces, constructing administrative systems and defining national boundaries. States whose rulers were successful in consolidating recognized territory and establishing effective governments tended to succeed while those whose rulers did not, failed. The usual consequence of failure was incorporation into another state. Among the failures were the now-extinct political forms of **city-states** and city leagues. At the time of Westphalia, all three forms coexisted yet only sovereign states endured. (Singapore can be seen as a surviving example of a city-state. After receiving independence from Britain, it merged with Malaysia in 1963 but withdrew again in 1965.) How can the emergence of a single model out of a plurality of working forms be accounted for? Why is the current international world not organized as leagues of metropolitan areas?

Recent scholarship argues that the state, because of its size and centralizing authority, was more efficient than city-states or leagues for organizing commerce. At the time of Westphalia, commerce in Europe was beginning to move from locales to regions and across the seas. For merchants and producers, commerce was risky because there was no authority to enforce contracts between buyers and sellers, no standard monetary units and no uniform system of weights and measures. Rulers who utilized their sovereignty to impose domestic order through expanded and centralized jurisdictions were able to provide those supports and lower the costs of doing business. That increased the profitability of commerce and encouraged economic growth and efficiency. For the rulers, that economic efficiency provided more income to tax, strengthening the material basis of the state.

These advantages were reciprocal; because of the lower costs of doing business, state-based traders preferred dealing with counterparts in other states. Those features made states with centralized jurisdictions and effective controls the most desirable trading partners, and the most effective ones flourished. That made them even more attractive business locations. Producers who could relocate moved to effective states, further expanding their economic base. In turn, prosperous commercial activity and expanding economic bases strengthened the rulers' political positions, adding further to stability. In sum, according to this argument, sovereign statehood was naturally selected from among the other forms because it proved to be best for organizing stable, profitable and expanding economic activity. That advantage came from the growth of centralized and effective political control that developed under the doctrine of sovereignty.[25]

FIGURE 6.3 The Hudson's Bay Company: Canada's First Corporate Citizen

The Hudson's Bay Company along with the British East India Company represented a hybrid form of statehood and marked a stage in the evolution of territorial sovereignty. The British government granted to trading companies not only business monopolies but also the powers of rule. The Hudson's Bay Company charter granted full powers to build forts, form their own armed forces, administer civil and criminal law and make treaties. The territory granted in the charter was a "virtual subcontinent" stretching from the western boundaries of Labrador to the Rocky Mountains, 1.5 million square miles or about 40 percent of present-day Canada.[26] There were certain limits: The company's charter did not permit it to make war on "other Christian Princes" without permission of the Crown or take territory claimed by them.[27] Nonetheless, the company's rights over its territory were "almost feudal, " and governors of the territories were employees not of the Crown but of the company. Aside from token payments that were almost never made, the company was not obligated to reimburse the crown for using the territory.[28]

The Hudson's Bay Company established and administered the Red River Colony. It made use of its authority to organize armed force in the face of the rival North West Company's attacks on the Red River Colony in 1815, which had driven out the settlers. Hudson's Bay Company organized a group of 100 Swiss mercenaries who were in North America following the War of 1812 to provide security for the colony's resettlement. It was again attacked in 1816, and most of the settlers were killed. The conflict ended when the two companies merged in 1821.[29] Later, the prospect of Hudson's Bay Company expansion south into the Oregon Territory prompted American settlement of the region and the negotiations that established the Canada-United States boundary from the Rocky Mountains to the Pacific.

Pressure to end this private land empire came from settlers who disliked the Company's administration and who wished to live under a civil authority and, more pressingly, from the growing economic and military power of the United States. To bolster its claim on prairie lands and thwart American expansion, the government favoured direct incorporation of Rupert's Land and the Northwest Territories into British North America. Two years after Confederation, the British bought out the Hudson's Bay Company's territorial rights and ended its trading monopoly.

Sovereignty, which had previously been exercised by the company, was transferred to Canada.

The Crucible of War

There is a more coercive interpretation of statehood's development. That school of thought regards the process as a struggle, begun in the 15th century, in which local rulers and landlords imposed taxation and police powers on unwilling populations. The rulers made this effort because they were aware of the state's great potential for organizing resources and consolidating power, and they wanted to control and utilize that potential themselves.[30] The two basic staples of power, wealth and soldiers, were acquired through taxation and conscription. In exchange for these impositions on the populace and for the general expansion of authority, rulers made concessions. One view sees the evolution of democratic rights and social programs as a set of bargains "hammered out by rulers and ruled in the course of their struggles over the means of state action, especially the making of war."[31]

War shaped the evolution of states in two ways. First, the threat of attack forced rulers to develop effective institutions, particularly those responsible for taxation and defence. Military preparations, especially against powerful states, required large permanent levies on populations. Although taxes are never popular, rulers did have the advantage of an external enemy as justification for requiring personal sacrifice from their subjects. As well, the threat of war provided a point of identification between subjects and the state, promoting national consciousness (if only out of common fear) and justifying the punishment of dissent.

Second, war eliminated unsuccessful states. The majority could not organize effective governing institutions and sustain adequate taxation and were defeated by stronger states and absorbed. In Europe, this stretched over several centuries, representing a continuous process of configuring and reconfiguring national territories and accommodating newly acquired populations. The European states that now seem homogenous in comparison to those elsewhere arrived at that condition through a long course of bloodshed and annexations. In the view of one scholar, the results were not all bad: "Weak states that were defeated then became the poorer regions of richer countries, but at least they had a chance to share in the revenue and resources of a viable state."[32]

Arms and Sovereignty

One of the hallmarks of sovereign statehood is indeed the ability to organize and deploy armed force. Symbolically, the association of military force with statehood can be seen in formal and ceremonial trappings many of which originated in the time when sovereignty resided in the person of a monarch and when military forces were at the personal service of the crown. Practically, military power is an abiding concern of states because recourse to war in the international system is always possible. It is easy to assume that this basic sovereign resource would have descended from some Westphalian prototype. In fact, according to recent research, armed force's evolution as an instrument of state is chequered. What we regard as the standard military apparatus—a recruited or conscripted force owned and controlled by the state—is only a century old. Before then the ability to organize and deploy armed force, one of the modern state's core prerogatives, was in a number of hands, many of them private.

Feudal obligations bound knights to fight for their lords, but that system began to break down in the 13th century when it became possible for people to buy their way out of military service. That gave rulers the money to recruit mercenary forces thereby enabling wealthy rulers to become formidable powers and making offensive warfare possible. That had two effects. First, military force became available for hire, and mercenaries were international agents. Second, rulers with sufficient wealth could greatly expand their power and upset balances with neighbours. The limitations of the feudal system kept warfare primarily local and defensive, but by the time of Westphalia whole private regiments, most of them raised in Germany, were available for hire and were widely employed to augment national forces. Officers were freely recruited from across Europe.[33]

The market was also maritime. Armed vessels were in private as well as government hands. Working on their own, private warships preyed on commercial shipping as pirates. Hired by governments to prey on enemy shipping, these warships were privateers. Part of their pay was a portion of the cargoes they seized.[34]

The result was an international market in military forces. States that did not have the ability to raise armies large enough for adequate defence could rent what they needed. Warships could be had on a profit-sharing basis. Not all foreigners serving in states' forces were there by choice. In 1807, Britain had impressed some 6000 American citizens into the Royal Navy, a practice that was one of the grievances leading to the War of 1812.[35]

Why did these alternative uses of military force end? One reason was threat. States suppressed piracy when it became a common menace to shipping on the high seas. On land, unauthorized free-lance activities complicated relations with other governments.[36] More generally, states assumed exclusive ownership and control of military forces as part of the broader evolution of their control and authority. The private and mercenary forms fell into disuse because they were less directly controllable than units which governments formed and staffed themselves. The result of this transition, which was completed only in 1900, was the relationship between statehood and military force that we know today. The important point to note is that the evolution from diverse antecedent forms paralleled the state's consolidation of authority.

European Statehood Expands

Because of the economic and military ascendancy of modern Europe, the state system that developed there spread around the rest of the globe. As Spain, Portugal, France, Britain, the Netherlands, Belgium, Denmark, Italy and Germany expanded into the Americas, Asia and Africa, they established colonies, protectorates and spheres of influence. Where there were existing monarchies or systems of tribal rule in place, the European states either subjugated them or included them under the umbrella of their own rule. To avoid war over rival territorial claims, the Europeans formalized their holdings by negotiating boundaries either bilaterally or in multilateral gatherings such as the Berlin Conference in 1884-1885. How the Europeans did so had far-reaching significance because the lines dividing their colonies became state boundaries when their colonies began achieving independence after World War II.

Many colonial boundaries were linear extensions from areas of occupation or some other convenient base point into the interior. When these lands were unoccupied by other colonial forces, it was often possible to agree on straight lines or on natural demarcations such as mountain ranges and rivers.[37] The frequency of such agreements can be seen on the map of Africa where long tangents drawn at right angles divided Egypt from Sudan and Libya and where connecting rivers separated the Belgian Congo from French West Africa. Some 44 percent of the boundaries in Africa "either correspond to an astrologic measurement or are parallel to some other set of lines."[38]

Another long and convenient line was the 49th Parallel between Canada and the United States, a line which Britain and the United States agreed in 1818 would form the boundary from Lake of the Woods to the Rocky Mountains. The lands west of the Great Lakes were largely unsettled by Europeans, and the two states believed that a boundary would be easier to decide while they still remained so. The 49th parallel had been part of an earlier unfinished negotiation in 1713 between Britain and France to demarcate Hudson's Bay Territory from New France. President Thomas Jefferson favoured the demarcation as did the British who had never been able to get France to agree to it.[39]

Some colonial relationships erased the distinction between colony and mother country. France formally annexed northern Algeria in 1848 making the districts of Algiers, Oran and Constantine integral parts of the French state. France gave up Algeria only after a costly and divisive war of independence. Algeria's metropolitan

FIGURE 6.4 Canada's Ohio River Boundary

Before the Seven Years War between Britain and France (1756-1763), France held Quebec and the lands of the Ohio and Mississippi Valleys. When Britain acquired New France in the Treaty of Paris in 1763, it received Quebec and all the land west of the American colonies, north of the Ohio River and east of the Mississippi River.[40] Britain's efforts to manage this huge and still unsettled territory resulted in two important boundary lines being drawn. The first, set out in the Proclamation of 1763, severed Quebec from the remaining territories to preserve them for aboriginals and discourage immigration from the American colonies. The line between Quebec and the Indian lands ran from the St. Lawrence River near present-day Cornwall northwest to Lake Nipissing. Eleven years later, the British, concerned about the lack of government in the lands and still wishing to discourage immigration, re-annexed them to Quebec. The legislation, the Quebec Act of 1774, produced a second line. The Act carefully recognized the western boundaries of the colonies of New York and Pennsylvania and extended the Canadian boundary south to the Ohio River and west to the Mississippi.

In the Paris negotiations that ended the American War of independence, Britain willingly gave the United States the former French lands east of the Mississippi. Had Britain kept them, Canada would have included the present states of Ohio, Indiana, Michigan, Illinois, Wisconsin and part of Minnesota. More land might have changed hands. The American delegation, refusing to accept the highly unpopular Quebec Act as a basis of discussion, referred back to the previous boundary—the Nipissing line from the Proclamation of 1763.[41] The American proposal was to use that line as the northern boundary of the United States and extend it west to the Mississippi. Had Britain accepted that line, southern Ontario would have been American. The two sides eventually agreed to a mid-channel boundary running through the Great Lakes.

United States Ambassador James Blanchard (left) and Canadian Revenue Minister David Anderson hold a news conference in Ottawa to release an action plan, which outlines steps taken in managing the Canada–U.S. border. Shown is an example of a card to be used, showing a picture of Prime Minister Jean Chretien.

status added deep political divisions in France and elements of civil war. People opposing independence regarded Algeria as a permanent and inalienable part of France, making the conflict one of separation as much as decolonization. The war ended in 1962 after years of bitter fighting in Algeria and political turmoil in France.

State or Empire?

Is a territory with a government in control but with diverse populations a state or an empire especially if those populations are not there by choice and are discouraged from leaving? In an empire, a political authority at the centre exercises rule over others. Viewing an empire as a set of concentric circles, it is possible to distinguish degrees of authority and layers of control. British IR scholars Barry Buzan and Richard Little present this depiction:

FIGURE 6.5   Perimeters of Authority

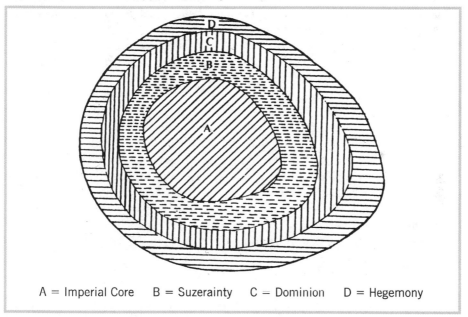

A = Imperial Core   B = Suzerainty   C = Dominion   D = Hegemony

In the centre of the figure is an "imperial core" of authority. Each concentric ring represents diminished levels of authority over political units. Level B is a suzerainty in which member units acknowledge their place in the order and concede authority to the imperial core. Level C is a dominion in which units have authority in some areas but have other areas under imperial control. Level D is a hegemony in which units are nominally independent but accommodate to the wishes of the core.[42] These relationships between units and the centre represent declining levels of control, but none is completely independent. That being the case, at what level does empire shade off into sovereign statehood? One could argue, for example, that a hegemony could include sovereign states since they accede to the centre's wishes voluntarily with the voluntary element reflecting sovereignty. Still, the boundary between state and empire is not well defined. That raises the question of whether countries that are characterized by central control, diverse populations and varying degrees of local authority are best thought of as states or empires.

Interesting cases are China, Russia, India, Indonesia and Nigeria. All have incorporated other populations, and all have acted forcibly to impose rule and prevent exit.[43] Biafra's struggle to secede from Nigeria in 1967 raised the question of granting or withholding diplomatic recognition. China's conquest and suppression of Tibet remains an issue in its relations with other states as does Indonesia's occupation and treatment of East Timor.

From Colonies to States

Former colonies began receiving independence after World War I when the Ottoman Empire's lands in the Middle East, which began as British and French mandated territories under the League of Nations, became independent. The full wave of decolonization started after World War II and reached its peak in the early 1960s. One of the final acts of European withdrawal was Britain's transferring rule in Hong Kong to China in 1997. Aside from Hong Kong, these colonies, almost without exception, became sovereign states. Upon receiving their independence, their statehood was recognized by other states.

They also became members of the United Nations, which admits "peace-loving states which accept the obligations contained in the present Charter and, in the judgement of the Organization, are able and willing to carry out those obligations." Admission is by vote of the General Assembly on the recommendation of the Security Council. Postwar tensions in the Security Council made early admissions contentious because the candidates were European states on opposite sides in the cold war, but by the time of decolonization in the late 1950s, the UN's practice was to regard membership as universal. For that reason, new states on becoming independent have made application one of their first official acts. One scholar refers to the UN as a "state-certifying organization."[44] At present, the UN's membership stands at 185.

Colonial boundaries were drawn without regard to ethnic composition, making two of statehood's prime attributes, territory and population, arbitrary creations. An interesting question is why the colonial powers did not give more regard to the actual ethnic distribution of people. A cavalier attitude on the part of the Europeans suggests itself. In Africa, where colonial boundary-making inscribed an entire continent, several other factors were involved. First, the pattern of settlement was nomadic, and populations were mobile. There were few cities, and rulers generally exercised their authority over "land but not over people." The Europeans had an informational deficit: it was not clear who lived where. Second, with some exceptions there were no large existing political units to enclose, and most political organization was village-level. Third, there were low levels of political mobilization, and ethnicity was largely undeveloped as a unifying force. Finally, the continent contained few natural demarcations such as mountain ranges.[46]

FIGURE 6.6   Instant Independence, Delayed Statehood

In 1958, the government of France put its new constitution, which established the current Fifth Republic, to a public vote of approval in both France and its overseas colonies. Charles De Gaulle, who would become President under the new constitution, warned the colonies that failure to ratify would be an act of immediate independence from France, broadly suggesting that all French obligations would cease. The only overseas territory to vote No was the west African colony of Guinea. De Gaulle declared Guinea to be immediately independent. Even though the French government said that some of the cadres of French administrators, soldiers and teachers would remain through a brief transition, they quickly began to leave. When they did so, they took equipment with them and destroyed much of what they left behind.[45] France terminated financial aid.

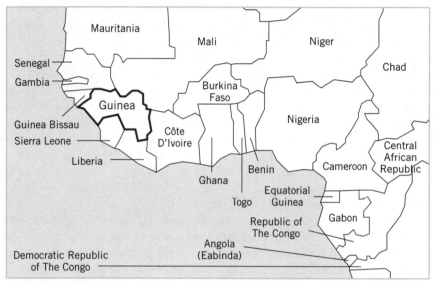

Republic of Guinea

Guinea, however, could not obtain immediate international recognition as a state because France, even though it had declared Guinea independent, refused for several months to grant diplomatic recognition. That delayed Guinea's accession to statehood because major powers such as Great Britain were unwilling to recognize Guinea until its relationship with France was clear. Several Soviet-bloc and African states did grant early recognition, but Guinea's international status remained indeterminate: it was no longer a colony, but most states had had not yet acknowledged it as a state. Independence was immediate, but statehood was not.

Another interesting question is why the leaders of colonial independence movements, given the opportunity to redraw boundaries to reflect local realities, did not do so. Instead, they adopted the boundaries as they stood. Even administrative divisions *within* colonies, in the case of French West Africa, became the boundaries of new states such as Mali and Niger.[47] Why were they simply accepted? There are two explanations.

The first focuses on the impact of colonialism in reproducing in Africa and Asia a political form that had evolved in particular circumstances in Europe. Social scientists refer to such transplanting as institutionalization. One of the indices of institutionalization is its taken-for-granted nature and its part of an understood and expected order.[48] By the 1950s, European sovereign statehood was so unquestionably entrenched as the way of organizing authority and territory that new states sought it without question. An index of that entrenchment is that it is still difficult to visualize any other form even in the face of the European Union's rapid modifications of statehood. Separatist movements, which have their own state as their objective, are wedded to that institution.

The second explanation is that recognition and maintenance of boundaries in Africa is rooted in mutual convenience. The European powers began that practice by agreeing among themselves not to interfere in territories where one of their members had even a nominal colonial presence. That custom, in the view of one scholar, has continued among Africa's leaders as a powerful norm of mutual recognition and non-interference. A "minimal domestic administrative presence" qualifies a government for non-interference from its neighbours.[49] Because these states are now independent, the rubric is sovereignty. That norm has been effective. No African state has conquered another since independence despite their lack of homogeneous populations and their weakly developed capacities to provide effective rule and services. Because of mutual recognition, African states so far have been spared the fate of their conquered European forebears. We will return later to the questions of weak states and non-intervention.

We saw earlier that exclusive state control of armed forces is a relatively recent development. By now, however, military forces have themselves become institutionalized, normal and unquestioned fixtures of modern states.[50] A recent example has been seen in the United Nations' creation of the new state of Namibia. "As a symbol of statehood, the incipient Namibian state created a flag and an army of more than a thousand soldiers." One might argue that given Namibia's location next to South Africa, which had made regular incursions, and to Angola where armed factions from the civil war were still present, an army was a necessity. Compared to its neighbours' forces, however, Namibia's army "was (and remains) essentially militarily insignificant." In view of that disparity, the army's role is largely symbolic, a demonstration of full statehood.[51]

Statehood: Legal and Empirical

All states, according to the doctrine of legal statehood, are sovereign and equal enjoying the same rights and responsibilities. Those of a great power are the same as those of a micro-state. One of **sovereign equality**'s most visible representations is the composition of the United Nations General Assembly where each member state has one vote. In the same way, all states enjoy the same protections against interference in their domestic affairs and the same recognition of their equal standing. These rights are embodied and upheld in international law. Until recently, sovereign equality had an additional element: each state was equally but individually responsible for its own support and survival and had no claim on other states for support. As sovereign entities, their survival was their responsibility. There was no legal guarantee.[52] States under that doctrine could fail.

According to the doctrine of **empirical statehood**, a political unit must be practically viable to be a state. The term empirical denotes the attributes we saw at the beginning of the chapter: a recognized territory, a population and a government in effective control—the requisites of effective existence as a state. The doctrine contains both ethical and pragmatic considerations. Ethically, one of the purposes of an effective control is to enable a territory's inhabitants to enjoy the civic protections available under independent rule.[53] Pragmatically, one of the purposes is international order, which stable governments exercising continuous authority over well-defined territories can help provide.[54] Empirical statehood remains one of the basic criteria states use in deciding whether to recognize new states: is there a government in effective control of a recognized territory and population?

FIGURE 6.7 Failed American Empirical Statehood: A Vignette from the War of 1812

During the War of 1812, Britain captured much of the state of Maine. When British forces took control of the port of Castine, they began charging British customs duties on entering goods. When American authorities once again took charge of Castine at the end of the war, they sought to collect duties on the goods imported during the British occupation. This double-billing was justified on the grounds that duty had not been paid to the United States. The issue made its way to the U.S. Supreme Court, which ruled in *United States v. Rice* that American customs could not collect the duties because Castine was not under American control when the goods were landed. In the Supreme Court's judgement, the United States was not empirically sovereign over Maine at the time and therefore could not claim the rights of sovereignty. One of these rights is to charge duties on imports.[55]

Do the legal and empirical doctrines conflict? As we saw earlier, European colonies were granted independence and were quickly recognized as new states. Legally, they were granted immediate and full international status. Empirically, many of these entities did not meet the requirements. Governments were weak, law and administration were incomplete and ineffective, the economic base for adequate public programs and services was insufficient or absent, military self-defence was weak or lacking and viability in the international economy including the ability to earn money through trade for necessary imports was weak or undeveloped. Instead of providing for their citizens' protection, these states' rule was usually authoritarian. Those conditions have tended to persist, and it is accurate to say that "a very high proportion of today's 185 UN members cannot meet traditional criteria of what constitutes a state."[56] Therein lies the conflict. Legally, these states are the full equivalents of stronger and more well established ones and enjoy their full measure of international status. Empirically, these states' deficiencies provide weak claims to statehood. In fact, without the protection of legal sovereignty, their empirical viability would be doubtful.

Because of these deficits, weak states have a particular reason to emphasize their legal status. Particularly important is the sovereign norm of non-interference in other states' domestic affairs and the prohibition, contained in the UN Charter, against armed aggression and conquest. Without those norms and in the absence of other states' adhering to them, weak states would be vulnerable to conquest, annexation or colonization. Because these norms are widely acknowledged, they can be seen as exemptions from sovereignty's previous provision that all states are equally entitled to fail. Instead, there are "new normative regulations: weak, marginal or insubstantial states are now exempted from the power contest at least in part and treated as international protectorates... Ramshackle states today are not open invitations for unsolicited external intervention."[57] Instead, the current doctrine of sovereign equality of states holds that weak states require immunity from empirical statehood's traditional requirements.

To what extent is that doctrine an international obligation? The early 1990s saw several major UN interventions into places where the pillars of empirical statehood had collapsed: Somalia, Bosnia, Cambodia. In Africa, regional interventions took place in Liberia and Sierra Leone. The reason for collapse was civil war and profound governmental breakdown. Much of the motivation behind the interventions was humanitarian: under those conditions, civilian populations were at acute risk of starvation and massacre. Much of the motivation was also to rescue failed states.

What changed the earlier sink-or-swim doctrine of sovereignty? Before World War II, traditional international law recognized sovereign states and "various formal dependencies." Under the self-help doctrine, rulers who were colonized could not demonstrate empirical statehood. Several factors converged after World War II. One factor was the doctrine of **national self-determination**. This became an important international influence during World War I when President Woodrow Wilson's Fourteen Points embraced self-determination and statehood for nations under the Hapsburg and Ottoman empires and after the war supported the constitution of new states in Central and Eastern Europe. Extending that principle beyond Europe set a precedent for recognizing colonial statehood and undermined the legitimacy of the other colonies.[58] After World War II, the principle of self-determination was placed in the United Nations Charter. Domestically, Western states increasingly recognized the rights of minorities in their own societies, and having embraced the notion of political equality at home they came to see colonialism increasingly illegitimate. Internationally, the principle of equality was extended to all states. As the colonies gained their independence, the gap between the empirical basis of their statehood and that of the rest of the UN membership added the notion of obligation not just to independence but to empirical survival. Ever since, the UN has taken on the responsibility of setting the standards of proper modern statehood. That purpose underlay the UN's interventions after the end of the cold war in civil conflicts such as Cambodia and El Salvador in which the task was not only reconstituting a state after civil war but of instituting the beginnings of democratic rule and respect for human rights. The UN justifies this intervention into domestic state practices as an extension of its obligation to promote peace and security. Human rights and democracy, in that equation, promote peace.[59] We will see more about the democratic peace in Chapter 9.

In both Europe and the colonies, independence and sovereign statehood became requisite. As one scholar has written of that time, "No other status was any longer considered legitimate; and empires, zones of influence and even hegemony were widely regarded as too reprehensible for objective study."[60] The result was an expansion of international obligation not just to recognize the new states but also to help ensure their survival. The pivot of that change was the norm of sovereign statehood.

FIGURE 6.8   Sovereignty and an Independent Canadian Foreign Policy

Along with the authority to govern and raise armed forces, one of the central points of sovereignty is the authority to conduct foreign policy. In Canada, that authority developed slowly. When Canada was a colony, management of foreign affairs rested squarely with Britain. As practice evolved during the nineteenth century, Britain would sometimes allow Canadian representatives in treaty negotiations that affected Canada although the treaty-making power—the original sovereign authority granted to princes at Westphalia—was still solely Britain's. On other matters involving foreign countries, the channel of communication was from the Canadian Prime Minister to the Governor General who would deal with the Colonial Office in London himself.

An index of the extent of Britain's management of foreign policy can be seen in the sharing of diplomatic documents. After the Alaska boundary settlement in 1899, Canada requested and received a copy of the agreement from Britain on the grounds that the contents would be necessary for dealing with issues arising out of the settlement. Britain, however, made it clear that it had not set a precedent for sharing diplomatic documents with Canada. In 1907, when Canada was negotiating an informal agreement on immigration with Japan, a member of the Canadian cabinet wrote to the British Foreign Secretary asking for a copy of the papers relating to the British-Japanese Treaty of 1894, which might contain information Canada would need to know. The Foreign Secretary declined to send the papers on the grounds of confidentiality although he said he would do his best to furnish documents requested individually.[61]

Canada's Department of External Affairs was created in 1909, but it was World War I that marked the transition. In 1914, Canada agreed without question to contribute all the forces Britain needed and was strongly supported by public opinion. As the war progressed, Canada's relationship with Britain became increasingly less satisfactory. When fighting stalemated into trench warfare and Canadian casualties mounted, the Borden government became increasingly alarmed at Britain's war strategy, but Britain insisted on managing the war itself and would not consult with the dominions about how it was using their forces.

In the face of mounting dissatisfaction, Britain eventually agreed to an Imperial War Conference that met in 1917. By this time, Canada and the other Dominions were resolved to push for a much greater voice in managing their foreign affairs. Looking forward to constitutional changes following the war, the Conference established this central principle: the Dominions were to enjoy "full recognition...as autonomous nations of an Imperial Commonwealth."[62] That principle opened the door for Canada and the other Dominions to begin conducting their own foreign affairs although Britain did not acknowledge their right "to participate in international society as equal sovereign states" until the Imperial Conference of 1926.

Canada sent its own delegation to the Paris Peace Conference, signed the Treaty of Versailles and became a member of the League of Nations. Canada appointed its own ambassador to the United States in 1920 although the ambassador still worked out of the British Embassy in Washington. In 1927, Canada opened its own embassy in Washington. Along the way, Canada carefully began to detach its foreign policy from Britain's. In the Chanak crisis of 1922, Prime Minister W.L. Mackenzie King demurred on sending a Canadian contingent to reinforce a British force in a skirmish with Turkey. The next year, Canada objected to not having been invited to the Lausanne Conference that made a final peace with Turkey and formalized a number of postwar territorial settlements.

The end of this evolution came in 1931 with the Statute of Westminster in which Britain officially set forth the principle that all Dominions were autonomous and free to conduct their foreign and domestic affairs within a British Commonwealth. Canada, officially, was sovereign. The Statute, however, only recognized what had already transpired. International lawyer and diplomat Allan Gotlieb characterized the post-World War I transition as "one of the most impressive examples of peaceful change in this century."[63] The Dominions' accession to sovereignty proceeded on a different basis than that of the former colonies after World War II. Canada and Australia claimed their status on the basis of their participation in World War I as well as on their signing of the Versailles Treaty.[64]

International Recognition: A Chequered Pattern

An important attribute of statehood is international recognition. As we saw, one form of recognition is admission to the United Nations. A longer practice has been diplomatic recognition by other states. In principle, recognition is based on empirical statehood: a recognized territory, a population and a government in control. According to the same principle, states can also withdraw recognition if these conditions no longer prevail. The most likely failure is a collapse of government and sovereignty. The relationship between sovereignty and recognition is not at all direct. States with virtually no sovereignty have been recognized as if everything were normal.

That was true of Lebanon during its long civil war in the 1970s and 1980s when the government had lost most of its control to militias and when parts of its territory were under Syrian and Israeli military occupation. Continuing recognition reflected another aspect of sovereignty's international practice: "Other members of the international community do not normally withdraw recognition of a state on the grounds that its sovereign status has been forfeited through loss of domestic control."[65] A state, in other words, can still be recognized by others even when its authority is incomplete or, in Lebanon's case, virtually absent. Conversely, states that definitely do have a territory, a population and a government in control may not be recognized. Taiwan is a good example. There the issue is China's insistent claim that the island is a renegade province.

Some IR theorists see diplomatic recognition and formal respect for sovereignty as reflecting a shared interest in maintaining sovereignty as a strong international norm of proper conduct among states. By containing a widely understood standard of behaviour, the norm also makes it possible to define violations of sovereignty and conduct. The purpose of the norm is to preserve states and the formally equal basis on which they deal with each other.

The norm, however, has not been consistent historically. Instead, it has gravitated between two points of emphasis. One point emphasizes the sanctity and integrity of existing states. According to this doctrine, the foremost consideration must be preserving existing territories, boundaries, populations and governments. The overriding purpose is international stability. Boundary changes and population transfers always represent absolute gains and losses for the states involved. In an international condition of anarchy, one of the foundations of order is a system of stable and territorially consistent states. The emphasis of this view is to preserve states already in place.

The rival norm is national self-determination. According to that norm, every nation deserves its own state. If a nation of people is confined within an existing state as a minority or oppressed population, the obligation of the international community is to recognize its aspirations for its own territory and government. If achieving that status requires dismembering an existing state or assembling parts of several states, such measures are justified. National self-determination trumps state integrity.

According to recent scholarship, which norm has prevailed has varied historically.[66] At times such as the end of World War I when the rights of nations have been treated as paramount, international practice has supported the creation of new states from parts or remnants of older ones. At other times the stability of existing states has taken precedence. At the time of decolonization after World War II, the prevailing view was that peoples' aspirations could be achieved through independent statehood and proper self-government. Independence had to be realized within the existing colonial boundaries. National *self-determination*, which would have required redrawing the boundaries according to ethnic settlement, was not equated with colonial *independence,* and so the colonial borders were kept with their various admixtures of peoples. Self-government within those borders was the objective.[67] Because that priority prevailed at the time, the new states got their old boundaries.

Since then the international community has supported the refusal of African states to back any secessionist or irredentist movements on the continent regardless of the arbitrary way in which different peoples were assembled into colonies and subsequently into states. At the same time, breakaway Yugoslav states were recognized. Germany earned international censure by recognizing Croatia almost immediately, but the main objection was that Germany's action helped to inflame incipient civil war. What the international attitude will be at any particular time is a question that a separatist movement seeking international recognition of its state-hood must reckon with. The practice varies.

Non-Intervention: A Variable Protection

The doctrine of non-intervention preserves all states from acts against their domestic sovereign jurisdiction. The most severe breach is armed aggression. The UN Charter strongly forbids it. Invasion violates all three pillars of empirical statehood: a state's territory, its population and by challenging its rule, its government. The Charter provides for a collective response by UN member states including military action. Two basic principles are involved. The first is the preservation of peace, the UN's prime mission. The second is the sovereign equality of states. All states, regardless of their size and power, are equally entitled to exclusive jurisdiction within their boundaries. The principle of collective security holds that all states share the obligation to retaliate against aggression directed at any state. We will see more about the workings of UN collective security in Chapter 11. Iraq ran afoul of the norm against armed aggression when it invaded Kuwait in 1990. One reason for the universal condemnation and the willingness of many states, including Canada, to join a military coalition against Iraq was to avoid the precedent of flagrant aggression particularly by very strong states upon small and weak ones. In that, the members were defending not just Kuwait but the broader principle of sovereignty and their own interests as states.

States also have the right to be free from interference in their internal affairs, a right that the Charter also recognizes. Outside intervention covers a variety of deeds from arming breakaway or revolutionary fighting forces to officially supporting a particular party in another state's election. This norm is particularly important to weak states, which are vulnerable to subversion and political disruption. By encouraging and supplying such movements, another state could do considerable mischief. Arab states during the 1950s and 1960s were under serious threat from such interference. The doctrine was Pan-Arabism, and the threats were fellow Arab states. Pan-Arabism's central idea was the natural unity of all Arabs and the arbitrary and artificial divisions within that unity posed by Arab states. Movement toward unity required existing governments to abandon their sovereignty in favour of a common political bond. Acting upon that doctrine, Egypt and Syria merged in 1958, a union that lasted for three years.

Pan-Arabism's requirement that all Arab leaders act according to common aims and principles undermined their sovereignty because it imposed an external standard on their behaviour. One leader could threaten another by charging betrayal of Pan-Arabism. The availability of mass media, particularly radio, enabled populations to be addressed directly, and the overthrow of the offending leader could be urged. "In general, Pan-Arabism represented a potential threat to the Arab state's domestic and international basis of existence, and an Arab leader who wielded the Pan-Arab card could be dangerous indeed."[68] In the face of Pan-Arabism, the doctrine of non-intervention was a weak defence.

FIGURE 6.9   Non-Intervention and Canada's Centennial

In 1967 and not long before the Centennial celebration in Canada, French President Charles De Gaulle paid an official visit to Canada. In a speech on the steps of Montreal's city hall, De Gaulle electrified his audience by declaring "Vive le Québec libre!" This gesture was a dramatic and unambiguous endorsement of Quebec's still-young separatist movement. De Gaulle was giving his support as head of a major power to a cause aimed at the pillars of empirical statehood: territory, population and effective government control, unambiguously interfering in the domestic affairs of another state. A year later, the Republic of Gabon, a former French colony and one of France's closest allies in Africa, hosted an international conference of education ministers of francophone states. Instead of sending the invitation to Ottawa, however, Gabon sent it to Quebec City.

The Cabinet of Prime Minister Lester Pearson was divided on how to deal with De Gaulle's speech. Opinions ranged from mild protest to severing diplomatic relations. Pearson chose a middle option by terming the speech "unacceptable." De Gaulle, without apology, flew home the next day. In the Gabon affair, the federal government proposed a formula to Quebec Premier Daniel Johnson for Quebec representation on Canadian international delegations and left open the possibility that for conferences dealing with education or culture the delegation might be led by a Quebec minister. The Quebec government did not reply but sent its own delegation to the Gabon conference. Ottawa sent a diplomatic note of protest to Gabon accusing it of meddling in Canadian constitutional matters and of ignoring the federal government's sovereign responsibility for managing relations with foreign states and suspending diplomatic relations. The note made specific reference to international law and proper standards of relations between states. Far from apologizing, Gabon responded that Ottawa was merely seeking to paper over its own interference in Quebec's affairs.

In both incidents, the federal government believed that France intended to "destroy Canadian confederation or, at the very least, to challenge its stability by intervening in Canadian domestic affairs." Ivan Head, Professor of International Law at the University of Alberta and soon to become a key adviser to Prime Minister Trudeau (Trudeau became Prime Minister two months after the Gabon incident), believed that Gabon's invitation was "no less than a formal act of recognition of Quebec's independence."[69] By referring specifically to international law and making the public gesture of suspending diplomatic relations—something that states generally do only as signs of extreme aggravation—Ottawa invoked the international norm of non-interference to discourage further gestures. In doing so, it supported the interpretation of sovereignty that emphasizes the integrity of existing states. France and Gabon, for their part, supported the interpretation of sovereignty that emphasizes national self-determination.

Sovereignty and Human Rights

The principle of non-intervention in the affairs of sovereign states becomes contentious when states use their authority to protect practices to which the international community objects. An important area of contention is governments' treatment of their citizens. States' legal and criminal codes clearly are part of their sovereign jurisdiction. When one is in another state, one is subject to its laws. The popular travel guide *Let's Go Spain and Portugal* has a section on Morocco. In stringent language it warns its readers against buying drugs in Morocco where they are readily available. Morocco has strict drug laws, and foreigners who are arrested are beyond the help of their governments.[70] Canadian travellers are warned of these consequences in signs and pamphlets in airport departure areas. One poster shows a Canadian sitting despondently behind bars. Home governments may appeal for leniency, but states are under no obligation to comply. A Canadian couple was sentenced to life in prison in Brazil after being convicted of involvement in the kidnapping of a wealthy businessman. The Canadian government appealed to Brazil to allow the couple to serve their sentences in Canada but the Brazilian government was resistant, arguing that crimes committed in Brazil should be punished under Brazilian law. After years of appeals and pressure, Brazil allowed the couple to serve their sentences in Canada. They were subsequently parolled.

Sovereignty and punishment raise the question of the limits of proper and humane treatment of citizens by their governments. The issue arises from universal conceptions of human rights, which holds that all people share common and irrevocable rights. The corollary of obligation holds that those enjoying those rights should help those who do not. In an international system containing states that oppress and abuse their citizens, universal conceptions of human rights squarely contradict the norm of non-interference. States whose domestic practices can least withstand scrutiny have not hesitated to invoke their sovereign rights.

Which takes precedence? That question came up in 1992 in Haiti. Following decades of notoriously violent and horrible rule, the government, responding to international pressure, held an election in 1990. The new government was soon overthrown by the Haitian armed forces, and repression resumed. Speaking to the UN General Assembly, Canadian External Affairs Minister Barbara McDougall addressed the question of sovereignty versus rights. "The concept of sovereignty," she declared, "must respect higher principles, including the need to preserve human life from wanton destruction." Prime Minister Mulroney, in a speech that same week, advocated the same view: "We must recognize that there are certain fundamental rights that all people possess—and that, sometimes, the international community must act to defend them."[71] After a UN-authorized economic embargo and intensive diplomacy did not succeed in restoring the elected government, the United Nations in 1994 authorized an armed invasion. Canada contributed 600 troops and units to train Haitian police.

Can an argument be made for sovereign non-interference even when following that norm dooms people to brutal rule? Writing in a major international law journal, one scholar emphasized the broader purpose behind non-intervention. Article 2 Section 7 of the UN Charter, which "flatly prohibits the United Nations from intervening in matters within the domestic jurisdiction of states," is based, he argued, on *both* legal and empirical statehood. Force may not be used against a state that is under effective control—against, in other words, a state that is sovereign. The purpose behind that doctrine is to protect states from arbitrary actions by other states particularly when those states have the collective power to enforce their will. Comparing the intervention in Haiti with the Soviet intervention that overturned a democratic reformist government in Czechoslovakia in 1968, the author asserted, "To use force to install a democratic regime [in Haiti] was no more permissible than it was to install a socialist regime [in Czechoslovakia]."[72]

For less powerful states, collective action under the UN may simply reflect the interests and priorities of the larger states. The smaller states' fear is that although they enjoy a solid majority in the General Assembly, the Security Council, which authorizes collective action, is dominated by the five permanent members. These states define the occasions and rationale of intervention. Since these states have widespread interests and are subject to varying international and domestic pressures, their motives may be difficult to separate from humanitarian principles.[73] For states facing such attention, a strong international norm of sovereign equality is a necessary protection.

Promoting free and fair elections is a less draconian way of advancing human rights. Since governments that face voters regularly are less likely to be abusive than those that are unaccountable, promoting elections worldwide can be seen as an effective way of achieving broader human rights. To that end, a number of governments and non-governmental organizations have promoted international supervision of elections.

Governments have given their consent slowly. Prior to 1989, the principle of sovereign non-intervention limited the scope of activity. For the UN, electoral supervision was granted only in former UN Trust Territories that were making the transition to sovereign self-government. These were not contentious cases because the territories had not yet achieved sovereignty. Even then, the ground rules were very circumscribed, limiting the number of observers and restricting their presence to the time right at the election and their mobility to the national capital. Organization of American States electoral observers in Nicaragua in 1974 and in Guatemala in 1980 were under the same restrictions with the additional provision limiting their status as representatives of the OAS.[74] From these beginnings, international supervision of elections has become more widely accepted and has achieved greater monitoring capability.

Governments that grant access to international election supervision teams are acceding to international expectations and pressure. Governments that seek to avoid scrutiny or that are sufficiently large and independent to resist pressure may not agree to supervision. We will see more about human rights in Chapter 13. Here the point to note is that universal purposes such as human rights may directly contradict principles of sovereignty.

Voluntary Surrender

States surrender sovereignty when they enter into international agreements. Any agreement that requires certain standards of behaviour constrains states' latitude to act as they choose. Trade agreements are a good example. Their fundamental provision is to encourage trade by lowering or eliminating tariffs. States, as part of their territorial sovereignty, have the right to regulate what crosses their boundaries, and imposing tariffs is one form of control. As we will see in Chapter 12, states generally have used tariffs to protect their industries from foreign competition. Often such protection is part of a larger industrial policy to encourage particular sectors or, less positively, to sustain non-competitive or declining industries. By entering trade agreements, states agree to reduce their tariffs. Protective tariffs in particular, because of their discriminatory purpose, are generally the first targets for reduction in trade agreements. More generally, the basic principle of trade agreements is that member states may not act in ways that create artificial disadvantages for other members' exports. In making that commitment, states give up important authorities to manage their trade and domestic industries. States enter into such agreements expecting that the benefits they receive will outweigh the prerogatives they surrender. We will see more about trade advantages in Chapter 12.

FIGURE 6.10 Institutionalism and Sovereignty:
Interdependence and Cooperation

Rapidly increasing interdependence between states increases the need for cooperation. The demand for global telecommunication, for example, creates a demand for telecommunications agreements. The demand for international investment creates a demand for harmonized finance and banking regulation. In telecommunication, the benefits are increased speed and efficiency; in investment, they are increased international opportunities for states' banks and corporations and increased international sources of investment capital. In areas such as these, the international system offers the prospects of all states enjoying gains. This prospect establishes the basis of cooperation.

At the same time, the condition of anarchy makes states self-interested actors that rationally seek to maximize their individual gains. Anarchy also creates the paradox that selfish behaviour leaves all states worse off. Prisoner's Dilemma illustrates that selfish behaviour leaves all with less desirable outcomes. The task is to construct ways of supporting cooperation in the face of the tension between mutual and individual gains. The prospects of collective gains and protection against cheating provide the motivation. International agreements in areas such as banking and telecommunication furnish information, procedures and rules. In addition to standardizing activity, these arrangements reduce the costs of states seeking and monitoring agreements individually. Where the incentive for cheating is high, institutional arrangements that provide for effective monitoring and compliance are needed.[75]

Agreements in particular sectors have made possible global technologies, the benefits of which we often take for granted. International telecommunications agreements, for example, have opened the way for systems that support the Internet and ATMs. In industry those same systems enable production to be coordinated across continents with components and parts for assembly brought together from distant sources in finely coordinated sequences. As states pursue these advantages, they surrender degrees of freedom to manage their own economies and institutions. The efficiencies made possible may set the stages for new levels of integration, creating conditions requiring additional surrenders of sovereignty. The attractions of larger export markets and access to broader sources of investment make further integration hard to forego, particularly if other states are expanding their own involvement in international economic networks. In light of that pressure, the greatest challenge to sovereignty may not be conquest and war but the unifying forces of efficiency and technological advance. We will see more about the effects of economic globalization on domestic governance in Chapter 8.

States may also agree to surrender sovereignty as the lesser of bad alternatives. Such alternatives face states whose finances are so desperate that they cannot meet their obligations or maintain a currency. One option is to take the consequences, which may include not being able to pay government employees, defaulting on debt obligations, seeing banks collapse and not buying crucial imports such as medicines. The other option is to seek an emergency loan from the International Monetary Fund (IMF). The IMF frequently imposes conditions before lending the money, and some impinge directly on sovereignty. In the last 20 years, the IMF has required recipient states to sell off government-owned corporations and utilities, cut subsidies to industries or consumers and devalue their currencies. The IMF's purpose is to reform the behaviour that led to the financial crisis and bring government spending into line with revenues. In its response to the financial panics in Asia in 1998, the IMF had the additional motive of restoring international investor confidence and reversing a disastrous flight of capital. We will see more about the Asian crisis in Chapter 12's treatment of the state and the economy. In the poorer states that are the most likely to require IMF loans, some cuts such as eliminating subsidies on bread, rice or transit fares can be politically explosive.[76] Avoiding such measures is a major incentive for governments to keep their deficit and debt levels below critical levels and to keep their financial institutions solvent.

FIGURE 6.11 Sovereignty and Choice: The Liberal View

The fact of statehood and anarchy disposes states neither to conflict nor cooperation. Their behaviour depends on the issue, the configuration of domestic interests, the mediating role of state organizations and laws and the actions of other states. Refusal to enter into cooperative agreements such as trade liberalization reflects not categorical concerns with absolute or relative gains but rather the interests of dominant groups.[77] The inefficiencies imposed by trade barriers become politically unsupportable when groups bearing excess costs compare their situations to those in states where barriers and costs have been lowered. The groups' political demand is to cooperate with other states in lowering barriers to trade and investment.[78]

Summary

We have seen that sovereign statehood is, in the longer perspective of history, a relatively recent way of organizing political rule, populations and territory. Sovereignty, the exclusive right of states to rule within their jurisdictions, can be seen as the foundation not just of statehood but of the state-based international system. Sovereignty is both a legal right and a collective practice. Without an effective international authority to enforce sovereignty and protect states' jurisdictions, the practice depends upon reciprocity with each state recognizing the others' sovereignty.

Statehood itself evolved in a particular historical setting. Because of the effectiveness of that form compared to others, statehood has predominated. Diffused throughout the world by colonialism and by the absence of any feasible alternative form of organization, statehood has become institutionalized as normal practice. Upon independence, former European colonies were recognized as sovereign states. The international community has assumed the obligation of underwriting their survival.

An important dimension of sovereignty is variable. Diplomatic recognition, one of the practices that supports states, is drawn between two competing principles of statehood: preservation of existing states and support for national self-determination. That tension makes the international reception of independence movements unpredictable. In the same way, the principle of non-intervention in sovereign states conflicts with the obligation to assist oppressed people against their governments.

States surrender sovereignty when they enter international agreements. The trade-off is expected benefits against reduced degrees of freedom. States may place themselves in the position of more pervasive intrusions when they accept financing from international agencies such as the International Monetary Fund. Their position is limited by the critical financial circumstances that lead them to seek help.

ENDNOTES

1   Alan James, Sovereignty and Statehood: The Basis of International Society, London: Allen and Unwin, 1986, p. 13.

2   UNESCO Statistical Yearbook 1995, Lanham, MD: Bernan Press, 1995, pp. viii–xi.

3   Janice Thomson, "State Sovereignty in International Relations: Bridging the Gap between Theory and Empirical Research," International Studies Quarterly 39 (January 1995) 214, 23.

4   Louise I. Shelley, "Transnational Organized Crime: An Imminent Threat to the Nation-State?" Journal of International Affairs 48 (Winter 1995) 469.

5   Michael Ross Fowler and Julie Marie Bunck, "What Constitutes the Sovereign State?" Review of International Studies 22 (October 1996) 390.

6   Robert O. Keohane, "International Institutions: Two Approaches," International Studies Quarterly 32 (December 1988) 385.

7   Stephen Krasner, "Compromising Westphalia," International Security 20 (Winter 1995-1996) 116.

8   William E. Connolly, "Tocqueville, Territory, and Violence," in Michael Shapiro and Hayward Alker, eds., Challenging Boundaries: Global Flows, Territorial Identities, Minneapolis: University of Minnesota Press, 1996, pp. 153–54.

9   Kennan Ferguson, "Unmapping and Remapping the World: Foreign Policy as Aesthetic Practice," in Shapiro and Alker, eds, Challenging Boundaries, p. 169.

10 J.P Nettl, "The State as a Conceptual Variable," World Politics 20 (July 1968) 581–82.

11 Stephen Krasner, "Westphalia and All That," in Judith Goldstein and Robert O. Keohane, eds., Ideas and Foreign Policy, Ithaca: Cornell University Press, 1993, p. 235.

12 Ruggie, "Territoriality and Beyond: Problematizing Modernity in International Relations, International Organization 47 (Winter 1993) 157.

13 Christian Reuss-Smit, "The Constitutional Structure of International Society and the Nature of Fundamental Institutions," International Organization 51 (Fall 1997) 565–66.

14 Alexander Wendt, "Anarchy Is What States Make of It: The Social Construction of Power Politics," International Organization 46 (Spring 1993) 417.

15 Martha Finnemore, "Norms, Culture, and World Politics: Insights from Sociology's Institutionalism," International Organization 50 (Spring 1996) 325–348.

16   Barry Weingast, "A Rational Choice Perspective on the Role of Ideas: Shared Belief Systems and State Sovereignty in International Cooperation," Politics and Society 23 (December 1995) 456.

17   Krasner, "Westphalia and All That," p. 236.

18   ibid.

19   John Gerard Ruggie, "Continuity and Transformation in the World Polity: Toward a Neorealist Synthesis," World Politics 35 (January 1983) 274.

20   ibid. p. 275.

21   James, Sovereign Statehood, p. 4

22   Ruggie, "Continuity and Transformation," 274.

23   ibid, p. 275

24   Markus Fischer, "Feudal Europe, 800-1300: Communal Discourse and Conflictual Practices," International Organization 46 (Spring 1992) 462.

25   Hendrik Spruyt, "Institutional Selection in International Relations: State Anarchy as Order," International Organization 48 (Autumn 1994) 528–31.

26   Peter C. Newman, Company of Adventurers, Vol. I, Markham, ON: Viking, 1985, p. 87.

27   Janice Thomson. Mercenaries, Pirates, and Sovereigns, Princeton: Princeton University Press, 1994, p. 103.

28   Newman, Company of Adventurers, pp. 90, 91.

29   Thomson, Mercenaries, Pirates and Sovereigns, p. 60.

30   Charles Tilly, ed., The Formation of National States in Western Europe, Princeton: Princeton University Press, 1975, pp. 6–83.

31   Charles Tilly, Coercion, Capital and European States, A.D. 990–1990, Cambridge: Basil Blackwell, 1990, p. 102.

32   Jeffrey Herbst, "War and the State in Africa," International Security 14 (Spring 1990) 120–24, 137.

33   Thomson, Mercenaries, Pirates, and Sovereigns, pp. 27–28.

34   ibid., p. 22.

35   ibid., p. 31.

36   ibid., p. 147.

37   Friedrich Kratochwil, "On Systems, Boundaries, and Territoriality: An Inquiry in to the Formation of the State System," World Politics 39 (October 1986) 37.

38   Jeffrey Herbst, "The Creation and Maintenance of National Boundaries in Africa," International Organization 43 (Autumn 1989) 675.

39   Kratochwil, "On Systems, Boundaries, and Territoriality," 38.

40   Max Savelle, The Diplomatic History of the Canadian Boundary 1749–1763, New York: Russell and Russell, 1940, pp. 132–33.

41   A.L. Burt, The United States, Great Britain, and British North America, New York: Russell & Russell, 1961, p. 23.

42   Barry Buzan and Richard Little, "Reconceptualizing Anarchy," European Journal of International Relations 2 (1996) 417–18.

43   ibid., p. 432.

44   Charles Tilly, "War Making and State Making as Organized Crime," in Peter Evans, Dietrich Rueschemeyer and Theda Skocpol, eds., Bringing the State Back In, Cambridge: Cambridge University Press, 1985, p. 185.

45   Harold Nelson, et al, Area Handbook for Guinea, U.S. Government Printing Office, 1976, p. 38.

46   Herbst, "The Creation and Maintenance of National Boundaries in Africa," 679–80.

47   ibid., 675.

48   John Meyer and Brian Rowan, "Institutional Organizations: Formal Structure as Myth and Ceremony," in Walter Powell and Paul DiMaggio, eds., The New Institutionalism and Organizational Analysis, Chicago: University of Chicago Press, 1991, p. 52.

49 Herbst, "The Creation and Maintenance of National Boundaries in Africa," 689.

50 Tilly, "War Making and State Making as Organized Crime," pp. 185–86.

51 Dana Eyre and Mark Suchman, "Status, Norms, and the Proliferation of Conventional Weapons: An Institutional Theory Approach," in Peter Katzenstein, ed., The Culture of National Security: Norms and Identity in World Politics, New York: Columbia University Press, 1996, p. 82.

52 Robert Jackson, Quasi-States: Sovereignty, International Relations, and the Third World, Cambridge: Cambridge University Press, 1990, p. 21.

53 ibid., p. 22.

54 J. Samuel Barkin and Bruce Cronin, "The State and the Nation: Changing Norms and the Rules of Sovereignty in International Relations," International Organization 48 (Winter 1994) 112.

55 Fowler and Bunck, "What Constitutes the Sovereign State?" 385.

56 K.J. Holsti, "International Relations Theory and Domestic War in the Third World: The Limits of Relevance," in Stephanie Newman, ed., International Relations Theory and the Third World, New York: St. Martin's Press, 1998, p. 122.

57 Jackson, Quasi-States, p. 23.

58 Barkin and Cronin, "State and Nation," 122, 125.

59 Michael N. Barnett, "Bringing in the New World Order: Liberalism, Legitimacy, and the United Nations," World Politics 49 (July 1997) 537.

60 Adam Watson, "Foreward," in James Der Derian, ed., International Theory: Critical Investigations, New York: New York University Press, 1995, p. xv.

61 James Eayrs, "The Origins of Canada's Department of External Affairs," in Hugh Keenleyside, et al, The Growth of Canadian Policies in External Affairs, Durham, NC: Duke University Press, 1960, pp. 15, 19.

62 Philip Wigley, Canada and the Transition to Commonwealth: British-Canadian Relations 1917–1926, Cambridge: Cambridge University Press, 1977, p. 24.

63 Allan Gotlieb, Canadian Treaty-Making, Toronto: Butterworth's, 1968, p. 10.

64 Jackson, Quasi States," pp. 64–65.

65 Fowler and Bunck, "What Constitutes the Sovereign State?" 388.

66 Barkin and Cronin, "The State and the Nation," pp. 108, 125.

67 ibid., p. 125.

68 Michael Barnett, "Identity and Alliances in the Middle East," in Katzenstein, ed., The Culture of National Security, p. 405.

69 John P. Schlegel, The Deceptive Ash: Bilingualism and Canadian Policy in Africa: 1957- 1971, Washington, D.C.: University Press of America, 1978, pp. 243, 255.

70 Let's Go Spain and Portugal 1999, New York: St Martin's Press, 1999, p. 19.

71 Gerald J. Schmitz, "Human Rights, Democratization, and International Conflict," in Fen Osler Hampson and Christopher Maule, eds., Canada Among Nations 1992–1993: A New World Order? Ottawa: Carleton University Press, 1992, p. 241.

72 Michael Glennon, "Sovereignty and Community after Haiti: Rethinking the Collective Use of Force," American Journal of International Law 89 (January 1995) 72.

73 Tom Keating and Nicholas Gammer, "The 'New Look' in Canada's Foreign Policy," International Journal 48 (Autumn 1993) 743.

74 J. Taylor Wentges, "Third Generation Electoral Observation and the OAS-UN International Civil Mission to Haiti," Canadian Foreign Policy 4 (Winter 1997) 52–53.

75 Stephen Krasner, "The Accomplishments of International Political Economy," in Steve Smith, Ken Booth, Marysia Zalewski, eds., International Theory: Beyond Positivism? Cambridge: Cambridge University Press, 1996, pp. 111–113.

76 Graham Bird, "The International Monetary Fund and Developing Countries: A Review of the Evidence and Policy Options," International Organization 50 (Summer 1996) 477–511.

77   Andrew Moravcsik, "Taking Preferences Seriously: A Liberal Theory of International Politics," *International Organization* 51 (Fall 1997) 532–33.

78   Jeffrey Frieden and Ronald Rogowski, "The Impact of the International Economy on National Policies: An Analytical Overview," in Helen Milner and Robert Keohane, eds., *Internationalization and Domestic Politics*, Cambridge: Cambridge University Press, 1996, p. 31.

WEBLINKS

Data on individual states' governments, economies and politics appear on the Web site of the U.S. Central Intelligence Agency:
www.odci.gov/cia/publications/factbook

The Toronto Globe and Mail is a good daily source of news about particular states:
www.globeandmail.com

The Carnegie Endowment for International Peace's site includes an address directory of the world's politicians. The site's Embassy Page is a diplomacy database that will eventually have addresses for over 50,000 diplomatic posts around the world.
www.ceip.org

World Wide Government Information Sources. This is a central server for sites of individual governments, as well a server for intergovernmental organizations and bodies such as the G-7.
www.eff.org/govt.html

The United States Library of Congress has an excellent set of country studies at:
lcweb2.loc.gov/frd/cs/cshome/html

Chapter 7

Statehood and Unity: The Challenge of Ethnic Identity

IR thinks of security threats as being external, but in states where cohesion and stability have broken down, the main threat is domestic. That makes for an interesting juxtaposition. Compared to the record of the European states between 1648 and 1945, developing countries have had a substantially lower incidence of interstate war.[1] Far more people, however, have died since 1945 in wars within states than between states, and most of those wars have been in the Third World. Some civil wars such as Sierra Leone's did not attract much international attention, but others, particularly in Somalia, Rwanda and Bosnia, confronted the international community with massive levels of violence and misery.

Civil conflicts affect the integrity of states—the international system's central actors. Successful separatisms add new states to the system and weaken the norm of sovereignty. Conflicts that escalate to civil wars create humanitarian emergencies and have the potential to draw in outside powers. At the extreme, civil wars lead to state collapse. Civil wars have no single cause although ethnicity is usually an issue.

These wars were not supposed to happen. Ethnic identity was expected to diminish as a political force with political and economic modernization, and the image of the future was a homogenous European Union, not a fractured Yugoslavia. Ethnic identity, however, cuts across the categories of statehood. It is present in states large and small, developed and developing, democratic and authoritarian, federal and unitary.[2] Although the largest group of recent new states emerged from the collapse of the Soviet Union, aspirations for independence or increased autonomy affect many others ranging from Canada to India. These aspirations address the basis of sovereign statehood, the international system's central pillar.

There are limits to how much the standard model of sovereign statehood can be reproduced. Nigeria, for example, contains some 250 different ethnic groups. Statehood for each one would yield a belt of micro-polities each requiring its own governing structures, administrations, police and judicial systems, self-defence and base of economic viability. Instead of smaller political subdivisions, some scholars envisage a transformation of statehood itself, particularly in places of high ethnic density such as Africa. At this point, the actual form of such a successor system is difficult even for theorists to imagine.[3] For their part, Third World leaders are resolved to make the best of the states they have.

In examining ethnic identity and the international system, we need to remember five things. First, ethnic differences are not the only reason for divided states. The outcome of World War II left Germany and Austria occupied by the four allied powers and Korea divided between North and South. Occupied Germany became the German Federal Republic and the German Democratic Republic. Austria was reunified in 1955; Germany, in 1990. The cold war aftermath of French colonialism in Indochina left two Vietnams, North and South. In addition, the outcome of a non-ethnic civil war in China left the island of Taiwan in the hands of the losing side and claimed by China since then as a renegade province.[4]

Second, ethnic differences rarely produce violence. A statistical survey of communal violence in Africa between 1960 and 1978 showed that "the mean [annual] figure of actual violent communal events as a percentage of potential events hovers around zero... communal violence, though horrifying, was extremely rare in Africa."[5] That finding is particularly impressive because Africa's ethnic density and arbitrary boundaries make it the continent that is seemingly the most prone to ethnic violence.

Third, civil conflicts that appear ethnically based may not be. The popular notion of the massacre in Rwanda was that it was an ethnic war. However, the two peoples involved, the Hutu and the Tutsi, share a number of important characteristics: language, religion and common clan names. What differentiated them historically was economic status based on land ownership in which a small elite employed a much larger population of peasant labourers. Tutsi was the name the colonial administration gave to the landowners, and Hutu was the name for the peasants. The division remained after independence with members of each group bearing that official designation. Since those divisions were related to political and economic power, one scholar believes that it is more accurate to characterize the conflict as between unequal "status groups."[6]

Fourth, civil conflicts may begin for other reasons such as resistance to corrupt or brutal rule and may draw in ethnic groups as the stakes become clear. Besides ethnicity, in fact, a main cause of civil conflicts is ideological dispute over the way the state is to be governed.[7] Civil wars in El Salvador and Nicaragua, for example, were ideological.

Fifth, practical day-to-day economic interdependence compels ethnic groups living in the same communities and regions to coexist. A recent theory of successful coexistence holds that groups that are cohesive and localized enough to support information networks about their own members will know who swindles, assaults, rapes or steals. Among these groups, an interest in maintaining interdependence makes them willing to cooperate in identifying and punishing members who transgress against the other. The alternative is collective vengeance against the offending group, a recipe for protracted feuding or drastic escalations. Punishing transgressors in their own communities eliminates the need for such retribution.[8]

If inter-ethnic conflict is uncommon, what accounts for the civil wars and collapsed states that do occur? One condition, particularly likely in poor states, is the failure of the government to maintain its control. In Africa, in the two decades following independence, there was enough economic growth to provide revenue for basic government services including police and armed forces. In the 1980s, however, a combination of lower export earnings and international indebtedness forced many governments to curtail services and, importantly for state security, cut back their armed forces. That provided more favourable prospects for insurgents who could buy arms freely on the international market. Together with an "administrative reach" that often was limited to major cities, government retraction left much territory freely contestable to any insurgent forces that might organize.[9] In Yugoslavia, the collapse of communism left the state without effective central authority and with stocked military arsenals scattered across the country. A failing civil control is not determinate itself. Otherwise there would be far more civil wars. It does create the latitude for other factors to operate.

Nationalism, Civil War and IR Theory

IR theory, as we saw in the last chapter's boxes, has much to say about statehood and sovereignty. IR theory has little to say about civil violence and ethnic nationalism, something that several theorists believe is a significant shortcoming.[10] None of this textbook's three main theories treats those two topics directly. Neorealism and Institutionalism regard states as *unitary* actors, and internal breakdown is not part of that framework. Constructivism addresses national identity but as a product of interaction between states, not among groups within a state. Liberalism does focus on the domestic sources of political life and embraces both democratic and authoritarian states, but its premise is a political order that can accommodate various group demands. Civil wars begin when that order breaks down. Feminism and Postmodernism have distinctive views about national identity as we shall see.

Recently, Neorealism's notion of international anarchy has been applied to civil insecurity and violence. Constructivism's basic concept can be directed to domestic unity. Along with Feminism and Postmodernism, these will be this chapter's only IR theory boxes.

Collective Identity

Collective identity is the source of nationhood. A nation is a group of people who share a collective consciousness and feel a common bond. The personal rewards of such identity are substantial. One reward is a sense of equality. Regardless of how class-ridden and unfair a particular society is, people are equal as fellow nationals. The identical graves in military cemeteries are one manifestation: serving the nation makes all people equal. Another reward is hope and transcendence. The emergence or reinvigoration of one's nation can become, through personal identification, one's own renaissance. The nation's future surpasses one's own limited time and prospects. A third reward is escape from impoverished social relationships. National identity offers "rescue from alienation, solitude and anonymity." Finally, identifying with a nation provides a form of immortality "promising the members of each generation that their descendants will care for them as they, in turn, cared for their forefathers." Altogether, ethnic identity's strongest anchor is dignity and purpose—"redemption from personal oblivion."[11]

FIGURE 7.1   Individual, Nation, Transcendence

British composer Gustav Holst (1874-1934) wrote "I Vow To Thee My Country" in 1921. He was strongly influenced by English choral and folksong traditions, but the work's theme of transcendence makes it both personal and universal. The country, "entire, whole and perfect," exceeds human limitation and receives unquestioning love. In "the final sacrifice" one's devotion becomes consummate. "Another country," a place hereafter and indefinite, promises a sublime passage— of country and individual—to timelessness.

I Vow To Thee My Country
I vow to thee, my country, all earthly things above,
Entire and whole and perfect, the service of my love:
The love that asks no question, the love that stands the test,
That lays upon the altar the dearest and the best;
The love that never falters, the love that pays the price,
The love that makes undaunted the final sacrifice.

2
And there's another country, I've heard of long ago,
Most dear to them that love her, most great to them that know;
We may not count her armies, we may not see her King;
Her fortress is a faithful heart, her pride is suffering;
And soul by soul and silently her shining bounds increase,
And her ways are ways of gentleness and all her paths are peace.

Try playing the melody. It may sound surprisingly familiar:

The basis of national identity is a collective consciousness among people that makes them feel unified.[12] Although that consciousness may arise from a number of sources such as language and religion, it is the *sense* of unity that is central. Traditional views of nationalism emphasized the affiliations of language, religion and shared territory. These factors, however, do not always produce feelings of collective consciousness. Sharing the same territorial state, for example, did not unify

Yugoslavs or Czechs and Slovaks. Similarly, being Francophones has not unified Quebecers and Acadians. What is important instead is a perception of unity. A nation is "a community whose members share feelings of fraternity, substantial distinctiveness and exclusivity as well as beliefs in a common ancestry and a continuous genealogy."[13] When those feelings are present, a people becomes bounded and distinct from others.

A state and a nation are not the same. As we saw in the last chapter, a state is a legal and institutional entity of territory, government and international recognition. The state's population may or may not have the characteristics of a nation. If the state's population is unified by a single sense of affiliation, it is a nation-state: the state's territory encloses a single people. If the state's population contains more than one nation, the state is bi- or multi-ethnic. Nation-states are the exception. Of the 185 states now in the international system, only 11 percent are ethnically homogenous, having minorities that comprise less than five percent of the population.[14] Bi- and multi-ethnic states are the rule.

Identity and Statehood

Nation became wedded to statehood in particular historical conditions. As sovereign states replaced feudal rule in Europe, territorial boundaries began to become fixed and customary, governments began to extend their rule and influence and the property of individuals became a part of a larger entity demarcated from others and recognized in rule and in law. As that happened, individuals stopped according their allegiance to "local nobles or family elders" and began identifying with sovereign states, fostering the popular basis of state authority. That development represents a "change in the way in which people thought of themselves and their relationship with existing institutions." [15] The name often applied to that bonding of identity and statehood is **nationalism**. By the time of the French Revolution, that bond was strong enough to support armies based not on involuntary service but on a sense of civil obligation.

The idea that distinctive groups of people require their own states has two important rationales. The first is achieving democracy. The liberal political philosopher John Stuart Mill (1806–1873) believed that national statehood was a requirement for developing democratic political institutions. States with more than one national group in their population would fall under the sway of the strongest group and become repressive.[16] At the same time, liberals such as Mill believed that order and justice are most thoroughly achieved not at the state level but in international arrangements in which states cooperate under some broader authority. Statehood would be an interim phase of political organization, and for further progress to occur, statehood would have to be democratic and liberal. Even so, Mill feared, statehood may not be a progressive force. With concerns being focused on the interests of particular groups of people and not on all people collectively, loyalty to the national group works against aspirations of international authority, which require that particular interests be subordinated to collective ones.

The second rationale is to preserve the community's welfare and its distinct features by enlisting the authority of the state. Nationalists "seek to secure for themselves a public sphere where they can express their identity, practice their culture and educate their young."[17] The notion of national self-determination holds that people require statehood in order to achieve these aspirations. The prospect is difficult or impossible if the people are ruled as a subjugated minority. According to the notion of national self-determination, the "public sphere" needed for national self-expression and preservation is most reliably achieved when the nation controls the state. It is in seeking such a public sphere that ethnic identity aspires to statehood.

By bringing individuals, private property and rule under a single political order, sovereign statehood furnished an "exceptionally elegant answer to questions about political identity—about who the 'we' is that engages in political life." Domestically, sovereign statehood provided individuals with a "primary and often overriding political identity as participants in a particular community." Internationally, statehood provided the connection to the broader human community by dealing with other states on the basis of sovereign equality.[18] An international community of nations could be organized and function as an international community of states.

As we saw in the last chapter, the traditional way of determining the right to be a state was the doctrine of empirical sovereignty: does the state have effective control of its territory and population? States claimed their right to exist by demonstrating their capacity to be states. As we also saw, that doctrine changed radically at the end of World War II when the moral value of national self-determination was extended to former colonies. According to that doctrine, a state has a right to exist if it represents a people's independence. The recognition of sovereignty, as we also saw, has varied between the two principles: respect for existing states' integrity and recognition of peoples' aspirations for independent statehood. For former colonies, self-determination operated at the time of their independence followed by respect for state integrity. For many former colonies, as we saw in the last chapter, empirical statehood remains problematic.

FIGURE 7.2   The Two Faces of National Identity—A Feminist View

Feminists, as we saw in Chapter 5, argue that sovereign statehood, with its emphasis on independence and autonomy, reflects male notions of identity in contrast to female notions that emphasize community and interconnection. Is nationhood also a male construction? One feminist, Ann Tickner, sees two aspects.

On the one side, there is a long tradition of depicting nations as families and homelands as maternal. Home and hearth have both personal and collective significance. Individuals have found an important source of meaning and identification in viewing the nation as family. Communities, particularly in times of war and disaster, have found comfort and reassurance in their feeling of extended kinship. [19] The less attractive side of family symbolism has been separation between public and private spheres with home representing the place for women. Separating hearth from polis provided a rationale for denying women the same role in public life as men.

Not all national symbolism is peaceful. Modern states, as we saw in the last chapter, were founded in war and political conquest and more recently in anti-colonialism. "Defining moments in collective historical memories are often wars of national liberation, great victories in battles against external enemies or the glories of formal imperialist expansion."[20] Because soldiering has been a male responsibility with women performing ancillary functions behind the lines and at home, much of the most vigorous symbolism attached to nationality is martial and male. Women may tend the homeland in time of war, but men defend it. That powerful reinforcement of gender divisions is a principal reason why feminists object to the role of military force in international relations and to war as an available recourse.

Nationality itself is problematic because it is based on the construction of differences between those who are privileged and those who are defined as "other." For feminists, the other is both domestic and foreign: women and minorities at home and less powerful and wealthy states abroad. The solution lies at the core of collective identity: "The insecurities and conflict that arise out of these exclusionary identities will not be diminished until gender and other social hierarchies are diminished."[21] Change begins at the hearth.

Sovereign statehood on its own does not create identity or purpose. It is a condition that makes it possible for states to exist and to act among other states, but it provides no adequate justification itself. Identity can *form* the basis of a state's purpose. In addition to being a shared sense of nationhood, identity is also a fusion of values, understandings and roles.[22] Together, these help define a state among other states and provide the values and purposes for state action.[23] The result need not be limited to a single state: among a number of like-minded states, shared values and purposes can provide a set of "basic principles that define and shape international politics." When those values are shared by the dominant states in the international system, they form a structure of norms and understandings that defines the boundaries of proper behaviour.[24] One of the values that defines Canadian identity is political moderation, compromise and accommodation of differences. To the extent that other liberal democratic states share those values and to the extent that those values frame the actions of international bodies such as the United Nations and of individual states, Canada's identity is one source of international norms. We will see more about liberal governments and peace in Chapter 9 and about international norms in Chapter 11.

The Consequences of Self-Determination

National self-determination, as we saw in the last chapter, has been a powerful political force in this century. True to the Fourteen Points enunciated by American president Woodrow Wilson, the peace settlement after World War I created the new states of Czechoslovakia and Yugoslavia and reconstituted Poland. After World War II, the notion of national self-determination supported independence for European colonies in Africa and Asia. Many candidate populations remain. The world contains some 6,000 different language groups of which many have "dormant or manifest aspirations for statehood."[25]

In Europe, statehood and nationhood converged first through the consolidation of modern states such as France, Germany and Italy then through the construction of new states after World War I and finally through massive and forcible resettlements after World War II, particularly of German minorities from central and eastern Europe. The cumulative effect has been impressive. In 1820, more than half of the people of Europe lived as minorities either in single states or scattered among several states. By 1920, because of state consolidation and the peace settlement of World War I, that figure stood at 20 percent. Resettlements after World War II reduced the figure to three percent.[26] Nationalist movements in Europe such as the Scottish and Basque have attracted attention, but they represent tiny portions of the total population. Much more significant in number have been guest workers, refugees and immigrants from the developing world. Their challenge to the political order is not one of independent statehood but of accommodation within existing states.

Africa presents a much more complex picture. At the time of colonization, Africa's political organization was a variegated mosaic of "clan groups, city-states, kingdoms and empires without any fixed boundaries" that shared many characteristics with feudalism in Europe, particularly the fluid and mobile nature of political authority.[27] One account describes pre-colonial Africa as a "continental archipelago of loosely defined political systems." [28] When colonial boundaries were drawn, as was seen in the last chapter, they passed through existing ethnic and community domains. The result of decolonization in Asia as well as in Africa was a global belt of multi-ethnic states.

Also stretching across Asia was the Soviet Union's empire, comprised of an expanse of Turkic, Iranian and other peoples in Asia and of Caucasian (inhabitants of the Caucasus), Ukrainian, Baltic and Romanian peoples in Europe. The empire's collapse has reproduced the phenomenon of decolonization with residents within particular territorial boundaries assuming independent statehood. Ethnic groups in some areas have struggled over territory as Armenians and Azerbaijanis did in Nagorno-Karabakh, and all of the former Soviet entities contain minority populations, in most cases Russian. A bloody war was fought to keep the territory of Chechnya from seceding from Russia. Given the number of peoples, territories and minority populations, involved and the weakness of the former Soviet states themselves, the amount of ethnic violence in the transition has been surprisingly small.[29] The result has been another belt of states.

National Identity and the Potential for Violence

Although the overall incidence of ethnic violence has been low in light of the number of opportunities, the period between the end of World War II and the mid-1990s has seen a rising level of ethnic violence worldwide with the number of groups involved in serious conflicts increasing from 26 in 1945-1949 to 70 in 1993-1994. (To keep the *incidence* of ethnic conflict in mind, remember that there are approximately 6,000 different language groups in the world.) Most of these conflicts have taken place in developing states with the largest number occurring in Asia. The rate of increase was highest during the middle years of the cold war and has tapered off since the cold war's end.

One possible reason for the lower rate of increase is that ethnic nationalist movements seem to respond well to being allowed greater autonomy within existing states. The states with the most success so far in containing violent and separatist nationalisms have been democratic and industrial. Spain, for example, was able to contain Basque, Galician and Catalonian nationalism in the 1980s by granting measures of regional autonomy.[30] At the same time, in situations where a nationalist movement is strong enough to attempt secession and where the central government is weak or disorganized enough to encourage the effort but still strong enough to resist it, the results can be very violent as the world saw in the former Yugoslavia.[31]

The *potential* incidence of violence may be higher. One study found 230 ethnic groups around the world at risk of persecution. Of that number, 72 live in sub-Saharan Africa where they constitute 41 percent of the total population. Forty-nine of the groups live in Asia where they constitute 12 percent of the population.[32] Because the transition from colonies to statehood is so recent, some scholars believe that it is unfair to judge the new states harshly.[33] As we saw in the last chapter, Europe went through the same process of aligning borders and nations, but it took several centuries and cost millions of lives.

From Identity to National Movements

What conditions transform sentiments of national identity into movements for statehood? There are two views. The first view, inspired by Postmodernism, holds that there really are no fixed collective identities and that ethnicities and nationalisms are artificial constructions. Various influences including political manipulation can make people *believe* in a common identity. Ethnicity is an "identity that [can] be created and recreated anew to suit particular economic and political circumstances."[34] Its situational nature lends it to mobilization around particular causes. Such efforts are most likely to be successful in the face of serious threats to an ethnic group's interests or security.[35] The identity behind those interests is a social construction. The implication is that ethnic identities are situational and fluid and that nationalist aspirations can vary over time in intensity and focus.

FIGURE 7.3 National Identity: The Postmodernist View

We saw in the last chapter that Postmodernism takes a dim view of statehood. What about collective national identity? Individuals to postmodernists have "extraterritorial" identities—different parts of their identities are anchored in different locales. One's identity may have multiple and overlapping boundaries. Among many individuals, the result is multifarious diversity—a "panoply of discordant voices."[36]

Because each individual has his or her own particular points of connection and locale, any attempt to define a collective identity is to "separate out particular identities from their conditions of possibility." Confining people to particular definitions, expectations and rules makes arbitrary constructions out of a rich and natural disorder: "Cultural entities are, in effect, *all* boundary."[37] What those boundaries separate are parts of people's identities. The more naturally diverse a group is, the more arbitrary and fictitious any collective identity becomes.

The ability to assign categories and shape individual identities is an ultimate form of political power. Governments have particularly effective means of wielding such power. The same holds for political elites that construct and guide national-ist movements. The authenticity of such movements is therefore suspect, espe-cially those that embrace wide diversities of people and employ powerful means of communication. By imposing standardized identities and by limiting internal di-versity, nationalist movements practice a form of oppression. Compounding the oppression is the use of nationalist movements to realize the aspirations of states or of elites who wish to lead states.[38] States, to postmodernists, as we saw in the last chapter, are hierarchical instruments of subjugation.

Individual and collective identity make citizenship and immigration pertinent questions. By regulating the movement and residence of people, states distribute the entitlement of inclusion, differentiating between privileged self and excluded other. State boundaries are sites of control, and immigration policy sets the crite-ria of entry. The politics of selection and identity also affect people who are in-side the state but who are treated as other. Multiple identities among the citizenry make inclusion particularly contentious: "... debates about who belongs and who does not, about who we are and who threatens us, reveal large groups of people who may be inside the state but outside the nation, whose rights to residence, family re-union, access to social resources or a job are vulnerable at best... Both the inside and outside are unclear and are fought over."[39]

The other view, based in traditional scholarship, holds that peoples do in-deed possess common identities that draw on sources deeply rooted in collective myths and experience and passed from generation to generation. Modern mass communications make it possible to generalize and elaborate these myths and stories as music, drama and commentary and to distribute them widely. They would have no meaning unless they resonated with deeply held beliefs and un-derstandings.[40]

FIGURE 7.4 National Unity: A Constructivist View

Constructivism, as we saw in Chapter 4, is a theory of interaction. States do not have given or fixed identities. Instead, these are formed as states respond to each other's behaviour and form more general expectations about the relationship. States define themselves as enemies of each other on the basis of interacting and drawing con-clusions. That identity is sustained by hostile behaviour. The result is an inter-subjective understanding of opposition and threat. On the same basis, a state may define itself as having common purposes or interests with another state. Cooperation and reciprocity between them generate an intersubjective understanding of part-nership and shared interests.

States may develop sufficiently close intersubjective understandings that, con-sequently, their identities begin to merge. When that occurs, the states define their interests strongly in terms of their partners' welfare. When those intersubjective understandings expand to a whole range of common issues and when the states no longer treat those issues on the basis of their own interests, they can be said to have achieved a common identity. The best example of progress along that path is the strengthening ties in the European Union. Whether the EU will ever reach the stage when all members think only of common interests and not their own—the stage of political unity—remains to be seen. The underlying dynamic is the formation of a closer collective identity.

What conditions are needed for that to occur? The minimal condition is regular interaction and the latitude for positive intersubjective understandings to develop. Another is practical interdependence in which states' well-being to some extent depends on their actions towards each other. Collective identity formation also requires states to share common basic values. Whether that identity actually develops depends centrally on how states behave towards each other. When that behaviour is cooperative and reciprocal, it allows positive intersubjective understandings to develop. Supported by interdependence and common values, these understandings can lead to increasingly mutual perceptions of interests and, as those mature, increasingly common identities.[41]

In light of what we have been seen about the evolution of statehood, it is clear that these conditions also support successful domestic political orders. Regular interaction is guaranteed by the presence of a state, which organizes and facilitates it. The post-feudal states that best succeeded in organizing daily transactions, as we saw in the last chapter, are the ones that survived. Common values form the subjective basis of unity. A rich source of common values is ethnic identity. As with the development of collective identity between states, collective identity within states requires actual behaviour that supports intersubjective understandings of trust and confidence.

It is thus possible to envisage three paths of national life: An increasing collective identity, a stable and continuing collective identity and a deteriorating collective identity. All depend on the intersubjective understandings which the groups involved derive from their interactions together. A state in which identity is developing will see an upward path of cooperation and trust. A stable state will have a long pattern of satisfactory interaction among groups and a well-established set of intersubjective understandings. A deteriorating state will have a downward spiral of unreciprocated cooperation, increasingly unfavourable intersubjective understandings and an identity that begins to fracture.

From National Movements to Conflict

What makes ethnic awareness become a disruptive political force? The answer is complex partly because the phenomenon occurs across various kinds of states—unitary and federal, developing and industrial, small and large, developing and industrial. Several factors appear to be central although they do not operate consistently. For each case where one appears to be involved, one can find other cases where it was not.[42]

One factor is political and economic modernization. To both Marxists and Western sociologists, this is a paradoxical result because they expected nationalism and ethnic conflict to disappear with economic and political development. Marxists held ethnicity to be a false consciousness that elites fostered to divert people's attention from their economic subservience and from their natural solidarity with other exploited peoples. Marxists expected that socialism, in ending class exploitation, would end nationalism. Sociologists in the West, drawing on the theories of Max Weber (1864-1920) and Emile Durkheim (1858-1917), believed that economic development and industrialization would meld local identities into single national ones and eliminate ethnic differences.[43] Instead, socialism in the Soviet Union merely suppressed ethnicity, which quickly emerged when the Soviet system fell. Similarly, modernization in states such as Canada and Belgium has seen the emergence of traditional ethnic identities into modern political movements.

How can modernization promote ethnic awareness and mobilization? In many industrial states where nationalist movements have emerged in recent years, governments in the 1940s and 1950s, seeking to manage the economy, promote growth and employment and improve social welfare, expanded the scope of their activity through public programs and regulation. These activities, undertaken on a national basis, illuminated regional disparities. As governments sought to address those disparities, they raised popular expectations thereby making the disparities political issues. Where regional disparities also involved ethnic minority status, the two combined to produce demands to devolve authority from central to regional governments.[44] The combination of events served to link together expectations for improvement with expectations for autonomy, blending ethnicity and territorial jurisdiction.

Ethnic nationalism is also encouraged by political modernization, particularly the development of mass participation in elections. That, along with the availability of mass communication, makes it possible to mobilize large portions of the population in support of particular causes. Extremism is countered in liberal democratic states by the play of offsetting pressures and interests, by free and critical news organizations and by traditions of accommodation and tolerance. When elites can control mass communication for nationalist propaganda, when state institutions are seen as inadequate to deal with serious problems and when there is an ethnically based sense of threat or grievance, the instruments of modern statehood may indeed allow ethnic nationalist mobilization.[45]

In states that are undergoing economic and political modernization, the growth of the state and its ability to determine the allocation of resources and jobs makes control a point of rivalry and contention. Ethnicity may be one of the main pivots of struggle. In recently independent states, some ethnic groups may enter the contest with the advantage of having favoured status under colonial rule, which often relied on particular groups to fill administrative and military posts. Under independence, those groups may enjoy entrenched positions. Even if they do not, their previous status may leave them suspect in the eyes of other groups. If ethnic groups do in fact use their positions to direct resources to their own members, they make capturing the state the other groups' priority. Groups that fail are left subordinate and estranged. If particular ethnic groups are disproportionately represented in the armed forces, the police and the legal system—central organs of sovereign statehood—they may foster an even stronger sense of grievance because they wield the state's coercive power with the unmistakable mark of ethnicity. Exacerbating the problem is the inability of poor states to provide the kinds of practical benefits and services that would foster a sense of loyalty and attachment.[46]

In post-colonial Africa, two additional conditions were at play. First, the leaders of new states, seeking to consolidate their rule, paid the greatest attention to cities where the possibilities of rioting were the most dangerous and where political opposition could most effectively organize. In doing so, they neglected the rural areas and peripheries and the groups living there. Second, because these states were formed within set boundaries and because the international climate of opinion strongly supported the states' integrity, dissatisfied minorities could not leave. Because they were stuck within the existing arrangement, their claim on the central governments was weak. Periodic efforts to crush secessionist movements, usually taken with the approval of the international community, made the point clear in practical ways.[47]

These factors might be seen as facilitating conditions, but by themselves they do not account for the personal emotional force of ethnic nationalism. One source is a difference in values between the state or dominant population and an ethnic minority. As we just saw, values are a part of a collective identity. The greater the divergence in values, the more likely is an ethnic population to believe that a separate state is necessary to cultivate and preserve those values. The same is true of wide economic disparities. The wider the disparities are, the more credible and personal is the belief that ethnic discrimination is at fault. Finally, the more that a minority is excluded from the ranks of national government, the more likely are its members to support demands for a separate political structure.[48]

Another source of emotional force is common myths and experience. One important element is an enduring sense of "chosenness"—of possessing some exceptional and superior characteristic. Many folk myths and histories contain an idea of special selection or favour, and these can form the foundation for more modern elaborations of distinctiveness and character. The result can be a heady blend of pride, destiny and merit. National homelands may also be strong anchorages of identity. Most nationalist stories contain sacred or original sites, and over generations these become hallowed and immortal grounds.[49] Particular places can have immense significance. For Serbs, the locus of national identity is Kosovo, the scene of a military defeat in 1389 that ended Serbia's early independence and made it a part of the Ottoman Empire. To Serbs, it marks heroic struggle and martyrdom against invading outsiders. Although 90 percent of Kosovo's current inhabitants are Albanians, Serbs regard the region as inalienable.

These factors are sufficiently potent that any one of them may support ethnic mobilization. Conditions that encourage them are ineffective rule by the central government, particularly a weakening of that rule, support from outside the state, an international climate sympathetic to national self-determination and political separation, and a network within the ethnic community that can serve as the basis for a political organization and the recruitment of leaders.[50]

FIGURE 7.5   Quebec Nationalism and the State

The evolution of nationalism in Quebec illustrates the point that ethnicity has various elements depending on time and circumstance. Until the 1950s, francophone identity was firmly bound in church and private life, and the dominant political parties regarded Canadian federalism as an arrangement that would allow Quebec sufficient autonomy to preserve its traditional forms. The Quiet Revolution can be seen as political and economic modernization where the effect was to redirect identity from church and town to commerce and the city. That clashed with the established economic position of Anglo-Quebecers and made subordination a political issue. The federal government's rapid development of social programs in the 1960s expanded the state's role in economic and social life and raised expectations. Because these changes came in the public sphere, francophone Quebecers came to identify their aspirations with the political entity of Quebec and its government. Their aspirations could best be realized by Quebec's taking on increasing degrees of responsibility. To the extent that required securing them from the federal government, the basis for an adversarial "we-they" outlook was established. That in turn created the political basis for a program of autonomy and a constituency for the Parti Quebecois.[51] It also formed Quebec nationalism within the territorial boundaries of Quebec and included only the francophones living within them.

At the same time, ethnic mobilization is a contest against co-existing identities with the larger national state. The task of an ethnic political movement is to encourage people to redefine their identities exclusively as members of the ethnic community and to withdraw their attachments to the national state's values and identity. This process may be ambivalent and protracted and may never be sufficiently complete to produce consistent majorities or irreversible commitments. The failure of referenda in favour of sovereignty association illustrates the division and ambivalence. In addition to identity and values, popular support may be affected by pragmatic calculations. Potential supporters must weigh the risk that an independent state would deliver lower levels of personal welfare. Since an independent Quebec's actual success in an international economy cannot be known decisively in advance of separation, the calculation is beset with uncertainty.[52] Ambivalence and uncertainty may produce a protracted and undecided situation in which ethnic identity and aspiration continue to support increased autonomy but do not produce a strong consensus in favour of either option.

Leadership shapes ethnic sentiment into political force. Successful leaders are those who can persuade the population to identify with a nationalist vision. In contrast to the economic classes that produce goods, leaders in a political class produce dreams and inspirations. Their success is in getting others to follow even when doing so is not clearly in their personal material interest.[53] Such leadership produces independence movements when a "few cultural visionaries" manage to recruit a core of "political entrepreneurs." Movements take practical form when these entrepreneurs form a political organization to popularize an agenda of ethnic autonomy or separation and when that agenda embodies broader notions of ethnic values and identity. If the organization is successful in gathering support and if it can portray itself as a credible alternative, it may become significant enough to share power within the state or to advocate complete separation. People deciding whether to support such a movement must weigh their attachment to the existing regime, their identity as members of the existing state and the self-interests that may be put at risk. A successful movement will be able to convert divided identities and ambivalence into solid support.[54]

That political leadership may be motivated not by ethnic aspirations but by personal power. The civil wars following the breakup of Yugoslavia had been preceded by considerable ethnic cooperation and tolerance under the communist government. The collapse of communism produced the prospect of sweeping political change. To preserve their positions in power—something that their counterparts in other ex-communist states were not very successful in doing—Yugoslavia's political elite used the resources of the state to "create a domestic political context where ethnicity is the only politically relevant identity."[55] From the mounting crisis of their governments' political legitimacy, the leaders redirected their people's attention to a constructed crisis of threats from other Yugoslav ethnic groups. This diversionary tactic did keep leaders in power but at the cost of unleashing a wave of hatred and violence that produced Europe's bloodiest conflict since World War II. Serbian President Slobodan Milosevic set the tone of ethnic menace. For its part, Croatia's leadership officially singled out resident Serbs. Two of the Bosnian Serb leaders, Radovan Karadzic and Ratko Mladic, have been indicted as international war criminals for their role in encouraging and organizing the carnage.

These points summarize a complex reality. National identity has various sources, and the conditions under which it can be mobilized into a political movement depend upon local circumstances. The important thing to remember is that notions of collective identity may not be static and invariant but respond to particular stimuli and encouragements. Those that appear to be the most powerful are related to a general sense of inequality in status or condition and to a feeling of estrangement from a state's dominant values and identity.

Ethnicity, Separation and Civil War

Ethnic movements contain two prospects that affect the international system. The first is the destruction of the integrity of existing states. That weakens the norm of sovereign inviolability and, by adding more states to the international system, increases anarchy. Breakaway states may be too small or poor to be viable. Because they are new, unstable and used to violence, they may not know the "rules of the game" of other states in the region and create instability.[56] The second and much more grim prospect is civil war. Fought in the centres of daily life, these conflicts devastate economies and societies. Disrupted agriculture and distribution reduce the supply of food; closed or destroyed industrial facilities and infrastructures break down the economy's base. Added to these conditions is personal exposure to the fighting itself. Fully half of the world's refugees have fled from civil con-

Two Muslim women observe a funeral from behind barbed wire near Sarajevo. The funeral is for civilian war victims discovered in several mass graves. The victims were believed to have been killed by Bosnian Serbs during the war while Serbs occupied surrounding villages.

flicts.[57] At the same time, autonomy or separation may be an oppressed people's best hope for improved conditions—a possibility recognized in the international norm of self-determination.

What induces ordinary people to take up arms against their neighbours? What makes the fighting so brutal and generalized? There are two levels of explanation. In the first, particular conditions magnify ethnic identity's affiliations and differences into a malign and lethal spirit. In the second, the logic of insecurity itself makes normally peaceful people prepared to fight.

One magnifier of ethnic identity is rapid economic and social dislocation within a state. This situation may arise either from development and progress or from stagnation and decline. In either case, change creates competition to secure newly available benefits, especially jobs, or to retain threatened or disappearing ones. Ethnic minorities may be easy targets of blame and dissatisfaction. Fully aware of their exposed and unpopular position, minorities in turn may become militantly protective. At sufficiently high and undeniable levels of threat, minorities may become susceptible to "psychologically paranoid reactions."[58] Another magnifier is the political disruption and uncertainty that comes with the breakup of existing regimes and states. Such changes raise questions about the state's ability—or willingness—to continue providing security to ethnic groups. Political upheaval unfastens previously stable relationships of political power providing ethnic groups with both threats and opportunities. In such heightened circumstances, vigilance and security become more important, and threats become more dangerous.

FIGURE 7.7   Neorealism and (Domestic) Anarchy

The main tenet of Neorealism is that states have no international government to protect them. The result is an international anarchy in which each state must protect itself. War is always a possibility because there is no collective authority to prevent it. Adequate security requires states to be vigilant of the capabilities and intentions of other states. If those become threatening, states must arm. Failure to do so leaves them defenceless.

Recently, some neorealists have applied this reasoning to security within states and have found striking parallels. People at complete liberty to pursue their ambitions against one another produce Hobbes's fearsome "state of warre"—domestic anarchy. Hobbes's solution was a strong state to provide security. What happens if a state loses that ability or offers protection only selectively? Just as states do amongst other states, citizens must be vigilant and willing to defend themselves. Ethnicity, by forming citizens into communities, adds a collective element.

Under the logic of anarchy, every community must potentially fear the other. When to be fearful depends on the other's capabilities and intentions. Politicized threats are the most dangerous because they target particular adversaries and raise the prospect of organized violence. In the face of that danger, communities must arm. Failure to do so leaves them defenceless.

Each group, concerned about its safety and having no state for protection, must watch the behaviour of other groups. Two conditions give rise to grave concerns. The first is evidence of increasing hostility and militancy. Such evidence can arise as political leaders, in the wake of a stable political order, seek to mobilize followers along ethnic lines. Their motives may not only be the ones of clinging to power, as was just seen, but of creating new political movements, parties or states under their leadership. To other groups, the rhetoric that accompanies such mobilization becomes threatening when it voices grievances and stereotypes or aspirations for dominance. Militant or fanatical followers may use the agitation as an opportunity to act directly against other ethnic groups. Even though such incidents may be officially condemned or denied, they confirm perceptions of rising peril.

The second condition is the acquisition of arms and military organization. Even though the armed side may insist that its efforts are only for defence, the other side must reckon with the possibility of offence. Failure to do so risks underestimating the threat. Offensive force is not difficult to organize and may depend as much on morale and determination (or hatred) as on the number of fighters and the quality of arms. Small levels of arms and incipient degrees of organization may be enough to send fright into a neighbouring ethnic community since unarmed civilian populations are very vulnerable to attack even by small, informal and lightly armed forces. Groups living as separated islands in a larger population feel particularly exposed. Since members of every ethnically mixed community have ways of recognizing each other, individuals know that their identities cannot be hidden or disguised.[59] Their worst fear is being defenceless when invaders enter their neighbourhood, village or home. Such exposure and fear create strong incentives to organize and arm.

Both the stronger and weaker sides may have incentives to strike first. The weaker side may decide to initiate fighting to fend off attack, secure a better defensive position or capture arms. The stronger side may decide to act while it still has superior force. Since international interventions in such conflicts usually come well after fighting has begun and take the form of enforcing cease-fires and positions in place, both sides may decide to strike early and secure as many gains as possible.[60] Those gains are territories inhabited by the other group, and the purpose of seizing them is to consolidate a contiguous area, to "purify" areas of mixed residence or to establish more secure boundaries. To each side, the divide of ethnicity means that the other side can never become loyal and dependable. The objective of fighting is to remove the other group by terrorizing it into flight, rounding it up into camps or killing it. For non-combatants who are easy to find in the civilian areas where most of the fighting takes place, the result is the horror and atrocity that attracts international attention.

FIGURE 7.8   Common Rights, Diverse Identities

The belief that all persons have the same basic rights, inscribed as an international norm in the United Nations Universal Declaration of Human Rights in 1948 and in subsequent international conventions, holds freedom from arbitrary treatment and oppression to be unvarying and obligatory. We will see much more about human rights in IR in Chapter 13. Here the issue is cultural diversity. At what point does a universal code conflict with innate differences among peoples and cultures? Should respect for those differences constrain the reach of universal standards?

Postmodernists, as we just saw, believe that identity suffers whenever individuals are subjected to categories or standards that arbitrarily constrain their authentic experience and expression. Rights that emerge from particular cultural circumstances, like other common understandings, are socially constructed. Rights that are proclaimed by governments, like other authoritative definitions, are arbitrary acts of political power. As either social or political constructions, rights possess no inherent or categorical moral force.

Adherents of universal standards argue from the perspective of natural law and natural rights. In the natural law tradition, humans derive standards of proper conduct either from a divine origin or through reason. Rulers are obligated under natural law to govern justly. In the natural rights tradition, citizens are entitled to just government. In both traditions, the common condition of humanity confers on all people the same rights and obligates all governments to respect them.[61]

What follows from the postmodernist position? If beliefs and practices are socially constructed, norms and values are particular to time and locale. No state or group of states is in a position to assert the superior moral force of its own standards. Universal human rights codes are merely statements of Western values proclaimed by Western governments. Since any authoritative proclamations are exercises of political power, invoking the universal authority of the United Nations disguises use of that power to oppress local practices. Universal is in fact imperial. We should recognize that human rights, reflecting diverse experience, differ from place to place.

Advocates of universal norms note that the obligation of rulers to govern justly is common to most cultures. They also note that cultures themselves are complex amalgams that contain both permanent and changing elements and that societies are quite able to preserve the traditional parts while adopting new ones. They also argue that societies are constantly changing on their own, and their values change along with them. No particular set of cultural values regardless of natural authenticity is immutable. Finally, human rights advocates argue that political figures who charge cultural imperialism have arrogated the voice of their communities and often benefit personally from keeping practices the way they are. The bottom line is universal: "Human rights mean precisely that: rights held by virtue of being human."[62]

One political philosopher sees this basic disadvantage with taking human nature as relative and socially constructed: "Should I care about assaults on people's dignity or welfare if there is nothing fundamental about the human person itself that can be damaged?"[63] It is no solution to assume human characteristics categorically. "One way or another," the philosopher argues, "we cannot get around the question of what makes us human. Those who opt for a pre-packaged human nature and those who embrace a wholly contingent silly-putty image of human beings make life much too easy for themselves. The real challenge lies in sorting out whether we are dealing with certain rock-bottom fundamentals without which no genuinely *human* life is possible or, rather, with clusters of qualities and traits that the French find desirable, say, but the Samoans find wholly inexplicable and unnecessary."[64] What is required is a "complex orientation toward the truths of universal norms and aspirations as well as the many plural ways human beings have devised to live out their lives with and among one another."[65]

The External Side of Civil War

Once a civil war is underway, it becomes an international event. Sides in the conflict may seek allies and suppliers. The appalling human spectacle often tends to attract heavy international news coverage displaying destroyed villages, hunger and homelessness, and massacres. Because civil wars are fought within local regions and communities and because citizens become fighters, casualties tend to be widespread. The numbers of women, children and elderly in the toll magnify the human atrocity. Civilians who accounted for half of the casualties in World War II now account for four-fifths. Rape, often used as an instrument of civil warfare to demoralize and humiliate the other side, adds an additional dimension of horror. The particular exposure of women in civil war stems from its locales—homes, villages, rural fields and roads, refugee camps. Because of that exposure, women constitute some 80 percent of civil war refugees.[66] Civil wars confront other governments with the decision of whether or not to become involved. These hinge on three basic considerations: humanitarian, ethnic and strategic.

Television news coverage of civil wars emphasizes the humanitarian dimension and makes it easy for people to visualize themselves in the same situation. That sense of common humanity may create public expectations that their governments do something to ease the suffering. The normative dimension is obligation in an international community: to stand aside in the face of massive suffering and abuse is unconscionable. That obligation, as we recall from the last chapter, conflicts with the sovereign norm of non-interference in the domestic affairs of other states.

Humanitarian sentiments motivated major international interventions in the early 1990s into two civil wars—Somalia and Bosnia. The humanitarian objectives in Somalia were initially to provide security for food relief to people in refugee camps who were at risk of starvation. In Bosnia, the objectives were the more complex ones of maintaining cease-fires and preventing further bloodshed. The moral consequences of insufficient effort in the face of such civil disasters may linger well after the fact. There has been a sense of guilt in Europe and North America over the international community's doing far too little to stop the genocide in Rwanda in 1994. Although one could argue that the country's remoteness together with the speed and scale of the massacres would have required a rapid large-scale operation, the consequence was a horrific slaughter. Four years later, President Bill Clinton, during an official visit to Africa, apologized for the failure of the United States and the international community to act effectively.

Ethnicity may play a role in the decision to provide support for one side in a civil conflict. If the ethnic group involved in the conflict has fellow members living in another state, those members will identify with the group's plight and put pressure on their governments to support it in the conflict. Ethnic identity guides their policy preferences. Governments facing decisions on dealing with the civil conflict must heed such pressure because the ethnic community is a domestic political constituency whose support is necessary.[67] In multi-ethnic states such as Canada, pressure from various ethnic groups may politically cancel each other, limiting the influence of any one group allowing other rationales such as humanitarian obligations and peacekeeping to take precedence. Authoritarian governments can suppress ethnic sentiment in the population but must heed the preferences of institutions such as the military and police that provide important support. Some of those preferences may have ethnic elements.

States may intervene in civil wars because of strategic interests. Syria intervened in Lebanon's civil war in 1976 for four reasons. First, other states were backing various ethnic factions in Lebanon. Syria backed groups opposed to those backed by Syria's enemies. Second, Syria sought to prevent the war, which was fought on both ethnic and ideological lines, from crossing the border into Syria and destabilizing the situation there. Third, Syria acted to prevent the victory of either Christian forces supported by Israel or radical Muslim forces supported by Iran and Saudi Arabia. Either outcome would threaten Syria. Finally, Syria had a historic claim to Lebanon that went back to France's creation of the state under its League of Nations mandate following World War I. Intervention would be one way of establishing Lebanon as a special sphere of Syrian influence.[68]

Greece took great interest in the civil wars in the former Yugoslavia because one of the successor states, the Former Yugoslav Republic of Macedonia (FYROM), began publicly proclaiming its opposition to Greece's sovereignty over its portion of Macedonia. The region had changed hands among various local powers historically, and Greece got control of its part of Macedonia in 1913 (see Figure 7.9). Appeals against the legitimacy of Greek rule figured in the Greek civil war in the late 1940s with the Yugoslavian government actively encouraging Greek insurgents and invoking a common Macedonian heritage. Against that background, FYROM's agitation about the legitimacy of Greek rule greatly concerned Athens.

FIGURE 7.9   Former Yugoslav Republic of Macedonia (FYROM) and Greek Macedonia

Shown as a dotted line is the boundary created in 1878 by the Treaty of San Stefano, which incorporated Macedonia into Bulgaria. Greece and Serbia divided Macedonia following defeat of Bulgaria in the Second Balkan War in 1913.

To Greece's advantage, the Serbian government of Slobodan Milosevic was interested in re-annexing Macedonia. The Greek government supported the idea of Serbian hegemony over Macedonia as well as Bosnia and Montenegro under a federal arrangement. At one point President Milosevic proposed dividing Macedonia between Serbia and Greece. The Greeks refused and concentrated their efforts on persuading the international community not to recognize the new republic under the name of Macedonia.[69] More recently, Serb-Albanian warfare in adjacent Kosovo has raised again the question of legitimate statehood, complicated by the fact that a large Albanian minority also lives in Macedonia. The issue remains unsettled. Macedonia was admitted to the United Nations in April 1993 as the Former Yugoslav Republic of Macedonia, but both that name and Republic of Macedonia are used.

Problematic Resolution

Ethnic civil wars are very difficult to settle. Stopping the fighting and killing requires not only a cease-fire but also a commitment from each side to demobilize its forces. Fulfilling that commitment is very risky because each side's continuing ability to fight is its only assurance of survival. Prisoner's Dilemma is of earnest significance: the worst position is to disarm (cooperate) while the other side stays armed (defect). Keeping arms in place is a kind of insurance against cheating. Agreements cannot be trusted because there is no existing national government to enforce them and provide security. While the ability to resume fighting assures protection, retaining it keeps each side insecure and prevents a settlement. Outside forces, even peacekeeping forces already in place, may be too uncertain in their effectiveness or dependability. The situation creates an intractable dilemma: the possibility of one side's cheating creates such danger that continued fighting is preferable to negotiation.[70]

FIGURE 7.10 Is This Any Place for Peacekeepers?

In Somalia, the situation was one of civil war and disintegrated rule. The government of the authoritarian ruler Siad Barre collapsed in 1991, and by late that year the situation had deteriorated to generalized fighting. The conflict was not ethnic in the sense of language or religious fractures, but it was territorial. The groups in question were clans with the largest ones joined in alliances by some 15 smaller ones. All controlled or contested particular regions or locales and were heavily armed. Taking advantage of the disorder, armed criminals added further to the lawlessness and breakdown.

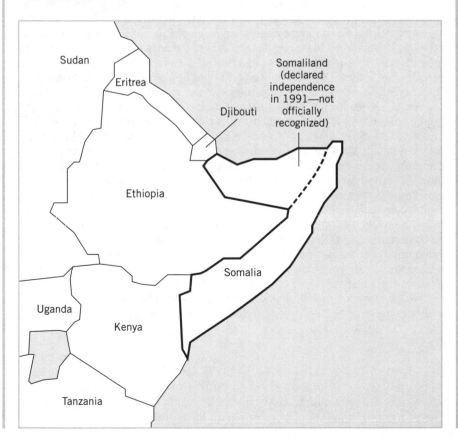

People fleeing the worst of the fighting settled in camps. Their major threat was starvation with clans cutting off access to the camps and seizing food supplies provided by international donors. Clans used the food for their own members and for money to buy weapons. Theft became so pervasive that Somalia's "entire political and economic systems essentially revolved around plundered food."[71] In 1992, the United Nations began a relief operation, and Canada contributed its Airborne Regiment.

The UN's involvement ended in 1995 without restoring stability. Among the participating states, that denouement left a sense of failure and futility. Adding to Canada's chagrin was revelation of a Somali teenager's beating and death at the hands of several members of the Canadian Airborne Regiment. The discovery of the event and of efforts in the senior command to cover it up prompted a lengthy investigation, disbanding of the regiment and public dismay. There was widespread feeling that Canada's reputation as a model peacekeeper had been tarnished.

The experience in Somalia also prompted reflection on when it is advisable to send outside forces into a conflict. Part of the problem was the nature of the Somalia mission. What began as protection turned into armed engagement. Safeguarding food supplies required disarming local clans who resisted fiercely. Losing their weapons would cost them opportunities for gain and would leave them vulnerable to other clans. Even more, because food represented power and money, stopping the theft amounted to disrupting Somalia's entire political economy.[72] Taking on the clans not only made outside forces direct combatants, thereby removing the mantle of neutrality, but also exposed them to close fighting and retaliation. The isolated locations of some forces, with Canada's contingent posted some 400 km from Somalia's main city, added to the insecurity.[73]

As the UN mission progressed with no sign of the clans' willingness to stop fighting, efforts turned to moving directly against the ones seen as key obstacles to a settlement. In a raid on the headquarters of General Aideed, one of the main political contestants, 18 American Rangers were killed, a helicopter was downed and the bodies of its crew were dragged through the streets by a jeering mob. That spectacle, carried vividly by television news, did much to confirm the American public's desire to avoid interventions not tied to key national security interests. The worst effects were felt by Pakistan's contingent, which suffered 24 dead and 54 wounded in a rash of ambushes. These events in Somalia were occurring at the same time as the Bosnian civil war where Canadian peacekeepers along with other UN forces were also frequently under fire and taking casualties.

The aftermath of the Somali involvement has prompted considerable reflection on the possibilities of effective and proper intervention. To be sure that Canadian forces are properly prepared for dangerous and trying situations, the federal government has sought to improve peacekeeper training. Even more basic has been the recognition, in Canada and elsewhere, that some kinds of conflicts are too hazardous for peacekeepers and that intervention may actually prolong fighting. Civil wars, in particular, are likely to generate such conditions. Recognizing that fact has led governments to seek ways of assessing conflicts *before* committing forces. Their outlook might be described as chastened and judicious.

Ethnicity complicates the dilemma. Returning ethnic group members to their communities restores the risks that caused them to flee. If the area is of mixed ethnicity, members are individually vulnerable to attacks by small bands and gangs whose incentive is to disrupt the peace settlement and complete the area's purification. If the area is mono-ethnic but small or isolated, it too remains vulnerable to attack because the surrounding group will have incentives to claim the area completely. To prevent that, the other group may launch pre-emptive attacks. The most stable solution, according to one scholar, is a resettlement of populations into areas they can occupy exclusively and defend effectively. That means massive uprooting of civilians and abandonment of homes and communities. The alternative is continuous insecurity and the possibility that the fighting will erupt again as soon as outside forces leave.[74] A more optimistic view is that resolution can occur through a gradual process of conciliation under a secure peace. In those conditions a workable level of tolerance may develop. Constructivism (see box) provides a model of how a collective identity could form. Successful leadership and fatigue with war may provide favourable conditions. The initial stages of postwar resettlement are underway in Bosnia and Croatia. Whether multi-ethnic communities there can be restored to a peaceful condition over time remains to be seen.

Secessionist conflicts pose legal problems for other states. Under the norm of the sanctity of existing statehood, recognizing a breakaway region violates the integrity of a fellow state and weakens the institution of sovereignty. Under the norm of national self-determination, failure to recognize a breakaway region is a denial of a people's aspirations for independence. A beleaguered group may plead for international recognition as necessary to its very survival, but any expression of support for a group's aspirations for statehood can be seen as an unfriendly and meddlesome act. We saw in the last chapter the response to President De Gaulle's endorsement of Quebec aspirations. For the same reason, the official American position on the Quebec question has always been expressed in this formula: "America's interest is in a strong and united Canada." There is also a practical reason for that policy. If Canada did fragment, Washington would face a string of weakened and squabbling entities on its northern border and much more complicated political and economic relations.[75]

One proposal for solving the dilemma emphasizes the traditional notion of empirical statehood. The basic criterion for recognition should be whether the new political unit provides order and stability in its territory better than the existing government. The principal elements of that order and the basic foundation on which political and economic development could be constructed are the core pillars of statehood: military defence and law enforcement. The standard would operate on an empirical basis and judge each case on its practical merits. In practice such a standard would be demanding because a breakaway movement, particularly in a poor state, would have to be well developed and established to form the degree of empirical administrative control required for recognition.[76] As matters stand there are no clear guidelines for recognizing breakaway states.

Summary

We have seen that ethnicity is the collective expression of individual desires for affiliation and has multiple roots. Ethnicity is a foundation of communities, but aligning communities with states has been an incomplete process. In Europe, a set of ethnically unified states has evolved although through a history of conquests, annexations and, in this century, construction of new states (Czechoslovakia and Yugoslavia) after World War I and the expulsion of minorities after World War II. In Africa and Asia, decolonization left a belt of multi-ethnic states. Although the incidence of ethnic violence has been low, statehood remains an aspiration for many. In many states, ethnic identity provides an ongoing source of division and discontent. Sovereign statehood remains the ideal for full realization of ethnic identity although self-determination for all of the world's ethnic groups would create hundreds of new states.

The conditions that transform ethnic identity into ethnic mobilization include estrangement from the state's dominant values, a sense of unfair deprivation or exclusion and a belief in a common origin and destiny. Mobilization of these sentiments into a political force requires political entrepreneurship and a state that will neither fulfill nor suppress the community's demands.

Civil war becomes a prospect when communities face the same security dilemma found among states in the international system. That dilemma arises when order breaks down. Communities must then be vigilant to threats from other communities and be prepared to fight.

Civil wars implicate other states for humanitarian and pragmatic reasons. The same security fears that led communities to begin fighting make them very reluctant to disarm. Recent civil wars have presented daunting prospects to international peacekeepers and have left fractured states and instability.

ENDNOTES

1   K.J. Holsti, "International Relations Theory and Domestic War in the Third World: The Limits of Relevance," in Stephanie Neuman, ed., *International Relations Theory and the Third World,* New York: St. Martin's Press, 1998, p. 104.

2   Rita Jalali and Seymour Martin Lipset, "Racial and Ethnic Conflicts: A Global Perspective," *Political Science Quarterly* 107 (Winter 1992–1993) 586.

3   Jeffrey Herbst, "Responding to State Failure in Africa," *International Security* 21 (Winter 1996/1997) 120-44.

4   Alan James, *Sovereign Statehood: The Basis of International Society*, London: Allen and Unwin, 1986, pp. 137–38.

5   James D. Fearon and David D. Laitin, "Explaining Interethnic Cooperation," *American Political Science Review* 90 (December 1996) 717.

6   Rhoda E. Howard, "Civil Conflict in Sub-Saharan Africa: Internally Generated Causes," *International Journal* 51 (Winter 1995-96) 34–35.

7   Chaim Kaufmann, "Possible and Impossible Solutions to Ethnic Civil Wars," *International Security* 20 (Spring 1996) 138–40.

8   Fearon and Laitin, "Explaining Interethnic Cooperation," pp. 719, 727–29.

9   Herbst, "Responding to State Failure in Africa," pp. 122–24.

10 Yosef Lapid and Friedrich Kratochwil, "Revisiting the 'National': Toward an Identity Agenda in Neorealism?" in Josef Lapid and Friedrich Kratochwil, eds., *The Return of Culture and Identity in IR Theory*, Boulder, CO: Lynne Rienner, 1996, p. 105.

11 Yael Tamir, "The Enigma of Nationalism," *World Politics* 47 (April 1995) 433–34.

12 *ibid.* p. 424.

13 *ibid.*

14   David Welsh, "Domestic Politics and Ethnic Conflict," in Michael E. Brown, ed., *Ethnic Conflict and International Security,* Princeton: Princeton University Press, 1993, p. 45.

15   Rey Koslowski and Friedrich Kratochwil, "Understanding Change in International Politics: The Soviet Empire's Demise and the International System," *International Organization* 48 (Spring 1994) 224.

16   James Mayall, "Nationalism in the Study of International Relations," in Margot Light and A.J.R. Groom, eds., *Contemporary International Relations: A Guide to Theory*, London: Pinter, 1994, p. 185.

17   Tamir, "The Enigma of Nationalism" p. 425.

18   R.B.J. Walker, "Gender and Critique in the Theory of International Relations," in V. Spike Peterson, ed., *Gendered States: Feminist (Re)Visions of International Relations Theory*, Boulder CO: Lynne Rienner, 1992, p. 189.

19   J. Ann Tickner, "Identity in International Relations Theory: Feminist Perspectives," in Yosef Lapid and Friedrich Kratochwil, eds., *The Return of Culture and Identity in IR Theory*, Boulder, CO: Lynne Rienner, 1996, p. 153.

20   *ibid.,* p. 154.

21   *ibid.,* p. 158

22   William E. Connolly, *Identity\Difference: Democratic Negotiations of Politcal Paradox,* Ithaca: Cornell University Press, 1991, p. 199.

23   Christian Reuss-Smit, "The Constitutional Structure of International Society and the Nature of Fundamental Institutions," *International Organization* 51 (Fall 1997) 565–66.

24   *ibid.* p. 566.

25   Stephen Van Evera, "Hypotheses on Nationalism and War," *International Security* 18 (Spring 1994) 11.

26   Jalali and Lipset, "Racial and Ethnic Conflicts" p. 591.

27   Herbst, "Responding to State Failure in Africa," pp. 121, 127–130.

28   Robert Jackson, *Quasi States: Sovereignty, International Relations and the Third World*, Cambridge: Cambridge University Press, 1990, p. 68.

29   Fearon and Laitin, "Explaining Interethnic Cooperation," pp. 716–17.

30   Ted Robert Gurr, "Peoples Against States: Ethnopolitical Conflict and the Changing World System," *International Studies Quarterly* 38 (September 1994) 350, 365.

31   Van Evera, "Hypotheses on Nationalism and War," 16–17.

32   Jalali and Lipset, "Racial and Ethnic Conflicts," p. 588.

33   Howard, "Civil Conflict in Sub-Saharan Africa," 29–32.

34   Saul Newman, "Does Modernization Breed Ethnic Political Conflict?" *World Politics* 43 (April 1991) 456.

35   Jack Snyder, "Nationalism and Crisis in the Post-Soviet State," in Michael E. Brown, ed., *Ethnic Conflict and International Security,* Princeton: Princeton University Press, 1993, pp. 86–93.

36   David Campbell, "Political Prosaics, Transversal Politics, and the Anarchical World," in Michael Shapiro and Hayward Alker, eds., *Challenging Boundaries: Global Flows, Territorial Identities*, Minneapolis: University of Minnesota Press, 1996, p. 20.

37   *ibid.*

38   William E. Connolly, "Tocqueville, Territory, and Violence," in Shapiro and Alker, eds., *Challenging Boundaries,* p. 154.

39   Jan Jindy Pettman, "Border Crossings/Shifting Identites: Minorities, Gender, and the State in International Perspective," in Shapiro and Alker, eds., *Challenging Boundaries,* p. 268.

40   Anthony D. Smith, "Culture, Community and Territory: The Politics of Ethnicity and Nationalism," *International Affairs* 72 (July 1996) 445–46, 452–54.

41   Alexander Wendt, "Identity and Structural Change in International Politics," in Lapid and Kratochwil, eds. *The Return of Culture and Identity in IR Theory,* pp. 55–56.

42   Holsti, "International Relations Theory and Domestic War in the Third World," pp. 109–119.

43   Jalali and Lipset, "Racial and Ethnic Conflicts," p. 585.

44   Newman, "Does Modernization Breed Ethnic Political Conflict?" pp. 473–74.

45   Snyder, "Nationalism and the Crisis of the Post-Soviet State," pp. 90–93.

46   Howard, "Civil Conflict in Sub-Saharan Africa," pp. 31–32.

47   Herbst, "Responding to State Failure in Africa," p. 131.

48   Subrata K. Mitra, "The Rational Politics of Cultural Nationalism: Subnational Movements in South Asia in Comparative Perspective," *British Journal of Political Science* 25 (January 1995) 67.

49   Smith, "Culture, Community and Territory," pp. 445–46, 452–54.

50   *ibid.*

51   Newman, "Does Modernization Breed Ethnic Political Conflict?" pp. 473–74.

52   Hudson Meadwell, "The Politics of Nationalism in Quebec," *World Politics* 45 (January 1993) 217.

53   Andrew Janos, "Paradigms Revisited: Productionism, Globality and Postmodernity in Comparative Politics," *World Politics* 50 (October 1997) 133.

54   Meadwell, "The Politics of Nationalism in Quebec," pp. 216–17.

55   V.P. Gagnon, Jr., "Ethnic Nationalism and International Conflict: The Case of Serbia," *International Security* 19 (Winter 1994–1995) 132.

56   Van Evera, "Hypotheses on Nationalism and War," 10, 21.

57   Jalali and Lipset, "Racial and Ethnic Conflicts," p. 589.

58   Donald Rothchild and Alexander J. Groth, "Pathological Dimensions of Domestic and International Ethnicity," *Political Science Quarterly* 110 (Spring 1995) 75–76.

59   Kaufmann, "Possible and Impossible Solutions to Ethnic Civil Wars," pp. 145–46.

60   Barry Posen, "The Security Dilemma and Ethnic Conflict," in Brown, ed., *Ethnic Conflict and International Security*, pp. 104–111.

61   Rhoda E. Howard and Jack Donnelly, "Introduction," in Rhoda E. Howard and Jack Donnelly, eds., *International Handbook of Human Rights,* Westport, CT, Greenwood Press, 1987, pp. 2–5.

62   *ibid.,* pp. 18–20.

63   Jean Bethke Elshtain, "Back to Nature," *The New Republic*, August 3, 1998, 12.

64   *ibid.*

65   Jean Bethke Elshtain, "The Right Rights," *The New Republic*, June 15, 1998, p. 12.

66   Kimberley Manning and Barbara Arneil, "Engendering Peacebuilding," *Canadian Foreign Policy* 5 (Fall 1997) 55–56.

67   Stephen M. Saideman, "Explaining the International Relations of Secessionist Conflicts: Vulnerability versus Ethnic Ties," *International Organization* 51 (Autumn 1997) 722–26.

68   Roberet Cooper and Mats Berdal, "Outside Intervention in Ethnic Conflicts," in Brown, ed., *Ethnic Conflict and International Security*, p. 190.

69   Nikolaos Zahariadis, "Nationalism and Small-State Foreign Policy: The Greek Response to the Macedonian Issue," *Political Science Quarterly* 109 (Fall 1994) 662–63.

70   Barbara F. Walter, "The Critical Barrier to Civil War Settlement," *International Organization* 51 (Summer 1997) 335–36, 338–39.

71   Walter Clarke and Jeffrey Herbst, "Somalia and the Future of Humanitarian Intervention," *Foreign Affairs* 75 (March/April 1996) 74.

72   *ibid.*

73   David Carment, "Rethinking Peacekeeping: The Bosnia and Somalia Experience," in Fen Osler Hampson and Maureen Appel Molot, eds., *Canada Among Nations 1996: Big Enough to be Heard*, Carleton: Carleton University Press, 1996, pp. 226–27.

74   Kauffman, "Possible and Impossible Solutions to Ethnic Civil Wars," 147–51.

75   Charles F. Doran, "Will Canada Unravel?" *Foreign Affairs* 75 (September/October 1996) 103.

76   Herbst, "Responding to State Failure in Africa," pp. 136–37.

WEBLINKS

Leftlinks in Australia has links to sites of independence movements:
www.alexia.net.au/~mutton/links/independ

The University of British Columbia Library has an online listing of sources on nationalist, ethnic and religious conflicts:
www.library.ubc.ca/poli/international

One of the research focuses of the International Institute of Strategic Studies is ethnic and civil conflict:
www.isn.ethz.ch/iiss

An excellent site for studies of ethnic conflict is operated by the University of Maryland:
www.bsos.umd.edu/cidcm.
Select the Minorities at Risk option.

Website for the Bloc Quebecois:
www.blocquebecois.org

Chapter 8

Statehood and Unity: The Challenge of Globalization

The entertainment industry provides familiar examples of globalization: worldwide promotional strategies for recording groups; international audiences of millions for films such as *Titanic*; Chinese and Indian editions of *Cosmopolitan*. Similar examples can be found in manufacturing. The foreign content of cars produced at the Ford plant in St. Thomas, Ontario qualifies them as imports. The components are sourced from five continents (only Africa and Antarctica provide no parts), and an integrated computer network organizes their arrival for assembly on a just-in-time basis. Some Ford cars made in North America, such as the Contour and the Escort, share platforms (chassis and driveline) with Fords built abroad. The Ford Probe and the Mazda MX6 not only used the same platform but also were made in the same factory. Working at a higher level of standardization, computer manufacturers use components such as microchips and disk drives that are made by companies supplying the entire industry. Common to entertainment, cars and computers are three features: widespread and integrated production, international markets and standardization.

These were made possible by three related developments. The first, beginning after World War II with the General Agreement on Tariffs and Trade, has been a lowering of trade barriers, which has opened national markets to foreign suppliers. The second development has been a removal of national monetary restrictions, which has created an international market of investment capital and made it possible to finance new production facilities around the world. The third has been technological progress in telecommunication and transport, which provide fast and inexpensive linkages. Telecommunication conveys currency transactions and enables corporations to manage far-flung operations. Transport brings complex arrays of components to assembly sites and distributes finished products globally. Intermodal container shipping is a highly integrated form which uses ships, railways and trucks to provide seamless supply and distribution channels. Together, these three developments have removed the major obstacles to internationalization: access, finance, coordination and logistics.

A more fundamental transition is occurring in the European Union, which adds to these developments the political element of formal integration. Beginning by forming the Coal and Steel Community in 1952, the EU, of the entire world's groupings of states, has gone the farthest towards creating a single international entity. It started by eliminating tariff barriers among its members and continued by removing non-tariff obstacles such as differences in national product standards and restrictions on labour movement. From removing barriers, the process has proceeded to constructing increasingly powerful institutions to administer common policies. The most significant act of unity has been creating a common currency to eliminate the cost and inconvenience of differing exchange rates. Belonging to that common currency requires all member governments to manage their national finances within a set of strict requirements.

In Europe and elsewhere, an equally striking transformation is beginning as regions and cities in neighbouring countries forge their own ties thereby creating the outlines of new international entities *below* the state level. Central governments in Europe and North America facilitate this development by devolving some of their responsibilities. Although devolution is occurring for a number of reasons, which include reducing spending, recognizing regional demands and bringing some government functions closer to the people, it provides regions and municipalities the latitude to pursue their own objectives. In the EU, the cities most actively forming ties pay more attention to each other and less to their own governments.

The Future of the State

In all these cases, the propelling force is economic: larger markets and rationalized production. In all these cases as well, the enabling conditions are connective technologies and the removal of state controls. We will see more about the role of the state and the economic basis of trade in Chapter 12. Here our concern is with statehood itself. The pervasiveness of these changes and the industrial advantages of scale and efficiency have raised questions about sovereign statehood's future. Will it turn out to have been a transitional form of human organization? Will functions that have been regarded as sovereign prerogatives, such as regulating the trans-border movement of capital and goods and managing national economies, pass into either the private sector or international institutions?

Bringing the state into question raises queries about IR's basic notion—the essential divide between the domestic and the international. As we have seen, the state evolved as the source of domestic order with sovereignty providing the authority to organize economic life and to regulate transactions with other states. Evolution favoured states that were able to organize the most effectively. The result was the conception of IR that we have seen so far: adjoining jurisdictions, separate zones of sovereign control and an international system that is an aggregate of individual states' behaviour.

All of IR's three main theories—Neorealism/Institutionalism, Liberalism and Constructivism—are predicated on the centrality of states, and on this basic point they all agree: because sovereign powers are so determinate, the international order prevailing at any particular time is the result of states' actions. As states withdraw their controls and concede areas of decision either to the private sector or to international agreements and institutions, do they eventually become secondary? There are two schools of thought.

The first sees statehood as seriously compromised. Bending before commercial forces, states retain shrinking vestiges of their ability to manage their economies and provide basic supports. Control over money, goods and employment shifts from domestically centralized points in the public sector to internationally dispersed points in the private sector. This trend is particularly troubling to people who cherish the state for the protections it can provide: for domestic industries and culture through control of investment and trade and for regions and individuals through subsidies and social programs. Setting these protections aside makes it more necessary for those affected by international economic forces—regions, industries, individuals—to fend for themselves.

The second school of thought regards statehood as a continuing institution and the current levels of international trade and investment as variations in a much longer pattern. The state has not disappeared although the conditions in which it exercises its authority have been altered. Some basic state functions such as providing public revenue, a legal order and defence cannot be dispensed with; indeed, commerce depends on them. States are also not helpless pawns. They have changed their policies not because they have fallen under the sway of international capital but because they have sought to secure advantages in a changing world economy.

The progress toward a European Union and the emergence of regional integration raise further questions. Does IR have any way of conceptualizing concessions of sovereignty that are significant enough to alter the traditional practices of Westphalian statehood? Even more to the point, can IR conceive of an international *system* of conceded and modified sovereignties? At the end of the chapter, we will see four possibilities ranging from the deliberate accommodations of Institutionalism (sovereign states choosing to cooperate in specific areas) to the ambiguous patterns of Neo-Medievalism (traditional state boundaries blurring and overlapping).

Globalization has been used in so many contexts that it can refer to almost anything that is international and widespread. In looking at globalization in an IR context, it is easiest to focus on the source: harmonization of monetary, investment and trade controls. The internationalization of manufacturing, finance and marketing follows as banks and corporations take advantage of expanded commercial opportunities. What *caused* the **harmonization** is a major point of difference between the two schools, as we shall see.

Harmonization

Reducing **trade barriers** set the stage. After World War II, for reasons explained in Chapter 12, the General Agreement on Tariffs and Trade was instituted. In the half century since then, a series of GATT rounds of negotiations has decreased tariffs dramatically, making goods increasingly easy to buy and sell internationally. Lower tariffs affect both the input and output sides of production. On the input side, they eliminate the need to use only domestic suppliers. Using foreign suppliers is an advantage if their products are cheaper, better or inconvenient to make at home. On the output side, access to foreign markets multiplies sales potential, and raising production makes it possible to specialize and become more efficient.

The first phase of overseas expansion began after World War II as corporations sought cheaper raw materials overseas. In the next phase, they began opening foreign subsidiaries to supply components and sub-assemblies and to produce for local markets. Subsidiaries themselves were not new. Foreign corporations began setting up production in Canada, as we will see in Chapter 12, at the end of the last century under John A. Macdonald's National Policy. What changed after World War II was the breadth and scope of international expansion. Depending on the industry, the advantages could be considerable. On the input side, overseas locations could offer favourable costs, particularly of labour and materials, and on the output side, they enabled firms to operate as domestic producers in other countries. In the most recent phase of expansion, many firms have begun assigning to overseas branches tasks that were previously performed in the home offices: product planning and design, engineering and marketing. Decentralizing is possible because telecommunications provide instant transmission of directives, data, money and plans.[1]

Those stages of foreign expansion required increasing amounts of investment capital that could be acquired and positioned easily. To meet that demand, states lowered restrictions on the international movement of capital and adopted more uniform banking and currency exchange rules. In doing so, states removed jurisdictional boundaries that had kept their financial markets national and separate.[2] Their efforts have produced "much of the regulatory environment in which trans-border capital has thrived."[3]

A remaining impediment was national regulatory barriers to foreign investment. The principles of **right of establishment** and **national treatment**, which are basic rules of the GATT and its successor, the World Trade Organization, oblige states to treat foreign firms the same as domestic ones. States may not exclude foreign firms from their markets or subject them to different rules or taxes. Barriers to investment do remain, and states continue restricting access to particular sectors. Most states, for example, exclude foreign carriers from their domestic transport markets. When Canada and the United States signed an open-skies agreement in 1995, they gave each other's air carriers the right to offer cross-border service between virtually any pair of cities in the two countries (Calgary-Houston, for example), but they still reserved domestic service for their own airlines.

As restrictions fell and capital became widely available, international investment began to increase. The results have been mutually reinforcing. The advantage and ease of locating overseas has led more firms to do that. In turn, rising levels of international production have led to demands for even lower trade restrictions. Those demands come from the firms themselves as they seek to expand and rationalize their production networks and also from governments as they seek to improve export opportunities for their home enterprises. Increased opportunities clearly serve the enterprises' interests; they also serve state interests by stimulating employment and fostering favourable trade balances.

With these liberalizations in place, attention has focused on remaining barriers to investment and multilateral negotiations on an agreement begun in 1997 under the auspices of the Organization for Economic Cooperation and Development. A still further stage of harmonization would be negotiating a set of uniform competition, labour, occupational safety and environmental standards. Those would allow firms the same regulatory treatment in all jurisdictions and make integrated operations more convenient. Compared to trade and capital, eliminating investment barriers and harmonizing regulatory standards would reach even deeper into sovereign practices.

FIGURE 8.1 Canadian Culture in a Globalizing World

Early in this century, it became possible to mass-produce popular magazines. That led to concern that imported American publications, whose price and content showed the advantages of large markets, would drive out Canadian publications. The same concerns arose when American commercial radio broadcasting began and later when American television and cable TV became available. The advent of satellite TV multiplied the available channels.

The Canadian government has had two options:

1) It could allow popular taste to prevail. If Canadians preferred American— and more recently global—entertainment products, that was their prerogative. In taking this option, the state would stand aside from the expression of personal preferences.

2) It could regulate the entry and content of foreign entertainment. Doing so is a state's prerogative. In taking this option, the state would manage the availability of those products.

In following the second option, Canadian policy has accepted the premise that "commercial cultural products made by Canadians differ significantly from those made by foreigners." Because the size of the Canadian market cannot support all the costs of producing entertainment, some intervention by the state is needed. The rationale for intervention goes beyond commerce. Canadian entertainment products have "special properties such as promoting national identity, unity and sovereignty as well as creating employment in Canada."[4]

The means of intervention have been control at the border of printed material, restriction of foreign ownership in cultural industries, subsidies through discounted postal rates for Canadian publications, the power to evict foreign firms and direct government ownership of broadcast media.[5] Cultural policy was called into question in 1997 when the World Trade Organization ruled against Canada for giving postal subsidies to Canadian magazines and for imposing an 80-percent excise tax on advertising in split-run magazines. A split-run magazine is a magazine produced for the American market and transmitted to Canada where some Canadian editorial content is added. The basis of the ruling was the GATT principle of national treatment, which forbids discrimination against foreign firms. Tax and postal benefits, by that principle, would have to be available to all magazines in Canada. The WTO ruling caused dismay in Canada's cultural community and raised the question of how to manage national culture in a globalizing entertainment market.

Canadian magazine publishers were particularly unhappy. Split-run editions of magazines such as *Sports Illustrated* and *People* already cover their costs in the American market and can afford to discount advertising rates in their Canadian editions. Since all magazines depend on advertising for most of their income, split-run magazines draw away vital revenue without adding significant editorial employment in Canada. Canadian magazine publishers did not want direct subsidies but did demand some means of protecting their advertising.[6]

In October 1998, the Liberal government of Jean Chretien introduced legislation that would impose heavy fines on publishers of split-run magazines for accepting advertising directed to the Canadian market. The measure was expected to draw a trade complaint to the WTO on the same grounds of national treatment. As the legislation neared enactment in Parliament, American trade officials made known their intention to get the legislation overturned. Entertainment products, particularly films and music, are major American exports and are important sectors of the economies of California and New York. Although the United States agreed to exempting culture from NAFTA, its general policy is to treat entertainment products like any other kind of commodity and cultural protections like any other kind of trade protectionism. NAFTA allows retaliation against members' actual use of their cultural exemption. The Canadian government passed the legislation in early 1999, and as of this writing the two sides were negotiating the terms of implementation.

In favour of continued government intervention, one could argue that controls are needed now more than ever in the face of entertainment conglomerates such as Sony (which owns Columbia Pictures and CBS Records) and Walt Disney (which owns ESPN, A&E, ABC Television and MGM Studios). Ways must be found to protect and encourage Canadian culture. Failing to do so leaves Canada's market and its national identity exposed to increasingly standardized global products from corporations with formidable market power.

In favour of non-intervention, one could argue that communications technology is outstripping the means of containing it.[7] Satellite TV is just the beginning. In store are ways of using telephone lines and even hydro connections to transmit images and programs. The increasing array of communications media is also an opportunity for Canada to abandon its "inward-looking" policies and enter the global market. The British Broadcasting Corporation has already done so, and a recent initiative has been exploring a joint venture with an American cable TV company for a new news channel. For their part, Canadian film and TV producers are already international in their interests and ambitions.[8] Canadian corporations are also as Seagram's shows in its ownership of Universal Studios and PolyGram Records and its 80-percent stake in MCA.

These initiatives may reach too far. The international negotiations on investment rules, for example, encountered so much resistance that they were discontinued in 1998. One reason for the controversy was the prospect of losing remaining protections for particular sectors and industries. Canada, for example, strives to protect its cultural industries and had them exempted from NAFTA. A new investment agreement, it was feared, would remove restrictions against large international entertainment, publishing and broadcasting firms dominating the Canadian market and replacing national culture with commercialized global culture. In the same way, uniform rules on competition would remove states' latitude to regulate industry.

Some of the areas affected would be mergers and acquisitions, monopolistic practices, advertising and pricing. One group of states that has sought comprehensive harmonization in these and other policy areas is the European Union. Its purpose has been to create a seamless environment for trade and investment.

Two Schools of Thought:

I) States in Retreat

After World War II, governments in the capitalist industrial states sought to play a mediating role between large corporations and smaller firms. As corporations began expanding internationally, their interests became increasingly affected by international conditions, particularly ones related to access to foreign markets, finance and competition with foreign firms. In general, those interests favoured liberalization of trade and monetary controls. Small domestic firms, in contrast, had no overseas markets to pursue but were threatened by the power of corporations at home and by imports from abroad. Their interests favoured shelters and supports. Governments sought to reconcile these two sets of demands with a combination of liberalization abroad and selective protection at home. (More on the state's role in trade will be seen in Chapter 12.) While balancing those demands, governments also sought to maintain the social programs put into place earlier and expanded in the postwar years. This combination worked as long as there was both domestic and international economic stability.[9]

The crisis came in the 1970s when a combination of inflation and unemployment at home and oil price shocks abroad drastically upset that stability. Dealing with unemployment put heavy demands on government budgets just as high interest rates escalated the cost of financing them. Raising interest rates was necessary to deal with the rash inflationary consequences of the oil price shocks, which states around the world struggled to absorb. The combined effect was to limit governments' ability to continue financing the existing level of social programs and protecting vulnerable domestic industries. Given the fewer resources available, the best way to help those industries, it was decided, was to remove protections and encourage them to export. For their part, corporations already operating abroad felt rising pressures as international investment and competition continued to climb.

The result was a transformation of the state's mission. No longer able to balance between domestic and international requirements, states turned their efforts to adjusting "national policies and practices...to the exigencies of the world economy of international production."[10] In so doing, states internationalized themselves. The role of an internationalized state is to adapt to its position in a global system fashioned by private investment: "The nation state becomes part of a larger and more complex political structure that is the counterpart to international production."[11] That political structure is composed of other internationalized capitalist states that join together in removing national barriers to commerce. Less exactly, that structure is composed of common institutions and rules designed to coordinate increasing levels of economic integration and of common ways of thinking that justify such measures.[12]

As states remove barriers and coordinate their policies, they surrender their ability to act divergently particularly in policy areas that affect corporate costs and operations. Competition among states takes the form of attracting capital and persuading investors not to leave.[13] *National* competitiveness is the watchword, and the focus is on creating the most favourable conditions for business. The emphasis is not on trade itself but on removing government regulatory controls, promoting a skilled and productive labour force and providing a stable financial system, all to invite and keep international capital.[14] In a feminist perspective, this relationship duplicates the dependent position of women. Both women and states must "pretty themselves up or rather make themselves highly available and exploitable in order...to attract foreign investor 'boyfriends.'"[15]

Power in civil societies, in the view of British political economist Susan Strange, has shifted "from territorial states to non-territorial TNCs [transnational corporations]." States justify themselves as assisting their firms in world markets and encouraging investment. Harmonization, they maintain, fosters competitive levels of flexibility, speed and efficiency.[16] Particularly important sectors are those that are directly involved in the movement of capital, information and goods: banking, telecommunications and transport. The result is that states have "lost control over some of the functions of [their] authority" and the ability to act independently. Corporations do not seize state power themselves. It is "handed to them on a plate—and, moreover, for 'reasons of state.'"[17]

Pressures to remove state controls come not only from external investors and international corporations. Domestic firms, including small businesses, that bear higher costs than international competitors may also seek relaxed controls. Vulnerable firms have often been shielded from lower international costs by various protections and subsidies. Aside from maintaining often inefficient operations and imposing related costs and distortions on the economy, those measures pose no particular problems as long as there is no international competition. As trade expands, world and domestic prices become direct points of comparison. The pressure is particularly felt by firms that face international competition but that operate under higher domestic costs resulting from various protective measures. The differences show in "shadow" prices, which reflect the true disparity and tell domestic producers how uncompetitive they actually are. The differences become sharper as international transactions become easier.

The high cost of maintaining closed or sheltered economies generates compelling domestic political pressure towards equalization. The prospective benefits are highest in the most closed economies, and it is there that pressures to liberalize will be most keen.[18] The stronger the state has been in its use of protections, the stronger will be the pressures to remove them. There may, in fact, be self-interested political advantages in doing so: "The greater the deadweight loss from a prevailing arrangement, the likelier it becomes that some political entrepreneur will succeed in changing it."[19]

Another scholar, Richard Rosecrance, takes a more passive view. Instead of conceding powers, states have simply become marginal to the production process. Corporations make their investment decisions according to efficiency and locational advantages and have international horizons. For the developed states, that means standing by as production is reorganized and dispersed, often to developing states. For the developing states, it means having industrial growth guided as much by overseas investment decisions as by state objectives. Mutual downsizing is the result in the developed states as corporations hollow out their home production and governments, finding it harder to justify large spending in light of their reduced role, scale-back programs.[20]

FIGURE 8.2 State Autonomy: The View from Critical Theory

Read Antonio Gramsci to learn why states act as they do (see pp. 76-77). His theory of hegemony holds that states rule in the interests of the prevailing arrangement of political and economic power and that hegemony is formed in capitalist states by corporations and their allied political parties. In liberal capitalist states such as Canada, the hegemony is peaceful, reflecting people's belief that the order serves their interests. In fact, the role of the state is to "reflect and perpetuate the dominance ... of the capital-owning class." State policies are guided accordingly.[21]

Internationally, there is a harmony of interests based on a capitalist order. Although there is a hierarchy of states led by the most powerful, the ruling domestic hegemonies in all capitalist states benefit from the exiting order and seek to preserve it. Cooperation occurs because the capitalist elites of states at the various levels of the hierarchy seek to maintain their respective positions and advantages.

Canada's active involvement in the harmonization of trade and finance reflects the interests of its domestic capitalist hegemony, which benefits from Canada's place in the international hierarchy. Acceptance of the idea of harmonization by both the elite and the public reflects the influence of hegemonic consensus.

Altogether, meeting the demands of international competition subjects states to two sets of pressures. On the one hand, retaining divergent laws and regulations makes a state's economy and industry less attractive internationally. States must keep their laws and regulation in line with those of other states, or trade and investment will gravitate to them. Being seriously out of step, through state ownership of industry, restrictive investment and banking rules or high taxes, risks being bypassed by investors unless there is some offsetting attraction.

On the other hand, states cannot discontinue their functions altogether because international capital prefers stable states with efficient infrastructures. It avoids states that lack those conditions and abandons states that lose them.[22] Abandonment means shrinking revenue bases, deteriorating domestic conditions and increasing undesirability. To attract and keep capital, states have to remain involved in their economies. States thus need controls and taxation that are liberal enough to compete with other states for investment but effective enough to maintain stable and efficient conditions. Still, the bottom line remains: states must adapt to the demands of international capital and be willing to do what is necessary. The global position of capital leaves little choice.

II) States Persevering

The other view of states is that they remain robust. States have not surrendered control by harmonizing their trade, monetary and investment policies. Instead, harmonization serves those interests that states seek to promote: favourable conditions in the world trading system for everyone and positional advantages for themselves.[23] States' interests are also not necessarily tied to their home corporations. Uniform monetary practices, for example, make it easier for states' central banks to coordinate with one another in managing interest and exchange rates to maintain stable currencies. Far from being the captives of capital and corporations, states remain quite able to pursue their interests.

Current levels of international trade and investment are nothing new. Between 1880 and 1914 world trade as a percentage of world gross domestic product (GDP) was higher than it was in the 1950s and 1960s. World trade reached 11 percent of GDP in 1880, 1890 and again in 1913. Trade, post-World War II, stayed below that percentage until 1970. By 1995, after a quarter century of rapid expansion, trade was still only 19 percent of world gross domestic product.[24] That percentage, we should note, measures trade as a portion of total economic activity. The *volume* of trade has increased with world GDP, which has grown since the mid-1960s at an average rate of 3.9 percent.[25] As well, trade's increase from 11 to 19 percent of GDP since 1970 represents a gain of almost two-thirds. Even so, adherents of this school would emphasize the relative levels (trade as a portion of total economic activity) and argue that economic life within states is not disappearing in an international tide. The vast portion of economic activity remains domestic.

International investment shows an even clearer pattern. In 1929, international investment represented 24 percent of world GDP. In 1938, the figure was 27 percent. In both 1960 and 1970, it had declined to 12 percent, but by the period of 1976-1983 it was back to 24 percent. From 1992 to 1997, the figure was 23 percent each year. In an even longer perspective, the figure in 1840 was 19 percent.[26] Again, although the *volume* of investment has grown with world GDP, adherents of this school would emphasize that investment as a portion of economic activity has been relatively consistent over time. The interruptions in trade and investment patterns were due to this century's three consecutive disasters—World War I, the Great Depression and World War II.[27]

It is also inaccurate to see liberalization of trade and investment as producing a single homogenous global market. The world economy remains a set of markets each of which is governed by conditions particular to the industries and technologies involved. Instead of a "borderless world made up of a single playing field," one scholar writes, there is a "profusion of playing fields in which different market actors and firms interact."[28] No particular kind of corporate organization, scale of operation or mode of production has an inherent advantage. Instead, the competitive conditions in particular markets and industries determine success and failure.

Corporations themselves are also not homogenous global entities. A comparative study of German, Japanese and American international corporations found that in their internal governing and in their management of long-term financing, research and development, overseas investment and relations with other firms, they "diverge fairly systematically." That divergence reflects the influence of their home states' national institutions and ideological traditions, particularly understandings of the proper relationship between business and the state. The result is a world market that remains plural: the "foundations of corporate markets are not converging" nor are corporations displacing states and political leadership: "National structures remain decisive."[29]

States' withdrawal of barriers and regulations has altered their relationship to corporations but has not ended their role in the international economy. What is changing is territorial organization. States no longer constitute "holistic national economies" with production contained neatly within sovereign borders. Now, industrial structure is shaped by international supply networks and markets, creating a "profusion of playing fields" in which both states and corporations are actors. Competitive advantages on the various playing fields are "created in ways which are not dependent on the nation-state as a social, economic and/or political unit."[30] Whether production concentrates within a single state or disperses among a number of them depends on the characteristics of each particular industry.

Reorganizing production does not mean the disappearance of states. States remain the only entities possessing sovereignty. They may act under domestic and international economic influences, but they still remain the centres of authoritative decisions whether dealing with corporations, with one another or with international bodies such as the International Monetary Fund or the G-7. Because of that authority, some scholars question whether the new context of state action "should be understood as 'internationalizing of the state.'"[31] It is states that control the territories in which economic activity takes place. "Global spaces of the kind formed through telecommunications, trans-world finance and the like interrelate with territorial spaces where locality, distance and borders still matter very much."[32]

Far from eroding state strength, others argue, involvement in the international economy bolsters it. Surveying the statistical data, one political economist asserts that "greater reliance on trade is associated with an increased role for the state rather than a diminished one." Over the last 30 years, the states that have succeeded most with international trade have been the ones with the most actively involved governments. Instead of diminishing governments, exposure to trade has expanded them. That pattern also characterizes developing states. Over the last 30 years, the ones with the most open economies are the very states where government sectors have grown the most. Far from being a disadvantage, "high stateness may even be a competitive advantage in a globalized economy."[33] What explains that apparent contradiction?

The most attractive places to invest are states that have coherent and well-managed policies and economic stability. Those conditions are the results of effective government. To prospective international investors, such states proffer "a predictable set of rules and competent rule makers with whom to dialogue." And even though states have harmonized their rules, they are still needed to administer them assertively: "The operation of the international financial system would descend quickly into chaos without responsible fiscal and monetary policies on the part of international actors... Those who sit astride the international financial system [investors and corporations] need capable regulators."[34] Since these states provide the necessary conditions for international production and commerce, they are positioned to pursue interests quite apart from corporations, both foreign and domestic. The states with the most highly professional bureaucracies are the ones that are best able to negotiate effectively.

It is such states, particularly in East Asia, that insist on retaining controls over industrial sectors not just through regulation but through state sponsorship and direction.[35] The purpose is to guide national industries, particularly in leading or strategic sectors, according to the state's international interests. That determined and active exercise of sovereignty is one of the reasons why trade relations between East Asian states and those with less interventionist governments are often strained. Altogether, in the view of the second school, the relationship between states and international capital is not dependent. States still have significant powers and advantages, and the relationship is interdependent.

FIGURE 8.3   Institutionalism In Action

Institutionalists, as we saw, are interested in the ways states may cooperate to achieve common benefits or tackle common problems. How would an institutionalist regard globalization? First, an institutionalist would regard states as predominant actors. The high levels of economic transactions that characterize globalization are possible because states, through cooperation and exercise of their sovereign powers, establish the necessary regimes and institutions. (Regime is an institutionalist term for sets of rules and common practices covering particular areas of interaction.)

Second, an institutionalist would recognize that interaction and cooperation reinforce one another. As states increase cooperation by forming common rules, they set the stage for increased economic activity. That, in turn, generates the need for even more cooperation and rules. An institutionalist would regard that as evidence of states being well able to formulate workable arrangements together and of potentially large areas of cooperation. Economic cooperation is only one area; others include the environment, scientific research and cultural preservation.

The sum of rules and agreements even in very specific areas can be impressive. When IR scholar Mark Zacher began a study of regimes for international transportation and communication, he was "amazed by the number of treaties and books of regulations that exist for these industries."[36] What these dense accumulations of rules show is "states' increasing enmeshment in a network of international institutions." The network's weavers are states themselves.

What should we make of this transformation? In the same scholar's words, "It is simply quite impossible to deny that international economic regimes have led to the creation of greater commercial openness and predictability and to a strong political order that permeates international relations."[37]

The two schools of thought agree on the rising level of international investment and trade and the facilitating role played by states. The two schools diverge on the position of the state. The first sees states as having abandoned management of their economies to such an extent that they are left competing with one another to be the most agreeable hosts. Unable to manage independent policies, they accommodate their economies into the international niches fashioned by private capital. The second school sees states as providing needed conditions and resources available from no other source: stable monetary systems and financial markets, capable administration of rules and controls and policy-making competence. States, according to this school, remain quite capable of pursuing their own interests. In the view of the first school, the position of states is dependent: international capital sets the terms to which they adjust. In the view of the second school, the position of states is interdependent: their ability to make rules and supply needed conditions puts them on an equal footing with international capital.

FIGURE 8.4   Financial Crisis, Capital Flight and the State: Indonesia in 1998

Until 1997, Indonesia had been regarded as a dynamic and growing economy and attracted high levels of international investment. All of the promising indicators seemed to be present: a large domestic market (Indonesia is the world's fourth most populous state), a hospitable government committed to growth and industrialization, low labour costs and location in the centre of one of the world's liveliest economic regions. Supported by exports and investment, Indonesia appeared well on the way to long-term growth. Instead, devaluation of a neighbouring currency, Thailand's baht, shook investor confidence throughout the region. (We will see more about the crisis of the Asian economic model in Chapter 12) For Indonesia, the result was a drastic currency devaluation, bank failures, massive layoffs, a flight of capital and a political crisis that brought down the president. In this debacle, adherents of both schools of thought can find support for their positions.

The first school can display Indonesia as a victim of dependence and abandonment. Indonesia's reliance on foreign capital left its economy and ultimately its political system exposed to private decisions made abroad. At the first signs of trouble, international capital took flight, sending the economy into perilous descent. Even the massive emergency loan package assembled by the International Monetary Fund, as much to bolster investor confidence as to rescue Indonesia, was not enough. Capital continued its exit, and the economy continued its fall.

In negotiations with the IMF, the government of President Suharto sought to avoid some of the measures imposed on Indonesia's economy as a condition for financial relief, but his position was weakened by the worsening crisis. In the end, he had to agree to most of the terms. As prices soared, employment collapsed, and banks plunged into insolvency, popular discontent and fear focused on the government. With his political base undermined, Suharto resigned amidst mounting disorder. The lesson: the changeable judgements of international capital can transform a state from dynamism to pauperism within weeks. The wages of relying on international capital show in Indonesia's fate.

Adherents of the second school can exhibit the need for competent and honest government. As one of several Asian practitioners of crony capitalism, Indonesia

Associated Press/AP photo/CP archive/Firdia Lisnaweti

Students riot in the streets of Jakarta in May 1998 demanding the resignation of President Suharto. The demonstrations began in protest of the government's handling of the economic crisis that began the previous year.

violated the standards of prudent banking and investment. Instead of lending on the normal basis of risk assessment, Indonesian banks were guided by family connections most of which involved President Suharto's immensely wealthy clan. As long as the investments appeared to be productive, they supported the confidence of foreign lenders, and capital streamed in both as direct investment and as loans to Indonesian banks. The economy grew, and the system continued.

The bubble burst when the currency crisis in Thailand prompted investors to look more closely at Indonesia. What they saw was questionable banking practices, low transparency (reporting of corporate information to investors) and massive corruption. Believing that the Indonesian system could not withstand the growing regional uncertainty, investors who could get out began to leave. The haven for much of their capital was the United States, an exemplar of a transparent and carefully regulated financial system. The lesson: investors will stay as long as they believe that conditions are adequately profitable and safe. A considerable measure of safety is provided by capable and honest government. In leaving Indonesia, investors voted with their feet against inadequate and risky standards.

Formal State Integration: The European Union

Formal integration among states involves not only policy harmonization but also the pooling of government functions and the construction of common institutions. Our focus here is on how this process affects statehood. The best way of assessing this is to look first at constitutions, the legal bedrocks of sovereignty and rule. Integration at that level is a much more radical transformation than economic interdependence because it represents a "structural merger of constituting principles."[38]

The difference is fundamental. Under the Westphalian practice of sovereignty, a state's laws are supreme within its jurisdiction. There is no hierarchy of legal sovereignty, and no one state's constitutional order is subordinate to another's. The terms of treaties are binding domestically, but that is because concluding treaties is a sovereign act in which a state agrees to those intrusions on its constitutional order. When states transfer authority to an international institution such as the EU, they create a hierarchy of legal sovereignty and place their constitutional orders in a subordinate position. Therein lies the revolutionary change.

In the European Union, the sovereign divide between international and domestic law has been breached. The precedent was set in a European Court of Justice decision in 1963 which held that the founding agreement, the Treaty of Rome of 1958, applied directly to citizens within the member states. This meant that the Treaty and other agreements did not require member states to enact enabling laws but could have uninterrupted force. That removed the intermediary role of the state. In the Westphalian order, states arbitrated between the domestic and international. To bring treaties into force domestically, they enacted enabling laws. The court decision bypassed that intermediary role, shifting the position of both citizens and states.[39]

For citizens, it is possible to appeal directly to laws at the EU level. Under Westphalian sovereignty, they would have appealed to their governments, but now EU jurisprudence takes precedence. For states, EU jurisprudence takes precedence as well. Judges in member states hearing a case that may fall under the terms of EU law now ask the European Court of Justice for a ruling. That ruling forms the basis for dealing with the case at the national level.

This jurisdictional transformation is not complete. It is proceeding case by case as courts establish the meaning and limits of EU provisions, and many cases are contentious. The fact that it is happening reflects a fundamental revision of Westphalian sovereignty. For EU members, there is no longer a clear separation between domestic and international law, and the state is no longer the exclusive mediator. The principle is established for a more comprehensive transfer of sovereignty from EU states to EU law and institutions. How much actually occurs remains to be seen.

Even in the EU, sovereign practice has by no means disappeared. One scholar, seeking to determine the actual degree of integration, surveyed four policy areas to determine the level of transfer from EU states to EU institutions. He examined policy areas beyond trade and investment as better indicators of fused state functions: nationality and culture, economic welfare, military security and environmental protection. The pattern of integration is variable.[40]

The highest level of integration is in the policy area of economic welfare in which states are "interacting to define and redefine governance, most often broadening its scope." High as well is environmental protection in which the trend has been to "supplement and increasingly supplant state governance." Integration does

FIGURE 8.5   Integration, Constructivism and the EU

Can state identities fuse? In the view of constructivists, that depends on their interactions with one another. Rising levels of interdependence and a convergence of values provide supporting conditions, but the important ingredient is the development of common intersubjective understandings through successful cooperation. "By showing others through cooperative acts that one expects them to be cooperators too,"[41] the process changes state identities, and a collective identity begins to form. If cooperation proceeds to greater levels of trust and responsibility, collective identities will eventually be strong enough to support transfers of authority from states to a common institution.[42]

As that happens, sovereignty begins to become segmented with states retaining some functions but transferring others. During that process, continuing areas of sovereignty provide a reservoir of psychological security by assuring that the state's "corporate individuality" will continue to be recognized. That security makes the transition to a collective identity less drastic and threatening.[43] At this point in the EU's integration with many functions transferred to common institutions but with others still in the hands of states, the situation can be described as a "disarticulated sovereignty in which different state functions are performed at different levels of aggregation."[44] As common institutions are given more responsibilities, they begin to become part of the expected order, making collective action seem increasingly normal.

This process need not lead to the end of sovereignty. In a constructivist perspective, sovereignty is only one identity a state may have.[45] Pooling state functions "is a way of reorganizing and redeploying state power, not a withering away of the state."[46] At the same time, a state's identity comes to include others by "endogenizing" them, making them less foreign and external. Psychologically, the transition is profound; for people in the EU, accommodating the remaining elements of sovereign identity with an emerging common identity amounts to nothing less than the "re-imagining of European collective existence."[47]

not extend to nationality and cultural policy. Because of the diversity of national cultures and because of the political importance attached to preserving them, especially in the face of growing economic and political integration, states have not only retained their activities in these areas but in some cases, particularly in smaller states, have expanded them.

The area where states retain the greatest degree of authority is national defence—sovereignty's traditional core. Keeping to that practice, EU members have agreed to cooperate but not integrate. The implication of this variable pattern: EU member states still decide the areas in which they will pool state functions. Retaining the largest degree of control over defence and security shows that, where the most basic Westphalian concern is involved, states prefer to direct their own polices and not cede them to an external authority.

Many of the parties involved in those four policy areas were not EU members. In all areas except culture, other state groupings besides the EU were present: NATO and the Conference on Security and Cooperation in Europe in national se-

FIGURE 8.6 European Integration: An Uncompromising Neorealist View

The dream of Jean Monnet (1888-1979), one of the visionary parents of European integration, was that economic interdependence would become so close that war among the member states would never again be possible. That compelling vision supports much of the idealism for a European Union, but is it warranted? May the 15 members never again worry about going to war against one another? One neorealist, John Mearsheimer, warned against such complacency.[48]

His reasoning follows Neorealism's structural analysis. Europe during the cold war was a region in a global bipolar system. War among the European states was prevented by the two superpowers whose alliances embraced Western and Central Europe. The superpowers' common interest was avoiding crises that could lead to nuclear war. Stability between the superpowers protected the Europeans from each other.

Since the end of the cold war, Europe has become a regional **multipolar** system. Multipolar systems, in the neorealist view, are inherently more unstable and dangerous than bipolar ones because they contain more than two possible alliances. States may align against other states in many combinations. The worst fear of states is to have an alignment form against them. The obvious response is to be a member of a counter-alliance. Those calculations are straightforward in bipolar systems because there are only two alliances. Calculations are more complicated in multipolar systems because many configurations are possible and because states can switch alliances. As states keep balancing, the combinations keep shifting. The result is a fluid situation that generates uncertainty and invites miscalculations. The dangers multiply when the states involved have high military capabilities.

Economic interdependence and trade remain secondary to military security. As long as neighbouring states have military capability and as long as they can form hostile alliances, military security remains the top concern. The international system, including the EU, remains anarchic, and states remain the centres of action and threat. The only way of preventing war is to stay armed.

Mearsheimer's advice: Since the three strongest European powers (Britain, France and Russia) have nuclear weapons, the fourth power, Germany, should acquire them as well. Only in that way can it balance against attack and be fully secure. As one might expect, Mearsheimer's advice provoked intense controversy. "Reckless" was one senior IR scholar's characterization.[49] Mearsheimer defended his advice as an accurate application of neorealist logic.

curity, the Organization for Economic Cooperation and Development, the World Bank and the IMF in economic welfare and an array of regional groupings and United Nations organizations in environmental protection.

What do these patterns mean? Some observers see common EU institutions gaining. In highly integrated policy areas, the EU can be quite autonomous: "In [the EU's] thousands of councils, committees and working groups, national ministers increasingly find themselves working with their counterparts from other countries to oppose colleagues in their own government; agriculture ministers, for example, ally against finance ministers."[50]

Other observers see the member states guiding the process according to their own interests. According to that view, states pick and choose which policy areas to cede to the EU and select those areas that will respond best to common direction. Full policy integration requires states to relinquish their authority. The only states that are likely to do that are those that face domestic demand for action that is serious enough to threaten their legitimacy, a fairly drastic and unusual circumstance. Even that kind of demand is limited to particular policy areas and not to the state's control across the board. States under less pressure will prefer to work cooperatively but keep their authority. What option states choose varies by policy area with states favouring integration in some but simple cooperation in others. The outlook, in this view, is that EU member states very much have the latitude to choose and will continue to guide the process.[51]

This pattern of varying integration both within the common framework of the EU and among other international institutions and groupings has been termed "**complex governance**."[52] The degree of integration depends on the policy area and how much authority governments are willing to concede. We will return to complex governance shortly when we consider the future of the state. For now, we need to note that the EU has gone the farthest in establishing common policies and institutions and remains at the forefront of state integration.

Regions

Shared functions and responsibilities are also being forged between regions and cities in neighbouring states. Although the supporting conditions exist elsewhere, the process again has gone the farthest in the EU. It raises a pertinent question: If states have been the traditional basis of organizing economic activity and if the kind of integration seen in the EU results from state action, why is international economic integration proceeding *below* the state level?

One explanation focuses on changes in the way industrial technology is organized. The traditional way (often called **Fordism** after Henry Ford, the parent of standardized mass production) was based on fixed and immense facilities located according to supplies of material and labour and proximity to markets. Since the 1970s, industrial activity has been based increasingly on the fluid and intangible assets of information and knowledge.

One result is that the importance of information has grown in relation to the importance of materials. Another result is that the informational content of work, assisted by computerized data management and telecommunications, has climbed dramatically. A third result is that industrial locations are no longer determined by material inputs. Information and expertise are often more important. Economists have been fascinated by these trends and their implications for industrial organization and development.

The nature of productive knowledge is the key. Some of the most important knowledge is not readily moved. Called "tacit knowledge," it cannot be transmitted through traditional communication—scientific articles, instructions or directives. Instead, "it is embedded in the institutional and social settings of specific intra- and inter-firm practices." It is conveyed through direct interaction. Ideas and applications arise from experts working on the same general problems and in regular contact with each other.

Because tacit knowledge's application depends as much on context and situation as on its actual content, it tends to localize. It is most readily put to use in places where there are networks of people involved in related activities and possessing overlapping or complementary expertise: researchers in universities, suppliers of equipment, engineers in neighbouring firms, consultants and venture capital investors. The implications are directly territorial: regions where such knowledge is concentrated will tend to be centres of innovation.[53] That innovation in turn provides competitive advantages in an international economy. California's Silicon Valley is an early example.

Such regions do not need to be particularly large. In one view, a region must be "small enough for its citizens to share certain economic and consumer interests but of adequate size to justify the infrastructure—communication and transportation links and quality professional services—necessary to participate economically on a global scale."[54] The result is a fusion of globalism and localism: "...despite the increasing attention paid to the trend towards globalization, paradoxically, the new [knowledge-based] paradigm is highly dependent on localized, or regionally based, innovation."[55] How much that potential is realized depends on the ability of knowledge networks to form.

That brings state boundaries into question. Boundaries that separate knowledge networks impede the development of innovative regions. These barriers become particularly intrusive as the ones to capital and trade disappear. One might expect that regional and local politicians, keen to grasp opportunities for economic growth and high-tech development, might be particularly interested in encouraging local networks, even ones extending into neighbouring states. That has been a recent pattern in the EU.

Two regional corridors—termed the "two bananas" because of their curved shapes—have developed. The first runs from southeastern England across the Netherlands, Belgium and northern France through the Rhine valley to Switzerland. The second, termed "Europe's Sunbelt," (see Figure 8.7) arcs from Barcelona through Marseilles into northern Italy.[56] The connections already show in trade and investment flows. In the sunbelt, the city of Toulouse, one of France's high-tech centres, trades more with the neighbouring Spanish region of Catalonia than with the rest of France. For its part, Catalonia's political leaders are working closely with counterparts in France and Italy to forge closer ties. The cities of Lyon, France and Turin, Italy are planning a high-speed rail link to provide attractive logistics. The purpose is to draw in more foreign investment and encourage knowledge-based industries and networks. The significance of these initiatives is that they are being guided by local ambitions and are not part of national industrial plans.

In one commentator's view, integration at the regional level poses an even greater challenge to sovereign statehood than does EU integration at the state level.[57] The regional challenge results from a strong push-pull combination. The

FIGURE 8.7   Map of Europe's sunbelt

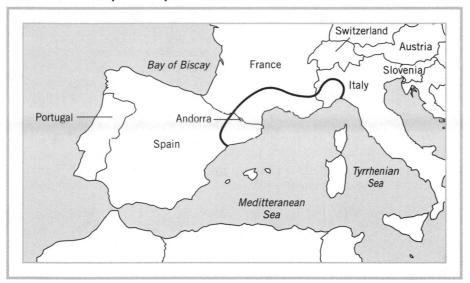

push comes from governments themselves as they decentralize responsibilities to regions and municipalities and give them more control over revenues. The pull comes from global trade opportunities, the availability of investment capital and the concentration of knowledge and expertise in adjoining locales. Together they support the idea of cultivating a SiliconValley in one's own vicinity. That vicinity is defined by resources and networks, not by state boundaries.

FIGURE 8.8   Ontario as a North American Region State

Until recently, Ontario was Canada's political and economic heartland, the province that most reliably supported federalism and national unity and whose industrial base was the national mainstay. A combination of push and pull factors, in the view of Queen's University economist Thomas Courchene, has changed that dramatically.[58]

On the push side has been the evolution of fiscal federalism with Ottawa transferring to the provinces responsibilities that had traditionally been those of the federal government. The crucial move came in 1989 when Ottawa imposed a five percent cap for "have" provinces on increases to the Canada Assistance Program, a conduit of federal funds to provincial programs.[59] That happened just as Ontario's social program expenditures were increasing sharply under the government of David Peterson. The 1990 recession expanded welfare claims just as provincial tax revenues began to contract. Ottawa's financial squeeze, coming when it did, left Ontario with a massive budget deficit.[60]

The disenchantment did not stop there. The Peterson government, as well as the successor NDP government of Bob Rae, strongly opposed the federal government's embrace of free trade with the United States. An irritant to the federal side was Ontario's high level of borrowing to finance its deficit, which hampered Ottawa's efforts to lower interest rates. The treatment of program funding continued under the Liberal government of Jean Chretien, which in 1995 extended the earlier cap on federal transfers and made further cuts this time affecting health care. The move was part of efforts to cut the federal deficit, but it downloaded more responsibilities.

Altogether, in Courchene's view, these developments changed the basis of Ontario's long-standing identification of its interests with Ottawa's. With those interests no longer aligned, Ontario would have to assess its position in a new light. The latitude was there for basic reformulations.[61]

On the pull side is the enormous North American market opening under two additional Ottawa initiatives—the Canada-U.S. Free Trade Agreement and its successor, the North American Free Trade Agreement. Ontario is extraordinarily well positioned to benefit. Within a one-day's trucking radius of Toronto is a market with US $2 trillion of disposable income and over US $1 trillion in retail sales.

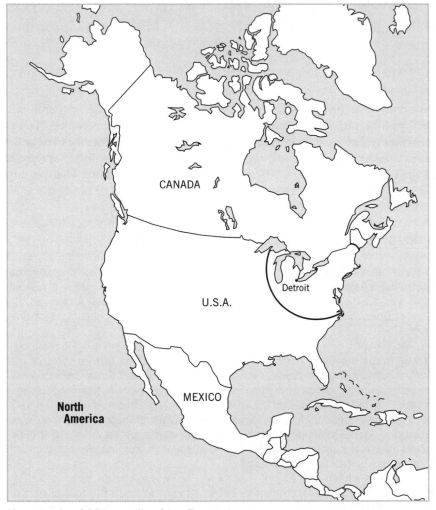

Map showing 800 km radius from Toronto.

The American portion of that market is 17 times the size of the Quebec and Manitoba portion. Because Toronto's location is in the centre, its share exceeds Boston's, New York's and Detroit's.

Ontario is already heavily engaged in north-south trade, and its exports as a percentage of provincial GDP are higher than the levels of the G-7 states (Canada, United States, Great Britain, France, Germany, Japan and Italy). Almost all of Ontario's exports go to the United States, and the level is expected to continue increasing. As it does so, the share of Ontario's trade with the rest of Canada will continue declining. Ontario's trade benefits with the United States are so enticing, in Courchene's view, that the trend is "not reversible."[62]

Instead, the benefits have interested the Ontario government in creating favourable conditions and infrastructures. These intentions reach down to the municipal level. In 1995, the NDP government of Bob Rae formed the Task Force on the Future of the Greater Toronto Area. The task force's final report, which appeared in 1996, framed the reorganization of Toronto's government in economic globalization. The starting point of any reforms should be "the status of Toronto as a regional city-state attuned to the international economy."[63] That view has proved to be highly compatible with the philosophy of the successor Conservative government of Mike Harris although for different reasons. The Rae government was interested in restructuring urban government to improve services, and the Harris government is interested in consolidating them. Both governments "were able to entertain the idea of a regional economy based on export-oriented industries sprawled across a high-tech metropolis held together with new (and sometimes privatized) high-efficiency infrastructure."[64]

One effect of creating such conditions is to encourage the clustering of knowledge and resources in particular locations. Because innovation is based on human networks of knowledge, at some point barriers to labour movement between Ontario and neighbouring American states may become limiting enough to warrant regional agreements probably on an industrial-sector basis.[65] Altogether, "Ontario's North American economic integration is sure to intensify."[66] Foreseeable is a wealthy and active Great Lakes economic region.

Preserving a workable Canadian state, in Courchene's view, requires imaginative and adaptive ways of accommodating regional attachments while maintaining a core of cohesion. The key areas of adjustment are funding and programs. The ingenuity required will be considerable.

Statehood and the Future Order

As we saw at the beginning, IR's basic understandings have centred on a separation between the domestic and international and on states being the primary actors. We have seen a set of developments that undermine those understandings: controversy over the power of the state in the face of pressures and incentives to harmonize practices, the far-reaching precedent of formal integration in the EU and the increasing ability of economic regions to form close connections across state boundaries.

What has been IR's response? At this very preliminary stage, four basic alternatives have been identified. All share the notion of the state as an important actor, but they differ in the degree and coherence of state authority they envisage. Figure 8.9 shows state authority on a sliding scale, moving from cohesion at the left end to dispersion at the right. The alternatives range from institutionalist cooperation at the left to Neo-Medievalism at the right.

FIGURE 8.9   State Authority on a Sliding Scale

Authority			
Definite, ordered concentrated			*Indefinite, overlapping, diffuse*
Institutionalist Cooperation	*Philadelphian System*	*Complex Governance*	*Neo-Medievalism*
Alternatives			

Representing the greatest degree of state coherence and authority is Institutionalism. The intermediate positions of the Philadelphian System (which we will see momentarily) and Complex Governance represent lesser degrees but stop short of the dispersed authority of Neo-Medievalism (which we will also see momentarily). That difference is indicated by the long gap on the right side of the scale. None of the alternatives envisages a disappearance of organized political authority although the conceptions of statehood become progressively fluid and ambiguous from left to right. We begin at the left end of the scale.

Institutionalism

The central actors are states that cooperate to get mutually beneficial conditions. The incentive is to generate absolute gains (making everyone better off). The task is to construct rules and institutions that prevent cheating, provide common pools of information and expertise and monitor compliance. Rules and institutions for trade and investment have been important achievements in cooperation, but many other areas exist.

The more elaborate and formal the common institutions are, the better they will be at providing the information and verification that ensure fairness. Although the results of cooperation are uniform practices among states and much higher levels of interaction, states control the process through their sovereign ability to negotiate rules. If building stronger institutions ends up transferring power from states, that occurs because states themselves have made conscious choices and taken sovereign action.

The Philadelphian System

The **Philadelphian system**'s title comes from the arrangement of government in the United States under its Articles of Confederation and early constitution.[67] In the Philadelphian System, careful attention was given to the need to coordinate certain common functions, particularly defence, while allowing the member states to retain sovereign control (which they had acquired as individual ex-colonies) over their domestic affairs. Central authority was limited and specific and was carefully balanced against the states' sovereign interests. These were protected by such measures as the states' right to keep militias.

Although the Philadelphian System's careful balance and fixed terms allow less discretion among its member governments, its arrangement of authority is orderly and coherent. That justifies locating it on the scale after Institutionalism (because of less discretion) but before Complex Governance (because of greater coherence). The Philadelphian System's fixed terms limit the member states' latitude of action, but in exchange they get a balanced and predictable structure. Some scholars believe that a form of Philadelphian System might be the next step along Europe's road to integration replacing ad hoc agreements with a formal federal framework. If the EU's present practices actually do represent Complex Governance, adopting a Philadelphian System would be a move towards greater order.

Complex Governance

The central actors remain states, but they have agreed to pool some areas of their authority in common institutions. Complex governance, as we saw, has been used to describe the EU's mixed system in which member states retain high levels of responsibility in some policy areas such as defence and delegate responsibility in other areas to EU institutions. Integration is not total but is selective and sectoral. States retain a primary ability to decide which responsibilities to pool and which to keep. The result may be quite discontinuous and disorderly.

Complex governance fits two concurrent requirements. First is the need in some sectors for common policies and administration. That need leads to pooled responsibilities and joint institutions. Second is the need for some government activities to be moved even closer to the people. That need leads in the opposite direction to regional and local governments.[68] The result is a composite: integration in some areas, continuing national rule in others, local devolution in still others.

As governments pool more functions, the balance between retained and pooled authority will shift. With enough authority and time, common institutions can form interests of their own and tip the balance in their direction. At that point the governments' ability to choose and delegate becomes impaired. These institutions, however, gain power irregularly. As they do so, they form a chequered pattern of control. Whether these institutions eventually add up to a harmonious and rational structure and whether that structure reflects the states' preferences depends not on master planning but on evolution. As with Institutionalism, states do make sovereign choices, but once underway the process of complex governance is more open-ended and potentially self-advancing than the case-by-case, sector-by-sector bargains envisaged by Institutionalism. The results may not be particularly coherent.

Comparing Complex Governance to Institutionalist Cooperation and the Philadelphian System is a convenient way of showing their similarities and differences. Like Institutionalist Cooperation, the Philadelphian System preserves sovereign discretion although only in designated areas. And like Complex Governance, the Philadelphian System delegates some responsibilities—but not all—to a central authority. There are three important differences. The first is permanence. Once the Philadelphian System's constitutional bargain is struck, the divisions are fixed and not subject to member governments' discretion. Changing those divisions involves renegotiating the constitution. Neither Institutionalism nor Complex Governance requires such binding transfers. The second difference is comprehensiveness. Neither Institutionalism nor Complex Governance entails commitments across the entire span of policy. The third difference is careful counterbalance between needs and interests at each level. Institutionalist Cooperation is very concerned with fairness and cheating but arranges counterbalances agreement by agreement and sector by sector. Complex Governance is a continuous process of negotiation, and if counterbalances emerge, they do so from particular and changeable conditions. Because that process is disconnected, Complex Governance may allow common institutions to accumulate their own authority, affecting permanence, comprehensiveness and counterbalances altogether.

Neo-Medievalism

Moving along the scale beyond Complex Governance, we find progressively less direction and coherence. The state does not disappear, but its functions become more indeterminate and scattered. The international system becomes a mixture of overlapping authorities and functions. At the end of the scale we encounter **Neo-Medievalism**. Because Neo-Medievalism is so different, envisaging it takes some imagination. Boundaries are a good starting point.

Begin by thinking of two sets of boundaries—of sovereign states and of international industries. Placing international boundaries around particular industries is reasonable. As we have seen, international industries are no longer confined within individual state jurisdictions but operate across state boundaries in international markets. Since firms in any particular industry are joined together by supply and product markets and are operated according to common understandings (that, in fact, is one way of defining an industry), we can depict that set of interrelationships by enclosing them within a boundary. Within the boundary are the industry's producers, suppliers and customers. The world's steel industry can be imagined as a single-bounded entity. The world's automobile industry would have boundaries of its own. This is also true of the world's pulp and paper industry. The boundaries of these industries would overlap those of the Canadian state although at different places. They would also overlap each other—automobiles and steel, for example. A complete depiction would include boundaries for all the world's international industries.

Now imagine a global system that is a set of overlays of state and industrial boundaries. They are easy to visualize as a stack of different map transparencies viewed through an overhead projector. The combined image would be a composite of economic activity and political control with different boundaries enclosing different domains. The pattern would be one of multiple overlappings between states and industries. As long as the states' own functions stayed within their boundaries (as they normally do under the practice of sovereignty), the variable components would be those of the industries. The state system could be represented on one transparency; all the others in the stack would be those of the industries.

But what if some state functions themselves internationalized and flowed across state boundaries? Is there any reason why state governments could not operate some of their services beyond their borders?[69] The possibility is not that outlandish. The Dutch postal service has entered the European courier market and competes with Federal Express. The postal service is now privatized, but it continues to provide its regular national service along with its new international offerings. Go one step farther: Imagine that the Dutch postal service and Federal Express are under an international regulatory body's jurisdiction and are also still subject to their own states' rules and those of the states in which they operate. Some of those rules—governing accounting standards and employment practices, perhaps—may be extraterritorial and apply anywhere the firm operates. Imagine yourself, as an international manager of one of those operations, keeping track of which rules apply in which situations.

Now imagine many internationalized governmental services. Again, the possibilities are not that outlandish. After the cold war, when the international community was pondering Russia's areas of comparative advantage and economic viability, the half-serious suggestion was made that Russia exploit one of the former government's prime areas of investment and infrastructure, incarceration, and operate its prisons as a service industry, saving other states the costs of building more of their own. More positively, we can imagine these possibilities: OHIP operating as an international health insurer, the Canadian mint as a currency and coin manufacturer (it already markets gold coins), Via Rail as a commuter carrier in Los Angeles or London. Imagine the same thing for other states operating in Canada: The Centers for Disease Control providing epidemiological services on contract. Those international extensions of government functions would add additional overlays to the stack, one for each service.

Where do these possibilities leave states? One prospect is an irregular mosaic of state activities and controls, private activity and partial regulation through international bodies.[70] Those conditions sound surprisingly similar to medieval Europe. As we saw in Chapter 6, the medieval system was one of flexible territories and jurisdictions, overlapping political authorities and multiple allegiances. Globalization, in the view of a few scholars, may be restoring some of those conditions. We can begin with territory.

As we saw in Chapter 6, territories in medieval Europe could have multiple allegiances. Jurisdiction and responsibility were difficult to define because it was often unclear who controlled exactly what. Today, globalized production and telecommunication can make jurisdiction and responsibility problematic as well. What is the national origin of a good made at an offshore site from components sourced from several states and designed in still others? Who holds the intellectual property rights (ownership of ideas, designs and technologies) for innovations of international joint ventures? And where in cyberspace do electronic money transactions actually occur? Which state has jurisdiction when databases are located in one country, buyers and sellers in other countries and banks in still others?

There are more puzzles. When states delegate authority and pool responsibilities, they may do so incompletely. They may grant authority to an international institution but keep on performing the same function—or parts of it—themselves. If international institutions, states and even regions all have some responsibility over a policy area, authority exists at multiple levels, and the locus of responsibility becomes blurred. Unless the authority is exactly apportioned and the different levels operate with complementary purposes (as the Philadelphian System's design makes possible), some levels may conflict with others.

Environmental protection invites such overlaps because so many diverse activities are involved. When those overlaps occur, it becomes difficult to identify a single responsible centre. Even within single states, where lines of authority should be more definite, there may be requirements from each level of government and multiple compliances. Domestically and internationally, the governments involved in those kinds of policy areas may find their authority either duplicated or incomplete. Again, the medieval parallel is tantalizing: Overlapping and concurrent authority riddled that system.

Loyalty and identity are the final comparison. If these are shaped in part by being subject to rule, multiple rule will form multiple loyalties and identities. Medieval Europe was crisscrossed with lines of affiliation and obligation.[71] Today, formal integration is the clearest source of multiple rule: A citizen of the EU may be both Danish and European. And regional loyalties? It is quite possible to be Catalonian, European and Spanish (in that order according to Catalonian nationalists). Will Catalonians develop an additional identity as Europe's sunbelt coalesces and evolves?

In a broad historical span, the medieval period was not that long ago. Has the Westphalian state system that followed been an exceptionally tidy episode in an extended and disorderly progression? In search of the answer, two scholars surveyed Mesopotamia, Mesoamerica, feudal China and medieval Italy. They concluded that the Westphalian state system can indeed be seen as a fairly recent and specific way of organizing human activity. Particularly exceptional is the system's clear distinction between domestic and international. Much more common historically are blended orders of empires, cities and clans. "All but perhaps the very earliest 'primitive' (pre)historical epochs have been characterized by layered, overlapping, and interacting polities—coexisting, cooperating and/or conflicting."[72]

FIGURE 8.10 Medievalism and Postmodernism

Multiple identities are our natural condition. The possibilities in our condition are preserved by ambiguous authority, which diffuses locales and power. Identities will be found not within enclosed territories but at crossroads of people and ideas. Open frontiers and indeterminate spaces multiply the sites of connection and experience, allowing a dynamic interaction between self and environment. The identities that emerge may be multiple and contradictory, requiring continuing reformulation.[73]

Instead of clearly demarcated boundaries, it has been more accurate historically to speak of frontiers—flexible and indistinct zones of contact. A single source of government has also not been the norm. Instead, a number of centres of rule have directed particular areas of activity, exclusively in some and shared in others. Ancient Mesopotamia provides a good illustration: Cities in Mesopotamia were economic, political and cultural centres, but they coexisted with kingdoms, tribes, temples, estates and merchants. An overall order prevailed.

Today, the closest example of these overlapping patterns is the EU. As we saw, integration is proceeding in jurisprudence and in a number of policy areas. At the same time, member states are retaining some authority and localizing still others. Concurrent to that is the integration between EU cities and regions. How does that pattern look in the light of history? The parallels, the two scholars concluded, are too *limited*: "There is no historical model that can do justice to the patterns of authority taking shape in modern Europe." [74] What can we expect for other states? Again, the two scholars: "History contradicts assumptions about the universality, exclusivity or permanence of any polity. The record reveals the presence of constant pressure both toward larger and more inclusive polities and the fracturing of existing polities."[75] We shall see.

Summary

We have seen that economic forces can have a powerful effect on statehood. With technology providing the means of organizing production across national boundaries and with trade and monetary agreements providing the latitude, the economic role of the state has come into question. Those who view the state as seriously compromised in its ability to manage its economy and regulate its domestic life place emphasis on the independent position of international capital and the competition among states to attract and keep investment. Losing investment or being ignored by capital costs jobs and economic welfare. Those who view the state as robust emphasize the conditions that only effective states can provide: legal and monetary systems, economic regulation and capable public management. Those conditions are at least as important in attracting capital and are best exercised by competent states.

The European Union is evolving into a complex political order as it removes barriers among its member states and expands common institutions. A principal purpose for doing so has been to create a seamless single market. In the process, states have kept some areas of authority and ceded others to the EU. At the regional level, cities are forming their own economic networks across national boundaries, producing a parallel set of connective relationships. No one can yet say what the EU's eventual structure will be. At present it is dynamic and evolving.

A challenge for IR is to imagine the organizational forms that follow from increased interdependence among states. It is helpful to see the possibilities along a continuum with the most moderate possibility being represented by Institutionalism and the most open-ended and exotic possibility being represented by Neo-Medievalism. How statehood evolves in the next decades will be fascinating to observe.

ENDNOTES

1   Neil Richardson, "International Trade as a Force for Peace," in Charles W. Kegley, Jr., ed., *Controversies in International Relations Theory: Realism and the Neoliberal Challenge*, New York: St. Martin's Press, 1995, p. 287.

2   Gilbert Winham, "International Trade in a Globalizing Environment," *International Journal* 51 (Autumn 1996) 640.

3   Jan Aart Scholte, "Global Capitalism and the State," *International Affairs* 73 (July 1997) 432.

4   Keith Acheson and Christopher J. Maule, "Canada's Cultural Policies: You Can't Have It Both Ways," *Canadian Foreign Policy* 4 (Winter 1997) 66.

5   *ibid.,* pp. 67–68.

6   Southam Newspapers, September 15, 1998

7   Keith Acheson and Christopher J. Maule, "Is There Life after Deathstars? Communications Technology and Cultural Relations," in Fen Osler Hampson and Maureen Appel Molot, eds., *Canada Among Nations 1996: Big Enough to Be Heard*, Ottawa: Carleton University Press, 1996, p. 101.

8   *ibid.*, pp. 108–09.

9   Robert W. Cox, *Production, Power, and World Order: Social Forces in the Making of History*, New York: Columbia University Press, 1987, pp. 219–30.

10 *ibid.,*p. 253.

11 *ibid.*

12 Randall D. Germain and Michael Kenny, "Engaging Gramsci: International Relations Theory and the New Gramscians," *Review of International Studies* 24 (Jaunary 1998) 16.

13 Joachim Hirsch, "Globalization of Capital, Nation-States, and Democracy," *Studies in Political Economy* 54 (Fall 1997) 45.

14 Vincent Cable, "The Diminished Nation-State: A Study in the Loss of Economic Power," *Daedalus* 124 (Spring 1995) 32.

15 Anne Sisson Runyan, "The Places of Women in Trading Places: Gendered Global/Regional Regimes and Inter-nationalized Feminist Resistance," in Elonore Kofman and Gillian Youngs, eds., *Globalization: Theory and Practice*, London: Pinter 1996, pp. 238–39.

16 Susan Strange, *The Retreat of the State: The Diffusion of Power in the World Economy,* Cambridge: Cambridge University Press, 1996, pp. 42–43, 79.

17 *ibid.,* p. 45.

18 Jeffrey Frieden and Ronald Rogowski, "The Impact of the International Economy on National Policies: An Analytical Overview," in Helen Milner and Robert Keohane, eds., *Internationalization and Domestic Politics,* Cambridge: Cambridge University Press, 1996, pp. 32–34.

19 *ibid.*, p. 43.

20 Richard Rosecrance, "The Rise of the Virtual State," *Foreign Affairs* 75 (July/August 1996) 45–62.

21 Mark Neufeld, "Canadian Foreign Policy and Hegemonic Order," *Studies in Political Economy* 48 (Fall 1995) 11.

22 Philip Cerny, "Globalization and the Changing Logic of Collective Action," *International Organization* 49 (Fall 1995) 620.

23 Eric Helleiner, *States and the Reemergence of Global Finance: From Bretton Woods to the 1990s,* Ithaca: Cornell University Press, 1994, pp. 18–19.

24 *Statistical Yearbook 1995,* New York: United Nations, 1997, pp. 159–176, 706.

25 *World Economic Outlook May 1998,* Washington, D.C.: International Monetary Fund, 1998, p. 145; *World Economic Outlook April 1985,* Washington, D.C., International Monetary Fund 1985, p. 205.

26 Janice Thomson and Stephen Krasner, "Global Transactions and the Colsolidation of Sovereignty," in Ernst-Otto Czempiel and James N. Rosenau, eds., *Global Changes and Theoretical Challenges,* Lexington, MA: Lexington Books, 1989, pp. 199, 201; *World Economic Outlook May 1998,* p. 214.

27 *ibid.*

28 Philip Cerny, "Globalization and Other Stories: The Search for a New Paradigm for International Relations," *International Journal* 51 (Autumn 1996) 628.

29 Louis W. Pauley and Simon Reich, "National Structures and Multinational Corporate Behavior: Enduring Differences in the Age of Globalization," *International Organization* 51 (Winter 1997) 1–2, 5.

30 Cerny, "Globalization and Other Stories," p. 626.

31 Germain and Kenny, "Engaging Gramsci," p. 16.

32 Scholte, "Global Capitalism and the State," p. 442.

33 Peter Evans, "The Eclipse of the State: Reflections on Stateness in an Era of Globalization," *World Politics* 50 (October 1997) 67–69.

34 *ibid.*, pp. 70, 72.

35 Sylvia Ostry, "Globalization and the Nation State," in Thomas J. Courchene, ed., *The Nation State in a Global/Information Era: Policy Challenges,* Kingston: John Deutsch Institute for the Study of Economic Policy, 1997, pp. 62–63.

36 Mark W. Zacher with Brent A. Sutton, *Governing Global Networks: International Regimes for Transportation and Communication,* Cambridge: Cambridge University Press, 1996.

37 Mark W. Zacher, "The Global Economy and the International Political Order," in Courchene, ed., *The Nation State in a Global/Information Era,* p. 75.

38 James A. Caporaso, "Across the Great Divide: Integrating Comparative and International Politics," *International Studies Quarterly* 41 (December 1997) 580.

39 *ibid.*, p. 583.

40 Barry B. Hughes, "Evolving Patterns of European Integration and Governance: Implications for Theories of World Politics," in Kegley, ed., *Controversies in International Relations Theory,* p. 239.

41 Alexander Wendt, "Collective Identity Formation and the International State," *American Political Science Review* 88 (June 1994) 390

42 *ibid.*

43 *ibid.*, p. 388.

44 *ibid.*, p. 393

45 *ibid.*

46 Alexander Wendt, "Identity and Structural Change in International Politics," in Josef Lapid and Friedrich Kratochwil, eds., *The Return of Culture and Identity in IR Theory,* Boulder, CO: Lynne Rienner, 1996, p. 61.

47 John Gerard Ruggie, "Territoriality and Beyond: Problematizing Modernity in International Relations," *International Organization* 47 (Winter 1993) 172.

48 John J. Mearsheimer, "Back to the Future: Instability in Europe After the Cold War," *International Security* 15 (Summer 1990) 5–56.

49 Ole R. Holsti, "Theories of International Relations and Foreign Policy: Realism and its Challengers," in Kegley, ed., *Controversies in International Relations Theory*, p. 58.

50 Jessica Matthews, "Power Shift," *Foreign Affairs* 75 (January/February 1997) 61.

51 Mehmet Ugur, "State-Society Interaction and European Integration: A Political Economy Approach to the Dynamics and Policy-Making of the European Union," *Review of International Studies* 23 (October 1997) 483.

52 Hughes, "Evolving Patterns of European Integration and Governance," p. 229

53 David A. Wolfe, "The Emergence of the Region State," in Courchene, ed., *The Nation State in a Global/Information Era*, p. 221–24.

54 Kenichi Ohmae, "The Rise of the Region State," *Foreign Affairs* 72 (Spring 1993) 80.

55 Wolfe, "The Emergence of the Region State," p. 224.

56 John Newhouse, "Europe's Rising Regionalism," *Foreign Affairs* 76 (January/February 1997) 69.

57 *ibid.*, p. 84.

58 Thomas J. Courchene with Colin R. Telmer, *From Heartland to North American Region State: The Social, Fiscal and Federal Evolution of Ontario*, Toronto: University of Toronto Centre for Public Management, 1998.

59 *ibid.*, p. 78

60 *ibid.*, pp. 102–103

61 *ibid.*, p. 163.

62 *ibid.*, pp. 280–81.

63 Graham Todd, "Megacity: Globalization and Governance in Toronto," *Studies in Political Economy* 56 (Summer 1998) 194.

64 *ibid.*, p. 194.

65 Courchene and Telmer, *From Heartland*, p. 292.

66 *ibid.*, p. 281.

67 Daniel Deudney, "The Philadelphian System: Sovereignty, Arms Control, and Balance of Power in the American States-Union, Circa 1797-1861," *International Organization* 49 (Spring 1995) 191–228.

68 Hughes, "Evolving Patterns of European Integration and Governance," pp. 227–29.

69 David Elkins, *Beyond Sovereignty: Territory and Political Economy in the Twenty-First Century,* Toronto: University of Toronto Press, 1995, p. 126.

70 Cerny, "Globalization and the Changing Logic of Collective Action," 621.

71 Stephen J. Kobrin, "Back to the Future: Neomedievalism and the Postmodern Digital World Economy," *Journal of International Affairs* 51 (Spring 1998) 367–76.

72 Yale Ferguson and Richard Mansbach, "The Past as Prelude to the Future? Identities and Loyalties in Global Politics," in Yosef Lapid and Friedrich Kratochwil, eds., *The Return of Culture and Identity in IR Theory*, Boulder, CO: Lynne Rienner, 1996, pp. 22–23.

73 V. Spike Peterson, "Shifting Ground(s): Epistemological and Territorial Remapping in the Context of Globalization," in Kofman and Youngs, eds., *Globalization: Theory and Practice,* p. 12

74 Ferguson and Mansbach, "The Past as Prelude to the Future?". p. 32.

75 *ibid.*, p. 34.

WEBLINKS

The C.D. Howe Institute lists studies on Canadian political economy and trade and provides links to sites of other public policy institutes:
www.cdhowe.org

The site of the Council of Canadians, which opposes economic integration, is:
www.canadians.org

The site of the European Union is:
www.eurunion.org.
The site has links to member governments and issue groups.

The Eurocurrency site, with links to related governments and institutions, is:
www.King.ac.uk/~en_soo7/euro/eurolink

The site of the Organization for Economic Cooperation and Development, a research and coordinating body of the industrial countries, is:
www.oecd.org

Chapter (9)

Government and Foreign Policy

Why do states act as they do? This is an important question because states are the international system's primary figures. The system's condition at any particular time depends on what actions states choose to take. What shapes those choices? Two basic approaches have dominated the thinking in IR. The first, which we can call outside-in, looks to conditions external to the state. States rationally adapt to those conditions. The second, which we can call inside-out, looks to conditions within the state. States behave according to the interests and preferences generated by their domestic politics. In recent years, many IR scholars have recognized that neither approach is adequate by itself and have sought ways of melding the two. We can call that a fusion approach. To get a full view of state behaviour, it is worthwhile to see what constitutes both the outside-in and inside-out approaches. We will then look at what a fusion approach involves.

Outside-In: Conflict and Cooperation

The outside-in approach is exemplified by Neorealism. As we saw in Chapter 2, neorealists believe that anarchy is the international system's prime fact. Since there is no central authority to maintain order and since there is nothing to restrain states from aggressing on each other, security is every state's main concern. Regarding states themselves, Neorealism makes two crucial assumptions. The first is that all are alike in being sovereign and in sharing the need to act successfully in anarchic surroundings. The second is that all act rationally. What shapes states' actions is the arrangement of capabilities, particularly military, in the system. By knowing any individual state's position in the system, by knowing the arrangement of capabilities facing it and by assuming rational behaviour, it is possible to understand what the state does.

The cold war gives a good example of neorealist explanations of state behaviour. The arrangement of state capabilities during the cold war was **bipolar**—the Soviet Union and the United States had the greatest military strength. They constituted the system's two centres—or poles. Because of that cardinal fact, their relationship was inherently antagonistic. The determining influence was the arrangement of capabilities. The logic is expressed in these words: "Athens and Sparta, or the United States and the Soviet Union, [were] doomed to compete and to resist any substantial accretion to the other's power. To fail to compete [was] to risk the death of sovereignty or death itself."[1]

To see the basis for such a sweeping statement, remember Neorealism's basic tenets: in an anarchic system, there is no central power to protect states, and they must rely on themselves for security. When capabilities are concentrated in only two states, each one must fear any gain by the other. The temptation to exploit any gain gives both sides reason to be vigilant. Each one must pay close attention to the other's capabilities and match any gains. Failure to do so leads to a dangerous imbalance. The same is more broadly true of economic and political capability as these may be converted into military advantages. The bottom line: the two major states in a bipolar system will always be adversaries. The two sides' behaviour is a rational response to their position in the system and to the overriding importance of security. One needs only to look to the arrangement of capabilities.

Because maintaining a balance was so clearly necessary, neorealists believed that cold war bipolarity was actually a stable system. With the system centred on two key states, there was no room for alignments that did not include them. That made for simplicity and predictability. Nuclear weapons, in the view of some neorealists, provided another basis of bipolar stability by raising the costs of warfare to unacceptable levels.[2] As we saw in the last chapter, some neorealists also believe that post-cold war Europe will be less stable because bipolarity has given way to multipolarity and to more complex and changeable possibilities of alignment. Not all neorealists agree. One prominent scholar argues that bipolar systems are "extremely dangerous" because they create a stark win-lose situation. In those settings, neither side can allow the other to gain even a small advantage. Such vigilance encourages overreactions and crises.[3]

That disagreement aside, the attraction of Neorealism's outside-in approach is that state behaviour can be explained without having to look inside the states themselves. (The disagreement we just saw is over the influence of the *system*.) All that is required is the assumption that states behave rationally in light of their interests in security and in light of the capabilities facing them from other states. To understand the behaviour of states, focus on the system.

Is doing so an advantage? It is indeed. The best theories are those which are economical—or parsimonious, to use the formal term. A parsimonious theory can explain a phenomenon with a few factors. If that explanation is as accurate as one based on many factors, the parsimonious theory is clearly best. Using it saves time and effort and gets the same result. For neorealists, that means leaving out factors within states and focusing on the international system. "The most parsimonious explanation of a country's foreign policy behaviour is not found in the psychology of its leaders, its regime type or its political ideology. Instead, it is located in the relative position of the state in the anarchic international system as measured by its capabilities—its capacity for independent action."[4] As we saw in Chapter 2, a universal and parsimonious theory of IR was precisely the objective of Neorealism's main proponent, Kenneth Waltz. Simplicity is better than complexity. Less, in this context, is more.

Institutionalism, as we also saw in Chapter 2, starts from the same premise of rational behaviour. Its difference from Neorealism is assuming that states seek co-operation to get mutual gains. As rational actors, states will calculate carefully the prospects of gain and assess closely the likelihood of the other side's cooperating or cheating. The assumption of rationality makes it unnecessary to look inside the states themselves.[5] Again, the result is a streamlined procedure.

Outside-In: State Structure

It is also possible to explain the structure of states themselves from an outside-in perspective. Some scholars have been fascinated by the fact that states around the world all have similar basic organizations and institutions. As we saw in Chapter 6, all states have defence ministries and armed forces despite the fact that many either face no threats to their security or have resources that are completely inadequate. Nonetheless, a military establishment is a central arm of every state. Even the organization is the same with almost all states having a central staff, an army, an air force and, for states with coastlines, at least some naval units. Another area of similarity is education. There are many different ways of imparting knowledge to populations, but states tend to not only structure their systems in the same way, from national ministries to local administrators and schools, but also emphasize the same areas of learning. The question is: "Why do states in such radically different circumstances look so much alike?"[6]

The reason, in the view of some scholars, is that states look not only to each other for examples and experience but also to more basic international models and beliefs. Well-established models and beliefs are often a kind of common knowledge that is widely available. Such knowledge constitutes a source of authority that states may draw upon in deciding, for example, what to teach their 10-year-old children. Particular models may be transmitted more directly. A major structural change in many states in the last 20 years has been selling off state-owned industries. One pressure for that change has been conditions built into loans and grants from the International Monetary Fund and the World Bank, as we will see in Chapter 12. Backing those conditions is the two agencies' store of economic expertise. For reasons that are more difficult to pin down, liberal economics, which emphasizes the private sector, has been in fashion around the world since the early 1980s. The main point: it is possible to find external explanations not only for how states behave with each other but also for how they construct their own basic institutions and what priorities they emphasize. Here again we see outside-in reasoning at work: explanations of state action are achieved without looking into the state itself. The source of explanation is external.

Outside-In: Reservations

Is there any problem with an outside-in approach? Imagine shelving most of what you have learned in political science and government courses when you think about international issues. Imagine on the one hand a much more direct and simple way of thinking. The lack of clutter is very appealing. Imagine on the other hand doubts that may arise as you start setting aside a good portion of your knowledge. Is simplicity being gained at the cost of accuracy? A number of scholars believe that it is. Omitting conditions within states leaves out factors that may be very important.

We just saw that neorealists explained the relationship between the two cold war superpowers as inexorably adversarial. Arrangement of power in the international system ordained them to be enemies. But what if the Soviet Union in 1945 had had as its leader not Joseph Stalin but someone sharing the ideas of "Winston Churchill, Thomas Jefferson, Mahatma Gandhi, Alexander Kerensky or for that matter Mikhail Gorbachev?"[7] What also if the Soviet Union's military and industrial power in 1945 had been the same?

Even though the capabilities were there, cold war bipolarity might well not have followed. With liberal governments in both Washington and Moscow, it is easy to imagine their joining with other important democracies such as Great Britain, France, Australia and Canada in a joint world leadership to address common problems. There would have been a basis for the collective and moderate global management envisaged by the founders of the United Nations, and the last 50 years may have been very different. What accounts for that? It is not arrangements of power, for those are unchanged. Instead, it is the governing ideologies of the states' political systems. They, not capabilities, explain the relationship. Neorealism looks only at capabilities.

Here is another instance: Germany and Japan have been major powers since the 1960s yet neither has sought military capability anywhere near its economic and industrial level. Neither Germany nor Japan has been eager to play independent military and political roles. Germany has always sought to be a team player within NATO, and Japan continues to define its security in terms of its defence alliance with the United States. Instead of seeking to maximize their military capabilities and exercise greater influence, both have remained "profoundly ambivalent" about assertive roles.[8] To a neorealist, such behaviour was rational during the cold war when the bipolar balance left little room for independent action from second-rank powers, but the end of the cold war has opened the field for much more initiative. The two states' continuing abstention from military influence, for neorealists, is hard to explain.

That is so because such behaviour confounds Neorealism's assumption that states, pursuing security, rationally choose to maximize their power and influence. In the words of one prominent neorealist: "...as the power of a group or state increases, that group or state will be tempted to try to increase its control over its environment. In order to increase its own security, it will try to expand its political, economic and territorial control; it will try to change the international system in accordance with its particular set of interests."[9] Japan presents a particular puzzle. Japan not only deviates from Neorealism's assumption about maximizing military capabilities and influence but deviates even moreso from Neorealism's premise that military capabilities, in an anarchic system, are the ones that count. More bewildering is that other states regard Japan as a principal power.

These facts raise some awkward questions. Is it rational for major states to seek only non-military capabilities? Is it enough simply to be wealthy? One scholar puts the issue this way: "Suppose the president of a company could choose between two stories to tell the stockholders. One message would be: 'We enjoy great status, prestige and influence in the industry. When we talk everybody listens. Our profits are nil.' The other would be: 'No one in the industry pays the slightest attention to us or ever asks our advice. We are, in fact, the butt of jokes in the trade. We are making money hand over fist.'"[10]

These questions are awkward because Neorealism has difficulty accounting for objectives other than power and influence. Wealth is worth accumulating because it bankrolls military power, but what about wealth that has no objective of such power? The problem stems from Neorealism's view of state interest. "A theory of interests defined solely in terms of power," in another scholar's words, "is an impoverished theory of interests."[11]

Considering why that is so leads straight to one of Neorealism's key assumptions—states are alike in being rational and having a sovereign ability to act. But what if states are *not* alike? What if internal politics are in fact quite important? On war and peace—Neorealism's prime concern—some scholars believe that domestic influences are substantial.[12] Peace and safety will prevail "not when the distribution of external power is stable but rather when the distribution of internal power is just."[13] These considerations point inside the state.

Inside-Out

Inside-out approaches look within states for IR's foundation. In IR scholar John Ruggie's words,

...the fabric of international life is made up of micro cases: policymakers generally do not get to choose on the future of the state system; they confront choices on exchange rates, trade deficits, arms-control treaties, hostile acts against international shipping, terrorist attacks on airport lobbies and embassy compounds, and garbage that floats down a river or is transported through the air. If change comes, it will be the produce of micro practices. Hence, if we want to understand change or help to shape it, it is to these micro practices that we should look.[14]

What should we look for? The catalogue of domestic factors is extensive, and there is no agreement in IR on how to incorporate them or even on which ones to emphasize. In the words of one scholar, "Much of the existing literature on relations between domestic and international affairs consists either of *ad hoc* lists of countless 'domestic influences' on foreign policy or of generic observations that national and international affairs are somehow linked."[15] We can appreciate why parsimonious theories are so appealing. Where to begin?

The Liberal Perspective

A very convenient point of entry is provided by traditional Liberalism. Individuals, not states, are the primary actors in IR, according to Liberalism, because it is individuals who form groups and interests. Bargaining among groups determines which interests become politically paramount. It is those interests that guide states. In that way, foreign policy—the rationale directing state action internationally — has the same sorts of origins as domestic policy. Both represent the outcome of efforts by individuals and groups to have their views and preferences prevail. Foreign policy, like domestic policy, is politics, and individual and group preferences are the key.[16] That, as we saw in Chapter 3, is the starting point of Liberal IR theory. Because it also takes account of external factors, we will consider it later when we look at fusion approaches.

Interests do not need to be fixed and stable. Individual preferences change with circumstances. New situations prompt new definitions of interests. Groups align and re-align, and their demands for state action change just as events do. Interests are also not inevitably selfish. Liberal thought, as we saw in Chapter 3, has a long tradition of viewing people as capable of transcending self-interest and acting with altruism, common purpose and a sense of duty. Because state interests are an amalgam of individual ones, they can also change and can be selfish or generous. Just as with individuals, state interests are affected by circumstances and preferences. And just as with individuals, neither is fixed.

What translates interests into state policies and actions? Liberals are interested in the basic institutions within states because these affect which individuals and groups are influential, which kinds of issues get attended to and what sorts of interests are brought into the political arena. Liberals also are aware of the importance of economic systems and social values. Altogether, in the view of liberals, states are "embedded" in their own societies and cannot be understood apart from them.[17]

Authoritarian Governments: Restricted Channels

Whether a state is democratic or authoritarian matters. The important difference is in the openness of the political system to political interests. Authoritarianism in government breeds "a highly centralized, secretive, state-dominated polity."[18] Such governments dislike strong opposition and closely regulate individual and group activity. The more authoritarian a state is, the more that access to top decision-makers is restricted.

Authoritarian states may ignore or suppress many interests that naturally arise, and state action will reflect the preferences of a limited circle. How small and unvarying that circle is depends on the degree of authoritarianism. Some scholars believe that such systems are prone to inflexible outlooks and rigid policies because by restricting access they screen out offsetting views and information. With restricted access and controlled opposition, authoritarian governments come easily to believe that only their interests are correct.

Those same features, however, make it possible for authoritarian states to take decisive action because opposition exists only among cliques and factions within the government itself.[19] Strongly authoritarian states curtail even that opposition. Without the direct connections to their societies that are provided by political parties and groups, the leadership elite can focus more completely on external factors and take a more definitive approach to the state's interests. With that free hand, top leaders can change policy quickly.

Democratic Governments: Diversity and Access

The opposite features characterize democratic states. Their decentralized decision-making provides multiple points of access, allowing a diversity of views and information to be brought forward. One advantage is that policy can be based on a greater spread of information and opinion. Since more individual groups are heeded, another advantage is legitimacy. The disadvantage comes in implementing policy since individuals and groups also have multiple opportunities to press for changes or to divert the policy altogether.[20] If the pressure is effective, and especially if opposing groups apply it, state action becomes irregular and contradictory.

These three dimensions concisely summarize the differences between authoritarian and democratic states:

➤ *Political institutions*—especially their degree of centralization and ability to act autonomously

➤ *The structure of society*—especially its level of consensus or polarization and ability of groups to mobilize politically

➤ *The process of representation and accommodation*—especially the way interests are organized and expressed and the way government responds to political demands[21]

The main implication: the way political interests are mobilized and accommodated is an important feature of states. Authoritarian states have the advantage of decisive action but limited varieties of information. Democratic states have the advantage of rich information but limited decisiveness.

FIGURE 9.1   A Main Chance: NGOs and Canadian Foreign Policy

Non-governmental organizations (NGOs) operate outside of government but are involved in areas covered by government policy through direct action and advocacy. NGOs exist across the spectrum of domestic policy: aboriginal rights, homelessness, environmental protection, historical preservation. NGOs also organize around international issues: promotion of development and human rights, preservation endangered species and tropical forests, advancement of peace. Some states, including Canada, provide direct and indirect support to NGOs because they generally agree with their aims and because they desire to promote citizen involvement.

Many of the NGOs' interests, both domestic and international, are directly affected by government policy. Because influencing government is a prime mission for NGOs, their activity can be seen as group politics. NGOs contend with other groups, including other NGOs, to get the policies they want. As with group politics generally, this process is normally indirect with NGOs seeking to maintain relationships with senior officials in their policy areas and, where possible, to cultivate support and influence at the constituency level. As with group politics as well, the activity is a combination of issue-by-issue advocacy and maintaining a positive general image.

Governments and NGOs normally interact issue by issue, but occasionally governments invite more general contributions. Broad-scale policy reviews provide the best opportunities. A major review of Canada's foreign and defence policy was held in the late 1960s, and another was held following the 1993 election of the Liberal government of Jean Chretien. Under the rubric of "democratizing foreign policy," the Chretien government in early 1994 announced a parliamentary review of foreign and defence policy. Two joint Commons/Senate committees were formed, one for defence and one for foreign policy, and interested groups were invited to make submissions and proposals. The door was opened for NGOs. The promise of influencing the broad lines of policy stimulated NGOs to prepare presentations.

Some 125 Canadian NGOs are interested in international development and seek to increase (or at least preserve) Canadian government programs. Some of the NGOs include Canadian Crossroads International, Canadian Executive Service Overseas, the Canadian Friends Service Committee, the Canadian Labour Congress, Canadian Physicians for Aid and Relief, CARE Canada, Canadian University Service Overseas, OXFAM, the Canadian branch of Save the Children and World Vision. The Canadian Council for International Cooperation (CCIC) operates as a coordinating body. When the government announced the policy review, the CCIC, hoping for maximal effect, set out to organize a combined response.[22]

Motivating all of the NGOs to produce credible contributions was a common worry that fiscal cutbacks in the government reflected new priorities and threatened programs. Because the NGOs are often voluntary organizations for which organizing political pressure takes special effort, they value an open foreign policy process and welcomed the review's comprehensive focus. For greatest impact, the CCIC decided that it would meld all the NGOs' common concerns into a single thematic presentation and have the individual organizations emphasize experience "on the front lines."

How did they fare? According to IR scholar Denis Stairs, "many of the Members of Parliament and Senators came to feel that they were being bombarded over and over again by orchestrated repetitions of the same superficial and unsubstantiated message from a closely interconnected coterie of the like-minded. Fatigue set in, eyes glazed over... and with it an opportunity to buttress a powerful moral case with vivid displays of emotionally appealing evidence."[23]

The government reports that emerged from the review reflected an effort to summarize a mass of information and argument and produce a workable official document. Required was something specific enough to be a meaningful policy statement but general enough to address foreign situations as they arise. At the end of the process, the report "contained relatively few surprises." NGOs hoping for major policy changes did not get them.

There are two ways to view the outcome. One view is that citizens' groups, even when they are invited to take their advocacy directly to government, still have the disadvantage of being on the outside. They face an additional disadvantage if the government's attitude is not closely aligned. Another view is that NGOs have a political potential that is just now beginning to show and that another foreign policy review exercise five years in the future might see quite a different performance.

That potential comes from the possibilities for international joint action. With the availability of the Internet, scarce resources and dependence on volunteers do not doom NGOs to being politically ineffectual. The Internet makes rapid and widespread coordination possible. Skilled NGO managers can combine efforts, focusing on key constituencies, attracting media coverage and orchestrating political pressure. As NGOs gain political sophistication and influence and as they pool resources internationally, they will become more like other political special interests. Not all scholars see that as a good thing. Group interests are inherently narrow and specialized. With more groups in the game, governments may have even greater difficulty attending to broad-gauge problems because doing so will harm the interests of some groups. At acute levels of activity, governments may be hobbled by conflicting pressures.[24]

What About the State?

Liberal perspectives may put too much emphasis on preferences and too little on responsibility. The function of the state, as we saw in Chapter 6, is to define and manage successful action both domestically and internationally. Liberal views see politics as a matter of interests and effective expression. **Statism** sees politics as a matter of rule and control. Politics are more "concerned with issues associated with preserving order against international and external threats and less with the distribution of utilities [benefits] to political actors."[25]

That view depicts the state in a more independent position. Instead of being directed by whichever combination of interests is the most persuasive at the time, states have the ability to define and pursue their own views and preferences. Highly autonomous states have authoritarian features because they use their position to screen out most demands and representations. Democratic states can have a strong core at their centre to accommodate interests and demands but remain independent of them and embody a stable view of the state's interests and purpose.

Central bureaucracies are reservoirs of those views in both democratic and authoritarian states. Bureaucracies, as students in Introductory Political Science learn, exist to house expertise, advise governments and implement policy. Because the officials in democratic state bureaucracies are normally recruited and pro-moted independently of ruling political parties, are rewarded for their substan-tive knowledge and judgement and have job tenure independent of governments in office, they can apply professional knowledge to the state's interests and present their views at the highest levels. Because of their political independence, these views can be durable. Think of a bureaucracy as a state's long-term memory. Because of that inner resource, the statist view treats the state as "actor in its own right," interacting with groups and society but quite capable of having its own preferences and formulating its own action.[26]

Action and the State

How does the statist perspective affect our understanding of state behaviour? Statists tend to emphasize constraints. Individuals and groups are not completely free agents politically. State structures—channels of authority, entrenched views—surround political activity and impose limits. Because of the power and long-term tenure of state bureaucracies, they may even shape and determine individuals' and groups' understandings of their interests and the ways of acting on them.

The statist perspective also recognizes that not all participants are equal. Holding a senior position in government gives officials resources and options that are not available to private individuals. In contrast to Liberalism, "statist orienta-tions see political leaders as less constrained by societal forces. They can alter preferences using the state's own resources. They may even be able to change the distribution of political resources possessed by societal groups."[27]

In democratic systems, the state does not ordain political action as it does in authoritarian systems, but it has an important ability to shape and channel it as well as independence in molding and implementing the results.

Centralization v. Decentralization

Government organization can vary by the concentration of authority. A decen-tralized government is one that devolves responsibility for a particular policy area, such as international economic relations, among a number of agencies with no one agency having clear authority to act. A centralized government concentrates re-sponsibility for a particular policy area in a single agency that does have clear au-thority to act.

The advantages and disadvantages resemble those between democratic and authoritarian governments. A decentralized government, like democratic govern-ment generally, has many points of access and decision. Policy results from achiev-ing agreement among many agencies each of which is exposed to group interests and demands. A centralized government has more limited points of access and persuasion and a greater ability to act decisively. This is not to say that centraliz-ing government leads to authoritarianism. Democratic governments, including centralized ones, remain accountable through elections and organized opposition

and depend on legitimacy and public support. Centralized democratic governments do, however, concentrate authority in fewer places.

In choosing how to organize itself, government faces a trade-off between openness and the ability to act coherently. In the words of one scholar, "regardless of
which model is chosen, how does one best coordinate and integrate the different,
and differing, domestic interests that must be projected into the international
arena or, by the same token, ensure an efficient linkage between international developments and domestic politics?"[28]

This is a particularly interesting question in foreign policy because so many various concerns are involved: trade, relations with military allies, energy, drug enforcement, economic development assistance, human rights, environmental issues,
energy and migration. Centralization would involve concentrating all authority
within a single foreign ministry. Decentralization would involve subdividing responsibilities into separate agencies – perhaps one agency for international development, another for human rights and another for international environmental
issues. Decentralization can also involve sharing responsibilities with other existing agencies—human rights with a justice ministry, trade with a finance ministry
and international environment with an environment ministry.

Neither formula is clearly preferable. Highly centralized arrangements may
lead to "tensions within the foreign ministry where the units that do not deal in matters of war and peace per se itch to establish their own autonomous existence."
Decentralized arrangements, on the other hand, lead to "an equally powerful itch
on the part of both politicians and their fiscal advisers to amalgamate in order to
eliminate the financial costs and administrative overlap and the political costs of
problematic coordination."[29]

Canada and the United States:
Centralization and Decentralization

The trend in Canada over the last 25 years has been toward centralization. In
1982, the former Department of External Affairs was merged with the trade section
of the former Ministry of Trade and Commerce to form what is now known as
the Department of Foreign Affairs and International Trade (DFAIT). Canada has followed the pattern of foreign policy management of other smaller industrial states
that have a heavy involvement in international trade. Belgium, Denmark, Finland,
the Netherlands, Norway and Sweden have all combined foreign affairs and trade
within single ministries. "Not unlike Canada, these states tended to have open
economies with a mix of industrialized and primary sectors that were heavily dependent on export markets and thus which needed a foreign ministry that could
conduct both economic and political diplomacy in defence of national interests."[30]

The United States, in contrast, is highly decentralized. The Department of State
is officially responsible for managing foreign policy, but it shares authority in particular policy areas with other agencies: the Drug Enforcement Agency in international drug trafficking, for example, and the Treasury Department, the Office of
the United States Trade Representative and the Department of Commerce in trade

policy. Adding to the decentralization is the ability of Congress to affect foreign policy, particularly with legislation that includes specific requirements or that involves authorizations of money. The American system, in both foreign and domestic policy, is very open to expressions of interest, but its actions are often complex and difficult to predict. At their worst, highly decentralized systems can be contradictory and inconsistent—the result of seeking to reconcile different policies, agency positions and effectively articulated preferences. Other states may find dealing with them complicated and erratic. For the decentralized states, such variability makes it difficult to pursue coherent interests. That difficulty, in the eyes of some scholars, is weakness, and on that basis they have characterized the U.S. as a weak state.[31]

FIGURE 9.2   Canada, the Maghreb and Quebec

Does Canada have important interests in North Africa? Looking at external factors, those interests are not obvious. Algeria is one of the world's oil-producing states, but Canada has always had multiple sources of supply, including Alberta. During the 1960s and 1970s, Algeria had some influence in the Non-Aligned Movement, but its positions did not cause direct problems for Ottawa. For their part, Morocco and Tunisia are relatively small and poor states whose moderate views sometimes figure in Arab politics but whose influence is secondary. Why then, did Ottawa decide in the mid-1960s that Canada's relations with the Maghreb (North Africa) needed upgrading?

The effects of Quebec's Quiet Revolution focused attention on the fact that Canada's relations with the developing world were skewed towards English-speaking states, particularly those of the British Commonwealth. There was nothing comparable in Canada's relations with the francophone counterpart, the French Community —a group of former colonies under the stewardship of Paris. That situation, Ottawa believed, "would have to be remedied if French Canadians were to feel they had a direct stake in Canadian foreign policy."[32]

In 1965, the Secretary of State for External Affairs Paul Martin declared that the "bicultural" aspect of Canada would be reflected in all aspects of foreign policy. There followed an agreement with France to improve financial, economic and commercial ties and, with France's consent, to develop closer relations with France's former African colonies. Those included Algeria, Morocco and Tunisia. One of Ottawa's concerns was that Quebec, as its government began looking abroad, would find francophone states a natural initial focus and move to establish ties. Ottawa's stated purpose was promoting economic and political development abroad, but a collateral purpose was domestic: pre-empting the Quebec government's nascent interest in conducting its own foreign relations.

Deeper Inside the State

It is possible to burrow further into the state and consider individual agencies themselves. One view is that foreign policy and defence agencies, like all bureaucracies, develop their own "cultures"—sets of outlooks, understandings and procedures. **Agency cultures** arise from a many influences: the particular technologies or resources an agency works with, the professional and educational background of their members, the domestic and international political environments, their special responsibilities and their particular shares of information.[33] Agencies are adept at instilling their cultures in new members as the way things are done. Once in place, agency cultures are durable.

When do agency cultures affect a state's behaviour? Particular agencies are important when they have sole authority over an issue and the expertise to deal with it.[34] They are also important when an issue is complex. When these conditions come together, political leaders (the ones who normally make key decisions) may be unable to manage the issue closely. Exclusive authority gives an agency room to apply its special expertise, making it difficult for generalist outsiders, including political leaders, to intervene. Complex issues produce the same effect: generalists may have difficulty getting a full grasp. Both conditions favour delegating responsibility to the agency, and both give latitude to its culture. The result may strongly reflect the agency's way of doing things. Agency cultures may also be important in situations that develop rapidly. With little time for deliberation, the natural inclination is to follow normal procedures. Those usually reflect the agency's culture.[35]

Some scholars believe that parliamentary systems such as Canada's, because of party government and strong cabinet control, are able to put limits on agency cultures and keep them within close channels.[36] This is not to say that differences do not make themselves felt. In the Turbot War, which we looked at in Chapter 3, DFAIT's preference was negotiation. The attitude of the Department of Fisheries and Oceans was much more hard-nosed and confrontational. Its views, supported by public opinion and by maritime provincial and federal politicians, prevailed during the escalation of the conflict.[37]

What happens if we imagine less central control? One result is more ambiguous policies and decisions. These can occur as a result of compromises among political or bureaucratic factions. The advocates of a particular view may not be strong enough to have their way, and a bargain with a rival faction may have to be made. That faction may require accommodating some of its views even though they might be contradictory. The result, a half-measure of compromise and adjustment, may not address the problem or even contain a clear position. Without knowing of the politicking and maneuvering that went into the result, others may find it difficult to understand.

Serious divisions in a government may make even these compromises impossible. An important agency or faction might be excluded from the process, but its absence will be reflected in policy gaps and inconsistencies. If all factions are present, on the other hand, the result may be temporizing and indecision as each one cancels the other's influence. Worse, factions may succeed intermittently, producing a zigzag pattern of first one policy and then another.[38]

Special Individuals

We can go even further into the state and examine the role of individuals. The ones who are most interesting are those in the position to make key decisions.

Centralization tends to limit those positions and decentralization to expand them. Making decisions involves not only deciding the objective merits of an issue but accommodating and reconciling diverse views, preferences and advice. Key decision-makers have the authority to weigh these inputs. When they do so they determine which agencies and interests will be the most influential.

Is it necessary to go that far into the corridors of government? Are there reasons that justify micro-analysis? Some scholars believe that there are such reasons. Without taking the goals and understandings of key figures into account as well as their ability to make crucial choices and decisions, some state actions may appear inexplicable. One suggestive way of understanding the question is to see foreign policy as a way for political leaders to achieve their own personal goals. If the leader's own goals are the prime consideration, the choice of policy may be secondary. One policy may be substituted for another if it furthers the leader's goal. The result may be surprising changes of course. Without taking the leader's own goals into account, considering the regular list of external, domestic political or bureaucratic factors may miss the key ingredient.[39]

At the same time, personal goals may be genuinely altruistic: a leader may sincerely desire a more peaceful relationship with another state or may honestly want to help a particular domestic sector. When that goal is paramount, the policy choice is finding the most effective means. Without knowing the goal and the leader's attachment to it, the choice may seem puzzling, particularly to other states.

FIGURE 9.3   Individual Action: Pierre Trudeau's Peace Initiative

How much do government foreign policy actions depend on the beliefs and deeds of one person? Pierre Trudeau's personal peace initiative of 1983-1984 shows the latitude possible if a leader is determined to use it. Following a hopeful period of superpower detente in the early 1970s, the cold war became steadily more frigid. On the Soviet side, unprecedented interventions in Africa in the mid-1970s were followed by the 1979 invasion of Afghanistan. On the American side, Ronald Reagan, promising to restore national strength and resolve, was elected president in 1980. He adopted strident rhetoric, characterizing the Soviet Union as an "evil empire." Many feared equally fervent intentions.

Nuclear war became a growing concern. NATO adopted plans to station a new generation of intermediate missiles in Western Europe to match a new Soviet missile deployment in Central Europe. Apprehensions rose in March 1983 when Reagan announced his plans for Star Wars, an anti-missile defence system that many believed would de-stabilize the nuclear balance. Tensions and recriminations became acute when Soviet fighter aircraft shot down a Korean Airlines 747 on August 30, 1983, killing all aboard.

Prime Minister Trudeau, believing that the situation was becoming increasingly dangerous and seeing no moderating influences between the superpowers themselves, became convinced that someone had to act. In September 1983, he decided on a personal peace initiative. This idea went against the views of the Department of External Affairs (as DFAIT was known then). As professional diplomats, officials there believed that such efforts need elaborate advance preparation with other governments. Themes and points of agreement need to be negotiated carefully and quietly. Senior-level visits and ceremonies simply put the official stamp on exhaustive work at lower levels. A lone initiative would be a flash in the pan.[40]

Trudeau's long-time adviser and confidant, Ivan Head, felt differently. In a memo to Trudeau, Head stated:

"Canada is a respected member of the international community, has an enviable policy record, is regarded as being deeply affected by arms buildups because of its geographic location and has proved again and again its effectiveness an as actor. We have an obligation to contribute to resolving the impasse. Your reputation and your seniority combine to place an inescapable burden upon you."[41]

After consultation with other advisers, Trudeau decided to proceed.

Set up to work independently of the foreign affairs bureaucracy, a small group prepared a set of issues and a plan of events. Trudeau would visit with leaders in the principal NATO states, the Soviet Union and the United States. The message, set forth in a speech by Trudeau at the University of Guelph on October 27, 1983, emphasized the need to begin new multilateral measures towards nuclear controls and to renew commitments to peace.[42]

In Europe, he met with the French, German, British, Italian and Dutch governments and with the Vatican. A meeting with Soviet Party Secretary Yuri Andropov was thwarted because Andropov was gravely ill. Trudeau then took his message to the meeting of the Commonwealth states in New Delhi where his efforts were endorsed and then to Beijing. In early December he met with Reagan in Washington. His final stops, in early 1984, were meetings with United Nations Secretary General Javier Perez de Cuellar and with the governments of Czechoslovakia, East Germany and Romania. These last were added because Andropov's grave condition had created a leadership vacuum in Moscow. Later, at Andropov's funeral, Trudeau met with the successor, Constantin Chernenko.[43]

The European governments were moderately interested but made no commitments. Press coverage was positive but bland. Some Europeans saw Trudeau as a late-comer to arms control issues, which had occupied their governments closely for years. Chinese premier Deng Xiao-ping used his meeting to emphasize that nuclear tensions were entirely the fault of the two superpowers.[44] Reagan received Trudeau politely but was noncommittal. Chernenko called Trudeau's efforts "useful and practical."[45]

What did his initiative achieve? The polite receptions recognized his personal position and the reputation of Canada but showed little inclination to take his ideas to heart. To career diplomats who emphasize that senior encounters need thorough spadework, the initiative was noble but ineffectual. Its results were predictable.

At the same time, the European governments did proceed with one of Trudeau's proposals—upgrading their participation in the January 1984 European Disarmament Conference in Stockholm to the foreign minister level. That meeting initiated the Conference on Security and Cooperation in Europe, an East-West forum that would continue through the 1980s. The June 1984 meeting of the G-7 (Canada, United States, Britain, France, Italy, Japan) approved a statement, which Trudeau drafted, that expressed its members' commitment to peace. Reagan toned down his harsh anti-Soviet rhetoric.

A year later, Soviet General Secretary Mikail Gorbachev (Gorbachev became President of the Soviet Union in 1988) invited Trudeau to advise him on how to deal with Reagan at the approaching summit conference. Trudeau suggested that

Canadian Press/CP photo/Ryan Remiorz

Former Soviet Union President Mikhail Gorbachev says goodbye to former Canadian Prime Minister Pierre Trudeau during a visit to Canada in 1993.

the two leaders could do much to reduce tensions by making a joint statement and recommended emphasizing the futility of nuclear war. The two leaders issued a statement cast in the words Trudeau had offered: "A nuclear war can never be won and must never be fought."[46]

How much these changes stemmed from Trudeau's personal efforts is difficult to say in light of all the other influences at work. What the episode does show is that individual state leaders, when they are determined, can override the predilections of their bureaucracies—the central organs of state—and proceed on their own. The leaders' latitude is improved when domestic opinion is positive, and, in Trudeau's case, it was indeed.

One place where personal political goals can be decisive is developing states. As we saw in Chapters 6 and 7, these states often function with very low levels of popular support. The combination of governmental weakness and low legitimacy makes political leaders vulnerable to being overthrown. Their prime goal of staying in power may shape foreign policy, particularly alignments with other states. In the mid-1970s, for example, the new leadership of Ethiopia dropped its alignment with the United States and approached the Soviet Union. Although there were ideological reasons for the move, a prime consideration was to get support against the breakaway province of Eritrea (which has since become independent).

Eritrea's rebellion, along with ones in other provinces, was a serious threat to the Ethiopian leadership's hold on power. The leadership calculated that the Soviet Union, having had a hand in the origins of Eritrea's rebellion, was best placed to help contain it.[47] Ethiopia's choice violated the basic principle of balancing against threats. Acting on that principle, Ethiopia would have addressed one influence (the Soviet Union's) by offsetting it with another (the United States's).

The Soviet Union responded promptly by abandoning Eritrea and lavishing supplies and advice on Ethiopia. The Eritreans were very surprised to be left in the lurch. The Soviet action had personal elements of its own. The Soviet leadership, tired of aiding developing governments that claimed to espouse socialism but could not be depended on for support, saw in the new Ethiopian leadership not just socialism but Marxism-Leninism. Here was a future ally. The Ethiopian leaders' embattled position also reminded some Soviet leaders of the USSR's own perilous beginnings after 1917 thereby sponsoring a sense of kinship.

States Behaving Badly

How do we account for greedy, immoderate or impetuous behaviour? One might think that Neorealism, occupied as it is with security and capability, would provide the best perspective: sometimes drastic moves are necessary. From a neorealist's perspective, such situations should not arise. To maintain stability and protect their security, rational states should always seek to offset other states' gains, even marginal ones. Because rational states keep capabilities balanced, Neorealism can only explain drastic behaviour—a military invasion, for example—as a breakdown of the process. Attending to external configurations of power maintains a stable international system and keeps states out of such predicaments. That leaves radical action to be explained by domestic factors.[48]

One explanation emphasizes the collusion of political elites. A national leader may be bent on expansion but also understand that such a course involves risks and costs that have to be accepted. Even authoritarian leaders need elite support to impose such sacrifice. For their part, important elites may see advantages in expansion, particularly economic advantages related to military spending, and back the policy. Easing their decision is the fact that the general public bears the greatest burden. Other elites may be brought on board by political logrolling—agreeing to support expansion in exchange for backing their interests. The public may be carried along with nationalist appeals and promises of victory. Less positively, the public may be too disorganized to resist.[49]

A weak or suppressed opposition favours these accommodations, allowing elites and national leaders to define the states' interests according to their own wishes. Suppressed opposition allows huge costs to be imposed on the public. During the cold war the two superpowers courted allies in the developing states by providing lavish economic and military assistance. With a less wealthy economic base, the Soviet effort required considerable sacrifice at home. In the words of one scholar, such behaviour "demonstrates how hollow the concept of 'national' interest can become when a well-fed and privileged elite displays 'altruism' toward foreign clients even while imposing monumental sacrifices on its own subjects as the Soviet elite did for so many years."

The consequences are not merely deprivation. The same scholar describes "a Hitler or Saddam syndrome in which societies are put at risk and sacrificed, not for their own good, but for the 'higher interests' of their leaders."[50] In Saddam's case, the sacrifice was thousands of casualties that followed his decisions to attack neighbouring Iran and Kuwait. Thousands more were sacrificed to malnutrition and starvation as a consequence of his refusal to comply with the United Nations Security Council's resolution requiring inspection and destruction of his chemical, biological and nuclear weapons capabilities. Thwarting that resolution continued a punishing regime of economic sanctions. Intended by the Security Council as a short-term measure to speed compliance, the sanctions dragged on for seven years and fell most heavily on women and children.[51] The Iraqi leader's desire to keep his weapons was more important than feeding his people. The situation improved somewhat in 1998 when the UN permitted Iraq to sell more oil for food and imposed a compliance procedure to ensure that the food actually reached the needy. We will see more about economic sanctions in Chapter 11.

Elite ambition may be particularly dangerous if the states involved are principal powers and if domestic opposition provides no restraint. One of the rivalries leading to World War I was a naval race between Germany and Great Britain. Germany, which initiated the race, was guided by a powerful conservative political elite that favoured national power and expansion. The political opposition was against the higher taxes involved. The elite succeeded in getting naval expansion, but the opposition blocked the taxes to finance them.

Britain, faced with a direct challenge by its major rival, reluctantly followed suit and expanded its fleet. The decision was not an easy one because the Liberal government was elected in 1905 on a platform of social reform and had a strong faction committed to carrying through with new social programs. Diverting revenue to arms would thwart those objectives. Another Liberal faction, along with the foreign and defence bureaucracies, was very worried about German naval expansion and was determined not to let it go unanswered. The Liberal government's preference was to solve the problem with an arms limitation agreement, but Germany rejected that plan.[52] Because the British government's political legitimacy was higher than Germany's, the population reluctantly accepted the higher taxes, and construction went ahead.

Germany's elitism ended up being its disadvantage. The Conservatives were powerful enough to expand the navy but not to finance it. The result was a large deficit and an unfinished fleet. Germany had the worst of both worlds: provoking a rivalry with its major adversary at a particularly sensitive time—the decade before 1914—but not having the ability to carry it through. Compared to Britain, Germany entered World War I with less fleet and more deficit.[53]

FIGURE 9.4 Explaining State Action: India's and Pakistan's Nuclear Tests

In May 1998, India tested five nuclear devices in the Rajasthan desert, one of which was a bomb capable of being placed in a missile warhead. Several days later, Pakistan exploded five devices of its own. India had conducted an underground nuclear explosion 24 years earlier and was known to possess nuclear capability. Pakistan was known to be receiving technical assistance and equipment from several states for its nuclear program and was regarded as nuclear-capable. Both states had ballistic missile programs although Pakistan's development of medium-range missiles was regarded as being ahead of India's.

The tests caused much alarm and dismay in the international community and were roundly condemned. Some states imposed economic sanctions. Concerns about nuclear warfare, gone dormant after the cold war, rose again. Particularly unsettling was India's and Pakistan's record of three wars—one following independence, a second in 1965 and a third in 1971—and a serious war scare in 1990. Unlike the two superpowers who had elaborate control systems to prevent unauthorized missile launchings and who kept their forces in protected deployments, India's and Pakistan's forces were still in their initial, and vulnerable, stages. Since each side might reckon with the possibility of eliminating the other's nuclear force in a surprise attack, their posture was regarded as dangerously unstable. Instead of increasing their security, their nuclear advances exposed them to new risks.

How would the four IR theories account for the two states' behaviour?

Neorealism

Consider the capabilities facing India. To its north lies China with whom it fought a border war in the Himalayas in 1962 and with whom it has had unfriendly and suspicious relations since. China has steadily been upgrading its military power and has gained increasing ability to strike beyond its borders. One of the most worrisome improvements has been nuclear missiles capable of hitting India.

To India's west lies Pakistan with whom it has fought three wars since independence. Aligned with Pakistan since 1965, China, along with other states, has been assisting Pakistan in its nuclear development and has been providing missile technology. In the year before India's nuclear test, Pakistan had begun tests of its new missiles, and they proved to be capable of hitting Indian targets. Pakistan's missile classes have been named after historic conquerors of India.[54] West of Pakistan lies the Persian Gulf, itself a region of missile technology proliferation. Faced with nuclear neighbours on two borders, India had to demonstrate offsetting capability. Although the results may have been foreseeable in provoking Pakistan to follow suit, nuclear power had to be shown.[55]

Pakistan could not stand by as its neighbour upped the ante. India's new gain was not just a relative one—concerning enough in a neorealist perspective. Instead, because the devices tested showed direct applicability to nuclear ballistic missiles, India's gain was step-level. Faced with the fact of a major imbalance, Pakistan was compelled to create a new balance by testing its weapons. Failure to do so, Pakistan's government emphasized, would invite India to make dangerous estimates of Pakistan's political will.

Because neither state's capital is far from the border, neither side has the security of defence in depth. Major targets and assets are within striking distance. Pakistan's smaller size makes it particularly exposed. Such conditions invite offensive warfare, both conventional and nuclear, because the attacker can anticipate quickly defeating the other side. Force advantage and surprise are the key elements. Nuclear weapons can also provide deterrence against attack, and for its part India maintains that "if deterrence works in the West... by what reasoning will it not work in India?[56]

Institutionalism

India's test was a vote of non-confidence in the world regime of nuclear non- proliferation. That regime is based on two international agreements, the Nuclear Non-Proliferation Treaty and the Comprehensive Test Ban Treaty. At the time of the tests, neither India nor Pakistan had signed them. Successful regimes depend on consensus and on the membership of all states involved whether the activity be nuclear weapons or international banking. India's and Pakistan's abstention shows an incomplete world consensus on nuclear weapons.

From India's perspective, the regime is incomplete in a more practical way. China has pursued its own weapons development and has joined other states in aiding the weapons program of Pakistan but has drawn no serious consequences from the international community. India could draw two conclusions:

➤ The non-proliferation regime makes exceptions for powerful states with which members have important commercial ties and wish not to antagonize. States like China can bend the rules when it suits them, both in developing their own forces and in giving technical assistance to states in developing their own.[57]

➤ The regime might make the former superpowers and Europe more secure, but not South Asia. Its protections are adequate for some states but not for others.

In the face of India's and Pakistan's abstention and even more of their acquiring nuclear capability, other states must consider the non-proliferation regime. The crucial point in assessing their commitment comes when continued adherence is outweighed by security concerns. When that happens, rational collective action yields to rational self-help. As the regime weakens, institutional assumptions fade and neorealist ones rise. The collective task is to keep cooperative incentives in place.

Liberal IR theory

Domestic politics in India have been in transition. The Congress Party, India's dominant political force since independence, has fragmented and declined. In 1998, power was held by an unstable coalition government headed by the nationalist Bharatıya Janata Party (BJP), which came to office promising to restore India's international position. That position too had endured setbacks. India had intervened in the Sri Lankan civil war and failed to end it. The non-aligned movement of developing states, of which India was an important leader, lost much of its rationale with the end of the cold war and East-West rivalry. The end of the cold war also cost India its prime ally, the Soviet Union. Although India had been cautiously liberalizing its state-centred economy since the early 1990s, the world's attention focused instead on the high-growth economies of the Pacific Rim. Finally, there was the continuing problem of Kashmir.[58]

To counter these discouraging situations, the BJP government heralded the nuclear test as a blow for national pride. Showing that its strategy was both domestic and international, the BJP calculated that the test would be highly popular at home. The BJP hoped the test would curb fractious situations in its governing coalition and perhaps enable it to win a majority in the next election.[59] The consequence of these calculations was nuclearization of India's prime military relationship. A broader consequence was widespread international condemnation. Even the domestic effects may be temporary. Since the test, the Indian public's euphoria has waned, but the country's problems continue.

Constructivism

The nuclear tests provide striking evidence of how identities can reinforce one another. Unlike the interactive cycle that ended the cold war, the momentum between Pakistan and India is not cooperation and trust but antagonism and fear.

The two states have had the identities of enemies since the time of independence. With the exception of the war of 1971 when India sided with Bangladesh in its secession from Pakistan, the conflicts have all involved Kashmir, itself a site of contested identity. Kashmir's status was not resolved when independence created India and Pakistan out of British India. Kashmir has remained a problem ever since with each side claiming rightful sovereignty over this part of their northern frontier. The significance of Kashmir is not just territorial: its Muslim majority, backed by Pakistan, does not wish to be part of India.

Intersubjective understandings arising from this war-punctuated history have made military defence key national interests. Although India has the advantage, Pakistan has worked to keep its force levels high enough to discourage, if not defeat, invasion. India's nuclear test not only upped the military ante. The test-countertest cycle reinforced the states' identities as enemies, but now their intersubjective understandings support enmity at the nuclear level.

Marxism: An Alternative to Complexity?

These considerations make inside-out approaches inherently diverse and complicated. They also make it possible to arrive at more than one explanation of a particular episode depending on which factors were considered and how much weight was given to each.[60] Even more, delving very deeply into domestic factors soon leads away from IR's interest in finding general patterns and toward treating each state as a special case. That is the approach of foreign policy studies, which IR tends to regard as a separate kind of endeavour. Is there any way of reducing the complexity and increasing the generalizability? Is there any parsimonious approach at the domestic level? Actually, there is: Marxism.

A key assumption of Marxism is that the state acts according to the interests of the dominant class. The foreign policy of a capitalist state accurately reflects the interests of its capitalist class. We have seen one elaboration of that basic premise in Critical Theory. The ruling hegemony is a dominant alliance of economic and political power. The interests of that hegemony guide the state's actions. Such an approach eliminates a number of the complexities we have just seen, particularly when the hegemony rules peacefully. That peace reflects a popular consensus based on the ruling hegemony's abilities of popular persuasion. The arrangement can be quite stable over time.

Such parsimony and explanatory power rivals that of Neorealism. With Neorealism, as we saw, the main thing one needs to know in considering any state is its position in the international system; with Marxism and Critical Theory the main thing one needs to know is who constitutes its dominant class. In the words of one scholar, "This may explain why Innenpolitikers [people who prefer the inside-out approach] are drawn to neo-Marxist explanations. Only Marxist explanations can match [Neo]realism's generalizability."[61]

The Fusion Approach

Many scholars in recent years have appreciated the limitations of both external and internal focuses. Neither by itself is adequate. Outside-in approaches, as we have seen, omit potentially crucial domestic factors. Inside-out approaches, because they are complicated, have no consistent way of including the state's international position. Is there some way of combining both focuses? IR has recently begun grappling with that task. "We know that domestic politics, 'matter,'" asserts one scholar, "but we still do not know how to treat domestic and international politics as a whole."[62] Can the two be put together in a single way?

We saw the beginnings in Chapter 3 with Liberal Pluralism. State behaviour originates from the interests and actions of groups. Government seeks to reconcile these into a common policy. When governments act on that policy with other states, they create conditions that affect *their* groups' interests. Those interests, in turn, are reconciled into policy and acted upon, returning the effects. International politics, in this view, is an ongoing domestic and international process of adjusting interests. Because the conditions prompting the process arise both domestically and internationally, the Liberal IR Theory approach accommodates both Inside-Out and Outside-In factors. Now we can see how they interact.

We can begin by regarding the task of government as one of balancing: domestic demands and constraints against foreign threats and opportunities. Each side of the balance affects the other. In the policy area of security, domestic politics decides how much a public is willing to spend for military resources. That in turn affects the calculations of other states, both about the actual capability of the state and, more importantly, its willingness to support commitments abroad.[63] In the policy area of trade, domestic demands for openness or protection with trading partners affect those partners' interests, calculations and policies. These feed back to the originating state.

Although the structure of governments may differ, they do respond to each other's actions.[64] What follows? A successful policy reconciles both internal and external pressures. Internally, the policy retains the support of important constituencies or the public at large. Internationally, the policy deals successfully with the external situation. States may not always succeed. Addressing a compelling international situation may require more dislocation or burden than key domestic groups or the general population may be willing to accommodate.

For democratic governments in particular, going against public opinion may carry a high price: defeat in the next election or, more usually, depleted political capital. Political capital is one way of characterizing a government's ability to get its way through persuasion, rewards and appeals to public confidence. Political capital can be used up, and politicians guard it carefully, reserving it for the most important issues. For authoritarian governments, the price of going against resistance may be steeper yet. Because potential opposition in those governments rests in powerful institutions such as the military or a ruling elite, they can often organize the force to overthrow the government.

What if governments *can't* respond to important external situations? The result may be failure to address key situations in time, serious setbacks or half-measures that bring no remedy. The classic illustration is the governments of Europe and North America as they confronted the rise of Naziism. Public opinion did not favour active resistance until the danger had become grave.

The Right Balance

One scholar has combined domestic and external factors into four reactions to overseas threats.[65] They are:

> *Unresponsiveness to international events* The state has neither the resources nor the inclination to counter to external threats. Canadian and American isolationism in the 1930s, which avoided rearmament in the face of Nazi Germany's growing military power and stayed clear of security commitments with Britain and France, fits this category.

> *Underextension* The capabilities are present, but there is no willingness to undertake commitments commensurate with them. Japan's post-World War II avoidance of military roles outside of its defensive alliance with the United States and its more general unwillingness to participate in collective military ventures—such as the Gulf War in 1991—fits this category.

> *Overextension* Commitments are made that cannot be supported by capabilities. The American involvement in Vietnam is an example. Public opinion initially supported intervention, but as the war dragged on and requests for more troops kept coming, the public's support turned to opposition, putting pressure on the American government to end the war. The Soviet Union's chain of commitments in the 1970s and 1980s (Ethiopia, Nicaragua, Cuba, Angola, Afghanistan) ultimately exceeded its capabilities. Mikhail Gorbachev believed that commitments such as these were compounding the USSR's economic problems.

> *Realism/Extended Deterrence* A balance is struck between external threats and available capabilities. Domestic support is sufficient to sustain necessary commitments to allies and regional balances. Deterrence is the appropriate match between threat and capability. Threats are contained when such a balance prevails. Extended deterrence is stable over time. This combination supports other lengthy international endeavours. Canada's long-term commitment to peacekeeping, supported consistently by public opinion, is an example.

Schematically, the combinations of commitments and capabilities can be seen in Figure 9.5[66].

TABLE 9.5:   Tabulation

		Commitments	
		Constrained	**Unconstrained**
Capabilities	**Constrained**	Unresponsiveness to International events	Overextension
	Unconstrained	Underextension	Realism/Extended Deterrence

What is the main implication of this scheme? Domestic politics affect the latitude of governments to make commitments and the availability of capabilities to support them. The need for those commitments and capabilities originates externally. Domestic politics may or may not produce appropriate responses, and willingness to act may or may not match external threat. The most dangerous mismatches are unresponsiveness (failing to address challenges posed by aggressive adversaries) and over-extension (making commitments that cannot be supported).

Under-extension poses no difficulties if there are no threats. Japan can afford to under-extend because of its security cooperation with the United States and because that alliance so far has been quite adequate to meet any threats. That could change if threats increased either because American protection became inadequate or if China evolved into a powerful military adversary. At that point, the Japanese government would be faced with the other three options. If China's growth did militarily threaten Japan, under-extension would still be an available policy provided the United States cooperated by providing increased support. Unresponsiveness and over-extension would both be inappropriate. Stable deterrence would require a proportional matching of Japanese capabilities and commitments with China's. The ability to do so depends on domestic politics in Japan.

Economic ties also affect the choice. When there are ties of investment and trade with the threatening state, groups whose economic interests are put at risk may pressure the government not to take strong action. The states that are least likely to be affected by these pressures have weak economic ties with the threatening state and strong ones with other states facing the same threat. That combination produces the fewest domestic economic pressures against firm responses because there is no economic loss with the aggressor and because ties with the other states could be injured if failure to deter led to war.[67]

The Democratic Peace

Democratic states do not go to war with other democratic states. That statement, in one scholar's words, "is as close as anything we have to an empirical law in international relations."[69] Britain and the United States provide a striking example. In the early part of the 19th century their relations, punctuated by the War of 1812, were often rancorous. That changed in 1832 when Britain became a par-

FIGURE 9.6   Canada's International Roles: Government and the Public

Alignment (or mismatch) between a government's foreign policy and public opinion is not limited to national security. A survey of 808 foreign policy statements and speeches by Canadian foreign affairs ministers and the Prime Minister between 1989 and 1993 showed three strong role orientations. The statements are significant because they represent communication between government and the public. Because of the dependence of democratic governments on the public's support, these orientations, particularly the ones most frequently mentioned, can be assumed to reflect common understandings. The three most frequently mentioned were these:

➤ *Instigator and active participant in international/regional cooperative security* This role involves Canada using its influence in cooperation with other states against threats to international security, particularly the proliferation of weapons. Although Canada is not directly at risk in the short run, its role stems from long-run self-interest and recognition that such threats must be addressed collectively. The means of pursuing that role emphasize multilateral institutions including the UN, NATO and the Organization of American States. The means also include supporting existing agreements and using Canada's individual influence to promote further measures.

➤ *Advocate of human rights and democratic institutions* This role involves Canada using its influence to promote democratic reform in developing states, to assist former Soviet republics in their passages from communism to liberal democracy and to aid in monitoring elections in troubled states such as Cambodia. In the Western Hemisphere, the role includes working for recognition of the rights of indigenous peoples. This role treats democracy, respect for human rights and a market economy as a single cluster of related conditions.

➤ *Supporter of development assistance* This role involves Canada's continuing its long support of economic development by providing aid and continues in the face of pressure to scale back assistance.[68]

Given Canada's heavy involvement over the years in peacekeeping operations and its long support in both government and public opinion, one might expect peacekeeping to head the list. Interestingly, peacekeeping ranked last. This could indicate that the role enjoys such a long-standing consensus that, in contrast to human rights and anti-proliferation, it needs no support through official statements. It was also in this period (1989-1993) that peacekeeping missions in both Bosnia and Somalia were encountering enough difficulty and frustration to bring the activity into question in Canada as well as elsewhere.

These roles reflect an internationalist tradition in Canada that goes back to the end of World War II when Canada committed itself to supporting the United Nations, efforts to promote peace and security and international development. The ranking just seen can be regarded as a stable long-term consensus between government and public.

liamentary democracy. In North America the results showed in a willingness to negotiate differences including ones over boundaries and a common interest in avoiding conflict—even though interests were badly at odds during the Civil War when Britain resented interruption by Union blockades of its profitable trade with the Confederacy.[70] Britain and France, although they were often keen colonial rivals, nonetheless formed an entente against Germany before World War I. They were joined by Italy, which abandoned an alliance with Germany and Austria in order not to fight fellow democracies.[71]

Liberal democracies are not peaceful across the board. They have been quite willing to go to war against non-liberal states. Part of the pattern may be accounted for as defence against aggressive authoritarians, but there are less pleasant aspects. Under liberal and democratic governments, both Britain and France engaged in ambitious colonial expansion in the 19th century. The United States fought an expansionist war with Mexico, intervened repeatedly in the affairs of Caribbean states and waged a war of conquest against the Indians. If liberal states are not inherently peaceful, they have kept a separate peace among themselves. Because liberal states in this century have included many of the world's most powerful, the phenomenon is significant. As former authoritarian states become democratic, the area of the **liberal peace** expands beyond Europe and North America.

The liberal peace has sparked much research in the last 15 years. Some scholars have denied that such a pattern actually exists, but a very recent study reanalyzing the data used to disprove the liberal peace finds that they actually confirm it.[72] One reason for the controversy is that the liberal peace contradicts two IR theories: Neorealism and Critical Theory.

Theory Contradicted

Neorealism explains peace as a result of successful deterrence: peace is preserved because states arm themselves against potential aggressors and discourage them from attack. States that are not strong enough to deter on their own align with others for the necessary level of force. For that strategy to work, states must be willing to align in whatever combinations provide the most discouraging prospects to an adversary. In picking partners, states should not hesitate over type of government.

A survey of state alignments in international conflicts between 1816 and 1986 belies that strategy. Liberal states align with each other and avoid authoritarian states. Authoritarian states do the same thing among themselves. Both democratic and authoritarian states stick with their own kind. That finding alone confounds a major tenet of Neorealism. Even more striking is that only authoritarian states were influenced by power calculations in their alignment choices. Liberal states were not. They align with each other even when doing so produces a less powerful union than they could get by aligning with authoritarian states. The determining factor is the nature of the domestic political and economic system and not considerations of power. Neorealism would predict power to be the determinate consideration. Instead, the historical record shows, states align with others like themselves.[73]

The other IR theory confounded by the liberal peace is Critical Theory. Peaceful hegemony, according to Critical Theory, exists because a dominant power maintains order by coercion and consensus, but dominant powers have come and gone, and liberal states, including smaller ones, have maintained continuous peace among themselves.[74] They have also refused to allow non-democratic states to become dominant, cooperating to resist Nazi Germany's and Imperial Japan's effort to displace Great Britain and to resist the Soviet Union's effort to displace the United States.

Also confounded is the Leninist expectation that imperial rivalry among capitalist states would lead to war. There has been rivalry but not war. Instead, warlike rivalry diminishes as states become democratic. As they do so, they abandon policies of hostility and widen the sphere of the democratic peace. The sphere increases with the expansion of democracy. "No matter how we look at it," declares one scholar, "democracy, rather than any other *ad hoc* explanation, accounts for the drastic reduction in levels of international conflict."[75]

Explaining Peace

What accounts for the peace among liberal states? Examining the question provides a good way of filling out the fusion approach with concrete items. The factors involved are a liberal checklist: institutions, public opinion, the articulation of interests and economic interdependence. They provide a concise way of concluding this tour of government and foreign policy. We begin with institutions.

Institutions, as we saw in Chapter 3, are not only the formal agencies of government, such as parliaments, cabinets and bureaucracies, but also the laws and understandings that frame expectations of proper behaviour and guide action. One important institutional feature is the tolerance of opposition, which increases with the level of democracy. Governments that tolerate dissent are more likely to be open to pressures and opinion, and that responsiveness tends to make the processes of decision, which can include the decision to go to war, transparent to the public. Openness and transparency tend to produce moderation, and on issues of war and peace, "The complexity of the decision-making process makes it unlikely that leaders will readily use military force unless they are confident of gathering enough domestic support for a low-cost war."[76]

Constitutions provide formal assurance of that responsiveness, and elections provide practical assurance. Representation, the vehicle of popular consent, is crucial. Toleration of multiple pressures also reflects the norm of moderation and compromise. Applied to decision-making, this norm supports "nonviolent and compromise-oriented resolution of political conflicts, the equality of the citizens, majority rule, tolerance for dissent, rights of minorities."[77] In liberal states, these norms are firmly anchored in constitutional practice and political culture and passed from government to government.

Toleration moves from domestic to external politics when the other states share the same norms. The relations among democratic states reflect their own domestic practices and not the idea of anarchy.[78] That moderation discourages perceptions of threatening intent, promotes negotiation and supports an interest in mutual gains. In contrast, authoritarian governments, because they do not rule by popular consent, are "in a state of aggression with their own people." Used to seeing their own populations as threats to be contained, their dealings with other states, particularly liberal ones, are wary and suspicious.[79]

Some constructivists dispute the liberal emphasis of domestic political practices. It may be assuming too much about the strength of democratic values and institutions to argue that the influences that guide domestic decisions govern the very different domain of war and peace even when the other states are democracies. The constructivist alternative explanation stresses intersubjective understandings: democratic states do not fight one another because they do not apprehend each other as enemies. Their mutual experience and expectations have prescribed forms of managing conflict that do not include war.[80]

Liberals emphasize the influence of the public: it dislikes unnecessary burdens and bears the cost of war. Political leaders know this. The better the public is represented, the less leaders will be able to impose heavy and unpopular costs. In authoritarian states, in contrast, "privileged individuals can easily pass on costs to others."[81] Because such governments also control or monopolize mass communication, they are more able to mobilize nationalism. An "amoral and technically rational" view of politics prevails.[82]

The quality of public opinion is important. Two scholars cite cosmopolitan outlooks as a force for moderation. Cosmopolitan views can briefly be characterized as open and tolerant: they "affirm universal values but appreciate diversity (within bounds)."[83] The basis of cosmopolitan views is prosperity. Prosperity depends on commerce, which in turn depends on peace. A combination of enlightened attitudes and economic self-interest is the result. In democratic states, government officials themselves tend to be cosmopolitan, providing a receptive political context.

Other scholars point out that democratic public opinion is not particularly receptive to aggressive hyper-nationalism. One factor is a political climate of free speech and opposition. That climate supports a critical mass media, which makes it difficult to promote myths of national superiority and expansion. Democracies that have succeeded in narrowing the distance between social classes remove some of the resentment and alienation that feed those myths. A moderate and critical public opinion is perhaps the single most important foundation of peace.[84]

A final base of the democratic peace is economic. Early in this century, a British peace advocate, Norman Angell, argued that war among the industrial states would not be profitable because the close financial ties among the major states would transmit the economic shock and disruption from one state to the other. That interdependence gave all major states a common interest in preserving stability. As well, trade and finance were such powerful generators of wealth that conquering territory for gain, a traditional goal of aggression, was no longer profitable. A state may no longer, in Angell's words, "enrich itself by subjugating another or imposing its will on another."[85]

Trade and industrial integration, seen in Chapter 8, do disperse production among a number of states. In economic terms, as we will see in Chapter 13, this represents an international division of labour in which each state contributes its particular resources. The benefits are larger markets, efficiency and a much wider array of goods than states could enjoy if they tried to meet all of their needs themselves. Price transactions, not political intervention, regulate those arrangements.

Leaving those transactions to the market, according to the Liberal Peace explanation, promotes a sense of shared purpose in avoiding disruptions. In the modern world economy, institutions such as the International Monetary Fund whose purpose is to maintain financial stability apply their own resources to the process. Allowing play to market forces also reduces the interventionist role of the state making it less easy to blame undesired economic outcomes on another state's malign or selfish actions. The market receives the blame instead.[86]

Neorealists and Critical Theorists Rebut the Democratic Peace

What rejoinders could neorealists and critical theorists make? One neorealist argues that the democratic peace overemphasizes several points. One point is the shared democratic values of moderation and compromise. Emphasizing them confuses peaceful values with practical interests: it is simply more convenient and safe to negotiate than to fight.[87] A second point is that government may put safeguarding "aggregate social welfare" ahead of public opinion in deciding to go to war. The public itself may find that rationale persuasive, and by appealing to it, a government may win the public's support. A third point addresses the burdens borne by the public and the reluctance of a free and informed public to accept them. The public may actually consider both the *costs* of war and the possible *gains* from war. Publics are also not always calm and judicious. In some circumstances they can become fervent and crusading. Authoritarian governments, free of public opinion, may be more pragmatically mindful of costs.[88] Finally, trade and commerce get a skeptical neorealist eye. The prospect of trade disruption and interrupted supplies are not a deterrent to war as long as there is a functioning world market. If states in a conflict risk losing trade and supply by going to war, the market, which functions to connect buyers and sellers, will provide alternatives and substitutes. Interruption is a problem only when those alternatives and substitutes are not available.[89]

How would a critical theorist respond to the democratic peace? The fact that hegemons come and go is less important than the fact that states in any hegemony have a common interest in cooperating to share the benefits of their position. Because the ruling elites at various levels of the hierarchy all see advantages for themselves, cooperation is pragmatic and not principled. Popular support does not express moderate values and altruism either. Successful hegemonies instill consent by persuading their citizens that the order works in their interest. On this point, Critical Theory and Neorealism share the same ground: Common interests explain peace better than democratic institutions and trade.[90]

Summary

Explaining state behaviour in the international system is a complex task. That is so because the behaviour responds to both domestic and external conditions. To see

FIGURE 9.7 What Do Middle Powers Have in Common?

The idea of a middle power originated with Canada. During the negotiations in 1945 that produced the United Nations Charter, the Canadian government worried that granting permanent seats on the Security Council to only great powers would lead to a dangerous concentration in the postwar order's executive body. Canada's argument for a seat emphasized its interest and willingness as a moderately sized but wealthy and democratic state to contribute to the maintenance of peace.

Canada did not get a permanent seat, but the idea of being a responsible and active agent for peace took hold. This idea crystallized into the role of middle power. The role was defined not just by capabilities but by internationalist and active intentions. Middle powers would use their influence to work for cooperation in international organizations such as the United Nations and, where necessary, seek to mitigate the dangers of great-power behaviour. As world politics polarized during the cold war, being a middle power took on the role of providing a moderating influence.

Being an effective middle power stems not from material capabilities but from membership in a plurality of international organizations and active relationships with the organizations' members. That, in turn, requires a level of engagement beyond that required by simple pragmatic interests and a reputation for capable, helpful and impartial behaviour.[91]

The role emerged in Canada as the public adopted the idea and supported it. One could argue that, after over 50 years, the idea of being a middle power has become a part of Canada's identity. Ideas that are entrenched to that degree can be strong forces that shape government's action: certain behaviour is simply expected both from the domestic population and from other states. Such expectations, plus a reasonable level of positive returns, perpetuate the role.

The role of middle power, defined as it is by patterns of behaviour, is not rigid, and various states have claimed that label over the years. The core members are generally regarded as Canada, Australia, the Scandinavian states and the Netherlands.

what those conditions might be we looked at Outside-In explanations, which focus on external conditions and Inside-Out explanations, which focus on domestic conditions. By assuming rational behaviour, it is possible to construct very concise Outside-In explanations—exemplified by Neorealism. The same is not true of Inside-Out explanations, which must account for an array of potentially important factors.

Liberalism provides a convenient way of organizing those factors by emphasizing the individual and group basis of politics. Ways of understanding the state are provided by approaches that regard it as possessing a measure of autonomy. Bureaucracy, the core of the state, is a pertinent focus because of its expertise and ability to formulate independent views. Taking account of the role of particular individuals often provides a needed dimension.

Accommodating both domestic and international factors into explanations of state behaviour compounds the task. IR has made recent efforts to combine the two sets of factors, and we saw one that poses commitments and capabilities against external threat.

One of IR's most striking facts is the peaceful record of liberal states, at least in their dealings with one another. States with the same kinds of domestic orders tend to align with each other. The implications of the liberal peace, if the conditions maintaining it so far continue to hold true, are an expanding order free of war. Examining the explanations for the liberal peace provides a convenient concluding overview of state behaviour.

ENDNOTES

1   Bruce M. Russett, *Controlling the Sword: The Democratic Governance of National Security*, Cambridge: Harvard University Press, 1990, p. 126.

2   Ole R. Holsti, "Theories of International Relations and Foreign Policy: Realism and Its Challengers," in Charles W. Kegley, Jr., ed., *Controversies in International Relations Theory: Neorealism and Its Challengers,* New York: St. Martin's 1995, p. 40.

3   Robert Gilpin, *War and Change in World Politics*, New York: Cambridge University Press, 1981, pp. 89–91.

4   Ethan Kapstein, "Is Realism Dead? The Domestic Sources of International Politics," *International Organization* 49 (Fall 1995) 755.

5   Martha Finnemore, *National Interests in International Society*, Ithaca: Cornell University Press, 1996, pp. 8, 9.

6   Martha Finnemore, "Norms, Culture, and World Politics: Insights from Sociology's Institutionalism," *International Organization* 50 (Spring 1996) 335–36.

7   John Mueller, "The Impact of Ideas on Grand Strategy," in Richard Rosecrance and Arthur A. Stein, eds., *The Domestic Bases of Grand Strategy*, Ithaca: Cornell University Press, 1993, p. 52.

8   Thomas U. Berger, "Norms, Identity, and National Security in Germany and Japan," in Peter Katzenstein, ed., *The Culture of National Security*, Ithaca: Cornell University Press, 1996, p. 320.

9   Gilpin, *War and Change*, p. 95.

10 Mueller, "The Impact of Ideas," p. 61.

11 Joseph Nye, "Neorealism and Neoliberalism," *World Politics* 40 (January 1988) 239, 248.

12 Jack Levy, "Domestic Politics and War," *Journal of Interdisciplinary History* 18 (Spring 1988) 657, 73.

13 Fareed Zakaria, "Realism and Domestic Politics," *International Security* 17 (Summer 1992) 180.

14 John Gerard Ruggie, "International Structure and International Transformation: Space, Time, and Method," in Ernst-Otto Czempiel and James N. Rosenau, eds., *Global Changes and Theoretical Challenges: Approaches to World Politics for the 1990s*, Lexington: Lexington Books, 1989, p. 32.

15 Robert Putnam, "Diplomacy and Domestic Politics: The Logic of Two-Level Games," *International Organization* 42 (Summer 1988) 430.

16 Mark W. Zacher and Richard A. Matthew, "Liberal International Theory: Common Threads, Divergent Strands," in Kegley, *Controversies in International Relations Theory*, p. 118.

17 *ibid.*, p. 119.

18 Matthew Evangelista, "The Paradox of State Strength: Transnational Relations, Domestic Structures, and Security Policy in Russia and the Soviet Union," *International Organization* 49 (Winter 1995) 1.

19 Jeffrey T. Checkel, *Ideas and International Political Change: Soviet/Russian Behavior and the End of the Cold War,* New Haven: Yale University Press, 1997, p. 8

20 Thomas Risse-Kappen, "Ideas Do Not Float Freely: Transnational Coalitions, Domestic Structures, and the End of the Cold War," *International Organization* 48 (Spring 1994) 186–87.

21 Evangelista, "The Paradox of State Strength," p. 9.

22 Denis Stairs, "The Public Politics of the Canadian Defence and Foreign Policy Reviews," *Canadian Foreign Policy* 3 (Spring 1995) 97.

23 *ibid.*, p. 98.

24   Jessica Matthews, "Power Shift," *Foreign Affairs* 75 (January/February 1997) 60–65.

25   Stephen Krasner, "Approaches to the State: Alternative Conceptions and Historical Dynamics," *Comparative Politics* 16 (January 1984) 224.

26   *ibid.*, p. 225.

27   *ibid.*, p. 229.

28   Kim Richard Nossal, "Contending Explanations for the Amalgamation of External Affairs," in Donald Story, ed., *The Canadian Foreign Service in Transition*, Toronto: Canadian Scholars' Press, 1993, p. 49.

29   *ibid.*, p. 50.

30   *ibid.*, p. 56.

31   Stephen D. Krasner, "U.S. Commercial and Monetary Policy: Unravelling the Paradox of External Strength and Internal Weakness," *International Organization* 31 (Fall 1977) 635–72.

32   Louis Delvoie, "Bilateralism in Foreign Policy: Canada and The Maghreb Countries," *Canadian Foreign Policy* 4 (Fall 1996) 56.

33   Anthony Downs, *Inside Bureaucracy,* Boston: Little, Brown, 1967, p. 50; James March and Herbert Simon, *Organizations*, New York: John Wiley, 1957, p. 152.

34   Michael Atkinson and William Coleman, "Strong States and Weak States: Sectoral Policy Networks in Advanced Capitalist Economies," *British Journal of Political Science* 19 (January 1989) 51.

35   Jeffrey Legro, "Culture and Preferences in the International Cooperation Two-Step," *American Political Science Review* 90 (March 1996) 122.

36   Kim Richard Nossal, "Allison through the (Ottawa) Looking Glass: Bureaucratic Politics in a Parliamentary System," *Canadian Public Administration* 22 (Winter 1979) 610–26.

37   Donald Barry, "The Canada-European Turbot War: Internal Politics and Transatlantic Bargaining," *International Journal* 53 (Spring 1998) 280–82.

38   Robert Jervis, "Rational Deterrence: Theory and Evidence," *World Politics* 41 (January 1989) 203–05.

39   Benjamin Most and Harvey Starr, "International Relations Theory, Foreign Policy Substitutability, and 'Nice' Laws," *World Politics* 36 (April 1984) 387.

40   J.L. Granatstein and Robert Bothwell, *Pirouette: Pierre Trudeau and Canadian Foreign Policy*, Toronto: University of Toronto Press, 1990, p. 365, 366

41   Ivan L. Head and Pierre Elliott Trudeau, *The Canadian Way: Shaping Canada's Foreign Policy 1968-1984*, Toronto: McClelland and Stewart, 1995, p. 301.

42   Granatstein and Bothwell, *Pirouette*, pp. 366–67, 368, 369.

43   Head and Trudeau, *The Canadian Way*, pp. 306–07

44   Granatstein and Bothwell, *Pirouette,* pp. 369–70.

45   Head and Trudeau, *The Canadian Way*, p. 307.

46   *ibid.*, p. 308.

47   Steven R. David, "The Primacy of Internal War," in Stephanie Neuman, ed., *International Relations Theory and the Third World,* New York: St. Martin's Press, 1998, p. 87.

48   Zakaria, "Realism and Domestic Politics," pp. 192–93.

49   Edward D. Mansfield and Jack Snyder, "Democratization and the Danger of War," *International Security* 20 (Summer 1995) 26–30.

50   Andrew Janos, "Paradigms Revisited: Productionism, Globality and Postmodernity in Comparative Politics," *World Politics* 50 (October 1997) 133.

51   Lori Buck, Nichole Gallant and Kim Richard Nossal, "Sanctions as a Gendered Instrument of Statecraft: The Case of Iraq," *Review of International Studies,* 24 (January 1998) 80–84.

52   John H. Maurer, "Arms Control and the Anglo-German Naval Race Before World War I: Lessons for Today?" *Political Science Quarterly* 112 (Summer 1997) 288-290, 295–96.

53   David D'Lugo and Ronald Rogowski, "The Anglo-German Naval Race and Comparative Constitutional 'Fitness,'" in Rosecrance and Stein, eds., *The Domestic Bases of Grand Strategy,* pp. 93–95.

54 *Economist*, May 9, 1998, p. 42

55 Jaswant Singh, "Against Nuclear Apartheid," *Foreign Affairs* 77 (September/October 1998) 48–49.

56 *Economist,* May 9, 1998, p. 43.

57 *Economist*, May 23, 1998, p. 37.

58 James Manor and Gerald Siegel, "Taking India Seriously," *Survival* 40 (Summer 1998) 63.

59 *Economist* May 16, 1998, p. 15; July 11, 1998, p. 43.

60 Helen Milner, "International Theories of Cooperation Among Nations: Strengths and Weaknesses," *World Politics* 44 (April 1992) 489–94.

61 Zakaria, "Realism and Domestic Politics," p. 196.

62 Kapstein, "Is Realism Dead?" p. 772.

63 Richard Rosecrance and Arthur A. Stein, "Beyond Realism: The Study of Grand Strategy," in Rosecrance and Stein, eds., *The Domestic Bases of Grand Strategy*, pp. 17–19.

64 Bruce Russett, "Processes of Dyadic Choice for War and Peace," *World Politics* 47 (January 1995) 268–69.

65 Arthur A. Stein, "Domestic Constraints, Extended Deterrence, and the Incoherence of Grand Strategy: The United States, 1938–1950," in Rosecrance and Stein, eds., *The Domestic Bases of Grand Strategy*, p. 100.

66 *ibid.*

67 Paul A. Papayouanou, "Economic Interdependence and the Balance of Power," *International Studies Quarterly* 41 (March 1997) 118–22.

68 Andre P. Donneur and Caroline C. Alain, "Canada: A Reassertion of Its Role as a Middle Power," in Philippe G. Le Prestre, ed., *Role Quests in the Post-Cold War Era: Foreign Policies in Transition*, Montreal and Kingston: McGill-Queen's University Press, 1997, pp. 233–35.

69 Levy, "Domestic Politics and War," 662.

70 Michael W. Doyle, "Kant, Liberal Legacies and Foreign Affairs, Part I," *Philosophy and Public Affairs* 12 (Summer 1983) 216.

71 Michael W. Doyle, "Liberalism and World Politics Revisited," in Charles W. Kegley, Jr., ed., *Controversies in International Relations Theory*, p. 89.

72 Zeev Maoz, "The Controversy over the Democratic Peace: Rearguard Action or Cracks in the Wall?" *International Security* 22 (Summer 1997) 164–77.

73 Suzanne Werner and Douglas Lemke, "Opposites Do Not Attract: The Impact of Domestic Institutions, Power, and Prior Commitments on Alignment Choices," *International Studies Quarterly* 41 (September 1997) 534–44.

74 Doyle, "Liberalism and World Politics Revisited," p. 94.

75 Maoz, "The Controversy Over the Democratic Peace," 181.

76 Thomas Risse-Kappen, "Collective Identity in a Democratic Community," in Peter Katzenstein, ed., *The Culture of National Security*, Ithaca: Cornell University Press, 1996, p. 366.

77 *ibid.*

78 Randall Schweller, "Domestic Structure and Preventive War," *World Politics* 44 (January 1992) 250.

79 Michael W. Doyle, "Liberalism and World Politics," *American Political Science Review* 80 (December 1986) 1161.

80 Ted Hopf, "The Promise of Constructivism in International Relations Theory," *International Security* 23 (Summer 1998) 192.

81 Andrew Moravcsik, "Taking Preferences Seriously: A Liberal Theory of International Politics," *International Organization* 51 (Fall 1997) 531.

82 Schweller, "Domestic Structure and Preventive War," p. 250.

83 Nicholas G. Onuf and Thomas J. Johnson, "Peace in the Liberal World: Does Democracy Matter?" in Kegley, Jr., ed., *Controversies in International Relations Theory*, p. 192.

84 Steven Van Evera, "Primed for Peace: Europe After the Cold War," *International Security* 15 (Winter 1990-91) 26-29.

85   Richard Little, "The Growing Relevance of Pluralism?" in Steve Smith, Ken Booth, Marysia Zalewski, eds., *International Theory: Positivism and Beyond?* Cambridge: Cambridge University Press, 1996, p. 71.

86   Michael W. Doyle, "Politics and Grand Strategy," in Rosecrance and Stein, eds., *The Domestic Bases of Grand Strategy*, pp. 33–34.

87   Joanne Gowa, "Democratic States and International Disputes," *International Organization* 49 (Summer 1995) 516.

88   John Mearsheimer, "Back to the Future: Instability in Europe after the Cold War," *International Security* 15 (Summer 1990) 49–50.

89   Gowa, "Democratic States and International Disputes," 520.

90   *ibid.,* 522.

91   Laura Neack, "Linking State Type with Foreign Policy Behavior," in Laura Neack, Jeanne A.K. Hey and Patrick J. Haney, eds., *Foreign Policy Analysis: Continuity and Change in Its Second Generation,* Englewood Cliffs: Prentice Hlll 1995, pp. 224–26.

WEBLINKS

The site of Canada's Department of Foreign Affairs and International Trade is:
 www.dfait-maeci.gc.ca

The Department of National Defence's site is:
www.dnd.ca

The University of Keele has links to official government web sites:
www.keele.ac.uk/depts/po/official.htm

Respected studies of particular countries' foreign policies can be found at the Brookings Institution's site:
www.brookings.org

A Web site for diplomats emphasizes negotiation and law of the sea issues:
www.clark.net/pub/diplomat/DiploNet.html

The Carnegie Endowment for International Peace's site includes an address directory of the world's politicians. The site's Embassy Page is a diplomacy database that will eventually have addresses for over 50,000 diplomatic posts around the world.
www.ceip.org

Sources of Peril

Warfare as Human Practice

Is warfare inextricably tied to human history? Has there ever been a time when the threat of war did not hover even distantly over societies and states? One scholar, drawing on a mass of anthropological, archeological and historical data, has studied war over the last 10,000 years. That time span provides a more representative record than is found in the most recent centuries, which contain less than three percent of humankind's total history.[1] Organized warfare, he concludes, is not a modern invention but reaches back at least to the end of the last Ice Age.[2] The fate of the Neanderthals who inhabited Europe during the Glacial Period (100,000 to 10,000 years ago) may have been unsuccessful warfare. They appear to have been killed and dispersed by *homo sapiens* (modern man) in what may have been "history's first genocide." War has been relatively constant since then although it was "somewhat less frequent in antiquity."[3]

Was war a practice that some civilizations learned from others? There seems to have been no single point of origin. Instead, organized warfare appears to have arisen in three widely separated areas: in the Middle East in the Tigris-Euphrates Rivers Basin between 2900 BC and 2750 BC, in China in the Yellow River Basin between 2400-155 BC and in North America along the Gulf of Mexico between 1600 BC and AD 1. There is some evidence that warfare also originated independently in the upper Nile and central Andes regions.[4]

In each region, wars were fought, and states rose and declined. Warfare was a well-practiced institution by the time the civilization that evolved from the Yellow River basin encountered the civilization that evolved from the Tigris-Euphrates, and the two were relatively well-matched in their experience with war and governance. As a result, contact between them did not result in the fate of the Neanderthals. The Han Chinese, Mongols and Romans not only survived but prospered through trade.[5] The same was not true later when the successor civilization, spearheaded by Spain, encountered the Amerindian civilization in the New World. Favouring the Europeans, the scholar asserts, was a much longer evolutionary base of organization and war. Having less than a third of the Europeans' experience, the Amerindians were unable to resist them.

What does this massive historical study say about humankind and warfare? The conclusion is succinct: "Warfare is robust, cross-cultural and universal. It did not diffuse out of one area nor was it learned from a single area." Warfare also did not stunt the growth of civilization. On the contrary, "high levels of civilized life within stable and prosperous polities occurred synchronically with high levels of bloody cruelty and barbarity."[6] The threat of war and violence, it appears, pervades the past, and dread has been one of humankind's regular companions. Security continues as one of IR's focal concerns. Traditionally understood in terms of war, security recently has been seen to encompass a broader range of threats.

Security

Security has a concise definition: it is a "low probability of damage to acquired values."[7]

This definition leads to very specific considerations:

➤ *which* values are threatened?
➤ *who* threatens them?
➤ *what* is the agency of threat?

This definition also makes the response concrete:

➤ *which* values are to be protected?
➤ by what *means*?
➤ at what *cost*?[8]

Traditionally, security has been understood in military terms. By distinguishing between values and means, this scheme gives military threats two faces. The power to injure and kill threatens the personal value of physical integrity. Organized as military force and directed against whole populations, the power to injure and kill threatens the collective values of political, economic and social integrity. It is the prospect of individual and collective harm that connects military threats to values and makes military force an instrument of coercion. Military force is not the only agency of threat. Separating the elements of threat—to what, from which source and by what agency—identifies others. Economic and environmental threats address important values but have little to do with military force. We will see economic and environmental threats momentarily. Military threats begin on familiar ground.

Sovereignty and Independence

What values can military force threaten? Sovereignty and independence are the most basic. Armed invasion violates sovereignty and threatens a state with the loss of territory, people and resources. If the invasion defeats the government, the state ceases to be sovereign. One consequence of losing sovereignty, which was frequent throughout European history as we saw in Chapter 6, is annexation to the victorious state. That consequence can still happen. Annexing the oil-producing province of Khuzestan was one of Iraq's purposes when it invaded Iran in 1981. Annexing all of Kuwait was Iraq's purpose in invading that state in 1990.

Annexation can mean more than just the loss of territory and sovereignty. Tibet was invaded by China in 1950 and was made an autonomous province in 1951. Since then, thousands of Chinese have been settled in Tibet, a tiny society compared to China. The practice of Buddhism has been brought under state control, ending a system of political and spiritual rule under the Dalai Lama who fled after an unsuccessful uprising in 1959. Although Tibet had been under Chinese influence or domination for much of its history and was independent only between 1912 and 1950, China's treatment of Tibet has been a focus in recent years of international attention. Human rights have been one concern, but a broader one is Tibet's survival as a nation. A defeated government and a territory occupied to dilute the resident population may indeed threaten values at that comprehensive level.

The Political Order

The familiar view of the cold war is that it was a massive military standoff. In the view of some scholars, the stakes of the cold war were as much political as they were military. The military threat was Soviet annexation of Europe's industrial and scientific resources. Even in their diminished postwar condition, those resources would have represented a major shift of military potential to the Soviet side. The political threat was the "Soviet domestic order, combined with Soviet behaviour in Eastern Europe, [which indicated] a willingness to expand Communism beyond the USSR." That put at risk the domestic order of Western Europe.[9] Had Stalin been content to leave the east European states nominally independent as he did with Finland, the cold war might not have happened. Instead, his installing Soviet-controlled governments in Eastern Europe raised the same prospect for the states of Western Europe. The dual nature of the Soviet threat is reflected in NATO's original purpose, which was to preserve the political systems of the European members through a military alliance. As a strong advocate of the alliance in 1949, Canada's aim was political: to help protect democratic rule in Europe. In a constructivist view, the enemy had a different identity for different allies. For the United States, the enemy's identity was communist while for the Europeans, it was Russian.[10]

The Economy

Thinking about security as threats to important values readily includes economic threats. These may include deliberate and hostile actions by other states. Economic sanctions in which one or a group of states limits or cuts off trade with a target state are one example. We will see more about economic sanctions in the next chapter. Another threat is economic espionage in which one state uses its intelligence-gathering capabilities to get industrial secrets from another. What makes that practice more serious than simple theft of intellectual property is its impact on a state's economic competitiveness particularly when leading-edge technologies and products are involved. The danger is that the state stealing those secrets will apply them to its own products for trade advantages. If its economy gains at the expense of one's own, the threat can indeed be seen as a matter of national security. Industrial espionage becomes a military threat when the technologies have dangerous military applications. For both reasons, in the view of the Canadian Security Intelligence Service, industrial espionage is one of the most serious security threats facing Canada.

FIGURE 10.1 What Threatens Canada?

During the cold war, Canada's two prime security interests were Western Europe and North America. The Soviet threat to Western Europe was indirect as far as Canada was concerned, but, as with both World War I and World War II, Canada's interest was helping to protect against an important shift in the world balance of power and the loss of democratic rule in some of the most important states.[11] Canada's commitment involved stationing ground and air units in Germany. The threat to North America was nuclear war to which Canada, with population centres adjacent to American targets, was uncomfortably proximate. Canada's involvement was participating in a joint air defence arrangement with the United States under NORAD. Peacekeeping's original conception, which won Lester Pearson the Nobel Prize, was to interpose neutral forces in local conflicts to prevent their escalating and drawing in the superpowers. In that way, peacekeeping was part of the cold war.

With the demise of the Soviet Union and the militarily weakened condition of Russia, the threats facing Europe owe more to regional instability than to external aggression. As we will see in the next chapter, the Europeans have been seeking a means to provide for common security and have sought to re-direct NATO. There have been other proposals such as the revival of the Western European Union, an idea originally put forward in the 1950s for a European-based security system. These developments ended the rationale for keeping Canadian forces in Europe, and Canada withdrew its army and air force units from Germany.

North America no longer faces the prospect of a Soviet nuclear attack. NORAD remains, and Canada continued its participation in 1996 when the bilateral agreement came up for renewal, but both states have cut back facilities. NORAD's rationale has shifted to drug interdiction and monitoring North American airspace.[12]

Europe and the United States have become different security partners. Europe "is distinctly absorbed in its own problems, especially in the security area." For its part, the United States "has not had less need of Canada for many decades."[13] The end of the cold war has also changed the rationale for peacekeeping. While expansion of conflicts in places such as the Balkans could threaten regional security, they no longer risk superpower collision. Participating in international interventions advances other purposes including humanitarian ones and a commitment to global order, but its connection with Canadian security interests is not immediate.[14]

As always, Canada's position, apart from the world's active zones of conflict, provides a measure of distance, and threats tend to arise from conflict and instability elsewhere.[15] Two threats directly affect Canada. In its public report, the Canadian Security Intelligence Service identified terrorism and economic espi-

onage. Terrorism is a potentially immediate threat because of the ability of terrorist groups to operate in a variety of countries. Many, according to CSIS, have infrastructures in Canada and could carry out terrorist acts here. Economic espionage,
when sponsored by foreign governments, threatens economic security: "lost contracts, jobs and markets and a diminished competitive advantage." Efforts by nuclear weapons-seeking states to acquire technology and materials from Canada
pose a long-term threat because of proliferation.[16]

The reality of weapons of mass destruction was brought home by Indian and
Pakistani nuclear tests in 1998 and in Iraq's continued efforts to conceal its chemical, biological and nuclear weapons and production facilities from UN inspectors.
A North Korean test-firing of a medium-range missile over Japan and into the
Pacific in 1998 may have been intended to show its capabilities to potential buyers. The fact that those buyers exist and that North Korea would like to export missile and weapons technology provides a sobering reminder that international controls
on these weapons, while impressive, are not complete. To some, these conditions
have fostered an uneasy sense that international security may have gone through a
serene but temporary phase after the cold war, and although direct threats are not
manifest now, a more troubled and dangerous world order may be in store.

What kind of armed forces should Canada have? The question perplexes defence
planners who must cope both with Ottawa's budget-cutting and an uncertain international environment. The *1994 Defence White Paper*, which emerged from the
Liberal government's foreign policy review, concluded that "it seems prudent to
plan for a world characterized in the long term by instability." Because threats to
Canada may come in ways that affect other states, the *White Paper* maintained,
Canada requires a continuing commitment to collective defence and peacekeeping
and an ability to participate effectively. What kind of forces meet that requirement? The *White Paper* recommended that they be "multi-purpose and combat- capable."[17] In the face of uncertainty, it argued, the best posture is flexibility.

At the same time, economic threats may have nothing to do with hostile intentions and military capability. That was made clear to Canadians in 1998 when
major Asian economies went into recession. (We will see more about the Asian
crisis in Chapter 12) As large Asian firms failed or struggled for survival, employment and incomes fell, cutting demand for manufactures. That reduced demand
for important Canadian exports particularly mineral and forest products, which in
turn put speculative pressure on the Canadian dollar. Although Canada's economy itself remained healthy, as the government insisted to both Canadians and
foreign traders, the value of its currency on world exchange markets was pulled
down in reaction to events in Asia. In August 1998, the Canadian dollar fell to
an all-time low of 63 cents against the American dollar. The economic threat from
lower exports was damage to regional economies, particularly resource-based ones
in the West. The threat from a lower dollar was more expensive imports and ultimately a higher cost of living. Both posed harm to Canadian well-being. Another
threat was the much cheaper price of Canadian assets to foreign investors. Offsetting
these disadvantages was bargain-sale prices for all Canadian exports. Producers
selling not to Asia but to the United States enjoyed a windfall although the region
reaping most of the benefits was southern Ontario and not the West.

For the major industrial economies in general, the Asian crisis threatened economic stability. Some Asian states, hoping to keep existing shares of export markets and earn money for recovery, devalued their currencies to make their exports cheaper. For states such as China with competing goods to sell, the choice was either to devalue as well or to face lost export market share. Devaluation in Asia and the threat of more to come put pressure on Latin American states to follow suit or face damage to the export positions of their mineral commodities and manufactures. To make things worse, the Russian economy entered a severe crisis, forcing the government to devalue the ruble. These devaluations, and the prospect of further ones, threatened to introduce potentially dangerous instability into global financial markets. The United States, which depends much less than most industrial countries on exports, began seeing the results of the Asian crisis in reduced earnings of some of its largest corporations. Combined with anxiety about Russia, that crystallized in a massive sell-off in world stock markets in September 1998. The New York stock market lost 40 percent of its value within days. The Toronto stock market lost 30 percent. Aside from erasing trillions of dollars of asset values held by individual investors and pension plans, the global sell-off was an index of general economic insecurity.

The Environment

Environmental threats can take two forms. The first affects all states in common although some may be more exposed than others. Global warming is one common threat. Although its course and results are still unclear, one consequence is quite foreseeable: a rise in global temperature will begin melting the polar icecaps. For states with long shorelines and adjacent low-lying areas, the result could be widespread inundation—both of water-level metropolises such as Amsterdam and of entire regions such as southern Bangladesh. Some low-lying Pacific island states face the prospect of literally disappearing under the waves. Less clear are the likely climatic effects although shifts in the patterns of rainfall could have drastic consequences for the world's food-growing states. If less rainfall in some producing regions, perhaps the Canadian prairie, were not matched by more rainfall in others, perhaps the arid region of Argentina, the world would have to share the result—less food output.

The second form of environmental threat affects particular states. Deforestation and soil erosion, although they are collective problems, have the most serious effects locally because they affect states' ability to provide food and livelihood for their populations. The impacts on poor states are the most severe because they lack the wealthier states' economic and institutional capacity. Environmental damage, combined with poverty and economic underdevelopment, can worsen conditions in states already coping with major problems and stretched facilities.

Some scholars have argued that environmental scarcity leads to conflict among states. One common version of this argument is that heavy resource use by the wealthy states leads to depleted supplies and scarcities, placing states in direct competition with each other and increasing the risk of violent conflict. There is no common view on how scarcity could actually *cause* conflict. One reason is that scarcity may not be as compelling as one might expect. In many industries, as we saw in Chapter 8, raw materials have become secondary to knowledge and technology as the most valuable ingredients in production. Market forces may also blunt conflict by raising the prices of scarce commodities forcing users to find substitutes. Emergency-level scarcities may lead not to conflict but to common efforts as we will see momentarily with the G-7's origins.[18]

Meeting Threats

Threats posed by military force can be addressed by military force. This can be done in two ways. The first is active use to repel attack. The second is latent use to discourage attack. Since these uses of force are both protective, we will see them in Chapter 11 when we examine the sources of safety. We will see more shortly about the prospects of attack when we consider the security dilemma.

Meeting individual economic threats depends in part on the actions of individual governments. The central banks of states often buy up their own currency in world exchange markets to counter large-scale selling. (Selling lowers a currency's value on world markets; buying raises it). The Bank of Canada did so on several occasions in the summer of 1998 in an effort to prop up the falling Canadian dollar. Sometimes central banks of several states will cooperate in buying another currency to preserve its value and keep exchange rates in line.

Export markets narrow or close for reasons that governments may not be able to influence. There is not much that governments such as Canada can do on their own to revive the Asian economies and restore export volumes. Export markets may also shrink because of another state's protectionism (we will examine protectionism in Chapter 12). Here governments do have latitude for individual action. When a state's protectionist action violates the General Agreement on Tariffs and Trade, the threat can be met by filing a complaint with the World Trade Organization (as we will see in Chapter 12) or through diplomatic pressure. One reason why states such as Canada have supported expanding the powers of the WTO is to make trade remedy available in the interests of economic security.

Meeting general economic threats depends on collective action from many governments. The annual summit meeting of the Group of Seven states (United States, Canada, Britain, France, Germany, Japan, Italy) began in 1975 to coordinate responses to the inflation and stagnation that were hobbling the world's industrial economies and crippling the developing ones. The G-7 has developed since then into a cooperative forum for coordinating economic and monetary policy among the member states. They devote effort to the G-7 because they recognize that many economic threats require collective action by the world's major states. Because the G-7 members together represent almost half of the world's economic capacity, successful coordination can be widely influential. Like all summit meetings, the G-7 can act because the heads of government who attend along with their finance ministers and central bank directors have the personal authority to negotiate and to make commitments.

The International Monetary Fund (IMF) is an intergovernmental organization that was originally set up to restore monetary stability to postwar Europe and to prevent the individual state actions, such as competitive currency devaluations, that helped to worsen the Great Depression. Since then, the IMF has taken on a much larger role of being a lender of last resort to governments facing financial crises. In 1998, the IMF addressed the Asian crisis with a series of massive loans to the hardest-hit states, notably South Korea and Indonesia. That same year it provided an emergency loan to Russia to help stave off financial collapse, continuing a series of loans to that country stretching back to the early 1990s. One motive for providing these loans was to prevent an even worse breakdown. Since such collapses would affect all of the world's states—the developing ones in particular if North American and European economies also went into recession and cut their purchases of imports—the IMF's actions can be seen as a means of addressing a common threat to economic security.

Means of addressing environmental threats are more diverse. One way is cooperating to curb destructive emissions. The Montreal Convention of 1987, in which states pledged to reduce their production of chlorofluorocarbons, which attack the ozone layer, could be seen as a common measure against an environmental threat. Much more challenging is attacking the source of greenhouse gases because doing so requires reducing the use of fossil fuels. For states such as Canada and the United States, which rely on private cars for transportation, cutting emissions means less driving and more public transit. For China, which relies on coal for much of its energy, cutting emissions means adopting different industrial technologies. There is no equivalent of the IMF in the environmental area. The United Nations Environment Program was established in 1973 but has little direct power. It has served as a coordinator and clearing house for non-governmental organizations (NGOs) in their dealings with the UN. We will see more about environmental NGOs and greenhouse gases in Chapter 13.

Thinking about Security

If we focus on national and individual well-being, security can be construed very broadly. One scholar sees human disease as a good comparison. Both pose the fear of "pain and severe loss."[19] Because security in both cases is based as much on prospect (fear) as well as reality (pain and loss), it is as much a state of mind as well as an objective situation. That state of mind differs by locale. From the perspective of prosperous states such as Canada, the level of poverty and hardship common in the developing world appears extreme. From Canada's safely located perspective, the level of military threat faced by Israel is frightening.[20] On a more general level, the values that give personal significance to fear, pain and loss depend on what people believe, on their experience and on the meanings their culture and society ascribe.[21]

At the same time, viewing security in these terms risks having it mean everything and nothing. Believing that the most severe dangers to security remain military, some scholars argue that "defining security broadly will squeeze out work on the military aspects."[22] Others believe that military concerns make sense only in reference to values. In one scholar's words, "There is something peculiarly un-Clausewitzian about studying military force without devoting equal attention to the purposes for which it is used." (In his work, *On War*, Karl Von Clausewitz (1780-1831) stated the famous dictum that war is the continuation of politics by other means.) In that perspective, the central question to ask is: "Under what conditions should states employ military force and for what purposes?"[23]

One way of reconciling these two views is to see military force in the perspective of three concentric circles. The inner circle is the domain of traditional military science, which is concerned with resources, tactics and battles. The outer circle is the state's overall security ("everything that bears on the safety of a polity"). The middle circle joins the two: "how political ends and military means interact under social, economic and other constraints."[24]

There is one last point to consider about security. So far we have treated security for a state and its people as the same as security for the state's government and ruling elite. Are the two necessarily identical? Can a government have different security interests than its people? We had a glimpse of this problem in the last chapter when we looked at the foreign policy interests of ruling elites. In states where governments rule without popular consent, rulers face the prospect of being overthrown. For the rulers in question, that prospect is a direct threat to their personal security. Is there some way of incorporating that threat into our scheme? We can do so by adding regime security—a government's ability to protect itself from being overthrown.[25] Adding this element also makes us aware that the ability to define and act on security threats rests with government. As we saw in the last chapter, democratic governments have less leeway than authoritarian ones to pursue a political leadership's self-serving interests because of the greater variety of group interests that may be represented and because of the greater latitude for political opposition. As we also saw in the last chapter, one of the limitations facing democratic governments in dealing with security threats is persuading citizens to endure sacrifices. Democracies in the 1990s have shown themselves to be particularly unwilling to accept military casualties.[26]

The Security Dilemma

The **security dilemma** is a condition of uncertainty. A state creates a security dilemma when it develops or expands its military force. Other states are faced with the question of whether to be concerned. They need not be if the force is defensive. Other states can regard it as simply a prudent resource in an insecure world. But if the force is offensive, other states have every reason to worry. Acquiring offensive force can be read as preparation for attack.[29] Whether the force is offensive or defensive depends crucially on the state's intentions. How can they be known?

**FIGURE 10.2 Armed Forces in Developing States:
The View from Critical Theory**

Critical theory, as we saw in Chapter 5, focuses on hegemony. Domestic hegemony exists when the state is in the hands of a dominant bloc. In capitalist states, that bloc is formed of economic elites and like-minded political parties. The hegemony rules in its political and economic interests through a mixture of persuasion and coercion. Peaceful hegemony exists when citizens are persuaded to accept the existing order regardless of whether it rules in their interests. International hegemony exists when a group of powerful states manages international economic and political relationships in its own interests. Again, the sustaining means is a mixture of coercion and persuasion. International hegemony is peaceful when subordinate states accept their position in the prevailing arrangement.

In considering the position of developing states, the critical theory perspective focuses on colonial origins. Elites who achieved ascendance under colonial rule tended to continue as national leaderships after independence. The former colonial powers, members of the global hegemony, retained their dominance of the world's political and economic relations and were pleased to accommodate the new states as subordinate members. The hegemonic powers' interest was a stable supply of materials and favourable terms of trade, and their economic dominance kept developing states in a position of subordination. The economic relationship made the independent states tied to selling commodity exports, limiting their possibilities for development.

As managers of that unequal relationship in their own states and directly subject to domestic dissatisfaction with slow or absent economic development, Third World political leaderships have suffered problems of legitimacy. For them, security threats come as much from home as from abroad, and the safest form of military organization avoids putting large numbers of the citizenry under arms. Adequate defence thus relies on modern weaponry. Its suppliers are the hegemonic states.[27]

For their part, the hegemonic states appreciate the export opportunities for these high-unit value military commodities. Their interest in supply is enhanced by their interest in helping cooperative local elites stay in power. The rubric of national security furnishes an element of persuasion, justifying military ties with subordinate states and maintaining the coercive backstop of hegemony.[28]

Declarations may not be very helpful. What if the state insists that its purposes are purely defensive? That may indeed be true, and if it is, other states can rest easy. But what if the insistence is a deception to lull the others into a false sense of security? If that is the case, resting easy may give the state time to prepare a successful attack. Waiting to see more of its behaviour may not be a good idea. If its intentions turn out to be aggressive, time to prepare a counter force has been lost. What if the arming state is merely being insensitive? It has no hostile intent but takes actions that another state might consider offensive or makes irresponsibly provocative statements.[30] Again, the answer depends on its intentions. If they are defensive, the behaviour can be discounted. If they are offensive, the behaviour is a warning.

The difference is crucial to security. Defensive preparations signal that the state does not wish to upset the prevailing order. Its intentions are security-seeking, and they threaten no one. Offensive preparations signal that the state aims to overturn the prevailing order and take more for itself. Its intentions are greedy, and they threaten other states with aggression or by blackmailing into concessions.

How can others determine what the state's intentions are? Some kinds of military preparations are inherently suspicious. Adding more forces than are required to defend the state may reveal greedy intentions, and willingness to pay for those forces can be an important clue. A state that desires only defence will be less willing to bear the extra costs than a greedy state. Acquiring offensive weapons may also reveal greedy intentions. Although some defensive strategies involve offensive moves (such as striking first against an invading force), a greedy state is more likely to hold offensive outlooks more generally and to emphasize offensive capability. Those outlooks also make it less concerned about insensitive behaviour and alarming its neighbours: it *expects* conflict. Such behaviour itself may be an index of its intentions. Even so, acquiring arms is not always a sure tip-off. A greedy state that wants to disguise its intentions will build more weapons than it needs for defence but keep the level below the threshold of alarming others.[31]

Security-seeking states may generate uncertainty themselves. A state that is already quite secure may lead others to believe that it does not fear them. If it proceeds to acquire *more* weapons, the others may assume that it has become greedy. Why else would a state that does not fear others become stronger?[32]

Because the security dilemma exists in peoples' minds, it contains rich possibilities for false perceptions. Here are some kinds of thinking that complicate the task of estimating other states' intentions:

➤ *Ethnocentrism:* This kind of thinking puts national identity at the centre. By emphasizing differences, it aggravates the tendency to justify one's own motives and impugn the other's

➤ *Ideological or religious fundamentalism:* It adds doctrinal or moral absolutes to we-they thinking, posits implacable hostility and fosters uncompromising positions

➤ *Worst-case forecasting:* The job of military planners is to foresee and be ready for the worst. If such thinking carries over from planning to making real estimates, it can lead to inaccurately sombre conclusions

➤ *Excessive Neorealism:* Emphasizing conflict and relative gains (see pp. 17–19) promotes a sharply win-lose view of the world and an alarmist attitude about changes in force levels

➤ *Excessive Institutionalism:* Emphasizing shared interests and mutual gains (see pp. 19–23) promotes a benign and mellow view of the world that may underestimate genuine threats[33]

These possibilities are important. If they affect the thinking of people responsible for making threat estimates and strategic decisions, they may lead to drastic miscalculations.

What Causes the Security Dilemma?

There are two schools of thought. The first, exemplified by Neorealism, believes that the security dilemma is inherent in the condition of anarchy. The security dilemma arises because each state seeks to protect itself by arming. When it does so it makes its neighbours less secure. They, in turn, arm to protect themselves. "The means to anyone's security," writes Kenneth Waltz, "is a threat to someone else who in turn responds by arming." States are not the source of the problem. The security dilemma is produced "not by their wills but by their situations."[34] The problem resides in the system.

What about anarchy itself? Is it bound to breed the insecurity that prompts states to arm and threaten each other? Group identification provides a good case that it does, as we saw in the critiques of Constructivism (see pp. 65) in Chapter 4. When people affiliate with a group, they develop a sense of loyalty to it. As that happens, they make an increasingly sharp differentiation between those inside the group and those outside. The differentiation breeds disregard: "Group comparisons are not neutral: people generally do not strongly identify with groups they believe to be inferior to other groups." The result is invidious: "People who have [even] minimal identification with a group will discriminate against people in [another] group for no apparent reason."[35] Applying that same reasoning to states, popular identification produces mutual disregard between states, creating a climate of distrust, insecurity and concern with relative gains. International anarchy is "in-groupness" magnified. Mutual disregard gives states good reason to wonder about the others' intentions.

What about the states? Does anarchy doom them to permanent vigilance and suspicion? Not at all, according to the second school of thought. The system does not produce the security dilemma; states do.[36] Anarchy itself can accommodate either war or peace. Which condition prevails depends on the intentions and behaviour of the individual states. If the intentions are peaceful, anarchy can be benign. If they are aggressive, anarchy can be sinister. As we saw in the last chapter, there is strong evidence that a particular kind of states—liberal democracies—do not go to war against each other although they are quite capable of acting vigorously against authoritarian states. The constitution of the state (literally its basic political order) makes a big difference. Democracies can feel secure amongst themselves.

Can these two views of insecurity —system v. state—be reconciled? As we saw in Chapter 2, whether to be trusting or suspicious of a state depends much on previous experience (pp. 22). If that experience is one of deception and aggression, there is good reason to be wary and to treat any evidence of greed (such as acquiring offensive weapons) very seriously. If the experience is one of openness, cooperation and peace, offensive weapons do not pose the same threat because there is firm confidence that they are directed at some other state. Canada's view of American, British and French nuclear weapons was based on such experience.

FIGURE 10.3 Security: The Constructivist View

Constructivists side with the view that states—not the system—are the source of in-security. Anarchy is a neutral condition; it can be either safe or dangerous. States themselves have no inherent interests. (That view counters one of the central assumptions of Neorealism and Institutionalism: that anarchy makes all states rationally interested in gains for themselves.) Interests instead derive from states' identities, which form through interaction with other states. States whose interactions produce conflict and hostility define themselves as enemies. That relationship makes security an interest. In the same way, states whose interactions produce cooperation and peace define themselves as partners. That relationship removes security as a concern.

Relationships and interests can change. The cold war ended when positional conflict and armed confrontation were replaced by cooperation. That occurred because both sides changed their identities regarding each other.

Fear arises from particular kinds of interaction. States contending with an insecure international system do so " because their practices made it that way."[37] Does the same apply to states? Do greedy states arise because dealings with other states have made *them* that way? That is one possibility. "Victimization" may make some states aggressive.[38] Identities, however, can shift for purely internal reasons. One of those reasons is a change in government. The new Soviet identity that heralded the end of the cold war began, as we saw in Chapter 4, when Mikhail Gorbachev reconsidered the USSR's domestic problems in light of its international position and began conciliatory moves with the West. Identities can keep changing. Another political turnover in Russia—quite possible given its alarming deterioration—could transform its identity back to adversary. One possibility is a shift of political power to a "Red-Brown" coalition of former communists and right-wing nationalists. Forestalling that shift has been one reason for Western economic support.

Being a constructivist does not mean ignoring real danger: "One predator will best a hundred pacifists because anarchy provides no guarantees."[39] Predatory or greedy states create the security dilemma when their behaviour forces other states to define their interests in terms of security and monitor signs of aggressive intent.[40] Once the security dilemma does become entrenched in standing forces and normal routines, it may be difficult to escape. Those postures and outlooks mutually reinforce suspicious expectations—the nub of the security dilemma.

A community of states that desires only security has the potential to be quite stable because no state has forces (all are geared for defence) that lead others to fear attack. When those force postures are coupled with high levels of confidence and a long record of peaceful interaction, the makings are present for a security community. A security community, as we saw in Chapter 2, is a group of states whose levels of mutual confidence are high enough that none fears attack by the other. Firm and long-standing mutual trust can form the basis of a security community in which the members do expect force to be used amongst themselves. We saw the current roster of the security community on pp. 22.

Strong security communities can accept offensive capabilities by some members if it is clear that those capabilities are directed at external enemies. Such a condition characterized NATO during the cold war. The major members all had robust offensive capabilities, but it was clear to all that they were directed at the Soviet Union. That made it possible for states such as Canada, Norway and the Netherlands to remain confident that the forces of the major powers, particularly the United States and West Germany, would not be turned against them. Now that the cold war is over, states in NATO command smaller but still powerful offensive capabilities but still do not fear attack from each other. The same is by no means true among other states. Taiwan and China command similar capabilities, but their experience is one of hostility and threat. For them, changes in offensive capability and intentions are crucial.

How does a state signal peaceful intentions? One way is to indicate willingness to enter agreements to limit offensive weapons. Another is to show conciliatory behaviour generally and to forego opportunities to make unilateral gains.[41] The security dilemma does not go away. Conciliatory moves are very appropriate with states that also desire only security, and the result is heightened and reciprocal confidence. Conciliatory moves can be badly inappropriate with greedy states. The result is an emboldened aggressor who sees conciliation as appeasement and weakness. Intentions remain crucial.

The Utility of Force

Do some circumstances favour—even invite—the use of force? Ease of conquest is central. The prospect of a cheap victory makes aggression tempting. Calculated in the bare terms of prospective gains and losses, it is most rational to attack another state when the chances of success are high and the likely costs are low. When they have the choice, leaders prefer to avoid failure and heavy losses. Posing that prospect to potential aggressors, in fact, is the main reason for having strong defences: they raise the losses and increase the chances of failure. States that lack adequate defences face the choice of resisting attack against poor odds or capitulating. Their disadvantage—being easy quarry—tempts aggressors.

FIGURE 10.4 When to Worry: The Neorealist View

The security dilemma, in the words of one neorealist, forces states into a posture of "defensive positionalism." That attitude is necessary because the situation of states amongst each other is always uncertain and changeable. That makes gains in capabilities—even marginal ones—important because states may exploit those gains for advantages. Gains can be both military and non-military. Military gains improve the "efficacy of force" and pose direct threats to security. Non-military gains create problems in other areas by providing greater leverage in negotiations and the ability to make more advantageous deals. Military gains are the ones of concern here.

The key issue is uncertainty: situations that are safe today may become dangerous tomorrow. Even states that pose no threat now may become dangerous if they acquire an edge: "minds can be changed, new leaders can come to power, values can shift, new opportunities and dangers can arise."[42] The usability of military force can also change. A marginal improvement may tip the military balance just enough to encourage an otherwise circumspect state to become more aggressive and dangerous. Again, the present is no assurance: "states cannot be sure whether force, irrational today, would be irrational in the future."[43]

Is there anything to mitigate this prospect of perpetual uncertainty? The attitude of the other state makes a difference. (Taking this view modifies standard Neorealism, which posits that *all* states seek selfish gains). If the relationship is a friendly and cooperative one, the probability of change from benign partner to security threat is lower—*but still present since conditions can always change.* States with a variety of resources may also be less insecure if some of those resources can be used as effective substitutes for military ones in countering threats.

So: when to worry? The security dilemma provides the answer. Gains in capabilities matter, and intentions cannot be taken for granted. New capabilities may change intentions. New intentions may change capabilities. Both can become threats.

Ease of conquest may also invite **pre-emptive warfare** in which one side, anticipating attack, strikes first. The stronger side may pre-empt in the hopes of getting the cheapest possible victory. The weaker side (the one easily conquered) may pre-empt to offset its disadvantage with surprise. Finally, states that are easy to conquer "covet others' geographic strong points and strategic depth." Capturing safer boundaries gives *them* an incentive to attack. Safer perimeters are especially likely to be important if the neighbours are hostile and aggressive.[44] One of Israel's reasons for occupying southern Lebanon and the Golan Heights is to provide a security zone beyond its northern border (see Figure 10.5).

Ease of conquest is related directly to the balance between offensive and defensive force. Offensive force, which is geared for attack, is the destabilizing factor. The greater the offensive superiority facing a state, the easier it is to conquer. The easier that prospect becomes, the more dangerous are the conditions just seen.

What is the best way out? Matching offensive force with offensive force is not the best solution. If both sides are organized to attack, pre-emption and hair-trigger reactions are a problem. Each side's incentive is to take advantage of surprise and claim the initiative. Waiting risks losing because the attacking side's prime objective is to destroy the other side's offensive forces before they can be used. "Use it or lose it" has real meaning. Offensive postures also magnify the problem of relative gains because a small advantage may be enough to tip the balance particularly if that advantage can be combined with surprise.

A far more desirable posture is a strong defence. Well-defended states are not easily conquered and can impose high costs on attackers. The greater the prospect of strong resistance, the less likely is an aggressor to venture an attack. Even so, countering a highly effective offensive force requires a high level of defence.

The situation is prone to false estimates by both attacker and defender. For the defending side, avoiding attack requires persuading the aggressor that the defence is too strong to make attack worthwhile. That calculation may not be made. Offensive weapons and aggressive intentions, particularly against a state that wants to avoid war, may foster overconfidence.[45] For their part, defensive states may

FIGURE 10.5 Map of Israel and its Neighbours

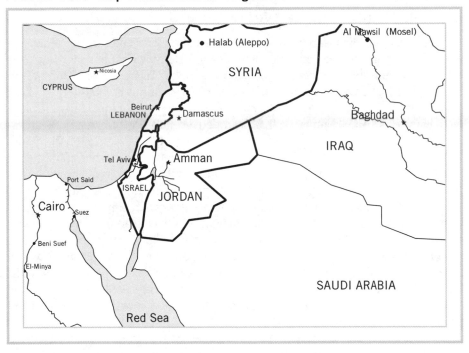

correctly gauge aggressive intentions but have difficulty estimating how much defensive capability is enough. These conundrums of offence and defence do not point promisingly to peace and stability. There is a better alternative.

For both safety and peace, both sides are on the best footing if they are geared for defence. In principle, defensive forces emphasize position and fortification over reach and mobility. If both sides have forces whose effectiveness is highest when they are fighting in place, neither is able to mount enough advantage for a successful attack. Instead, both sides are organized to stay put and wait. That discourages hostile initiatives and encourages stability.

Defensive arms, as we saw, indicate non-aggressive intentions. Mutually defensive postures signal that both sides neither can nor intend to strike first. In both capabilities and conveyed intentions, the result is a form of mutual assurance. At worst the posture produces a stable long-term standoff. At best, defence-defence provides the most favourable prospects for converting armed confrontation to more cooperative interactions because concessions entail less risk.

The same is not true with concessions from a defensive state to an offensive state. As we saw earlier, concessions from a defensive state may make an aggressor more confident and dangerous. Even riskier are concessions from one offensive state to another offensive state because marginal changes both in capabilities and perceived intentions are potentially so consequential. When hair-trigger force postures further magnify the dangers of wrong moves, offence-offence states may find their situation particularly difficult to escape.

Dual-Use and Smart Weapons

Are there any problems with this way of understanding force and security? There are two. First, distinguishing between offensive and defensive weapons may not be as easy as it sounds. In the words of one defence scholar, "a larger proportion of military technology than most analysts would prefer to admit is dual use...striking power, rapidity of fire and range are characteristics that are not inherently offensive or defensive."[46] Attack aircraft, which can deliver munitions to enemy positions and supply areas, would seem to be unambiguously offensive. They become defensive when they are used to halt advancing forces and destroy tanks and artillery. With their speed, mobility and firepower, tanks would seem to be clear-cut examples of offensive weapons. Those capabilities can also be used to disrupt attacks.

Second, recent technological improvements in weaponry, particularly the advent of "smart" weapons, make military force more attractive to use because attacks can be devastating. As the Gulf War showed, command, control and communications centres can be destroyed with precision, disabling the target state's ability to coordinate military force. Without that ability, its units are without overall direction. Destroying air defences also requires precision, and success gives use of the air to the attacker. All of these advantages are offensive because they lower costs and promise decisive results.

Because they are so effective, they stimulate the use of force in an unsettling way.[47] The prospect of quick and easy victory encourages weapons proliferation. While only a few states are technologically advanced enough to make the most sophisticated items, even a modest advantage can provide an edge over states that do not have them. As we saw, offensive weapons can foster ambitions. A greedy state can contemplate its own smaller version of the Gulf War. One factor limiting the aggressive potential particularly against well-armed major powers is intelligence information. Some scholars believe that accurate and precise information is at least as important as force because it selects the pinpoint targets to hit. That technology, particularly its ability to cover large areas anywhere with high accuracy, is available to only the most advanced powers. The United States possesses the greatest amount of intelligence capability, and more than any other state it knows where targets are located. What about conflict between two advanced states with full arrays of smart weapons and excellent intelligence? "Such an engagement [could be] as sanguinary for soldiers as the trenches of the Western Front."[48]

The Origins of War

The Peloponnesian War by Thucydides (460?—404? BC) is one of the most powerful and elegant explanations of the cause of war. The origins of that war (431- 404 BC) lay in rival power and fear of hegemony. Athens and Sparta headed alliances of smaller Greek city-states. The path to war began when conflicts between two of the smaller city-states drew in others. Athens intervened to prevent the naval fleet of one, Corcyra, from falling to a Spartan ally and tipping the balance of power. Athens intervened again in a revolt in a neighbouring city. Athens's actions and power concerned Sparta. If Athens became too strong, Sparta feared, it would dominate Greece. Sparta went to war.

Because Thucydides emphasized power and rivalry, he has been read in IR as an early realist. Certainly the arrangement of capabilities was central. From a modern perspective, ancient Greece was a bipolar system of Athenian and Spartan alliances. Even though Thucydides is regarded as one of IR's earliest thinkers, some scholars see scant evidence of systems-level thinking in his work. The one exception is the speech of Demosthenes to the Megalopolitans, which regards Greece "in terms of many states, all concerned with the relative power of all the others." For the rest, strategic thinking is "little more than the notion of gaining a numerical advantage over one's enemies."[49] Nonetheless, because of Thucydides' cogency and care, *The Peloponnesian War* has been regarded as one of IR's classic works. His question why war happens remains one of IR's central concerns. There is a large amount of IR literature on the causes of war, and this section merely surveys some of the main themes. We can begin by seeing briefly how contemporary scholars have treated the question of rising power and challenges to hegemony.

Rising power threatens states in two ways. First, accumulating power gives a state increasing ability to act because it can bear greater expenses than weaker states. That ability lowers the cost of changing the system. Second, ambition accompanies capability. The stronger a state becomes, the more willing it becomes to change the system to its liking.[50]

Will strong states inevitably seek to expand? If expansion provides more benefits, and if the expenses can be borne, the answer would be yes. States will expand until the benefits of doing so are outweighed by the costs.[51] Once achieved, hegemony need not be permanent. Capabilities can change, and when they do they give rise to new aspirants who struggle for position. Human history, in this perspective, is a long procession of rises and declines. Is the process inexorable and automatic? A neorealist would answer yes. Unless a rising state is blocked by a counterbalance of other states, it will continue to expand. The ultimate counterbalancing act is war.

Expansion is affected not only by capabilities and benefits but also by the nature of the state. Not all states exploit their capabilities for political and military dominance. Domestic politics and the interests of groups and political leadership affect expansion. Japan and Germany, as we saw in the last chapter, have discreetly abstained from military power politics for the last half century. External conditions including those affecting the use of force also intervene.[52] It is thus not possible to say that all states inveterately seek expansion. It *is* accurate to say that states seeking to expand disrupt an existing status quo, threaten other states and create the conditions for war.

The expanding state may not instigate conflict. States threatened by a rising power may take the initiative because they fear their weakening position. Their incentive is to wage preventive war before the shifting balance further erodes their capability. The immediacy of their motives depends on:

➤ how rapidly their military advantage is declining

➤ how serious their future military inferiority is likely to be

➤ the expected probability of war in the future

➤ the probability that fighting now will produce victory at acceptable cost[53]

We saw preventive calculations earlier with offensive weapons. Here the calculations are magnified from immediate contingencies to longer-term national capabilities.

Acts with belligerent intent are one prospect that make declining and other vulnerable states fearful. These acts include not only attacks and armed confrontations but also preparations for attack. As we saw earlier, acquiring offensive weapons is reason for other states to be concerned because those are weapons of attack. Seen as an act with belligerent intent, acquiring offensive weapons can be seen as a cause of war. The attempt to blackmail another state with threats of force is also. [54]

Alliances: Balancing, Bandwagoning and Buck-passing

States facing a rising power have another choice: forming **alliances** with other states. The purpose of alliances is to pool military power to counterbalance the other power. Alliances can also form to balance an opposing alliance. Equally matched alliances discourage war because neither side can count on victory at an acceptable cost. Such stability characterized NATO for almost 50 years although the ultimate guarantee was the two superpowers' nuclear weapons. If war does occur, the chances for either side to avoid defeat are best if the two alliances are equally matched although equal balances can produce long and bloody stalemates. Alliances are formed not only to counter a rising power. A rising power may form an alliance to assemble superior force for aggressive war.

For states seeking to counter a rising power, the prospects for an alliance would seem favourable: in principle, there should be available partners who also prefer the status quo. Calculations may be less straightforward. If the rising power's prospects look good, it may attract allies. Joining a rising alliance is called **bandwagoning**. Like other bandwagons, the alliance gets larger as it proceeds—it "collects those on the sidelines."[55] As more states join, it becomes increasingly unappealing for the remaining ones to stay away. If the logic of balancing power would direct states to join an opposing alliance, why would they side with a rising one? They may decide that the rising power is too strong to resist and must be accommodated through cooperation. They may decide that the opposing coalition is too unpromising and join the stronger one to avoid being defeated. They may also want to be on the winning side to help divide the gains.[56]

Another complicating calculation is the alliance members' actual willingness, when the time comes, to fight. An alliance cannot always count on a full turnout. Instead, members may expect others to do the fighting. This behaviour is called **buck-passing**. Allies have an incentive to pass the buck when the efforts of only some will be enough to protect the security of the rest. Standing aside saves the costs of participating without sacrificing security. Well-defended states can also afford to pass since their security is strong. A more devious calculation is to stand aside while larger powers exhaust themselves in the hope of improving one's position.[57] These calculations are particularly likely if the alliance has one or several strong members. Multipolar systems also encourage buck-passing because the lines of conflict may not be sharply drawn and because members of the system may have interests involving both their alliance partners and states on the other side.[58] Those with compromised interests have less incentive to take active part. Buck-passing is also a possibility if some of the members have a higher motivation to fight than others—a more exposed and vulnerable position, for example, or a greater stake in the outcome. The motivated states are likely to have others delegate responsibility to them.

Buck-passing can hobble an alliance at the worst time, and the likelihood of that happening tempts aggressors. For that reason, alliance agreements tend to have explicit commitments. Buck-passers may reveal their inclinations by showing resistance to binding agreements. As we will see in the next chapter, some scholars believe that post-cold war security arrangements in Europe will be prone to buck-passing, particularly by the smaller members.

Bandwagoning and buck-passing can combine in unfavourable ways. Bandwagoning states may be the most enthusiastic when prospects are good and be most likely to seek excuses when fortunes change, when the costs of participation become too great or when their own interests diverge. Whether that occurs depends on the nature of the common threat and the attitude of the states. Members of an outnumbered alliance may fight valiantly in the face of frightening odds—as the allies did in the first years of World War II—because of the dire consequences of losing.

When War Becomes Likely

Scholars have sought over the years to boil down all the factors that cause wars. The task, which involves searching for patterns in a large store of experience, has been monumental. This list, drawn from two efforts to identify the key conditions, provides a concise overview of a complex question.

War becomes more probable when:

➤ The achievements of at least one of the states falls short of its aspirations

➤ The experience of interaction identifies a particular state as a focus for military action

➤ The leaders of at least one of the states calculate that victory is likely and costs are acceptable[59]

Affecting the decision are:

➤ The balance of offensive and defensive capabilities

➤ The availability and usability of power resources

➤ The leaders' understanding of their position in the international system and how that position will be affected by going to war. Particularly important are the likely consequences of defeat [60]

This list combines most of the elements we have seen. Ambition and expansion are the basic motivation. Enemies and targets of military force do not appear at random. Experience and interaction shape those identities. States become military targets not only because of deficient military capabilities but because of the identity that has been established in the mind of the attacker. The actual decision to go to war hinges on pragmatic calculations of cost and success.

The availability of military capability and its offensive or defensive nature summarize the material considerations. The likely consequences, particularly those of failure, frame the strategic perspective.

Escalation, Accidents, Negligence

Even when powerful conditions such as these come together, wars generally do not happen out of the blue. There is normally an increase of tensions and a breakdown of possibilities for resolving differences. Escalation is one pattern in which a current of increasing hostility carries states into war. It is easy to imagine states blundering into wars through a drastic misperception of each other's intentions or through a series of unintended but worsening miscalculations. Such events would not produce war without broader predisposing factors. What about accidents and chance occurrences? War is not likely unless tensions already are strong. It may be more accurate to see such events as triggers that unleash a mounting set of circumstances.

Wars may also happen because states fail to act in time against aggressors. Scholars have been fascinated by the 1930s because Germany could have been contained had the major powers resisted while it was still weak. Instead, they temporized as Germany developed into a mortal threat whose defeat took six years and millions of lives. A number of explanations for this failure have been advanced over the years. A common one, as we saw in Chapter 2, was that the major powers placed their hopes on international law and on the League of Nations, which was "incapable of collective action."[61] As we saw in the last chapter, domestic politics can also be influential. Governments and the public may be unwilling to bear the costs of arming and preparing for war until the threat becomes dire. Halfway measures may magnify the problem by signalling irresolution.

Current Threats: Chemical and Biological Weapons

Chemical weapons were used in World War I by all the powers except Turkey.[62] Both sides in World War II possessed chemical weapons but did not use them because they feared retaliation. Iran and Iraq used chemical weapons in their war in the 1980s when both sides fired chemical weapons at each other's forces and cities. Iraq also used chemical weapons domestically against Kurdish villages in 1988. As we saw in Chapter 4, chemical weapons, because of the horror they caused in World War I, have borne a special stigma. There is concern now that these weapons will have particular appeal to aggressive and conflict-prone states. Chemical weapons can be both offensive and defensive. Offensively, they can devastate enemy forces or civilians. Defensively, threat of their use may discourage attackers.

Even threatened use can demoralize an opposing military force. Even if the other force has adequate protective gear and sufficient warning, having to wear that gear in combat imposes "severe restriction of hearing, vision, mobility, dexterity and the ability to communicate." That impairment reduces troops' effectiveness by 30 percent to 80 percent. The troops may suffer debilitating anxiety.[63] Unprotected forces face death and serious injury. Nerve gases, the most common form of chemical agent, are absorbed through the lungs or skin and kill by disrupting nerve transmission, which disables the ability to breathe. Threatening to inflict such results can be effective deterrence as we just saw with World War II.

Another attraction is that chemical weapons are cheap to make. Production costs are estimated to be as low as $10 to $20 per kilogram. The technology required is sophisticated but attainable. Chemical weapons also do not require ballistic missiles. An effective attack can be made by aircraft or cruise missiles. When Iraq attacked its Kurdish villages, it used helicopters that had originally been purchased for crop dusting.[64]

Finally, chemical weapons are more destructive than conventional explosives. How lethal chemical weapons are depends on the density of the target population and the concentration of the agent's aerosol mist in the target area. Simple open-air bursts tend to disperse the aerosol thereby preventing it from concentrating enough on the target area for high lethality. Ideal conditions require calm air and a densely situated target population. Much more deadly are chemical attacks within enclosed spaces such as the ventilation systems of large buildings.[65]

Although achieving enough concentration in large bursts would require "hundreds of thousands of kilograms per square kilometer," chemical weapons still pose a frightening prospect for urban populations. Based on calculations of the effects of a one-tonne missile warhead carrying sarin, its use without warning on a city with a population density of 35 per hectare (roughly the density of Tel Aviv or Riyadh), the expected fatalities would range, depending on weather conditions concentrating or dispersing the chemical aerosol, between 200 and 3,000 killed and somewhat more seriously injured. For comparison, that represents some 40 to 700 times more deaths and 20 to 300 times more injuries than would be caused by the same missile delivering a warhead of conventional explosives. That makes the prospect of use against concentrated civilian populations frightening, particularly in the developing world where population densities can be three to six times greater than in industrial states.[66]

What is worse is that civil defence against chemical attack is not promising. When the threat of Iraqi chemical attack on Israel came during the Gulf War, civilians tried to seal their windows and doors. "Even tightly sealed dwellings will not afford much protection unless they are thoroughly ventilated as soon as the cloud passes." If that is not done, "occupants will receive about the same dose as unprotected individuals but at a slower rate."[67] Ballistic missiles can be relatively inaccurate but still effective because the lethal agent is not a blast but a dispersing cloud.

Much of the same holds true for biological weapons. Instead of killing through poisoning as chemical agents do, biological weapons kill by spreading disease. The weapon delivers the biological agent, which infects its victims. Some pathogens are extremely virulent. One of the most dangerous is anthrax. Thirty kg of anthrax spores released in the air would provide fatal exposure to individuals below and downwind over a total area of six to 80 square km. That makes anthrax far more deadly than chemical agents. For the ability to kill populations, anthrax's rival is small nuclear weapons.[68]

Although the developed states have had chemical and biological weapons capability since World War II (Canada and Britain supplied chemical agents to the United States in the first year of the war), they have been seeking to reduce and control these agents. The areas of proliferation are China and the developing states. That poses two concerns. The first is that these weapons will be used in regional conflicts, adding greatly to the human devastation. The second is that, mounted on a medium-range ballistic missile, they could threaten developed states. Japan, as we just saw, had a North Korean ballistic missile test fired over its main island in 1998. With suspected chemical and biological weapons capability, North Korea clearly poses a threat to Japan. The same is true of European exposure to the Middle East. North America is more distant although in 1998 an American congressional committee study reduced CIA estimates of long-range missile development time for Iran from 10 to five years.

Finally, chemical and biological agents make excellent terrorist weapons. The potential use of sarin was seen in the Japanese Aum Shinrikyo's attack on the Tokyo subway in 1995. Even more sobering is the use of biological agents. Anthrax does not require delivery in warheads. Driving through city streets with a car-mounted dispenser is one possibility. Worse, the incubation period for biological agents may be hours or days, posing the initial problem for the target state of determining whether the appearance of widespread sickness is a disease outbreak or a biological attack. By that time, terrorists would be long gone, and responsibility would be harder to establish. Canada, in one scholar's view, may not be immune to terrorist attacks. As the United States continues its success in finding and prosecuting people who commit terrorist acts there—the bombers of the World Trade Centre, for example—terrorists may turn their sights to "highly visible, journalistically accessible cities in countries allied with the United States with porous national security systems...for 'demonstration' purposes."[69]

Those purposes may not involve chemical or biological devices. Another scholar believes that political terrorist groups and any states that might sponsor them are likely to stick to conventional explosives for several reasons. First, chemical and biological weapons are dangerous to handle and require considerable technical expertise. Second, killing huge numbers of people may defeat political terrorist goals both by unleashing determined retaliation and by poisoning public opinion against the terrorists' political cause. Political terrorist strategy requires casualties to be enough to assure media attention but not enough to cause widespread fury. Finally, the chance of detection makes it very hazardous for states to sponsor chemical and biological terrorism. These considerations may not restrain terrorists who are motivated by religious or ethnic fanaticism.[70]

Nuclear Proliferation

Until India's and Pakistan's nuclear tests in 1998, nuclear weapons seemed to be the most stable regime. The United States and Russia were scaling back their forces, and three states had abandoned their nuclear weapons programs altogether: South Africa, Brazil and Argentina. With India and Pakistan openly declaring their capability, many feared that the moderation would cease and that other states would accelerate their development. Given the insecurity and anxiety that were part of daily life during the cold war in states such as Canada and the United States and more immediately in Central Europe, why would any state now want nuclear weapons?

There are two schools of thought. The first school focuses on the security dilemma. When one state arms itself with nuclear weapons, it makes its neighbours less secure especially if relationships have been marked by suspicion and hostility. Compounding the security dilemma is offensive nuclear force. The most obvious use of nuclear weapons is attack, and any state possessing them has daunting offense particularly if its neighbours are non-nuclear. By that logic, India faced pressure to develop nuclear capability when China did so in the 1960s. When India displayed that capability, it provided motivation for Pakistan to follow suit. All three of those relationships are characterized by hostility and past warfare. Although that sequence stretched over almost 35 years, the progress was successive from acquiring state to neighbour. States facing non-nuclear but collectively formidable neighbours may seek to acquire nuclear weapons to right the balance. That was one reason for Israel's acquisition. The backlog was three wars against allied neighbours. One conflict, the Yom Kippur War of 1973, Israel came close to losing. But by the logic of the security dilemma, Israel's possession of weapons creates an incentive for its neighbours to acquire their own.

The second school of thought stresses emulation. As we saw in Chapter 9, some scholars, in an approach we called outside-in, explain state behaviour in reference to the international system. One influence, we saw, is on the institutions of states themselves. Some institutions, such as government science bureaucracies in states that are too poor to support

Associated Press/AP photo/Ajit Kumar/CP archive

Indian soldiers raise the Indian flag at the test site Shakti I, where India tested five nuclear devices, before a visit by Prime Minister Atal Bihari Vajpayee to Pokaran Wednesday, May 20, 1998. Vajpayee said that India was willing to "pay any price" for its security.

scientific endeavour, have been attributed to following the example of other states and seeking to meet the standards and program goals of international agencies.[71] For developing states, these standards and examples are associated with modernization, and building institutions such as science bureaucracies is to acquire its symbols. The same is held to be true of advanced weapons. They, like other modern accessories, herald being up to date. In this way, modern military forces are creations of the international system: "militaries [as in historic Europe, as we saw in Chapter 6] no longer build modern nations, but, rather, the world political and social system builds modern nation states, which in turn build modern militaries and procure modern weaponry."[72] Seen in that perspective, nuclear weapons—even though the superpowers are scaling down theirs and are glad to be rid of the insecurity—represent a giant step into modernity.

Desire for such progress may encourage factions in the state who favour nuclear arms. Bureaucratic interests and outlooks, seen in Chapter 9, may be at play. Agencies may see nuclear arms as furthering their interests and advocate acquisition. Sources of that pressure may be organizations and scientists involved in peaceful nuclear energy or nuclear-related research. Another source may be parts of the military that desire strategic weapons. The scientists may desire resources for their projects, and the military may wish to strengthen their forces.[73] Using this analysis, it is easy to become deterministic and assume that scientists and officers will always seek nuclear arms. Given the threats they face, military officers may see no need for nuclear weapons. As were many scientists in the West during the cold war, their counterparts elsewhere may be appalled by nuclear weapons and oppose them.

Even so, according to one scholar, the bureaucratic explanation fits well with India. Following China's nuclear test in 1964, a coalition of scientists and engineers, with allies in the armed forces, wanted to build an Indian bomb but were opposed by equally powerful factions in the government. That explains India's leisurely progress (10 years) in conducting its own test. An additional piece of evidence in favour of bureaucratic conflict is the fact that, as test time approached in 1974, senior military officials were not consulted about the impact of nuclear weapons on India's military posture and strategy.[74] In 1998, many quarters of the armed forces welcomed nuclear weapons.

Nuclear Proliferation, Instability and Third Parties

In the first stages of acquisitions, nuclear weapons can only be used for offence. As we saw, offensive forces create the incentive to strike first because the opponent's prime incentive in a crisis is to destroy the offensive force before it can be used. That pre-emptive element makes crises extremely unstable. Nuclear weapons of the kind likely to be held by proliferating states in the first stages of acquisition invite preemption because there are few of them and they may be relatively easy to hit. States that have nuclear weapons but no missiles must deliver them by aircraft and store the weapons nearby. Reasonable intelligence capability can find those locations.

If the state does have missiles, there will not be many. Although they will be protected by air defences, their emplacements will not be fortified enough to stand accurate bombing. The target state's incentive is to destroy offensive nuclear weapons if there is sufficient evidence that they will be used. The attacking state's incentive is to use them before they are destroyed. The combination is very volatile.

If both sides are on that nuclear footing, the chances of nuclear war escalating quickly from a crisis are considerable. The prospects are bad all around. The opponents themselves court devastation. Neighbours may face the risk of collateral harm, ruined regional trade and the prospect of nuclear war refugees at their border. For states in the system overall, the active risk weakens Hiroshima's taboo.

What should other states do? One response is to take a "safe sex" approach: if proliferation is going to proceed regardless of what other states do, the best policy is to provide assistance to lessen the dangers.[75] What assistance would do that? The superpowers managed to avoid war in the 1950s and early 1960s when their forces also were in first-strike postures and developed **second-strike** capabilities. Second-strike capability involves protecting or concealing a weapon so that it cannot be destroyed by an enemy first strike, but survive and retaliate. Whatever an enemy does, if second-strike capability is robust, there is no assurance that it will not suffer devastating retaliation. Attack is literally self-defeating. That being so, a rational enemy will not attack. Second-strike capability converts nuclear weapons from offensive to defensive weapons greatly improving safety. Two emerging nuclear powers such as India and Pakistan are stable when both sides are in second-strike postures. Those incentives are one of the clearest demonstrations of defence-defence. The incentives work the most powerfully when each side's nuclear weapons are highly secure.

The superpowers secured their weapons by placing them in underground blast-proof silos and by putting them at sea aboard submarines. Both retained bomber forces that could be sent aloft and dispersed in times of crisis. Each of these was vulnerable to countermeasures. As missile accuracy improved in the 1970s, direct hits on silos became a possibility. To retaliate, bombers would have to penetrate excellent air defences. The safest platform proved to be submarines. As *Hunt for Red October* dramatized, both superpowers had mapped the ocean floors to find canyons and deep areas where submarines could transit undetected or hide. Anti-submarine warfare—the countermeasure—never did catch up to the abilities of super-quiet submarines for evasion. To prevent the nightmare scenario depicted in the film *Dr. Strangelove,* in which a maverick flight crew decides to stage its own nuclear attack, the superpowers also developed elaborate multiple-key firing systems to prevent unauthorized launches. Retaining that control continues to be a concern as Russia's military deteriorates and political uncertainties increase.

Although these expedients helped protect the superpowers from nuclear war, they were expensive. For proliferators' safety and stability, they are too expensive either to develop independently or, assuming them to be available, to buy. That produces a new version of the north-south axis of wealth and poverty. Proliferating states may be kept in unsafe postures indefinitely.

Technologically advanced states could take a pragmatic approach and give assistance to make these forces more secure and capable of surviving. Doing so would reduce the risk of pre-emptive war. Aid would include control systems and protection. Doing so acquiesces in a practice that most of the world's states condemn and, worse, weakens the strictures against proliferation.[76] To this point, states including Canada possessing the technology have chosen to stand aside. If India and Pakistan proceed further with their programs or if Iran declares a ballistic missile and nuclear weapons capability, this question may become more than academic.

How bad is the prospect of proliferation for peace and safety? How likely is it that we can count on the next 20 years being as free of nuclear war as the last 50 have been? There are two schools of thought. The first, drawing on the tradition of Thucydides, emphasizes the power of expansionist intent. States that are seriously bent on changing the international order are not likely to be constrained, even by the prospect of nuclear retaliation, if they are sufficiently dissatisfied, angry or desperate. Nuclear weapons also do not promise peace even for states on a defence-defence footing. Even an unintended nuclear exchange would produce grievous levels of devastation. That continuing insecurity cannot be equated with peace.[77]

The other school of thought is that the international world has learned, through the superpowers' long experience, not to love nuclear weapons. The remarkably low number of states developing nuclear weapons is testimony that international society has moved beyond that stage of warfare and symbolic aspiration and sees the weapons for what they are. The number of states like Canada, which have ample technology for a weapon but choose not to develop one, is testament to an achieved maturity. How true that perception is will be seen in the coming years. Was the decade following the end of the cold war a halcyon interlude between nuclear epochs or was it a turning point? Immediate clues may be found in the international aftermath of India's and Pakistan's tests.

Regime Security

We saw at the beginning that security threats can be internal as well as external. Internal ones threaten governments with overthrow or more generalized disorder. States that do not face violent breakdowns or organized plots must still worry about their public's support. Authoritarian measures are effective to a point, but ultimately popular acquiescence is necessary. One condition threatening acquiescence is outside ideas and political contacts. It is far easier to govern a population that is unable to organize privately or to agitate even discreetly. For those reasons, it is not uncommon for such states to regard internal security as equally important to international security and to use agencies of the state for defence both abroad and at home.

All governments depend upon armed force as an ultimate guarantee against internal disorder. One expression for this function of armed force is aid to civil power. In democratic states, use of armed forces in time of civil unrest may be necessary to prevent bloodshed and public breakdown. Such uses in states such as

Canada are controversial because military units confront their fellow citizens. Two episodes in Canada were use of the armed forces in Quebec under the War Measures Act in 1970 and more recently during the Oka crisis. The controversy was over whether the events warranted that level of intervention. At the same time, disorders that require supplementing the police with the military are worrisome because they are the first stop on a continuum of greater and more generalized levels of violence, the rise of organized armed factions and ultimately civil war. In evaluating whether such uses are justified, one question to ask is whom they are intended to protect: the public or the state's leaders. Rhetoric alone may not be an accurate guide. Authoritarian governments justify actions that serve the government as actions demanded by the people.

States that define internal security in terms of protecting a leadership elite take a different view. Like democratic states, they also regard disorders and uprisings as contingencies to be avoided. In successful authoritarian rule, the population complies. Achieving compliance is achieved through various kinds of intimidation. The former government of East Germany, for example, used a wide-reaching domestic security organization, the Stasi, to gather information about individuals thought to oppose the government. Its operations were known, but its operatives—relatives, teachers, co-workers—were not. The possibility that anyone could be an informant discouraged active dissent and encouraged compliance. One of the decisions the German government faced after reunification was whether to open the Stasi files to the public. Doing so would disclose devastating personal secrets. The files were opened.

The Internet can pose a threat to authoritarian states because it makes it possible for opposition to form informal networks and coordinate activities with partners abroad. The government of Singapore, wishing to discourage use of the Internet by political opponents, in 1994 used the pretext of searching for pornography to examine the e-mail files of some 80,000 Singaporean subscribers. Political reasons did not have to be disclosed. The mere fact of demonstrating the ability to search without notice was enough.[78]

Threats to both the public and state leaders can arise from social and economic breakdown. States experiencing this breakdown typically have multiple crises: unemployment, hunger, overcrowding, deteriorating or absent state facilities, rapid inflation, organized crime and violent lawlessness. Environmental problems, particularly soil erosion, drought, overgrazing and deforestation, may exacerbate these conditions by removing important reserves and buffers. Active opposition may be born from popular despair. An example of such opposition was the rebellion that toppled Mobutu Sese Seko of Zaire, a wealthy and corrupt president. Support grew from the perception that things would only get worse. Breakdown can also be anarchic. Instead of transferring to a successor political movement, rule fragments into local units of warlords or gangs. Life becomes a struggle for control, and armed groups run at large. Public services, monetary systems and businesses close down, and public safety becomes random, nightmarish and individual. That situation characterized Beirut in the 1970s and Sierra Leone in the 1990s. Because there is no coherent political succession and because no force is strong to impose general order, the situation can continue as long as the sides are able to keep fighting. Ethnic divisions, as we saw in Chapter 7, add their own axes of conflict and intractability.

Summary

Security can be defined as the protection of important values. That view easily includes military threats, but it also includes less direct and immediate forms. Political threats address values of government. Economic threats address public and individual welfare. Environmental threats affect all states in common although some states may be more exposed to the hazard or vulnerable to the effects. States may be able to counter some threats on their own, but others, particularly economic and environmental ones, may be sufficiently generalized or momentous enough to require collective action. The G-7 was established to deal with common economic and energy problems.

The essence of security is the security dilemma. Views that emphasize its origins in anarchy regard it as an inveterate international reality and see insecurity as IR's enduring condition. Views that emphasize its origins in state behaviour regard the security dilemma as contingent on behaviour and interaction.

Crucial to security are the capabilities and intentions of other states. Security-seeking states pose no threats to other states, but expansionist and aggressive states do. Determining actual intentions is fraught with puzzles. One index is the weapons acquired. Defensive weapons mark a security-seeking state; offensive weapons, an aggressive one. Combinations of offensive and defensive weapons among states produce varying degrees of stability or danger. The most volatile combination is offence-offence.

Both intentions and force combinations can initiate war. Pre-emptive wars can occur when one side seeks to exploit an advantage or prevent a threat from becoming more dangerous.

Nuclear weapons embody these incentives in a special way. Fledgling nuclear forces are difficult to defend and invite pre-emptive attack making crises particularly volatile and dangerous. Protecting nuclear weapons from pre-emptive attack enhances deterrence and stability but involves expensive technologies.

Chemical and biological weapons also cause massive devastation but are cheaper to acquire and more readily deployed. Nuclear proliferation had fortunately been gradual until India's and Pakistan's tests in 1998.

Security can also be a domestic concern. Action on behalf of public safety can require military force in the face of severe disorder or breakdown. Leaders of non-democratic states may see the stakes in terms of their own tenure. More generally, domestic security may collapse under overwhelming pressures arising from poverty, inadequate public resources and deteriorating economic livelihood. Environmental misuse from excessive strain on resources magnifies many of the problems. At the individual level, insecurity becomes acute amidst generalized state breakdown.

ENDNOTES

1   Claudio Cioffi-Revilla, "Orgins and Evolution of War and Politics," *International Studies Quarterly* 40 (March 1996) 9.

2   *ibid.*, 8.

3   *ibid.*, 11, 12.

4   *ibid.*, 13–14

5   *ibid.,* 16–17

6   *ibid.*, 18.

7   David A. Baldwin, "The Concept of Security," *Review of International Studies* 23 (January 1997) 13.

8   *ibid.*, 23.

9   Thomas Risse-Kappen, "Collective Identity in a Democratic Community: The Case of NATO," in Peter Katzenstein, ed., *The Culture of National Security*, Ithaca: Cornell University Press, 1996, pp. 374–76.

10 Ted Hopf, "The Promise of Constructivism in International Relations Theory," *International Security* 23 (Summer 1998) 175, 187.

11 Joseph T. Jockel and Joel J. Sokolsky, *The End of the Canada-U.S. Defence Relationship*, Kingston: Centre for International Relations, Queen's University, 1996, p. 2.

12 Douglas Alan Ross, "Canada and the World At Risk: Depression, War, and Isolationism for the 21st Century?" *International Journal* 52 (Winter 1996-97) p. 11.

13 Hal P. Klepak, "Future Defence Policy in an *Epoque de vaches maigres*," in Fen Osler Hampson and Maureen Appel Molot, eds., *Canada Among Nations 1996: Big Enough to be Heard,* Ottawa: Carleton University Press, 1996, pp. 63, 66.

14 S. Neil MacFarlane, "Introduction," in S. Neil MacFarlane and Hans-Georg Erhart, eds., *Peacekeeping at a Crossroads*, Clementsport, N.S.: Canadian Peacekeeping Press, 1997, pp. 2–3.

15 Canadian Security Intelligence Service, *1997 Public Report*, Ottawa: Ministry of Supply and Services, 1997, p. 3.

16 *ibid.*, pp. 6–7.

17 *1994 Defence White Paper*, Ottawa: Ministry of Supply and Services, 1994, pp. 8, 12–13.

18 Nils Peter Gleditsch, "Armed Conflict and the Environment: A Critique of the Literature," *Journal of Peace Research* 35 (May 1998) 383–84.

19 Davis B. Bobrow, "Complex Insecurity: Implications of a Sobering Metaphor," *International Studies Quarterly* 40 (December 1996) 442.

20 Stephen Van Evera, "Offense, Defense, and the Causes of War," *International Security* 22 (Spring 1998) 19.

21 Bobrow, "Complex Insecurity," 440.

22 Richard K. Betts, "Should Strategic Studies Survive?" *World Politics* 50 (October 1997) 9.

23 David A. Baldwin, "Security Studies at the End of the Cold War," *World Politics* 48 (October 1995) 137.

24 Betts, "Should Strategic Studies Survive?" 9.

25 Nazli Choucri and Robert C. North, "Population and (In)security: National Perspectives and Global Imperatives," in David Dewitt, David Haglund and John Kirton, eds., *Building a New Global Order: Emerging Trends in International Security*, Toronto: Oxford University Press, 1993, 231.

26 Ross, "Canada and the World at Risk," p. 2.

27 Alexander Wendt and Michael Barnett, "Dependent State Formation and Third World Militarization," *Review of International Studies* 19 (1993) 330

28 *ibid.,* p. 335.

29 Nicholas J. Wheeler and Ken Booth, "The Security Dilemma," in John Baylis and N.J. Rengger, eds., *Dilemmas in World Politics: International Issues in a Changing World*, Oxford: Clarendon Press, 1992, p. 30.

30   Hidemi Suganami, "Stories of War Origins: A Narrativist Theory of the Causes of War," *Review of International Studies* 23 (October 1997) 412.

31   Charles L. Glaser, "The Security Dilemma Revisited," *World Politics* 50 (October 1997) 180–81.

32   *ibid.,* p. 180.

33   Wheeler and Booth, "The Security Dilemma" p. 40.

34   Kenneth Waltz, *Theory of International Politics*, New York: McGraw Hill, 1979, p. 186–87.

35   Jonathan Mercer, "Anarchy and Identity," *International Organization* 49 (Spring 1995) 251.

36   Stanley Hoffmann, "Back to the Future, Part II: International Realist Theory and Post-Cold War Europe," *International Security* 15 (Fall 1990) 192.

37   Alexander Wendt, "Anarchy Is What States Make of It: The Social Construction of Power Politics," *International Organization* 46 (Spring 1993)

38   *ibid.,* pp. 407–08

39   *ibid.,* p. 408

40   *ibid.*

41   Glaser, "The Security Dilemma Revisited," p. 181.

42   Joseph Grieco, "Understanding the Problem of International Cooperation: The Limits of Neoliberal Institutionalism and the Future of Realist Theory, in David A. Baldwin, ed., *Neorealism and Neoliberalism: The Contemporary Debate*, New York: Columbia University Press, 1993, p. 314.

43   *ibid.*

44   Van Evera, "Offense, Defense, and the Causes of War," pp. 7–9.

45   Robert Jervis, "War and Misperception," *Journal of Interdisciplinary History* 18 (Spring 1988) 676.

46   Andrew L. Ross, "The Dynamics of Military Technology," in Dewitt, Haglund and Kirton, eds., *Building a New Global Order*, pp. 116–17.

47   John Orme, "The Utility of Force in a World of Scarcity," *International Security* 22 (Winter 1997–98) 145.

48   *ibid.,* pp. 155–56.

49   Michael Sheehan, *The Balance of Power: History and Theory* London: Routledge, 1996, p. 27.

50   Gilpin, *War and Change*, p. 95.

51   *ibid.,* pp. 50–52.

52   *ibid.,* p. 55.

53   Jack Levy, "Declining Power and the Preventive Motivation for War," *World Politics* 40 (October 1987) 97–98.

54   Suganami, "Stories of War Origins," p. 411.

55   Stephen M. Walt, "Alliance Formation and the Balance of World Power," *International Security* 9 (Spring 1985) 6.

56   *ibid.,* p. 8.

57   Thomas J. Christenson and Jack Snyder, "Chain Gangs and Passed Bucks: Predicting Alliance Patterns in Multipolarity," *International Organization* 44 (Spring 1990) 141.

58   Ted Hopf, "Polarity: The Offense-Defense Balance and War," *American Political Science Review* 85 (June 1991) 476.

59   *ibid.,* 477–78

60   Paul Anderson and Timothy McKeown, "Changing Aspirations, Limited Attention and War," *World Politics* 40 (October 1987) 5;

61   Hans Morgenthau, "The Intellectual and Political Functions of Theory," in James Der Derian, ed., *International Theory: Critical Investigations*, New York: New York University Press, 1995, p. 40.

62   Julian Perry Robinson, "The Supply Side Control of Chemical Weapons," in Jean-Francois Rioux, *Limiting the Proliferation of Weapons: The Role of Supply-Side Strategies,* Ottawa: Carleton University Press, 1992, p. 58.

63   Erhard Geissler, "The Spread of Biological and Toxin Weapons: A Nightmare of the 1990s?" in *ibid.*, p. 99.

64   Steve Fetter, "Ballistic Missiles and Weapons of Mass Destruction: What is the Threat? What Should be Done?" International Security 16 (Summer 1991) p. 19.

65   Richard A. Falkenrath, "Confronting Nuclear, Biological and Chemical Terrorism," *Survival* 40 (Fall 1998) 46-47.

66   Fetter, "Ballistic Missiles," p. 22.

67   *ibid.*

68   *ibid*, p. 26.

69   Ross, "Canada and the World at Risk," 13.

70   Falkenrath, "Confronting Nuclear, Biological and Chemical Terrorism," 53–55.

71   Martha Finnemore, *National Interests in International Society*, Ithaca: Cornell University Press, 1996.

72   Dana Eyre and Mark Suchman, "Status, Norms, and the Proliferation of Conventional Weapons: An Institutional Theory Approach," in Peter Katzenstein, ed., *The Culture of National Security: Norms and Identity in World Politics*, New York: Columbia University Press, 1996, p. 82.

73   Scott D. Sagan, "Why Do States Build Nuclear Weapons: Three Models in Search of a Bomb," *International Security* 21 (Winter 1996-97), 63,

74   *ibid.*, p. 66–67.

75   Peter D. Feaver and Emerson M.S. Niou, "Managing Nuclear Proliferation: Condemn, Strike, or Assist?" *International Studies Quarterly* 40 (June 1996) 215.

76   *ibid.*, 216.

77   Robert Jervis, "The Political Effects of Nuclear Weapons," *International Security* 13 (Fall 1988) 89–90.

78   Gary Rodan, "The Internet and Political Control in Singapore," *Political Science Quarterly* 113 (Spring 1998) 77.

WEBLINKS

Assessments of Canada's security can be found on the site of the Canadian Security Intelligence Service:
www.csis-scrs.gc.ca

The site of the Canadian Institute of Strategic Studies is:
www.ciss.ca

Links to armed forces around the world can be found on the Canadian War, Peace and Security Server:
www.cfsc.dnd.ca

The site of the International Institute for Strategic Studies is:
www.isn.ethz.ch/iiss

A Web directory can be found at the International Relations and Security Network site:
www.isn.ethz.ch.linkslib

Information on arms sales and transfers, along with a list of related links, is available from the Stockholm International Peace Research Institute:
www.sipri.se

Chapter 11

Sources of Safety

Location, Location, Location

What makes states secure? Where they are situated is primary. Just as people cannot choose their relatives, states cannot choose their neighbours. Canada has possessed an enviable degree of military security because it has enjoyed over a century of peaceful relations with the United States and has common land borders with no other country. During the 1930s, that location supported complacency in the face of rising Naziism in Europe. Senator Dandurand's famous statement about Canada living in a "fireproof house" epitomized that outlook. The same geographic remove supported American **isolationism**. Such detachment depended on the ability of European powers to contain Germany, and as Britain struggled through the Battle of Britain, the chilling possibility emerged that it might lose. If that were to happen, there would be no remaining firebreak between a Nazi-dominated Europe and North America. A worse scenario would be a powerful German navy, augmented by a captured British fleet, at large in the North Atlantic.

As we saw in the last chapter, Canada's protective geography came into question again during the cold war. This time it was not the prospect of German warships free to menace the Atlantic coast but of Soviet bombers, and later missiles, traversing Canada's airspace on their way to American targets with nuclear weapons. Those transits would violate Canadian sovereignty, but much more serious was the prospect of direct and indirect harm. Canada's defence-sharing arrangements with the United States could make targets of Canadian factories and installations. Indirect but just as serious was the threat of collateral damage from strikes across the border (or from misses landing on the Canadian side) and of nuclear fallout drifting northward on the same air currents that bring acid rain. The third dimension of threat was the incalculable aftermath of a Soviet nuclear attack on the United States.

These geographic realities gave Canada an interest in continental air defence, prompting Canada to join the United States in NORAD to coordinate resources and responses (and in doing so, making targets of Canadian airbases and command centres). During the early years of the cold war when bombers were the main vehicles of attack, interception by Canadian and American aircraft was an important role, and many of the sites of interception would be over Canada. Since the end of the cold war, as we saw in the last chapter, threats to Canada have again become indirect and diffuse although not prudent to ignore. Not all states are as fortunate as Canada, and many face threats that are uncomfortably proximate.

Unstable neighbouring states are sources of uncertainty and potential danger. The European Union faces that prospect with Russia and Eastern Europe. Instability in the Balkans, the Ukraine or Russia may not produce direct threats of military attack, particularly if the forces involved are as deteriorated as they are now, but internal and regional conflicts may develop in unpredictable ways. The threats may be of expansion as other states are drawn in, of disrupted trade and of masses of refugees arriving at border crossings.

Instability may have no military elements at all but still constitute a threat. Again, proximity is the key. For the United States, whose border with Mexico is long and porous, economic collapse would create a humanitarian emergency and, if governmental breakdown occurred as well, perhaps widespread and violent civil strife. Security, in fact, was one argument the American executive branch used to persuade a skeptical Senate to ratify NAFTA. A Mexico developing through trade, according to that argument, would be a more stable and orderly neighbour. The possibility of domestic breakdown in Indonesia has long made Australia mindful of its large neighbour to the north. A brutal seven-year civil war has drawn France's attention to its neighbour and former possession, Algeria, and has made France a target for Algerian terrorists.

Unstable neighbours can invite intervention in the name of security. In 1998, one of the strongest factions in the Afghan civil war, the Taliban, consolidated power over much of the country. Supporting the Taliban was Pakistan, hoping that, of the various contenders in Afghanistan, it would pose the fewest security threats. A stable western border, Pakistan's government hoped, would allow it to concentrate on defending its eastern border with India.

Offensive military power, direct hostility and a history of conflict and war produce more actively dangerous neighbours. These conditions describe the Middle East, which amply qualifies as the world's most insecure region. Israel is a prime case of a chronically insecure state. Although none of Israel's immediate neighbours is strong enough to defeat it single-handedly, all three of Israel's wars—in 1948, 1967 and 1973—have been waged by its neighbours in coalition. Israel is not the only insecure state in the region. Saudi Arabia fears *both* its neighbours, Iran and Iraq, and Israel's capabilities make it a third threat. For their part, Iran and Iraq fought a devastating war through the 1980s and remain threats to each other. Hostile coalitions can form against states other than Israel. The coalition assembled for the Gulf War against Iraq included Syria and Egypt. Jordan, Syria's neighbour, sided with Iraq as did the Palestine Liberation Organization. And though fearful of Iran, Saudi Arabia shared Iran's interest in a weakened Iraq (see Figure 11.1).

Adding to the insecurity is the fact that, with the exception of Israel, the states in the region are authoritarian in varying degrees. Because authoritarian governments, as we saw in Chapter 9, tend to concentrate power in small leadership elites or in individual rulers themselves, they can change policies quickly and

FIGURE 11.1 Map of Middle East: a Region of Dangerous Frontiers

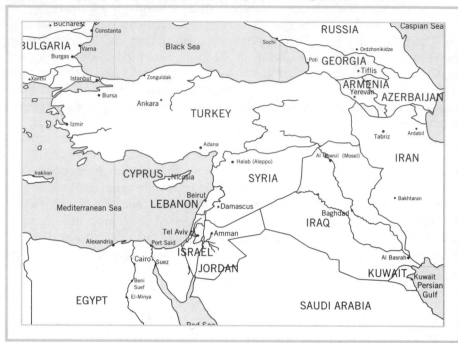

without notice. President Anwar Sadat of Egypt, who launched a surprise war against Israel in 1973, stunned the world when he made a trip to Jerusalem four years later to advance peace negotiations. Democratic governments, when enough voters are persuaded that security policy needs to change, are also capable of dramatic swings. Israel, a parliamentary democracy, took a much more uncompromising approach to peace with its neighbours and the Palestinians after 1996 when the government of Benjamin Netanyahu replaced Yitzhak Rabin's successor by appealing to voters' worries about security. Rabin was assassinated the previous year by an Israeli extremist who opposed his conciliatory approach.

The common element in all these examples is the luck of geography. From the perspective of a highly secure state such as Canada, we can only imagine how it must be to adjoin a state rent by extremism and civil war with other states in the region intervening openly and with a government whose intentions, when they can be discerned in the confusion, are alarming. Pakistan and Iran face such a threat in neighbouring Afghanistan. We can only imagine how it must be to stay carefully out of a nearby war but to have one's cities attacked by missiles from a state known to have used chemical weapons. Israelis experienced that terror from Iraq in the Gulf War. Saudi Arabians did also although their state was a direct participant. To a considerable degree, safety is a matter of proximity.

The Safety of Statehood

Statehood itself is a source of safety. As we saw in Chapter 2, the nightmare depicted by Hobbes is a situation in which all people are perfectly free to pursue their ambitions with each other with no limitations on the means they might use. Since some people are greedy and violent, an absence of effective control enables them to become predators. Hobbes's solution, as we saw, was to construct a state with a powerful authority. Only then could individuals be safe from each other. The same idea, as we also saw, applies to states themselves whose governments can assemble and organize resources for protection against external predators.

In the absence of an effective world political authority, each state's protection is ultimately a choice between self-help and cooperation—of meeting threats on one's own or of pooling resources with other states. Self-help can be a reasonable choice when one's resources are ample and may be the only choice if no partners are available for joint efforts. If one's defensive capabilities are enough to meet the threat, self-help saves the complications of partnership particularly if the basis of cooperation is unsteady, as we saw in the last chapter with buck-passing. When the basis of cooperation is firm, military alliances are one way to find safety. When the threat is high, alliance membership can become a central priority. Throughout the 1950s and 1960s, membership in NATO guided much of Canada's foreign policy toward Europe.

The same choice applies to political, economic and environmental threats. Some threats, such as a neighbouring state's damming a river upstream, are essentially bilateral and must be dealt with individually. Canada faced that situation with the United States in the 1970s when the U.S. Army Corps of Engineers proposed an extensive irrigation scheme for North Dakota. The problem was not diverting water from Canada but sending agricultural pollutants into Canada. Syria, whose territory is mostly desert, depends heavily on the Euphrates River for water. Across the border, Turkey is committed to a massive irrigation and hydro project, giving it control of the amount of water entering Syria. Canada and the United States were able to reach an accommodation that addressed the environmental concerns. Syria and Turkey do not enjoy that level of accord. Instead, Turkey's government makes a point of keeping cooperative relations with Syria's arch-enemy, Israel (see Figure 11.2).

Many economic and environmental threats are generalized and require collective action. In these areas as well, statehood can be an asset. True, it is states that generate, or at least do not stop, some of the conditions that create economic and environmental threats. Imprudent banking practices and lax state regulation, as we saw in Chapter 8, helped cause an economic collapse in Southeast Asia severe enough to threaten world financial stability. Failure by states to limit logging and land clearance produces the ecological threat of widespread deforestation. But states also, in the view of many scholars, remain the most promising participants

FIGURE 11.2 Map of Syria and Turkey

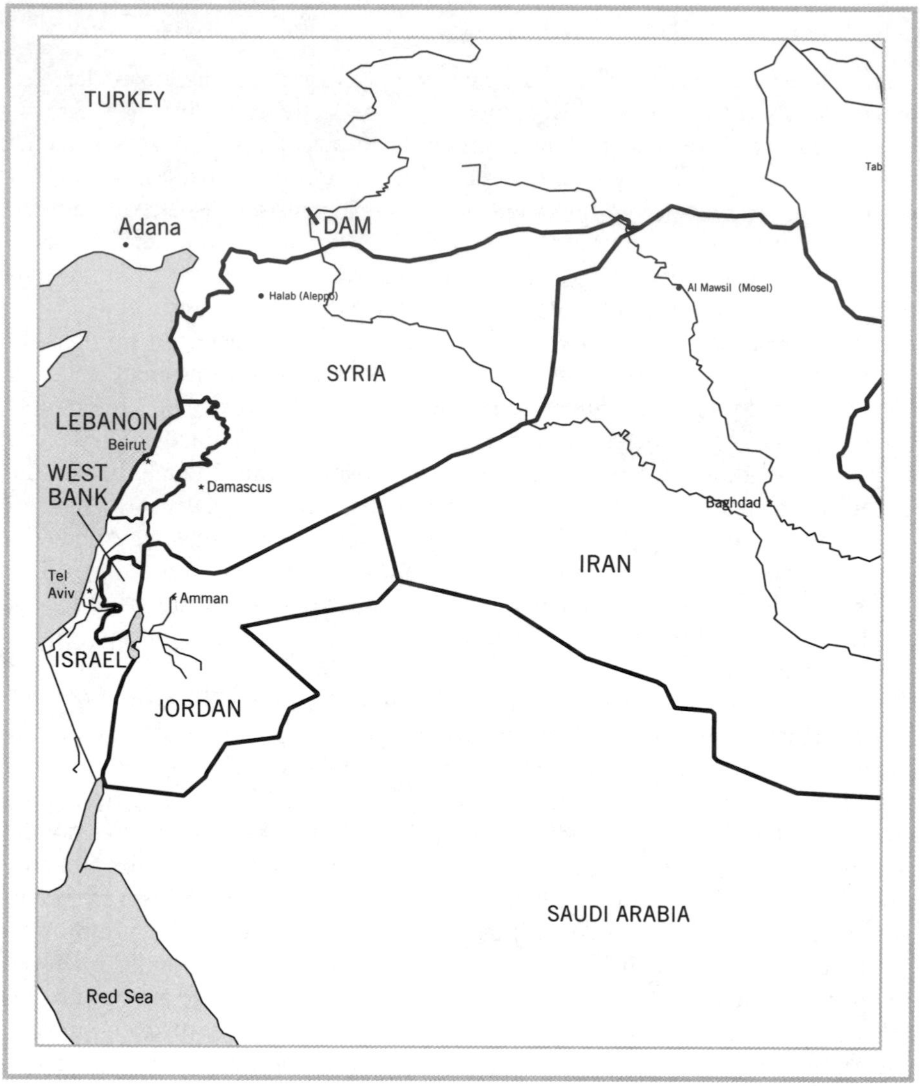

in joint endeavours. In 1998, as we saw in the last chapter, the G-7 member states sought to coordinate their economic policies to contain the Asian crisis's threat to the world economy.

When states agree to stop harmful environmental practices, as they did in the Montreal Convention of 1987 that phases out production of chlorofluorocarbons that attack the ozone layer, they are capable of effective environmental action. That is so because states can make authoritative decisions. Common action may depend on negotiating with other states, often under the auspices of international agencies, but once agreement is made states can commit resources and enforce rules. For their part, international agencies depend on the resources that states contribute and the authority they are willing to delegate. The difference is that the member states are sovereign, and the agencies are not.

It is easy to regard sovereign statehood, as neorealists, postmodernists and some feminists do, as the source of selfish and harmful behaviour. It is true that self-interest and the lack of central authority do invite abuse. At the same time, sovereign statehood may also be a friend of safety and joint action in a world subject to violence, economic instability and ecological dangers because statehood provides the means to act authoritatively.[1] We will look at collective measures later. First, it is useful to look at ways for states themselves to improve their safety.

Power: A Variable Resource

The basic resource in dealings with other states is **power**. This term has been debated in IR for decades. For realists and neorealists, as we saw in Chapter 2, power means military capability. This is the easiest form of power to visualize because it is direct, coercive and material. Although military capability is the ultimate resource in settling differences, it is not the only form of power, and most differences that arise between states do not warrant using it. More common are situations in which interests are in conflict but military capabilities are unusable.

One way of understanding why that is so is to recall the security community. As we saw in Chapters 2 and 10, a security community exists among states that do not resort to force among themselves. The global security community, as we saw in Chapter 2, now extends beyond Western Europe and North America to parts of Asia. States in this community are interdependent economically, and so there is no shortage of conflicting interests. Military power is not only unusable but virtually unthinkable. To test that statement, imagine a conflict between Germany and France. Then consider the conditions in Europe that would have to change before those two states would consider military options against each other.

Another way of understanding conflict without the threat of force is to remember the democratic peace. The democratic peace, as we saw in Chapter 9, is a fact to be explained. Recalling the explanations is a quick way of seeing conditions that discourage using military capabilities between democratic states:

- An open decision process
- A public that is aware of the costs it will bear
- A domestic climate of compromise that extends to other moderate states
- A free political opposition and critical news media
- A market economy that makes it difficult to blame setbacks on others' intervention

This is not to say that democratic states and members of security communities have no differences. They do not, however, use military capabilities among themselves, and so they do not threaten one another's security. In fact, being democratic and belonging to a security community are sources of safety. If democracy does indeed produce peace, extending democracy enlarges the number of states that pose no military threats to each other.

Military capabilities are not the only sources of power. To understand what the other sources might be, remember Chapter 3's presentation of Liberal IR theory. Preferences, as we saw, are central. They form within states, are pursued in state strategies and are affected by the actions of other states. Power can be seen as a way of changing another state's strategy by altering its preferences. The threat of force clearly affects strategies and preferences but so do other kinds of capabilities. Since many are not as obviously material as military ones, it is best to think of them not as capabilities but as advantages.

What qualifies as an advantage? In general, an advantage is something important to the other side. We can see an example in Canada's effort to persuade Chile to join NAFTA. The Canadian government's strategy was guided by the preferences of Canadian businesses and investors for a more open trade arrangement with Chile. Ottawa's own preference was to keep any additional trade agreements in the hemisphere within NAFTA's multilateral framework. Ottawa did not want the United States to negotiate separate bilateral agreements with new partners. Doing so would produce a hub-and-spoke arrangement with the United States in the centre and would leave each member to deal with the United States on its own. Canada's preference was a multilateral arrangement that would allow states to ally, offsetting the predominant position of the United States. Expanding NAFTA's multilateral framework was the preferable alternative.

Building coalitions within international institutions has long been a principle of Canadian foreign policy. Pooling advantages with like-minded partners makes sense for states whose individual advantages are modest. That is not to say that modest advantages always require joint endeavours. They can also be effective state to state. The effectiveness of any advantage depends on the preferences involved and their ability to be altered. The Chilean government's preference was for a bilateral trade deal with the United States. Canada's diplomatic strategy was to persuade it to join NAFTA instead. To work, the strategy required a Canadian advantage that could alter the Chilean government's preference.

What advantage did Canada bring to the task? In 1992, 1993 and 1995 the largest portion of new foreign investment in Chile came from Canada. In total investment, Canada's share was exceeded only by that of the United States.[2] That gave Canada entrée to the Chilean business community whose own preference favoured NAFTA. Canada's diplomatic task was to help that community shift the Chilean government's preference. Canada performed that task by taking direct part in forging a pro-NAFTA consensus. Without the advantage of a strong economic relationship and the prospect of enhancing it through more trade, Canada would not have had the same standing with the Chilean business community and government, the same access to political connections and the same effect on the outcome.

Advantages are not absolute but are relative to particular relationships and issues: who is involved and what is at stake.[3] That is so because preferences vary from state to state and from issue to issue. Because different preferences may be involved, an advantage may be effective with one state and ineffective with another. Business ties and investment—Canada's advantage in Chile on NAFTA—would not have had the same impact in a state with little interest in a trade agreement or with little Canadian investment. The same is also true of different issues within the same pair of states. Canadian investment levels may have little impact on dealings with Chile about marine wildlife conservation because different preferences are involved. The effectiveness of advantages varies with preferences, state by state and issue by issue. There are no all-purpose advantages, even military ones. Power, which rests on advantages, is not absolute.

Power varies in another way as well. Any advantage that requires a state to use a resource imposes a cost.[4] Again, the costs are most visible with military force, which is expensive to deploy even in small missions, but there are others. When states impose economic sanctions, as we will see later in the chapter, they refuse to buy or sell with the target state. A **boycott** is a refusal to buy, and an **embargo** is a refusal to sell. Both carry costs. With a boycott the cost is a foregone source of supply, and with an embargo it is a foregone export market. Willingness to bear these costs varies.

Economic sanctions are easy to support if they impose low costs. That is true of a state that trades little with the target state or enjoys multiple sources of supply. Economic sanctions may be a much different proposition if the costs are high. Canada bore a high cost in 1980 when it joined a multilateral grain embargo of the Soviet Union in protest of its invasion of Afghanistan. The cost was high because the Soviet Union was a major customer. Those bearing the cost directly were Canadian wheat growers and the prairie economies. Canada also joined a boycott of the 1980 Moscow Olympics. The cost of that boycott was borne by the athletes who sacrificed a chance that comes once every four years.

In both cases, preferences were very much at issue and were tied to security and stability. Soviet behaviour was seen as increasingly confident and aggressive, expanding into areas of the world that had not been zones of superpower conflict. That new attitude was as important as the sites of involvement themselves. To governments participating in the sanctions, the implications were serious enough to warrant shouldering the costs.

The same is true for states on the receiving side. They may decide that continuing their actions (refusing to allow their preferences to be altered) is worth the cost. The government of Iraq, as we saw in Chapter 9, dragged out compliance with UN inspection of its weapons of mass destruction through seven years of very damaging economic sanctions. Its preference to keep its weapons-producing capability was stronger than its preference to sell oil and buy necessary commodities. We will see more about economic sanctions later in the chapter.

Advantages can also be positive. A state may offer another state something that makes altering its preference attractive. These kinds of advantages frequently appear in negotiations as trade-offs. One side may offer a concession in one area—an investment rule, for example—in exchange for a concession in a different area—an environmental rule, for example. Again, costs are relevant. How attractive the exchange is depends on the preferences involved. If what is offered is less important than what is being asked, there is no basis for a trade-off. If what is offered is more important than what is being asked, the exchange is attractive. Preferences affect what concessions each side is willing to offer.

Willingness to spend money can be an advantage. As we will see in the next chapter, states frequently intervene in export markets to help their companies sell products abroad. One form of intervention is a government subsidy. Subsidies offset true costs and can be paid either to sellers or buyers. Paid to a seller, a subsidy compensates for a deep price discount. Paid to a buyer, a subsidy provides low-interest credit for the purchase. Either way, the purpose is to induce the customer to prefer one's own product to that of another. Willingness to spend may be quite generous in product lines that a government wishes to promote internationally. That willingness in turn is guided by the government's broader international economic strategy.

In 1998, British Airways, which had been a customer of Boeing, made a large purchase from Airbus after intense efforts by both producers to win the order. Airbus is a European aerospace consortium of France, Britain and Germany and Spain. According to the financial press, Airbus offered an irresistably sweet deal. France in particular has been determined to advance Airbus in the world market against Boeing. Since the member governments heavily subsidize Airbus to support a European commercial airliner industry and gain world market share, it is reasonable to assume that additional inducements were offered to swing British Airways' preference from Boeing to Airbus. The advantage was money and the willingness to spend it. The purpose can be seen as a form of economic security: protecting a high-tech industrial sector, with its jobs and development potential, by preventing a competitor from out-selling it.

Even something as attractive as money can be a variable advantage. A different aircraft buyer may prefer Boeing (fleet standardization is one reason) and not be persuaded by generous discounts from Airbus. Product characteristics may also affect preferences: one producer's aircraft may simply suit the airline's requirements better than the other's. Also shaping preferences is co-production, in which some of the components are made by industries in the buyer's own state, offsetting the purchase cost with local employment and technological development. The ability to offer **production offsets** can be an advantage although their attraction may vary among states.

Not all preferences are monetary. An important non-monetary consideration is the position of any large purchaser facing a duopoly. With the world market for large commercial aircraft now supplied by only two producers, it is in every airline's interest to keep them both in contention. The alternative is dealing with a monopoly. Concern about Microsoft's unrivalled position in the software industry shows some of monopoly's disadvantages. One strategy for preventing monopolies is to manage purchases so that no producer becomes predominant.

A constructivist perspective sheds further light on advantages by focusing on relationships themselves. As we saw in Chapter 4, constructivists are interested in the understandings that develop from interaction. When these understandings continue over time, they form more general expectations. These understandings can be particular not just to states but to issues. States may see one another as cooperators in one issue area, such as telecommunications, and adversaries in another, such as missile technology. These differing role identities may affect which advantages may be applied.

Between states that have formed expectations of each other as cooperators or allies some kinds of advantages may violate the spirit of the relationship. Those restrictions may not apply between states with role identities of adversaries. The difference affects which advantages may be used with whom. The open use of coercion, appropriate behaviour for dealing with enemies, may incense friends even when the issue in question is the same. The same may hold true between the same pair of states over different issues. What is seen as normal hard bargaining on one issue—trade in steel, for example—may be seen as high-handed and overbearing on another issue—air quality standards, for example.

Soft Power

Lloyd Axworthy, Minister of Foreign Affairs in the Liberal government of Jean Chretien, adopted the term "soft power" to characterize Canada's use of its advantages. Soft power emphasizes persuasion and coalition-building. The currency of soft power is not military force or the ability to spend money. Instead, soft power is based on reputation, liberal and humanitarian political values and the ability to bring together like-minded partners in conjoint efforts. Canada's long involvement in international institutions such as the United Nations and its use of "quiet diplomacy" to moderate extreme positions and craft agreements has earned it the reputation of a skilled and internationally minded state. Canada can use that reputation as an advantage in forging agreements and understandings.[5]

Soft power works best in institutional settings—United Nations agencies, for example—that are responsible for policy in particular areas and that have multilateral memberships. The institutional setting serves two purposes: it allows focusing on particular problems and issues of interest to Canada, and it provides a forum for bringing together coalitions or blocs of states to shape the institution's agenda and forge blocs of votes. Proponents of soft power regard it as Canada's principal advantage in important world issues. Security is one such issue.

Canada's sponsorship of an international convention banning anti-personnel landmines was an instance using soft power to promote security. The security sought was "human security"—a concept that emphasizes not the defence of states but of ordinary people exposed to the dangers of war. A landmine convention fitted that concept because so many of the victims of landmines—often deployed in civil wars—are civilians, particularly children. In Axworthy's words, "a humanitarian crisis arising from threats to life and limb of millions of individuals should take precedence over military and national security interests."[6] Giving priority to human security assumes that states themselves are safe enough in their international settings to allow that shift of emphasis. The conditions following the cold war, in the view of soft power's advocates, provide states such as Canada with enough security to allow humanitarian ends such as landmines to become priorities.

The landmines convention, signed in December 1997 by 122 states, has been displayed as an example of soft power in action. Canada, along with other like-minded states, used its advantages of diplomacy and reputation to assemble a bloc dedicated to eliminating this weapon and then persuaded other states to join. Wielding soft power does not require a state to be a great power. The other states promoting the convention were moderately sized ones like Canada, but the collective result was an international agreement. Crucial to the development of a consensus was a worldwide network of anti-landmine NGOs, which used their resources of publicity and coordination to organize domestic political pressure on governments to sign. Part of Canada's soft-power strategy was to work with NGOs.

Not all scholars believe that soft power, relying as it does on relationships and reputation, is sufficient for security. That is so because not all international issues are amenable to persuasion and coalition-building. The most serious security-related issues are likely to involve determined adversaries who may be impervious to collective appeals and censure.[7] The problem can be seen in terms of preferences. Soft power may be enough to alter preferences that are flexible or not strongly held but not enough to alter preferences that are rigid. Rigid preferences may reflect powerful domestic pressures that limit or foreclose a state's flexibility. Israel's extreme reluctance to concede territory on the West Bank to the Palestinian Authority reflects pressure from a politically powerful minority of Israeli settlers and from a larger domestic bloc that fears compromised security. Rigid preferences may also reflect a determined resolve. India conducted nuclear tests in 1998 because its government was committed to modernizing its capability regardless of international condemnation. The same was true of France in 1995 when it tested nuclear weapons in the South Pacific in defiance of widespread protest.

More serious is the criticism that soft power fosters an illusion: foreign policy requires only intangible advantages like reputation and membership in issue networks and not tangible advantages like "an honourable development program, war-ready armed forces and long-reaching intelligence services."[8] Those tangible advantages are required when state preferences clash, when the issues at stake are important and when reconciliation alone does not work.

The United States was able to broker a deal between Israel and the Palestinian Authority in 1998 to proceed with the transfer of land on the West Bank, removing a principal obstacle to the Middle East peace process. Part of the American advantage was soft power—credibility with both sides to bring them to the table and diplomatic skill to induce them to be flexible. A key element was hard power—a large, expensive and sophisticated CIA that would be employed to verify Palestinian treatment of suspected terrorists and reassure Israel. Without that material advantage, the deal may not have been made. Hard assets such as these, critics argue, cannot be discounted in favour of soft ones.

At the same time, critics of soft power do not suggest that moderately sized states such as Canada have the material resources to act alone, particularly when formidable states or threats are involved. Collective efforts are required instead. But to be effective in those efforts and to play a role in shaping and executing them, states such as Canada, the critics argue, must be willing and able to bring tangible advantages—hard power—into play.[9] We will see more about collective efforts later.

Power: Context and Circumstance

What do these considerations say about power? Seen as advantages that bear on particular relationships and issues, power is circumstantial: advantages that are effective with some states and issues are useless with others. Power is also uncertain: another state cannot know for sure how its efforts—as exercises of either soft or hard power—will influence the other side's preferences. Liberal IR theory's insights into the inner life of states have shown us why that is so. Preferences arise from groups, and governments (which can have preferences of their own) seek to reconcile them into a common strategy. Affecting those preferences are both domestic and international conditions. Complex societies generate diverse preferences, complicating the government's formation of a strategy and complicating the task of anyone, including other states, wishing to influence that strategy. The greater the array of preferences in question, the more factors there are that bear on the government's choice of strategy. It may be difficult for another state to predict how its advantages, as only one of the factors involved, will affect the outcome. That is particularly true if the issue affects a diversity of preferences. With complexity comes uncertainty.

For these reasons, it is best to look at power as affecting the *probability* that the other side will act as one desires. Given the ways that preferences and strategies can be shaped politically, that is generally as specific as it is possible to be, particularly when one's efforts are only part of a broader set of factors weighing on the other side's preferences. For IR scholars and, more consequentially, for states themselves, power and its effects are inherently difficult to calculate. That makes safety, to the extent that it depends on power in its various forms, contingent and changeable. Such uncertainties may operate at both the individual state level, as we will see next with deterrence, and at the international community level, as we will see later with collective security.

Protective Force: Deterrence

Defensive military force is intended to be used only against an attack. Rational attackers, as we saw in the last chapter, weigh the expected gains against the expected costs and calculate whether the effort is worthwhile. Mounting enough defence to impose unacceptable costs deters the attacker. Deter means literally "to frighten from," and in that way deterrent force frightens attackers with high costs. Potential attackers also consider risk: how likely is an attack to fail? In the same way, deterrent force shifts the attacker's calculations towards failure.

In military terms, **deterrence** requires enough force to present a disheartening prospect. Force is not the only consideration. Natural protections favour defence. For centuries, Switzerland's alpine fastness has made conquest an unpromising proposition. States with open frontiers, such as Poland's, are less safe because they are much easier to attack, and defensive military force must compensate. States facing potential attackers that are geared for highly mobile and invasive offence require more robust deterrence than states facing slower-moving threats.

Because the purpose of deterrence is to make war costly for the attacker, highly destructive weapons strengthen deterrence when two conditions are present: the other side can gauge their effect, and the advantage is defensive. Again, the purpose is to tilt the calculus against the attacker. That calculus hinges also on the clear intention to fight if necessary. Irresolution can undermine powerful material capabilities. Because the ultimate effect of deterrence is in the eye of the attacker, its effectiveness depends on estimates and perceptions, just as we saw with the security dilemma in Chapter 10.

FIGURE 11.3 Deterrence as Weakness

Since independence, Africa has had "not one single involuntary boundary change." The two efforts to alter boundaries—Libya's invasion of Chad and Somalia's invasion of Ethiopia—failed. Tanzania invaded Uganda in 1978, but the purpose was to oust the dictator Idi Amin. South Africa made armed incursions into its neighbours during the 1980s, but the purpose was to intimidate not conquer. Otherwise the continent has been remarkably free of interstate war despite the fact that each state has armed forces.[10]

How would a neorealist account for that remarkable pattern? Mutual deterrence is one explanation. The fact that all states have armed forces means that no attacker can be sure of an unresisted invasion. In assuming that all states act rationally, neorealists believe that states will not attack unless there are good chances of success. How can a weak state be dissuasive?

Mutual weakness may be an advantage. Because all of the governments except South Africa are poor and have difficulty maintaining effective armed forces, the level of force necessary to discourage attack need not be very large.

Weak attackers may not be able to afford to acquire enough extra force to achieve quick success and may not want to risk the internal political and economic disruption of a long or indecisive war. Even low levels of deterrent capability may be enough. What about the neorealist concern with relative gains—the extra increments of power that may give one side enough marginal advantage to consider an attack? At low levels of capability, success, trouble and risk may not be amenable to close calculation. The prudent course for potential attackers is to stay put.

Deterrence is easiest to understand when the same kinds of weapons are involved on both sides: conventional deterrence against conventional weapons and nuclear deterrence against nuclear weapons. That line is not always so clearly drawn. During the cold war, NATO's war-fighting plan in Europe assumed a massive Soviet conventional attack. Since NATO's conventional defences were not seen as strong enough to stop the attack, the plan called for the early use of battlefield and tactical nuclear weapons. Much of the purpose was deterrent; a conventional attack risked a nuclear response. One objection to the plan was that the contest would not stop there. Use of nuclear weapons by NATO would invite Soviet retaliation, opening the way to general nuclear war. The alternative was a higher level of conventional force than NATO members were willing to support.

Israel's motives for acquiring nuclear weapons were based on similar calculations. Although its adversaries, with the possible exception of Iraq, are not nuclear powers, in the early hours of the last war in 1973 Egypt and Syria came close to defeating Israel. Since then Israel has acquired a weapon of last resort.

Although the destructiveness of nuclear weapons makes them unwieldy for direct offence, they can be used for intimidation. If Iraq had possessed nuclear (or biological) weapons and medium-range ballistic missiles in 1990, one analyst speculates, and had threatened strikes on Paris and London, would France and Britain have joined the Gulf War coalition? And with those two cities held hostage, would the United States have been as willing to attack?[11] That use of nuclear weapons would have been indirectly offensive since the purpose would be to subdue opposition to capturing Kuwait—the prime objective.

More common is the role of nuclear weapons as tools of deterrence. A nuclear weapon provides deterrence when the attacker must reckon with retaliation. That threat is credible when the weapons are protected or dispersed to survive attack so that, regardless of what the attacker does, devastating force will remain.

In practice, deterrence may not always be as clear-cut. As we saw in the last chapter, the difference between defensive and offensive weapons can be difficult to ascertain. That quandary faces states that are just acquiring nuclear forces such as India and Pakistan. Are the weapons intended only for defence? If they are, if they can be fortified to survive attack, and if both sides are on that same footing, nuclear deterrence can be stable. With neither side having incentive to strike first, defence/defence—the safest posture—obtains. The cold war term was Mutual Assured Destruction, or MAD. Because the destructiveness of nuclear weapons is so terrible to contemplate, according to MAD, neither side will risk retaliation. As instruments of mutual deterrence, nuclear weapons, according to that logic, are instruments of safety. A less sanguine view holds that if states are determined to have nuclear weapons, defence/defence is the least dangerous configuration.

Safety may not be so neatly determinate. Whether states with nuclear weapons actually follow the logic of MAD has often been questioned. As with deterrence generally, calculations of utility are pivotal—what will be gained at what costs and with what risks. Deterrence works when a potential attacker is persuaded that the costs and risks outweigh the gains. In the view of IR scholars Janice Stein and Richard Ned Lebow, potential attackers, acting perfectly logically and rationally, may not be deterred. That is so because their calculations are heavily weighted by subjective factors: their willingness to take risks and their valuations of costs and gains.[12] These in turn are affected by preferences. These may be known to the deterring side, but their subjective importance may not be known. Preferences can also change particularly in heightened and unstable situations such as crises.

MAD was an American doctrine. During the cold war it was hoped that MAD's logic would also be obvious and compelling to the Soviet Union. Although the Soviet leadership, like its American counterpart, was careful to avoid crises that might escalate to nuclear war, its commitment to MAD was not certain. In the words of IR scholar Robert Jervis, "Russian declaratory policy as well as its military posture seem to reject the logic of MAD." Instead, he argued, Soviet views of nuclear weapons and their role in defence emphasized preparedness for actual war. That supported the worry that the apparently stable situation of defence/defence was actually one-sided.[13] Others argued that the close balance of nuclear forces between the two sides produced a *de facto* situation of deterrence since attack by either side could never be thorough enough to eliminate significant retaliatory capability. The Soviet archives, accessible since the end of the cold war, have shown no evidence that it ever intended to attack the United States.[14] Such assurance was not available to American strategists at the time.

Would the stability that existed between the United States and the Soviet Union be duplicated by new pairs of nuclear adversaries? That question has practical implications now that India and Pakistan, adversaries since independence in 1947, have become nuclear powers. Their accession and the ability of other states to follow suit raises renewed questions about nuclear weapons, deterrence and safety. There are two schools of thought.

The pessimistic school emphasizes the vulnerability of fledgling nuclear forces to pre-emptive strikes. States in the early stages of nuclear acquisition, as we saw in the last chapter, have forces that are not protected enough to withstand an attack. Instead of deterring the other side, vulnerable nuclear weapons create the very different incentive of eliminating the weapons before they can be used. What is worse is fledgling nuclear powers lacking adequate ways to monitor the other side and warn of attacks. "Government leaders may be faced with speculations, assumptions and unverifiable intelligence reports that generate worst-case pressures either to use nuclear weapons or to make robust threats to do so."[15] Crises become more combustible because each side knows that the other's temptation to use its weapons is high. Surprise attacks are always a possibility; again, the incentive is to eliminate the weapons before they can be used. Unprotected nuclear weapons, in this view, make states less safe.

The optimistic school emphasizes the unforeseeable consequences of nuclear attack. That uncertainty adds to the attacker's risk and raises the costs of miscalculation. The price of a bad decision, in the words of IR scholar Karl Kaysen, is "so immense and immediate that it is almost inconceivable that haste or wishfulness will again play the roles in initiating wars that they have in the past."[16] World opinion also may be a restraint. International norms against the use of nuclear weapons have become so strong that states violating them face unforeseeable and perhaps severe repercussions.[17] Together, these costs may be high enough to eliminate the risk of attack and create long-term stability.[18]

What about India and Pakistan? One analyst sees high risks of pre-emptive war and believes that the two states are safer keeping their nuclear weapons undeployed.[19] Adding to the concern is severe political and economic instability in Pakistan. Nuclear safety depends on calm leadership and sure control. Instability undermines the other side's confidence and encourages worst-case thinking. In the eyes of other analysts, India's and Pakistan's record of strategic behaviour has been encouragingly circumspect and restrained. Although they have fought three wars since independence, these have not been all-out efforts. Attacks were directed at military targets and avoided civilian ones. The two states also have not engaged in superpower-style arms races. Compared to other states, their per capita arms expenditures have been moderate. Both sides have shown awareness of the risks of preventive war by mutually pledging not to attack the other's nuclear facilities and by exchanging information about them.[20] Which school of thought will turn out to be correct? Time will tell.

Safety and Collective Security

Collective security is a commitment among states to combine forces to resist aggression regardless of who the aggressor may be. The commitment is directed not to particular states but to any state that violates the peace. That generalized commitment makes collective security agreements fundamentally different from alliances, which are directed to particular states and contingencies. NATO's specified adversary was the Soviet Union and its allies, and the contingency was attack on Western Europe. Out-of-area operations in places such as the Persian Gulf were not in NATO's mandate. Specific provisions also characterize bilateral alliances. The American alliance with South Korea is directed to attack from North Korea. Members of a collective security agreement pledge to resist *any* act of aggression.

A good way of contrasting alliances and collective security is the scope of protection: alliances are intended to improve the safety of groups of states, and collective security is intended to improve the safety of the international system. The incentive to fight in an alliance is protecting oneself and one's partners; the incentive to fight under collective security is punishing violation of the peace. Safety purchased by alliance membership is local or regional; safety purchased by collective security membership is universal.

Ideally, collective security operates as a deterrent. Any state contemplating the costs, risks and potential gains of aggression must consider not only the target state but the international community. When collective security is strong, an aggressor faces a combined armed response. The prospect of isolation in the face of that response deters aggression and preserves the peace. Iraq's isolation and defeat by the Gulf War coalition in 1991 are collective security's object lesson to other aggressors. A safer international system for all states is the intended result.

For states such as Canada, which face no direct security threats and have modest resources for deterrence, collective security is an attractive proposition. Individually moderate levels of military capability can be pooled against a single violator and provide a formidable response. Canadian policy since the UN's founding has been based on the view that a stable world is in the common interest of all states and requires support. Improved international security, in turn, is a common benefit that all states, including Canada, can enjoy. Multilateral approaches to security have also suited Canada's preference for working through international institutions with other like-minded states to achieve foreign policy objectives.

Collective security is inspiring in conception but has been problematic in practice. The Covenant of the League of Nations provided for common action against violations and was the first effort to institutionalize collective security. One practical difficulty was that it would operate only if the aggressor virtually confessed to violating the Covenant. Another difficulty was that action could be taken only by a unanimous decision.[21] Seeking to rectify these paralyzing limitations, the founders of the United Nations created a Security Council with wide-reaching powers to identify aggressors and order armed collective action. The potential for amassing powerfully armed coalitions is considerable as shown by the Gulf War, which was waged under Security Council authorization.

That result was indeed the UN founders' intention. Article VII of the Charter forbids the use of armed force against member states and authorizes the Security Council to organize collective action against violators. The Gulf War was the Security Council's first decisive action to repel aggression in 45 years. The Security Council did authorize action in 1950 against North Korea's invasion of South Korea, but that decision was taken only because the Soviet Union had boycotted the Council in protest. The Security Council's impediment was caused by its basic structure of five permanent members (the United States, France, Great Britain, Russia and China) each of whom can veto resolutions and prevent the Council from acting.

In 1945, the founders expected that these five states, which had cooperated to defeat Germany and Japan in World War II, would continue as an international executive to keep the peace. Aware that the Article VII gives the Security Council a potentially formidable power, the great powers insisted on a provision allowing them to prevent action against themselves—the veto. During the cold war, when conflicting interests polarized the United States and the Soviet Union, vetoes paralyzed the Security Council. Neither side would allow action to be taken against itself, its allies or its interests. The other permanent members have used the veto for the same reasons.

The end of the cold war brought the promise of a Security Council finally able to perform its intended function. The strong authorization of action against Iraq, whose invasion of Kuwait was a clear violation of the Charter, supported hopeful talk of a new world order or rather a return to the order envisaged in 1945. The world's major powers, with no cold war fault line to divide them, would agree on identifying aggressors and authorizing collective action. The prospect was a more orderly world under the like-minded management of the Security Council.

In fact, maintaining such an order entails two important areas of agreement: who the aggressor is and what measures are required. Designating aggressors may not appear to be a difficulty, but Iraq's invasion of Kuwait was a relatively unambiguous case. More difficult are instances of preventive war in which the attacker claims that the threat from the other side was so imminent and dangerous that self-preservation required striking the first blow. By that argument, responsibility for creating the climate of aggression is with the side that is attacked. That possibility complicates establishing fault. Another complication is close bilateral ties between the Security Council members and the two sides. Members with close relations with one side may be more hesitant to name it the guilty party than are members without such ties.

Willingness to authorize armed force against a state may also vary. States may be reluctant if the aggressor is a principal power because direct military costs and indirect economic costs will be high. Iraq in 1990 had one of the world's largest armed forces and amply qualified as a powerful state, but other states are even more formidable. Collective action against China, for example, might be quite a daunting proposition. Military costs could be high particularly in the contiguous states where aggression would be most likely and where China has significant local advantages. The same would be true of economic costs because of China's importance as a host for international investment and as a purchaser of high-technology goods. Both depend on present and future cooperation and goodwill. States with investment and trade interests in China include all of the world's industrial powers including moderately sized ones such as Sweden and Canada.

Another consideration is an unequal ability to project military force. The United States is the only member state with the air- and sea-lift capacity to marshall significant force in distant places. Major operations, particularly those deploying large ground forces, require American participation. The strategic importance of the Persian Gulf made the United States a very willing participant in 1990, but its involvement in Bosnia, an area marginal to American security, came well after the European states' and Canada's. To minimize domestic opposition to risking American lives in Bosnia, involvement was conditional on cautious rules of engagement. For reasons such as these, skeptics believed that the Gulf War may not have been an index of collective security's future but an instance when the permanent Security Council members' interests happened to align.

After the Gulf War the Security Council was able to agree on interventions in Somalia and Bosnia, but these were very different kinds of conflicts. Unlike the cross-border invasions that constitute clear violations of the Charter, these were civil wars. Somalia's was self-contained, and there was no external aggressor. There was external aggression in Bosnia, and in 1992 the Security Council ordered economic sanctions under Article VII of the Charter against Serbia for its support and encouragement of Bosnian Serb forces. The Security Council's purpose in both cases was humanitarian and not repelling acts of aggression.

In Somalia, as we saw in Chapter 7, the UN redefined its mission as defeating the clan leaders who stood in the way of a settlement, and it was that decision that was later blamed for the disorderly and incomplete results. In Bosnia, when the Security Council did authorize military force—air strikes against Bosnian Serb positions—it acted indirectly by requesting NATO to carry them out. In both cases, the UN action was officially peacekeeping—a lower level of response than the direct use of armed force available under Article VII. We will see more about peacekeeping later in the chapter.

More recently, the Security Council has been divided on Iraq. The issue has been authorizing force in response to Iraq's efforts to block UN weapons inspections. France, China and Russia, for different reasons, have been unwilling to approve specific military action. Division in the Council, critics maintain, gives Iraq exploitable latitude and undermines the UN's effort to eliminate its weapons of mass destruction.

The difficulty reflects an underlying contingency and uncertainty. Collective security depends on states agreeing on common measures. The willingness to do so requires that the interest of states in maintaining peace, particularly the interest of the five permanent Security Council members holding vetoes, overrides all others. For five states with differing preferences and global strategies, that may be a formidable requirement. Those with close relations with an aggressor or with preferences that oppose action against it may be unwilling to authorize collective action even when violation of the Charter is clear. More generally, all five states must prefer the status quo and understand threats to peace in the same way.[22] If even one permanent member fails to see the threat as paramount, collective action is doubtful. Collective security requires potential aggressors to expect a combined response, but that requires convergent views.

Whether convergence will occur predictably enough to discourage aggressors is open to question, and as the 1990s progressed, talk of a new world order increasingly became a reference to one particular episode—the Gulf War—and not a stable expectation. Instead, it is possible to imagine more disorder as aggressive regional powers calculate their moves with an eye to Security Council division.

A second difficulty with collective security has been the unwillingness of member states to form the standing international force envisaged in the Charter. Such a force would be composed of designated units from the member states and be under a permanent command structure. UN members have not been willing to make this degree of commitment. As a result, the UN must assemble forces *ad hoc* once aggression has occurred and once the Security Council has authorized action.

Notwithstanding the concessions of sovereignty that we have seen throughout this book, control over armed force remains a bedrock of statehood. Even in the closely knit fabric of the European Union, as we saw in Chapter 8, member states have preferred to manage their own defence policy rather than to pool it in a common institution as they have done in other policy areas. There is also the question of conflicting purposes. When their own interests are at stake in a conflict, states may insist on keeping their forces under their own command. Otherwise, states risk having their military forces employed against their own interests. Such conflicts of interest also raise questions about the impartiality of participating forces, a crucial consideration for the legitimacy of UN operations.

There is also the question of due care and responsibility for the forces under command—one of the prime obligations of military leadership. States lack confidence that a UN commander "of any other nationality other than their own will take due care to minimize risks."[23] Finally there is the question of adequate resources. The UN's member governments all face budgetary limitations that affect their willingness to support UN operations. Although they may vote in favour of an operation, they may be much less willing to provide adequate backing, thereby resulting in forces that are too small and lightly equipped.[24]

Together these are significant limitations. At the end of the cold war, one IR scholar ventured that the future of collective security was by no means clear.[25] A decade later that view still appears to be accurate.

NATO and Regional Security

NATO was an alliance formed against a specific threat: a Soviet-led invasion of Western Europe. Although American nuclear weapons were NATO's ultimate guarantee, the alliance was designed not as a set of bilateral defence agreements between the United States and individual European states but as a multilateral alliance based on the principle of joint obligation. NATO was also a political alliance of democratic states. Its core principle was equal treatment of all members, and its institutional structure was integrated. Those features may not have been necessary from a purely military standpoint, but they did reflect a political commitment to building a unified Europe.[26] In maintaining a deterrent force against Soviet invasion, NATO was a military success. More interestingly, in uniting European neighbours with long histories of warfare and competition, NATO was an institutional success.

After the cold war, the alliance did not disband even though the threat from Russia had greatly decreased. One explanation is that any established organization seeks to preserve itself and resists termination. Finding a new mission is one way of surviving. Another explanation is that NATO's multilateral and democratic structure has made it very much a part of a united Europe. The security community on which European union depends, some scholars argue, owes much to NATO. As an institution of democratic states, NATO has fostered the trust, cooperation and interdependence that has helped eliminate centuries of military rivalry, particularly between France and Germany.[27] Preserving NATO's structure and process keeps in place one of Europe's institutional pillars.

Now that the threats to NATO's security come from its periphery in Eastern Europe and the Balkans as aggravated civil conflicts and instability, its role has changed fundamentally. Although NATO remains committed to providing defence against attack from Russia, including nuclear attack, it now intervenes in conflicts outside the alliance. This new role has been recognized by the UN, which regards NATO as a regional security organization and its standing forces as a military asset. In 1992, NATO agreed to consider requests from both the UN Security Council and the Organization for European Security and Cooperation to enforce their decisions.[28] Previously, NATO had been careful to keep to its specific role as an alliance and avoid affiliation with organizations such as the UN.

Following the 1992 decision, NATO took an increasing part in the war in Bosnia, beginning with supervising the UN's arms embargo. By 1994, NATO had increased its involvement to conducting air strikes against Bosnian Serb artillery positions around Sarajevo. In 1995, UN Secretary General Boutros Boutros-Ghali acknowledged the UN's inability to mount a military force that could take direct action in Bosnia against Serbian violations and recognized NATO as the only effective multilateral standing force available for the job. Three years later, NATO was given the role of conducting airstrikes against Serbia again, this time to enforce Serbian commitments to disengage its forces in Kosovo. For NATO, these assign-

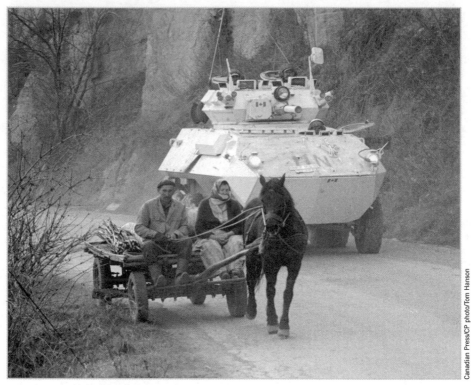

Canadian Press/CP photo/Tom Hanson

A Canadian Peacekeeping Cougar Armoured Personnel Carrier passes a horse-drawn carriage just outside of Visoco, Bosnia-Herzogovina, March 11, 1994, on its way back to base following a reconnaissance mission.

ments have marked a fundamental change of purpose: "NATO's members are now theoretically willing to use military force to uphold group standards of behaviour throughout Europe."[29]

NATO is not the only potential security organization in Europe. The Organization for Security and Cooperation in Europe (OSCE) began during the cold war as a forum for negotiations between NATO states and the Soviet bloc. The OSCE has become more institutionalized since the end of the cold war with the UN's recognition of it as a regional security organization and with NATO's declaring itself in 1992 to be the OSCE's military arm. Neither Russia nor the United States sees the OSCE as effective although European states have been interested in its possibilities as an organization for themselves.

The same interest in a security organization without the United States has supported revival of the Western European Union (WEU). Originally formed during the 1950s to coordinate European defence independently of the United States, the WEU never became an active security organization during the cold war. Since then, Germany and France have seen a use for it as the basis of a European core defence force in situations when American and Canadian forces will not be participating and when an alternative framework to NATO is needed.

NATO still remains the pre-eminent organization. European participation in the Bosnian war, the continent's first post-cold war conflict, was through the UN and NATO and not the OSCE or the WEU. The OSCE's role was limited to the ancillary task of providing monitors in Macedonia against Serbian invasion.[30] Finally, there is the Maastricht Treaty. Adopted in 1992 to promote closer integration in the European Union, it too provides for closer defence and foreign policy coordination among the member states.[31]

European interest in these alternatives does not mean that they wish American involvement in NATO to end. The Europeans still see a military role for the United States in underwriting the continent's security and an institutional role in supporting a key multilateral framework. Some scholars see the institutional role as particularly important now that the cold war's powerful external threat is ended. NATO's open and integrated command structure creates "a climate in which members' policy processes [are] mutually transparent," helping to maintain the confidence and stability that underwrite Europe's security community.[32] That security community, in turn, provides the safety and assurance for continued integration under the European Union.

Looser Ties

A NATO conference in Madrid in July 1997 expanded membership and changed the terms of obligation. Poland, the Czech Republic and Hungary, NATO's adversaries when they were members of the Warsaw Pact, were allowed to become members. Some of the three states' motivation was security against Russia and some was movement into Europe's institutional network. The obligation of all NATO's members changed as well. No longer must they respond together in time of danger. Now they may take action as they choose.[33]

These changes mark the transition from an alliance to a regional security organization and the addition of new functions: preventive diplomacy, collective security and peacekeeping. One name for this new blend is **common security**. Although not as well defined as either NATO's alliance obligations or the UN's collective security provisions, common security emphasizes prevention of war through negotiation and peaceful settlement. If hostilities do occur, common security emphasizes intervention while the stakes are local, force requirements are low and conjoint missions are feasible. Common security's attraction is its emphasis on peaceful settlement and its flexible approach to military involvement.

That same feature has attracted criticism. Some argue that common security is too vague to be of much help to policymakers.[34] Others argue that it is too unspecific in its obligations. When NATO was a cold war alliance, all members were required to fight together. Now, each state's latitude makes it easy to pass the buck. As we saw in Chapter 10, buck-passing occurs when some other state, one either more powerful or with more direct reason to be involved, can be expected to act. Buck-passing is especially likely when states do not share the same exposure to threat and when their participation is not fully obligatory. Secure states where the need to act is low can pass the buck to the less secure states where the need to act is higher. Because buck-passing is such an obvious temptation, alliance agreements often specify precisely the situations requiring joint action.

Two conditions in post-cold war NATO may encourage disjointed efforts. The first is the low-level and roundabout nature of threats. They stem not from direct attack but from spillovers from civil conflicts. The second is the location of the threats on NATO's periphery. The link between those conflicts and member states' national security is not immediate and compelling thereby making it easier to decline participation. One result is that the larger members such as Britain and France may end up with a disproportionate burden. Another result is dithering and irresolution. Although NATO did participate in Bosnia, purposes were divided, and direct force was avoided even when risks were low. Hesitancy and division, in the eyes of critics, encouraged Serbian recalcitrance and prolonged the suffering of the war's victims.

FIGURE 11.5 Should Canada Stay in NATO?

Canada's membership in NATO was based on three motives. First, Canada shared American and European concerns about the threat to a weakened postwar Europe and believed that the continent's falling under Soviet domination would represent a serious shift in the global balance. Second, Canada believed that the United States on its own could be prone to actions that endangered stability. NATO's consultative structure would, it was hoped, provide adequate military security while moderating any American tendencies toward unilateralism. Finally, NATO gave Canada a seat at the table with the United States and the Europeans. Such entree in strategic issues, it was hoped, would be the basis for participation in broader questions in which Canada had interests. Being a faithful member of NATO would provide benefits in other institutions such as the Organization for Economic Cooperation and Development, which has headquarters in Paris and a heavily European membership.

In 1969, the Trudeau government, believing that the worst of the cold war was over, decided to scale back by half Canada's forces in Europe. Critics at the time said that such a move would be seen by the Europeans as a lessening of commitment to defend them. The level of forces involved was not as important as the continuing reliability of partners across the Atlantic. The other trans-Atlantic partner was the United States whose force commitments and ultimate willingness to use nuclear weapons were central to European confidence. By the mid-1960s, when the Western European economies were well recovered from the war, the United States was becoming dissatisfied that the European NATO members were not shouldering more of the defence burden. In 1966, Senator Mike Mansfield introduced a resolution that called for a substantial reduction of American forces in Europe. Because of the perceived threat from the Soviet Union and its bearing on American security, the United States did maintain its level of support, but burden-sharing remained an issue for the rest of the cold war. Because commitment to Europe was an issue, Trudeau's withdrawal of forces evoked more disapproval from Brussels than from Washington. On the Canadian side, critics argued that the move sacrificed Canada's political standing in Europe at a time when Canada hoped to offset its economic ties with the United States with increased ties to Europe.

Canada withdrew the remainder of its NATO contingent after the cold war and no longer has forces stationed in Europe. With Europe's security shifted from a Soviet threat to more low-level and ambiguous threats in its neighbouring states, is there now any rationale for Canadian membership? This question was actively considered in the Liberal government's parliamentary review of foreign and defence policy in 1994. In favour was a coalition of academics and politicians who called for a Canadian commitment to common security, which emphasizes preventive diplomacy, non-obligatory action from members and peacekeeping.

People in Canada and Europe holding that view favour the evolution of NATO into a voluntary regional security organization that can reconcile conflict and create the foundations for peace. The concept was popular with members of the federal Liberal party as a positive rationale for continuing Canadian involvement in Europe and was stated formally in a policy document prepared for the defence policy review.[35]

Common security has not been without criticism. One criticism is that it provides the mantle of engagement without the need for real commitments. Instead of a NATO that is a "harsh military and political alliance led (as the image goes) by militaristic American generals," common security "costs little and downplays the actual and potential use of force in favour of conflict resolution and peacekeeping."[36] Without contingents stationed in Europe, critics assert, it would be difficult to marshal adequate forces on short notice, particularly from Canada's down-sized military. Worse is the absence of a firm requirement to participate, making any decision to use force politically contentious and raising the temptation to stay home. Given the voluntary nature of present NATO commitments, other governments may be tempted to buck-pass as well.[37] For other critics, common defence provides a rationale for further reducing Canada's armed forces. In one scholar's words, the result has been the "destruction of the Canadian armed forces as a usable, militarily consequential instrument."[38]

Canada, along with Britain, sent a warship to the Persian Gulf in early 1998 to support an American naval buildup aimed at pressuring the Iraqi government to re-open UN weapons inspections. No other states contributed. There also has not been any reduction of Canada's official commitment to use its armed forces in multilateral peacekeeping missions.

Some people feel that a principal reason for staying in NATO is political and economic. By that reasoning, Canada's standing in the G-7 may depend on a willingness to share the practical responsibilities of the world's senior powers. The G-7's European members may regard commitment to Europe's security—even in NATO's looser and more volitional form—as one index of that willingness.

Other scholars see the prime threats to NATO as non-military. The European Union depends upon stable monetary and trade relations and democracy. These depend on healthy domestic economies. Economic and social breakdown, either in adjoining states in Eastern Europe or in NATO states themselves, would "upend the foundation of national political stability" that has supported European integration. A severe economic crisis might drive the most vulnerable members facing unrest and the possibility of collapse to protect themselves.[39] That would introduce once again the international conditions of the Great Depression when states protected their own economies by discriminatory treatment of their neighbours' exports. (We will see more about economic protectionism in the next chapter.) The result worsened the Depression by shutting down international trade and intensifying rivalry.

Such action would threaten the security of individual states as the effects ripple through their economies and of common institutions as protective interests pit states against one another and undermine collective policies. Further along that path is the "corrosive competition between states that preceded the Second World War."[40] That consequence would undo 50 years of institution-building in Europe and threaten the basis of its security community. To prevent the economic breakdown that would cause such desperation, security requires strengthening the institutions of economic cooperation. Safety, in this formulation, requires stable finances and healthy economies.

These issues return us to the nature of post-cold war security. Threats of war do exist in Asia, Africa and the Middle East. None of these affect the NATO states directly, but they show that security remains a concern in the international system and raise the question of suitable strategies and organization. For secure NATO states such as Canada, the question becomes even more pertinent: what force levels and international commitments does Canada need?

Peacekeeping

Peacekeeping differs from both alliances and collective security because its purpose is not to resist attack but to enforce cease-fires. The idea of peacekeeping originated in 1956. Israel, France and Britain had launched an attack on Egypt. A cease-fire between Egypt and Israel had been reached along the Sinai desert, but there was concern that fighting could easily resume. Lester Pearson, then Canada's Secretary of State for External Affairs, proposed the idea of an independent UN force to be placed between the two sides along the cease-fire line. Installed with Egypt's and Israel's permission, the force would serve as a neutral buffer, assuring each that attack would not occur. In keeping with their neutral role, the forces would be armed only for self-defence. A multilateral peacekeeping contingent containing Canadian units was placed along the cease-fire line. Lightly armed and dependent on both sides' respecting the cease-fire and honouring their neutrality, the forces would become exposed and vulnerable if either side changed its intentions.

Intentions came into question in the spring of 1967 when Egyptian president Nasser, in a climate of sharpening tension with Israel, demanded that UN Secretary General U Thant withdraw the peacekeeping forces. Fearing for their safety, U Thant reluctantly withdrew them whereupon Israel, fearing imminent attack from Egypt, launched a strike that began the six-day war between Israel and its three neighbours, Egypt, Jordan and Syria. That result was by no means the end of peacekeeping, but it did underscore the fact that peacekeeping requires a cease-fire, the consent of both sides to have neutral forces placed between them and, above all, the respect of both sides for the peacekeepers' impartial and non-combatant status.

The end of the cold war saw a rapid increase of UN peacekeeping operations, but even with the largest deployments, stable cease-fires were not obtained. Fighting would continue or resume, peacekeepers were placed at risk and people depending on them were not always protected. We saw in Chapter 7 the difficulties peacekeepers faced in Somalia. Peacekeeping in Bosnia began with safeguarding humanitarian relief and monitoring the safety of ethnic enclaves. The difficulties started almost immediately because each side, instead of ceasing hostilities, continued to seek territorial gains and stronger positions.

That placed lightly armed international forces, including Canadians, into zones of active fighting. Even if peacekeepers were not targets themselves, simply being in the midst of a civil war put them in danger. What was worse was that their mission of assisting civilians made them adversaries of the combatants whose objective was to displace and kill civilians. Any efforts to protect civilians were treated as acts of direct involvement and exposed the peacekeepers to attack and retaliation.[41] That left UN forces dispersed in a dangerous war zone without a dependably respected neutral status, subject to attack and being taken hostage and lacking proper means of defence. As a result, civilians were not adequately protected, UN forces suffered casualties and the war continued.

An international conference assessing the UN's experience in Bosnia was held at the University of Toronto in 1997. It reached several conclusions. First, the wrong instrument was applied to the problem: peacekeepers were introduced into a situation in which no peace had been achieved. The situation required some other kind of intervention. Second, the UN's mandate was so indefinite that General Lewis MacKenzie, commanding the Canadian contingent in Sarajevo, "had to invent a role for his troops." That role was providing security at the Sarajevo airport to keep humanitarian relief arriving and to aid workers to keep distribution running.[42] The peacekeepers' mandate was vague because the Security Council lacked a clear purpose.

Third, the resources were inadequate for the mission. The peacekeepers were too lightly armed for their tasks. Protecting civilians as well as themselves required more ability to use force. Because the conflict was a civil war, there were no continuous front lines where cease-fires could be properly observed. Instead, there were multiple areas of combat where fighting could continue with varying intensity. Even where lines of demarcation were present as in Sarajevo, mortars and artillery could continue to kill and injure civilians. Addressing those threats directly—attacking artillery sites, for example—would involve much higher levels of force and go well beyond the definition of peacekeeping.

Finally, the presence of peacekeepers did not induce the sides to stop fighting. It was only when NATO aircraft, authorized by the UN, threatened to strike Bosnian Serb positions that the Dayton Peace Accord was negotiated. "With hindsight," concluded the University of Toronto conference, "most analysts are sure it would have been better to 'go bigger and go earlier.'"[43]

These difficulties point to a need to rethink interventions. Peacekeeping's original formula of interposing a neutral force along a cease-fire line was addressed to conventional battlefields such as the Sinai Desert where regular military units face each other and not to civil wars where irregular forces circulate through villages and countrysides. The occasions for peacekeeping since the cold war have been civil wars, and the motives have been the humanitarian ones of protecting civilians and relief supplies.

FIGURE 11.6   Canada as Perennial Peacekeeper: Explanations from Neorealist, Liberal and Institutional IR Theory

Canada has been peacekeeping's most regular participant. Peacekeeping costs military resources, produces casualties and is performed in distant places of no direct security significance to Canada. What does IR theory make of such continuous support?

Neorealism has difficulty explaining Canada's involvement for two reasons. First, peacekeeping contributes only indirectly to Canada's security; the conflicts have been far removed and low-level. The Sinai missions had a closer connection to Canada's security because any war between Israel and its neighbours during the cold war could draw in the superpowers. Those stakes generalized the threat. Otherwise, the states gaining the largest security benefits from peacekeeping are those closest to the conflict.

Second, peacekeeping's rationale is that the security of all states benefits from containing and resolving local conflicts. This may be a one-sided endeavour. General security is a public good, something that a few suppliers can provide but everyone can enjoy. Because public goods are equally available to those who provide them and those who do not, rational self-interest expects someone else to do the job. Since states hesitate to pay for something they can enjoy for free, "getting work done for the common good is difficult."[44] There are many potential peacekeepers. Wherever conflicts arise, there are at least a few states confronted with self-protective needs to intervene. Canada, safe where it is, could leave the effort to them and still enjoy general security.

Liberal IR theory, as we saw in Chapter 3, focuses on preferences. Governments seek to reconcile preferences that emerge in their societies and in their own official ranks. Preferences can be both self-interested and altruistic. They can originate from both material considerations and ideas. And because interdependence transmits the effects of policies and actions from one state to another, preferences can be affected by external as well as domestic influences. Like domestic influences, external ones can be material as well as ideal.

Canada's consistent support for peacekeeping is a blend of influences—material and ideal, domestic and external. The clearest influence is ideal/domestic. The Canadian public has shown a consistent preference for international engagement and humanitarian purposes and likes foreign policy activism. A public opinion poll in spring 1998 found a "powerful streak of democratic moralism" in Canadians' international attitudes.[45] Peacekeeping satisfies that preference because it is direct and active, it is used in places where people's safety is most immediately in danger and it is aimed to ending armed conflict. This preference is not material because no practical gain is involved but is rather ideal: peacekeeping represents the Canadian public's values. Vivid media coverage of humanitarian crises abroad provides the external stimulus and reinforces a sense of responsibility.

Support for the idea of peacekeeping is also external. Because peacekeeping is a valued international contribution, Canada receives recognition of its efforts.

That recognition reinforces the Canadian public's view that Canada exercises positive international influence. Canadian governments have also found these ideas congenial, and both Conservative and Liberal governments have supported international operations.

Are there material factors in these preferences? Externally, putting actual forces in the field earns more international credit than merely supporting resolutions. A long track record of burden-sharing in one institution, the UN, provides reputation and credibility in other institutions. That is not material capital, but it can be useful in issue areas where material preferences such as air quality are under discussion. That view, as we saw earlier, underpins the notion of soft power. Domestically, acting consistently in accord with the public's preference for international involvement earns the government credit to offset acting against the public's preferences in areas such as taxes and social programs.

How would an institutionalist explain peacekeeping? As we saw in Chapter 2, Institutionalism is based on the premise that states prefer to cooperate but fear cheating. To enable cooperation states construct common institutions to pool contributions, facilitate common action and monitor compliance.

Promoting common security presents institutionalists with the most challenging case, and the issue is cheating. In institutions that enforce trade agreements, a state that cheats gains relative to the others, but the others are left no worse off. Military gains are different. One state's violating a security agreement by improving its military capabilities can leave the others much worse off.[46]

For that reason, states have been cautious about entrusting their security to international agreements and about depending on mechanisms such as collective security. A transparent institution can offset fears of cheating by enabling members to verify one another's compliance with the rules and obligations. NATO's open structure has been credited with supplying that confidence among states that had only recently been mortal enemies. Even so, security institutions work best when security is plentiful. That condition exists when states' military postures are all defensive and when all are committed to the status quo. That level of safety reduces the need for a security institution.

Peacekeeping is not subject to the same problem of cheating and relative gains. Cheating is not taking part in joint operations, and relative gains are the costs and casualties spared by staying out. Although peacekeeping operations cannot succeed without adequate material support, the participating members do not suffer losses to their security if other states do not take part. The multilateral composition of peacekeeping forces spreads out the costs, reducing an abstainer's margin of gain over any individual participant.

Institutionalists look at gains more broadly. The gains are both individual and collective. Individually, Canada's participation in peacekeeping underwrites Canadian membership in other international institutions. These serve Canadian interests when Canada can work with other members to pursue common interests. Credit earned in one endeavour may be spent in pursuit of other endeavours. This emphasis is quite consistent with Institutionalism. One advantage of international institutions is reducing transaction costs between states. Instead of negotiating with each one individually, states can concentrate their efforts in a common arena where all states are brought together over particular issues. International institutions also pool information, reducing the costs of each state gathering its own. The advantages multiply with additional institutions and additional policy areas. Emphasizing effective and widespread membership particularly for states with modest resources such as Canada is an efficient foreign policy.

> At the collective level, institutionalists, true to their liberal heritage, believe that institutions foster international cooperation and produce order. That order, as we saw earlier, can be seen as a public good from which all may benefit. Neorealists emphasize the incentive not to pay for public goods. Institutionalists take a positive view by emphasizing the ability of effective institutions to set rules and discourage cheating. Members abide by rules because doing so makes them all better off. By pooling resources toward common gains, international institutions are a bargain compared to the unilateral alternatives. Canada, along with other states, shares in the benefits. With peacekeeping, pooled military resources produce gains in general security and make all states safer.

The UN's activities blur the distinction between two traditional kinds of humanitarian intervention. The first involves active coercion. States, alone and in concert, intervene prepared to use force. France, for example, intervened in Rwanda in 1994, Canada led a refugee relief effort in Zaire in 1996 and Nigeria intervened in the civil war in Sierra Leone in 1997. In a collective act of coercion, the UN declared no-fly zones over northern and southern Iraq after the Gulf War to protect the Kurdish and Shiite minorities living there from attack by the government in Baghdad. Iraqi aircraft entering those zones are fired upon. The second kind of involvement is not coercive. Peacekeeping is such an intervention but so too are relief operations protected by outside forces. Another form of non-coercive intervention is providing the relief supplies and workers themselves.[47]

UN interventions in the 1990s have had elements of both. Part of the reason is that civil wars create humanitarian emergencies for which the obvious international response is non-coercive intervention. Civil wars also involve armed populations as well as regular armed forces, complicating the problems of enforcing cease-fires and of protecting civilians and relief workers. Providing that protection requires more robust forces and rules of engagement and crosses over into coercive intervention. The UN has been very reluctant to authorize such levels of commitment. The result is involvement that begins non-coercively but edges toward coercion as the need for armed protection becomes apparent. Reluctance to supply that level of force produces the kind of half-measure seen in Bosnia: more active than peacekeeping but not forceful enough to stop the fighting. One scholar refers to such operations as falling within a "gray area" between peacekeeping and fully armed intervention with no clear or stable political objectives, no "doctrinal understanding" of the military operations involved and no adequate UN command structure.[48]

What is clear from the UN's experience in the 1990s is that the situations most likely to require humanitarian intervention are not part of its previous repertoire. The remedies are both political and institutional. Politically, members of the UN Security Council must be clear about the objectives they seek from intervention and the force levels and rules of engagement that will be required. Institutionally, the UN must develop more senior staff capability so that the Secretary General who is responsible for implementing Security Council directives has a realistic understanding of the military factors involved and is supported by competent professional advice. Also required is a larger base of major force-contributing states.[49]

Economic Sanctions

The founders of the League of Nations, with World War I's devastation in mind, regarded economic sanctions as a civilized alternative to military coercion. **Economic sanctions** involve cutting off trade with the target state. Sanctions can be embargoes, in which states refuse to sell, and boycotts, in which they refuse to buy. Sanctions can be limited, covering only specified commodities, or general, covering all commodities. They can be partial with only some states involved or universal with all states taking part.

Sanctions work by raising the cost of aggression. Instead of imposing the cost directly through military force, as seen with individual self-defence, alliances and collective security, economic sanctions impose the cost indirectly through material deprivation. The prospect of these material costs can have the same deterrent effect as the prospect of military ones. With both, the purpose is altering the cost/benefit calculations of potential attackers. As we saw earlier with deterrence, a sufficiently strong defensive force raises the direct cost of attack. With economic sanctions, a sufficient level of trade deprivation raises the indirect cost of attack.

Applied after aggression has occurred, economic sanctions impose the actual cost of attack by cutting off trade. Like collective security, the purpose is to reverse the aggression. Sanctions do this by visiting general hardship on the population, confronting the government with domestic pressure to get them lifted. At acute levels of deprivation, sanctions are expected to lead to an overthrow of the government. Overthrows are particularly likely in authoritarian states where powerful elites, contemplating the growing effects of deprivation, may decide that the government has pursued a disastrous policy. The appeal of economic sanctions is that they work without military force providing material coercion in a peaceful form.

Do economic sanctions actually work? There is much scholarly debate. A study that surveyed 78 cases of economic sanctions between 1914 and 1983 concluded that they were effective 40 percent of the time—a rather impressive record.[50] Effectiveness depends both on the purposes being sought, the number of sanctioning states involved, the target state's level of trade exposure to them and the availability of substitute supplies. By purpose, sanctions were found to be most effective when they sought only modest policy changes, when they sought to destabilize the target state's economy and when they sought to undermine the target state's military activities.

At the same time, sanctions were not found to be particularly effective in impelling states to make major policy changes either in their foreign or domestic policy. That is true with sanctions imposed collectively as with ending apartheid in South Africa and with sanctions imposed individually as with American sanctions against Cuba. Sanctions are most likely to be successful when the target state's economy is much smaller and is dependent on trade. The same is true of states with weak economies; they are the most sensitive to pressure. Finally, the prospects for success rise with comprehensive participation. The fewer alternate suppliers there are, the more quickly sanctions exercise their effects.[51]

Economic globalization may have a mixed impact on success. On the one hand, globalization dilutes the effects of sanctions because target states are tied into networks of supply and production making them interdependent with potential sanctioners. Other members of the network may be reluctant to disrupt their production by taking up sanctions. For the target state, networks may provide alternative connections. If one source of supply becomes unavailable, adroit networking may generate others. On the other hand, international production networks have multiple connections *within* a state. When the network stops transmitting supplies, the effects follow the network connections throughout the target state's economy. And when systems of production are highly integrated, target states may find it difficult to find new suppliers and customers outside the network of sanctioning states.

There is also the temptation on both sides to violate the sanctions. Target states seek alternate suppliers and buyers, presenting potential sanctioners with attractive additional business. Prisoner's Dilemma, as we saw in Chapter 2, illustrates the incentives to defect from common ventures. For the sanctioners, cooperate/cooperate would provide the collective benefit of a strong campaign. If they all cooperate, the mutual gain will be forceful sanctions and an isolated target state. If they all defect, no sanctions will be applied. The best individual gain goes to the member who defects while the others cooperate. Why would a state do so? If all of the target state's other trading partners are applying sanctions, deprivation is indeed likely, and motivation to buy from anyone increases. The non-joining state becomes the remaining source of supply. The non-joiner's unilateral gain is uninterrupted trade and windfall sales. The more effective the sanctions are, the more willing the target state will be to pay top dollar. The same is true of sales from the target state. States joining the sanctions sacrifice their supply while states that do not join enjoy exclusive access. With both purchases and sales, the target state gains ability to resist coercion.

In the view of one critic, the pro-sanctions literature underemphasizes the target states' nationalistic determination to resist and their governments' ability to stay in power. Re-examining the 1983 study's data set just seen, Robert Pape found a much lower rate of actual success. How are the modest results explained? Authoritarian governments, Pape argues, can cushion the effects' popular deprivation and discontent by ensuring that their supporting elites receive adequate supplies. In more democratic states, resistance to sanctions may be more genuinely popular, inducing "citizens to rally around the government against the coercive foreigners."[52]

States also have unappreciated capacities to substitute and improvise in the face of shortages. A case in point is Iraq. As we saw in Chapter 9, Iraq has withstood seven years of UN sanctions that were drastic enough to eliminate almost half of its GDP. Iraq's government, as we also saw, has been determined to retain its capacity for weapons of mass destruction. How could the government resist such pressure? A ruthless disregard for the suffering of its own citizens is one reason. Another reason is that "modern states are not fragile."[53]

Why then are sanctions attractive? In the case of Iraq, they provided a way of coercing a determined state without a large and continuing military confrontation allowing the Gulf War coalition forces to disband. They are also a substitute for armed force when collective will to use force is not present. When the Security Council imposed economic sanctions on Serbia, there was strong support for sanctions but deep division over military force. The human impact of sanctions is also less visible than the human impact of war. There are no military casualties, no civilian victims of bombing and shelling and no camps of refugees. According to a feminist analysis, that is so because the effects of economic sanctions fall especially upon women who cope individually with food and medicine shortages in their homes and out of public view. For them the effects are providing care for weakened children and "being fed last and least."[54]

If the critics are correct, economic sanctions cause suffering but do not change state behaviour. That leaves problematic prospects in situations requiring coercion. Common security emphasizes settlement and low levels of force but may be prone to buck-passing. Peacekeeping is compromised by inadequate resources, but states have been reluctant to make more active commitments. Collective security, epitomized by the Gulf War coalition, provides a powerful response to aggression but may depend too much on special circumstances to be a reliable protection. To the extent that collective measures' prospects are chequered, armed force—deterrent and active—remains the final resort.

Summary

What makes states safe? Location is the immediate condition. States without dangerous neighbours and located in orderly regions have much more secure circumstances than states located next to enemies and in unstable regions. How much states must be concerned with safety depends greatly on where they happen to be.

States can pursue their safety, along with other interests, by finding ways of altering other states' preferences. Power is the general name given to that capacity, but seeing it as advantages provides a more accurately flexible appreciation. The effort to alter preferences can be seen as a common denominator of protecting safety.

In the presence of threats, states can seek individual or collective deterrence. Individual deterrence leads quickly to thoughts of nuclear weapons because of the devastating advantage they confer. Nuclear deterrence is simple in principle but complex and uncertain in practice. The superpowers survived their decades of nuclear deterrence by acting as though their mutual interest was avoiding nuclear crises. Whether such stability will be available to new nuclear states is a troubling question.

Conjoint efforts involve the active coercion of collective security and the indirect and non-combatant presence of peacekeeping. Both have been problematic in the 1990s. Collective security in its most forceful expression depends on a consensus in the Security Council where disparate global interests among the five permanent members holding vetoes may limit the number of strong responses to aggression. At the same time, the more common problem of the 1990s has been civil wars. Peacekeeping is not fitted to these conflicts because cease-fires are fragile and because sides frequently have incentive to keep fighting. The internecine nature of civil wars makes them dangerous and unpromising sites of intervention particularly for small and lightly armed international forces.

Economic sanctions are an ostensibly attractive alternative because they spare using military resources. Although governments use them—both India and Pakistan incurred various economic sanctions to punish their nuclear tests—their effectiveness is a matter of debate.

For all these reasons, it is probably best to regard safety as a mixture of the universal and the local. A peaceful international system can still be dangerous for states facing a hostile neighbour. In the same way, states divide their efforts between common international efforts and self-protective individual ones. How much the latter efforts are needed depends on the state's location. Canada, among other secure states, faces the decision of how much to scale back its military forces. Hopeful trends are suggested by the democratic peace. If democracies really do not fight one another and if they are the prime candidates for membership in security communities, expanding democracy will expand safety. That suggests two questions for the future: Will democratization continue? Will the security community expand?

ENDNOTES

1   Jean Bethke Elshtain, "Feminist Inquiry and International Relations," in Michael W. Doyle and G. John Ikenberry, eds., *New Thinking in International Relations Theory,* Boulder, CO: Westview, 1997, p. 88.

2   Glenn Bailey, "Canadian Diplomacy as Advocacy: The Case of Chile and the NAFTA," *Canadian Foreign Policy* 3 (Winter 1995) 99.

3   Alan Lamborn, "Theory and the Politics in World Politics," *International Studies Quarterly* 41 (June 1997) 192.

4   Andrew Moravcsik, "Taking Preferences Seriously: A Liberal Theory of International Politics," *International Organization* 51 (Autumn 1997) 524.

5   Lloyd Axworthy and Sarah Taylor, "A Ban for All Seasons: The Landmines Convention and Its Implications for Canadian Diplomacy," *International Journal* 53 (Spring 1998) 192, 193.

6   *ibid.,* p. 191.

7   Fen Osler Hampson and Dean F. Oliver, "Pulpit Diplomacy: A Critical Assessment of the Axworthy Doctrine," *International Journal* 53 (Summer 1998) 396.

8   Kim Richard Nossal, "Foreign Policy for Wimps," *Ottawa Citizen* April 23, 1998, A19.

9   Douglas Alan Ross, "Canada and the World at Risk: Depression, War, and Isolationism for the 21st Century?" *International Journal* 52 (Winter 1996-1997) 18–19.

10 Jeffrey Herbst, "War and the State in Africa," *International Security* 14 (Spring 1990) 123–24.

11 Steve Fetter, "Ballistic Missiles and Weapons of Mass Destruction: What Is the Threat? What Should Be Done?" *International Security* 16 (Summer 1991) 28.

12 Richard Ned Lebow and Janice Gross Stein, "Rational Deterrence Theory: I Think, Therefore I Deter," *World Politics* 41 (January 1989) 209.

13 Robert Jervis, "Security Regimes," in Stephen D. Krasner, ed., *International Regimes*, Ithaca: Cornell University Press, 1983, p. 191.

14 Robert C. Johansen, "Swords into Plowshares? Can Fewer Arms Yield More Security?" in Charles W. Kegley, Jr., *Controversies in International Relations Theory: Realism and the Neoliberal Challenge,* New York: St. Martin's, 1995, p. 659.

15 George Perkovich, "Nuclear Proliferation," *Foreign Policy* 112 (Fall 1998) 15.

16 Karl Kaysen, 'Is War Obsolete?" *International Security* 14 (Spring 1990) 61.

17 Robert Jervis, "The Political Effects of Nuclear Weapons," *International Security* 13 (Fall 1988) 89.

18 John Orme, "The Utility of Force in a World of Scarcity," *International Security* 22 (Winter 1997–1998) 139.

19 Perkovich, "Nuclear Proliferation," 15.

20 David J. Karl, "Proliferation Pessimism and Emerging Nuclear Powers," *International Security* 21 (Winter 1996-1997) 98–100.

21 Thomas G. Weiss and Laura S. Hayes Holgate, "Opportunities and Obstacles for Collective Security after the Cold War," in David Dewitt, David Haglund and John Kirton, eds., *Building a New Global Order: Emerging Trends in International Security*, Toronto: Oxford University Press, 1993, p. 262.

22 Jervis, "Security Regimes," p. 175.

23 Michael W. Doyle, "Strategies of Enhanced Consent," in Abram Chayes and Antonia Handler Chayes, eds., *Preventing Conflict in the Post-Communist World*, Washington, D.C.: Brookings Institution, 1996, p. 486.

24 Meryl A. Kessler and Thomas G. Weiss, "The United Nations and Third World Security in the 1990s," in Thomas G. Weiss and Meryl A. Kessler, eds., *Third World Security in the Post- Cold War Era,* Boulder, CO: Rienner, 1991, p. 110.

25 Robert Jervis, "The Future of World Politics," *International Security* 15 (Winter 1991-1992) 70–73.

26 Steven Weber, "Institutions and Change," in Michael W. Doyle and G. John Ikenberry, eds., *New Thinking in International Relations,* Boulder, CO: Westview, 1997, p. 250.

27 *ibid.*, p. 251.

28 Joseph Lepgold, "NATO's Post-Cold War Collective Action Problem," *International Security* 23 (Summer 1998) 81

29 *ibid.,* p. 82.

30 Hans-Georg Ehrhart, "The Contact Group, NATO and Peacekeeping in the Former Yugoslavia: European Security at the Crossroads," in S. Neil MacFarlane and Hans-Georg Ehrhart, eds., *Peacekeeping at a Crossroads,* Clementsport, NS: Canadian Peacekeeping Press, 1997, p. 49.

31 John G.H. Halstead, *European Security: What's in It for Canada?* Kingston: Queen's University Centre for International Relations, 1996, pp. 4–6.

32 Lepgold, "NATO's Post-Cold War Collective Action Problem" 85.

33 Eric Bergbusch, "NATO Enlargement: Should Canada Leave NATO?" *International Journal* 53 (Winter 1997-1998), 160

34 Michael N. Barnett, "Bringing in the New World Order: Liberalism, Legitimacy, and the United Nations," *World Politics* 49 (July 1997) 531.

35 *Canada 21: Canada and Common Security in the Twenty First Century*, Toronto: Centre for International Studies, University of Toronto, 1994.

36 Bergbusch, NATO Enlargement," 158–159.

37 *ibid.* p. 160.

38 Ross, "Canada and the World at Risk" p. 2.

39 James Sperling and Emil Kirchner, "Economic Security and the Problem of Cooperation in Post-Cold War Europe," *Review of International Studies* 24 (April 1998) 230.

40 *ibid.*

41 John G.H. Halstead, "UN Peacekeeping: The Lessons of Yugoslavia," in MacFarlane and Ehrhart, eds., *Peacekeeping at a Crossroads,* p. 67.

42 Metta Spencer, "Science for Peace Roundtable on the Lessons of Yugoslavia," *Canadian Foreign Policy* 5 (Fall 1997) 89.

43 *ibid.* p. 90.

44 Kenneth Waltz, *Theory of International Politics* New York: McGraw Hill, 1979, p. 196.

45 Quoted in Hampson and Oliver, "Pulpit Diplomacy," 379.

46 Jervis, "Security Regimes," p. 175.

47   Oliver Ramsbotham, "Humanitarian Intervention 1990–1995: A Need to Reconceptualize?" *Review of International Studies,* 23 (October 1997) 458.

48   John Gerard Ruggie, *Constructing the World Polity: Essays on International Institutionalization*, London: Routledge, 1998, p. 241.

49   Kessler and Weiss, "The United Nations and Third World Security," pp. 116–17.

50   Gary Clyde Hufbauer, Jeffrey J. Schott and Kimberley Ann Elliot, *Economic Sanctions in Support of Foreign Policy Goals*, Washington, D.C.: Institute for International Economics, 1983, p. 75.

51   *ibid.*, pp. 76–81.

52   Robert A. Pape, "Why Economic Sanctions Do Not Work" *International Security* 22 (Fall 1997) 93, 107.

53   *ibid.*, p. 107.

54   Lori Buck, Nichole Gallant and Kim Richard Nossal, "Sanctions as a Gendered Instrument of Statecraft: The Case of Iraq," *Review of International Studies* 24 (January 1998) 81.

WEBLINKS

A Canadian peacekeeping site can be found at:
www.pk.kos.netpk1a

The site of Project Ploughshares is:
www.watserv1.uwaterloo.ca/~plough/

The Organization of Security and Cooperation in Europe operates a site at:
www.osceprag.cz

NATO's site is:
www.nato.int/

NORAD's site includes an air defence map from the height of the cold war:
www.spacecom.af.mil/norad/

The European Platform for Conflict Prevention and Transformation has links to related NGOs and institutes:
www.oneworld.org/euconflict/guides/organisa1.htm

The Stockholm International Peace Research Institute is a major source of peace and disarmament studies and contains related links:
www.sipri.se

The site of the United States Arms Control and Disarmament Agency has information on treaties and agreements:
www.acda.gov

Chapter 12

Wealth

Wealth, the State and Economic Doctrine

Wealth is the most basic measure of material welfare. In absolute terms, sufficiency is the issue: Is there enough for food, shelter and daily requisites? In relative terms, comparison is the issue: What is one's condition respective to others? As absolute and relative measures, averages matter. Measured by average life expectancy, absolute welfare varies from 41.3 years for men and 44.4 years for women in Guinea Bissau to 76.4 years for men and 82.4 years for women in Japan.[1] The Human Poverty Index classifies serious deprivation according to longevity, knowledge and living standards. States with large portions of their population that are seriously deprived are classified as poor. At 62 percent, the poorest state is Niger.[2]

Averages measure relative levels as well. Gross Domestic Product (GDP) per capita indicates average individual contribution to the total value of goods and services produced in a state's economy. Switzerland's per capita figure of $42,416, the world's highest, indicates not only affluence (each individual's average share of the total product) but also an efficient and productive economy (a large average contribution). Averages invite comparison. Canada's GDP per capita is 67 times that of Bangladesh.

In both absolute and relative terms, wealth is important in IR. Low absolute levels reflect poverty, and low relative levels reflect subordinate status. The point of reference is wealthy states. In absolute terms they are materially better off, and in relative terms they enjoy a more desirable position in the international system.[3] The difference is not accepted as inevitable: "Since some countries are already developed, it is usually assumed that all countries at least in principle can reasonably hope to achieve this goal. It is also commonly posited that the knowledge required to bring this about either exists or can be acquired."[4] That belief makes the state a key agent. How to use its sovereign authority is a central issue.

A key structure is the international system. States exchange goods and services, and what is exchanged is directly related to economic development. That in turn is related to relative poverty and wealth. States with highly developed economies, as measured by GDP per capita, can produce goods with high unit value—computers, for example. States with less developed economies supply components and raw materials, which have lower unit value. The difference represents value added by manufacturing. Economic and industrial development expands the ability to transform materials and add value. That ability is created by investment—in human skills, technology, production facilities and infrastructure. Investment expands the complexity of goods that can be produced, multiplies their variety and raises the efficiency of production. The added value is reflected in the final price. A unit of computer, which represents high investment, fetches more than a unit of raw metal, which represents lower investment. The raw metal, in turn, fetches more than an equal unit of unprocessed ore. The difference shows when goods are traded. Goods with higher unit value earn more export income for their states than do goods with lower unit value. The results appear in the states' trade accounts.

Although there is a direct relationship between economic development and the ability to export valuable commodities, differences among states are not uniform and categorical. Export mixtures can contain both manufactures and raw or semi-processed commodities. Canada and the United States, which have well-developed manufacturing sectors, are both major exporters of coal and food grains. Mexico and Brazil, whose manufacturing sectors are not as developed, are both important exporters of automobiles (Mexico produces the world's supply of the new Volkswagen Beetle). Brazil's commuter aircraft competes on the world market with Canada's. Altogether, a state's relative position in the world's trading system is affected by what goods it produces at what prices. That makes managing the economy—for both the welfare of individuals and the relative position of states—a fundamental question. Domestically, it addresses the role and purpose of the state. Internationally, it addresses the structure of investment and trade. In both, absolute and relative levels of wealth is the point at issue. The state has sovereign power to affect them.

Since economic activity without involvement of the state takes place as private transactions, it is useful to see the state as a third party. The intervention of the state accompanied the development of sovereignty. As we saw in Chapter 6, the states that had secured the basis of private transactions emerged successfully from feudalism and became strong. The forms of intervention have expanded since then, and sovereignty provides potentially wide authority over economic transactions. Whether and how to exercise that authority is a political choice.[5] Fundamentally, we can see that choice as between state and market. Giving free play to the market allows economic transactions to be governed by private decisions. Introducing the state's authority into the market ranges from indirectly influencing private decisions to appropriating them altogether.

In practice, the choice of intervention is not an absolute one. The question is not *whether* states should intervene in their economies but to what *degree* they should intervene. Markets require some state involvement. Markets that are left entirely to individual private actors produce market failures—an economist's term for inefficient or distorted distributions of resources and benefits. To prevent those outcomes, a state role in the economy is needed. The most nominal role is a legal system to enforce property rights and commercial contracts and a monetary system to support transactions. The state's role extends from that base through increasing degrees of intervention to the ultimate stage of replacing the market completely. That is achieved when the state owns the means of production and designates prices and supplies through central economic planning.

The role of the state can reflect differences not only between political systems but also between societies. One scholar distinguishes between liberal and non-liberal societies. The state in a liberal society limits its role in the economy to regulation and providing public goods. Regulation is intended to ensure the fair and effective operation of markets and to control the by-products of economic activity such as pollution. The state does so by enforcing standards in particular industries such as banking and by maintaining required practices such as competition. Standards and required practices also control by-products—toxic substances, for example. Public goods, such as a currency system and a highway network, support economic activity more generally.

In non-liberal societies, the state is more autonomous, allowing it to take a more "intrusive and interventionist" role in the economy and to follow an overriding rationale. Intervention may range from helping to guide finance and export development in key industries, as Japan does, to owning and managing the means of production, as the Soviet Union did.[6] The rationale for Japan is to advance the country's international economic position. The rationale for the Soviet Union was to transcend capitalism. Since the collapse of communist systems, markets have come to be regarded as the "most efficient system available" for generating wealth, but the state's role has not disappeared.[7] The Soviet system represented an ultimate degree of economic involvement, but others are possible.

Three doctrines of political economy—mercantilism, dependency and liberalism—envisage very different roles for the state. Their views of the international economic system give them points of connection with theories of IR. Mercantilism and Neorealism both envisage win/lose competition among states. Dependency centres on an international hierarchy and a powerful centre—a structural view shared by Critical Theory. Economic Liberalism, like political Liberalism, is predicated on cooperation and mutual benefit. The three economic doctrines support very different state policies, and as approaches to IR they contribute very different perspectives.

The state's ability to affect material welfare makes it central to all three doctrines. The point of difference is the state's proper role. Because material welfare is such a fundamental human concern, because sovereignty endows the state with so much authority to act economically and because relative differences make such powerful comparisons, the role of the state has figured in this century's most fundamental ideological debates and continues as an issue in both domestic and international politics. We begin with Mercantilism.

Mercantilism

As we saw in Chapter 6, the modern state developed as rulers sought to harness the capacities of their societies and economies. The two initial instruments were conscription and taxation, which provided two potent resources—armed forces and money. The accompanying economic doctrine was **mercantilism**, which held that "economic activities are and should be subordinate to the goal of state building and the interests of the state."[8] Mercantilists in early modern Europe equated national power with economic wealth and calculated it literally in gold. States with the greatest stores of precious metals were held to be the wealthiest, and amassing those metals was a major national objective. With mercenaries widely used to augment national military forces, reckoning power as liquid wealth made some practical sense since mercenaries would fight only if paid.

Mercantilists also calculated national power as a balance of payments surplus. The balance of payments is the difference between the money earned in selling goods to other states and the money spent in buying goods from them. A personal chequing account makes a handy comparison. Deposits to the account are like a state's export earnings, and cheques on the account are like a state's import purchases. A chequing account has a positive balance when deposits exceed debits. In the same way, a state's account has a balance of payments surplus when income earned from exports and other activities abroad exceeds expenditures on imports and other payments that leave the country. Accumulating a balance of payments surplus, in the mercantilists' view, adds to the state's store of wealth.[9]

A personal chequing account shows the intuitive appeal of mercantilist thinking. A healthy chequebook balance supports a greater sense of welfare than a weak balance (or an overdraft). Mercantilists gauged state welfare the same way. To achieve the necessary balance of payments surpluses, states must use their authority to promote exports and restrict imports. Sovereignty provides the control over what enters and leaves the state. Sovereignty also provides the authority to finance or subsidize the production of goods domestically to avoid having to buy them abroad.

For states without supplies of precious metals, trade surpluses were held to be the sole source of wealth. To accumulate more, states would have to exploit trade relations to transfer other states' wealth to themselves. Promoting the state's advantage and defending its position guided economic decisions, introducing the expectation of rivalry. If successful states were seen as enjoying their position at others' expense and if wealth were a measure of state power, envy and fear would drive their relationships. With a limited supply of wealth, one state's advance would be another's decline. Win/lose was the chief principle.

These assumptions resonate with Neorealism. For both mercantilists and neorealists, sovereign states act competitively in an international anarchy and rely on their own resources. Relative position is their prime concern. International anarchy gives play to purposes and resources, infusing relationships with gain-seeking behaviour and conflict. The distribution of scarce goods is the central problem with each state regarding gains by others as losses to itself. Alien is the idea that states can expand the goods available through cooperation, generate absolute gains and improve their situation collectively. The supply of benefits is finite, and preventing others from getting them at one's expense is the task. Gains are relative; states end up better or worse off than others. The distribution of power in the system affects which states get what.[10]

Material resources figure centrally. Mercantilists assumed rivalry and conflict to be a basic condition of international relations and wealth to be the requisite for military power.[11] A wealthy state could "equip armies and navies, hire foreign mercenaries, bribe potential enemies and subsidize allies."[12] Neorealists also pay attention to military force and worry about relative gains in capability. They do not share the mercantilist view of a strictly finite supply of material goods, but they do doubt that self-interested states can cooperate for absolute gains. Each state's incentive to exploit marginal advantages undermines common efforts even when all stand to benefit. Exploiting trade advantages for selfish gains underpins modern mercantilism, as we will see later.

As states began to develop manufacturing sectors, the link between national security and the economy shifted from amassing gold to promoting industrial self-sufficiency. Alexander Hamilton, the American Secretary of the Treasury in the administration of George Washington, concisely linked security to industry in his Report [to Congress] on the Subject of Manufactures in 1791. In Hamilton's words,

"Not only the wealth, but the independence and security of a country, appear to be materially connected with the prosperity of manufactures. Every nation, with a view to these great objects, ought to endeavour to possess within itself all the essentials of national supply. These comprise the means of subsistence, habitation, clothing and defence."[13]

Such views brought mercantilism into the industrial age. States, instead of hoarding precious metal, would develop industry, but the purpose remained the same: promoting "economic self-sufficiency and political autonomy."[14] Internationally, industrial mercantilism could be either assertive or defensive. Acting assertively, the German government, influenced by the economic doctrines of Friedrich List, promoted industrialization in the 19th century to become a great power and the military equal of Britain. Acting defensively, the Canadian government, under John A. Macdonald's National Policy of 1879, promoted industrialization to stay free of the economic attraction of the United States.

In its assertive orientation, industrial development was the means of ascending the international order. In its defensive orientation, industrial development was the means of escaping domination. Mercantilist win/lose assumptions underpinned both purposes. For assertive states, industrial might provided the national power to compete for position and scarce resources. For defensive states, home ownership of industry kept control from the hands of foreigners. In either orientation, independence in a competitive international system required a national industrial base.

Economic Nationalism

Mercantilist assumptions are quite compatible with nationalism. As we saw in Chapter 7, nationalism is a popular doctrine that emphasizes one's own distinctiveness and virtue. As we also saw, nationalism developed with mass political participation and the growth of the modern state. Nationalism supports defending or advancing the nation and its interests and identifies the welfare of individual citizens with that of the nation. The means of action is the state.

By the late 19th century, states in Western Europe and North America were well along the way to democracy, and their industries were growing rapidly. The convergence of democracy and development brought economic policy into the political arena. The government leaders who set policy did so on the basis of three considerations: their own understanding of national economic welfare, the preferences of particular domestic economic interests and, increasingly, the views of the general public. Questions about the state's ability to remain separate and distinct and to act according to its own interests address nationalist concerns and make economic relations public issues.

In an expansive mode, a strong industry represents national power and achievement: wealth from foreign sales and prestige from respected products and world market position. The state's role is to promote its industries worldwide by penetrating overseas markets and by establishing its technologies and goods as world products. In a defensive mode, a protected industry represents national separateness and distinctiveness: markets reserved for home producers and an industry free from foreign control. The state's role is to support domestic industry and limit foreign penetration.

FIGURE 12.1 The National Policy

In 1879, the government of John A. Macdonald adopted the National Policy. Its main provision was to increase tariffs on imported manufactured goods, and its main purpose was to encourage the development of Canadian industry by giving it highly protected access to the Canadian market. Under the National Policy, Canadian industries "could get virtually the degree of protection they desired."[15] The tariff on agricultural equipment was 25 percent; on railway equipment the tariff was 30 percent.[16] Under the same rationale, the Macdonald government sponsored construction of the Canadian Pacific Railway to provide the means for distributing domestically made goods. With the railway in place, manufactures could be shipped east and west across Canada from factories in Ontario and Quebec. The tariff discouraged trade north and south.

The National Policy followed American abrogation of a reciprocity treaty in 1866 over dissatisfaction with raised Canadian tariffs on manufactures and displeasure with Britain's friendly relations with the Confederacy during the Civil War. Canada, backed by President Grant, sought a new agreement, but the American Senate refused to ratify a draft treaty in 1874.[17] One historian interprets the events as reflecting a thwarted Canadian preference for economic ties with the United States. Had the United States been receptive, Canada would have proceeded with closer economic relationships.[18] According to another interpretation, the National Policy was "conceived and implemented by a predominantly commercial elite" in central Canada, whose purpose was to create a protected hinterland in the other provinces for selling its products without competition and for enjoying privileged access to natural resources.[19] There is also not ageement that the National Policy was a second-best expedient to reciprocity. There was active debate in Canada during the two decades before the National Policy about how to develop Canada economically.[20] Nationalist sentiment was reflected in the National Policy's popularity, particularly in Canada's centres of commerce and manufacturing.

The aim of preventing Canada from becoming part of a larger American market has been compatible with all three national political parties. Implemented by Macdonald's Conservative government, economic nationalism was supported by the Progressive Conservative Party until the early 1980s, a position that reflected the views of much of Canada's business community. The Liberal Party, which contested the pivotal election of 1911 on the side of free trade with the United States, became interventionist and nationalist under the government of Pierre Elliot Trudeau. The New Democratic Party, advocating a strong role for the Canadian state and representing the interests of labour, was a consistent supporter.

Independence and economic relations with the United States were the central issues in the 1988 election. The decision facing Canadian voters was whether to re-elect a Progressive Conservative government pledged to implement a Canada-U.S. free trade agreement. For nationalists, the consequences were dire: closer commercial relationships would foster common economic and political interests. In prospect were diluted Canadian values, an undermined rationale for an independent Canada and a lowered resistance to integration with the United States. Much of the voters' travail stemmed from the "pervasiveness of economic nationalism in the Canadian political culture."[21]

People who believed they had benefited from protected industries saw their interests on the line. Their worry was that a century of protection under the National Policy had left Canadian industry unprepared for open competition with American industry. Blended with nationalist sentiment, fear about losing jobs through free trade produced one of the most rancorous elections in Canada's history. The Liberals and New Democrats split the anti-free trade vote, and the Conservatives returned to implement the agreement.

Modern Mercantilism: Export-Led Development

Export-led development represents an assertive and outward-looking form of mercantilism. Like earlier mercantilism, it reckons national wealth and international position with positive trade balances. By selling goods to others and by restricting purchases from them, a state transfers wealth from their economies to its own. To work, the strategy requires attractive and competitively priced goods to export, aggressive international marketing and restricted imports. The domestic population must be willing to do without imports, pay more for its goods (one of the consequences of protectionism) and see export profits reinvested instead of paid as higher wages. The state is a central actor. It identifies the industries most likely to succeed in world markets, channels investment to them and maintains strict controls on imports.

Japan set the lead for the Asian Tigers (South Korea, Taiwan, Hong Kong and Singapore) in export-led development. Between the end of World War II and 1960, the Japanese government kept the economy tightly protected. High tariffs were placed on imports, and absolute limits were set by quotas. Under a quota system, imports are restricted to particular quantities per year, and once the limit is reached, no more goods may enter. Sixty percent of the goods imported into Japan in that period were covered by quotas. As a further control, the Ministry of International Trade and Industry (MITI) was able to withhold foreign exchange funds to prevent import transactions.[22]

This tight policy intended to use the domestic market as a source of secure earnings to help finance the expansion of Japanese firms into the international market. As a further encouragement, the Japanese government allowed firms to act in ways that would be illegal in Canada: expanding by aggressively driving out weaker competitors, collusively setting prices, dividing up market shares and limiting competition to raise profits. To maximize the benefits of investment, MITI concentrated bank financing on improving cost advantages that enabled export industries to sell abroad at attractive prices. MITI also collaborated with Japanese firms to plan export products and design international marketing systems.

Japan required open international markets. The General Agreement on Tariffs and Trade, a series of agreements begun after World War II to liberalize trade, provided the framework (we will see more about the GATT later). By the time significant multilateral tariff cuts began to be made in the 1960s, Japan was well-positioned to supply inexpensive and attractive export goods in volume. The result was export earnings that accumulated to a massive trade surplus. Some of these returns were used to finance the development of new products and manufacturing techniques, furthering Japan's trading advantages, and some were used to finance income-producing investments abroad. Much of the credit for this remarkable success goes to the Japanese state for protecting the home market, coordinating industrial development and steering Japanese firms into international markets. The state's purpose was to rebuild a Japanese economy devastated by war and gain a pre-eminent position in the world economy. The policy was regarded as an immense success. Other Asian states sought to follow the same formula and also achieved rapid growth. By the 1980s, governments and corporations in Europe and North America were wondering what lessons from Japan they should learn.

There were costs. Major trading partners, particularly the United States and the European Economic Community (the European Union's predecessor), regarded Japan as an unfair trader that exploited their opened markets by not opening its own. One result was a number of unilateral trade restrictions aimed at limiting Japanese advantages. (Worry about these same trade restrictions being applied to Canadian exports was an important incentive for negotiating a free trade agreement with the United States.) Trade friction became a continuous ingredient in American and European relations with Japan. Events in 1998, as we will see shortly, brought to light serious weaknesses in the Japanese economy, and the state's policy, which had once seemed dynamic, came to look stagnant.

South Korea, Taiwan, Hong Kong and Singapore, with varying patterns of state involvement, developed export-oriented industries and achieved impressive growth. For its degree of state activism, South Korea is perhaps the most interesting case. In contrast to Japan, which had the remains of a large pre-war industrial base, South Korea after World War II amply qualified as poor and underdeveloped, making its growth and international success even more impressive.

The role of the state in South Korea's development was direct and powerful. It was an "overwhelming presence," and its intervention in the economy was "ubiquitous."[23] In the early 1960s, when South Korea began its drive for industrialization and export growth, the state was directed by senior military officers, political leaders and senior administrators who shared the goal of industrial development and economic growth.[24] The state had considerable autonomy and latitude to act. A strong bureaucracy had been set up during the Japanese colonization from 1910 to 1945, and the post-war Korean government centralized power further. Takeover of the government by the military in 1961 strengthened the state even more. By controlling banking and credit, the government channeled funds to companies that had good export prospects.[25] By granting favourable tax treatment, lucrative construction contracts, disbursements of American foreign aid and by tolerating "large-scale tax evasion," the government encouraged the companies to grow rapidly.[26] To steer export promotion and foreign marketing, the government established the Korea Trade Promotion Corporation.[27]

With the government's acquiescence, Korean industries grouped together into huge family-owned conglomerates called *chaebol,* some of which have familiar names: Hyundai, Samsung and Goldstar. Because of their size and income, *chaebol* came to dominate the economy with the largest five accounting for over half of South Korea's total production of goods. The *chaebol*, in fact, became so powerful that the state, which had encouraged their growth in the name of industrialization and exports, ended up in a complex political contest with them in the early 1980s over the direction of the economy and the evolution of democratic rule.[28] South Korea's policies and the export success of the *chaebol*, however, did achieve the purpose of development and industrialization with South Korea attaining one of the world's highest growth rates through the 1970s and 1980s and with South Korean labour enjoying wage rates comparable to those in Europe.

Export-Led Development and the Asian Economic Crisis

The Asian economic crisis of 1998 badly undermined confidence in Japanese and Korean-style economic strategies. The problem began in July 1997 when Thailand devalued its currency, shaking investor confidence not only in Thailand's economy but also in its neighbours in Southeast Asia. The impact, as we saw in Chapter 8, was particularly severe in Indonesia as banks, which had borrowed heavily abroad to finance industrial growth, found themselves badly overextended. Confidence turned quickly to panic as investors, fearing currency devaluation and the depreciation of Indonesian assets, sold holdings and withdrew financing. Many took heavy losses. With capital flight and devaluation making foreign debt much harder to service, liquidity shrank and the financial crisis deepened.

One of the roots of the crisis was banking and investment practices. Banks, it turned out, had lent vast amounts to Indonesian businesses without the inspection and guarantees required in Europe and North America. Instead of lending on the basis of sound finances and good business plans, banks were guided by family connections. Another root of the crisis was over-enthusiasm by foreign investors and insufficient estimation of risk. Encouraged by the Southeast Asian economies' high growth rates and taking too little account of their weaknesses, foreigners over-invested, bidding up values, putting pressure on currency exchange rates and encouraging the belief that sound business and banking practices did not matter. Because standards of accountability in Indonesia were low, the businesses themselves were often badly managed, heavily overextended and corrupt.[29] These practices did not withstand the scrutiny prompted by the Thai crisis. When the foreign investors got out, many of Indonesia's over-financed industrial edifices collapsed amidst debt, inflation and unemployment. Recovery meant ending an entrenched system of political cronyism and developing an effective regulatory state.

Unlike Indonesia's economy, South Korea's was under closer state direction and was guided by comprehensive development objectives. South Korea too fell into economic crisis and, like Indonesia, needed a massive loan from the International Monetary Fund to avoid collapse. *Chaebol*, which had appeared robust and successful, turned out to be marginally profitable if not money-losing. Instead of insisting on reform, the government had directed South Korea's banks to keep finances flowing, sending good money after bad.[30] The sums left the banks badly overextended, and many became insolvent. When the financing did stop, many of the *chaebol* went bankrupt. Worse, because the *chaebol* were so large, their needs outstripped the state's resources, necessitating help from the IMF. Of all the Asian states hit by economic crisis, South Korea is regarded as having made the strongest efforts at recovery. One of the key measures has been banking and financial reform. In all quarters, there have been massive and painful efforts to get out of debt.

Japan avoided these extremes of difficulty, but its largest banks by the mid-1990s were also insolvent. The banks' problems were due largely to real estate speculation in the 1980s and the subsequent crumbling of property values although they had also invested heavily in southeast Asia. Japan's economy itself was stagnant. The banking sector was unable to provide credit for economic expansion, and consumers, worried about their jobs, were not spending enough to stimulate a recovery. In the views of some analysts, Japan's economic immobility was perilously close to a deflationary spiral—the general collapse of prices and asset values.

The problem was widely held to reflect rigidity in the management of Japan's economy. What was required, in that view, was wide-ranging reform. Banking was only one sector requiring change. Needed more generally was an opening of long-established and cozy business networks to competition, both domestic and foreign. Without that change, there would be little incentive to offer lower prices to consumers and stimulate spending and little incentive to end close, restrictive and often inefficient relationships among suppliers and distributors.

Achieving that change would require the state to loosen its close bonds with business. For both political and economic reasons, the Japanese government was very slow to act. Politically, the large Japanese corporations that had benefited from the alliance with the banks and government were very reluctant to end a comfortable and predictable arrangement. The government, depending on corporations for political support, was just as reluctant to push hard for change. Economically, reform would mean abandoning a system that had worked spectacularly well for almost 50 years.

South Korea's and Japan's troubles have cast doubt on their models of state-led industrial development. South Korea's model, in light of the crisis, has been criticized as being too single-mindedly focused on growth. Not enough attention was given to sound finances, efficiency and good management. The state should not have allowed its cooperation with the *chaebol* to override prudent lending. Japan's model of close cooperation between the state, banks and business looked invincibly dynamic in the 1960s, '70s and '80s when the economy was growing rapidly and exports were robust. Since then the model has come to appear inflexible, leaving the system unable to adapt to change and innovation. How South Korea and Japan resolve these questions will be interesting to see. In both cases, the role of the state is a central issue.

Associated Press/AP photo/CP archive/Chung Ang

Workers of the Samsung Group collect gold items from its employees to procure U.S. dollars at the Samsung headquarters in Seoul, Wednesday January 7, 1998. The month-long campaign, launched by a bank and state-run TV, was intended to help South Korea repay $57 billion owed to the International Monetary Fund in emergency rescue funds.

Dependency

Dependency analysis looks to the international economic system to explain differences in states' levels of economic development. At the core of the theory is a centre-periphery view of the world with industrial states occupying the centre and developing states occupying the periphery. The role of the peripheral states is selling commodities to the centre for processing and manufacture. The relationship is unequal because of the **terms of trade**. Terms of trade are the ratio of exchange: how much of one good must be traded to obtain another good—the number of carloads of iron ore, for example, that must be sold to buy a CAT-scan machine. Terms of trade favour states that import commodities and export manufactures. Price stability does as well. The prices for manufactured exports from the centre are relatively steady while the prices of commodity exports from the periphery decline with oversupply. Developing economies cannot advance by exporting more commodities.[31] The result of this relationship is that states at the centre gain wealth and power while states at the periphery stagnate and decline.

Dependency analysis is an admixture of Marxism and nationalism, and there are both Marxist and nationalist variants. The Marxist variant emphasizes imperialism and class analysis. Imperialism describes the relations between centre and periphery. Capitalist production in industrial states depends on cheap sources of materials and overseas destinations for surplus capital and goods. The industrial states have the power to dominate the relationship. Commodity prices are kept low, and investments in developing states are made for the industrial states' benefit. Class analysis describes the relations within the developing states themselves. Local elites dominate class relations and exploit workers. Foreign investment entrenches the elites' position, making them allies of foreign capital and perpetuating class oppression.[32]

Domestically, the relationship maintains a large subordinate class of workers; internationally, the relationship maintains a large subordinate class of states. The result is a chain of capitalist exploitation reaching from the wealthy states in the centre through local elites in the periphery to poor classes in the periphery. Exploitation transfers surplus from the peripheral poor to local elites and on to the centre. The relationship is epitomized by transnational corporations whose homes are in the centre, who cooperate with local elites and who exploit workers. Because the arrangement suits the interests of those in power at every level of the hierarchy, none has any incentive to distribute wealth more equitably. Despite inflows of investment, exploitation and underdevelopment remain the future of the periphery. Its condition is rooted in the world capitalist system.

The nationalist ingredients of dependency analysis emphasize terms of trade and domestic economic structures. After World War II, Argentinian economist Raul Prebisch worried that commodity prices, which had been driven up by wartime, would decline and resource-based economies such as Argentina would sink into poverty. The existing international and domestic conditions produced rigidity and stagnation. Internationally, the rigidity was terms of trade. Commodity exports themselves would never generate enough income for industrialization. Domestically, the rigidity was lack of economic growth. Labour and social mobility were paralyzed because there were no new jobs to seek, and allocations of financial resources were frozen because there were few incentives to invest.[33] The only way of breaking the cycle was to industrialize.[34] Domestic firms would be the agents of growth.

The strategic choice was producing for export or the home market. Export-led development had the attraction of large world markets—an attraction, we saw, that guided Japan. Entering international markets against well-established and powerful producers was "not for the faint-hearted or indolent."[35] Prebisch did not advocate complete reliance on domestic markets. He believed that escaping dependence on commodity trade required venturing into export markets, but this could only be done once the economy was industrialized. That required the "temporary seclusion" of the domestic market.[36]

The Marxist and nationalist variants of dependency share important ideas with Critical Theory. By adopting the notion of centre-periphery, they accept a structural view of the world that emphasizes division and inequality. Centre denotes power and privilege, and periphery denotes subordination and marginality. Hierarchy and marginalization also resonate with Postmodernism and Feminism as we saw in Chapter 5. In the words of one feminist scholar, "Even as we in IR learn about a capitalist order of hierarchically arranged economic zones, which is fueled by the circulation of commodities and enforced by statist military power, we also learn that it is alive with racist and sexist logics that roost in local places."[37]

Dependency and Critical Theory also share the notion of an international capitalist hegemony as a pervasive system of power and control. The hegemony operates from a dominant centre and embraces local elites whose interests make them the centre's allies. Critical Theory regards hegemony not just as material power but as ideological power. The dominance of the centre's values and ideas causes people in the periphery, particularly their elites, to accept the prevailing arrangement as a natural order, making their subordination cognitive as well as material. The prevailing influence of capitalist modes of thought is ideological hegemony. Together these ideas—a juxtaposed centre and periphery and a domination that pervades relationships and understanding—depict illegitimacy at the international system's core.

Breaking the Bonds

Both the Marxist and nationalist variants of dependency emphasize the role of the state. They differ over what the state should do. The issue is economic **autarky**—economic self-sufficiency and independence from trade. Some Marxists, along with some nationalists, advocated autarky as the solution. From a Marxist perspective, a world capitalist system is an all-embracing set of relationships. Because the centre is so powerful, breaking free requires severing the ties of dependence. That view readily embraces revolution: The way out of permanent subservience is through "radical acts of will" that overthrow domestic elites and cut the hierarchical capitalist chain.[38] Socialism can indeed be autarkic. Joseph Stalin sought self-sufficiency when he introduced the policy of "socialism in one country" in the Soviet Union and undertook rapid industrialization. Socialist alternatives to autarky are also possible. One alternative is to trade within a socialist community of states. Another alternative is to emphasize class exploitation within the state as the focal problem. With that problem resolved by socialism, states do not need to withdraw into autarky but may exist within world capitalism.[39] In all cases, state ownership is the vehicle of change.

Prebisch and other nationalists favoured a strong role for the state but did not advocate complete autarky. They recognized trade in needed goods such as food but emphasized the importance of protecting the industrial sector and encouraging its development.[40] **Import Substitution Industrialization** (ISI) was the strategy. Because ISI did not require the wholesale transformations of socialism, it was attractive in the developing world and was widely used in Latin America, Asia and Africa until the late 1970s.

ISI aims to promote domestic industries through protective tariffs, but, unlike Export-Led Development, ISI focuses on the growth potential at home. Creating a protected market encourages domestic entrepreneurs to begin business shielded from "bruising competition from foreigners."[41] ISI provides three kinds of encouragement. First, tariffs make imports expensive and cause consumers to buy from domestic producers. Second, domestic producers do not have to compete on variety and quality. Finally, sufficiently high tariffs assure healthy profits even to inefficient producers.

ISI is also attractive to governments. The tariffs are a source of revenue. They are also a source of political capital. Because tariffs are set by individual commodity and confer sizeable benefits to producers, they provide governments with valuable favours to distribute. Readily viewed as patronage and corruption, this practice becomes part of progress and growth under ISI. Most importantly, ISI can produce quick and robust industrial expansion, making the government appear successful. That is especially true in an economy that is already prosperous because existing demand supports immediate sales particularly if that demand had already been created and serviced by imports. Demand is strongest in the consumer goods sector because the items are widely used: clothing, homewear, appliances and automobiles.

ISI also enables a state to skirt the long and expensive stage of forming a capital goods industrial sector to produce the needed equipment and technology. These can be imported, or foreign firms can be allowed to set up production and bring in their technology. With capital goods readily available, industrialization can proceed quickly and cheaply, producing vigorous manufacturing activity and the appearance of healthy economic development.[42]

Economic nationalism in the developing world supported ISI. The governments had either just gained their independence or, as in Latin America, wanted to escape the status of commodity producers. In the newly independent states, there was also a sense of beginning afresh and a confidence in the ability of governments to guide economic development. ISI, it was hoped, would produce balanced industrialization while keeping free of post-colonial economic entanglements with wealthy industrial states. Industrialization priorities were recognized under Article XVIII of the General Agreement on Tariffs and Trade, which allowed developing states tariff levels and other forms of economic intervention that were forbidden to the wealthy states. Some states, such as Mexico and Indonesia, had moderately high tariffs of 20 to 25 percent, but there was latitude for much greater protection. Nigeria's tariff, for example, was 222 percent.[43]

Developing states also used high tariffs on manufactures to manage balance-of-payments problems that arise because of unfavourable terms of trade. Because terms of trade favour manufactured goods and penalize unprocessed natural resources, developing states are vulnerable to balance-of-payments deficits caused by paying more for manufactured imports than is earned from commodity exports. Since these deficits represent foreign indebtedness, poor states with small financial resources can end up borrowing heavily abroad and devaluing their currencies. Doing so brings even lower prices for their exports and worsens the terms of trade. To prevent that, states may use tariffs to discourage import buying. They may also limit the amount of their currency that can be exchanged for foreign currencies, again discouraging imports. Another expedient is dual exchange rates with favourable rates for exports and unfavourable ones for imports. Balance-of-payments concerns, in fact, may override industrialization as a reason to erect high tariffs. One state for which that was true was Mexico.[44]

To encourage domestic entrepreneurs, the governments of some developing states opened development banks and corporations to make finance capital available on easy terms. Some governments also created state-owned corporations in industries that were seen as important parts of a manufacturing sector or in which the investment required was too much for individual entrepreneurs. In some states, notably Brazil and Argentina, military governments invested in state-owned armaments industries for both national security and potential arms exports.

Problems with ISI

By the 1980s, states that had adopted ISI were deeply in debt and were being rapidly outstripped by the Asian Tigers. What had gone wrong? Was ISI a flawed strategy? Those questions prompted earnest consideration in the governments of developing states and vigorous debate in the universities of developed states where dependency analysis had sparked considerable interest.

Non-dependency explanations emphasized domestic markets and industrial structures. ISI was a limited strategy because expansion was restricted by the production level a home market could support. The result was small and inward-looking industries. The comfort and predictability of serving a domestic market behind a tariff wall encouraged complacency and business conservatism, and there was little incentive to venture into international markets. That created an industrial glass ceiling: once growth reached the level of satisfying domestic demand, it stopped. Viewing Argentina's development, Prebisch beheld "an industrial structure virtually isolated from the outside world."[45]

Political economist Albert O. Hirschman traced the problem to capital goods— the machinery and technologies for producing other goods. ISI, he argued, makes it easy to bypass the stage of forming a capital goods industrial sector, but doing so limits the possibilities of industrial development. More favourable is building a base of suppliers and a network of linkages, which stimulates further growth. Forward linkages are created when an industry's products are used as inputs by another industry, and backward linkages develop when an industry requires the products of others as inputs. Without that network, economic development is shallow and limited to a few sectors.[46]

The alternatives to developing a broad industrial base are attractive, and it is easy to see why they were often preferred. One alternative, widely used earlier in this century, is to import the technology under licence. Licenses grant the right to produce another company's products in return for royalty payments. This option provides needed technology along with recognized foreign brands and designs. License agreements, however, were not a stepping stone into export markets because the terms generally forbade foreign sales.[47] Another tempting option, also widely used, is to purchase capital goods outright. To stimulate ISI, the governments of some developing states set lower tariffs on capital goods and parts needed by domestic industries. That encouragement added another disincentive to establishing domestic capital goods industries.

A third option is allowing foreign corporations to operate. High tariffs actually attracted foreign direct investment. Setting up local production qualified for treatment as a domestic firm, escaped the tariffs and accessed a protected market. Foreign direct investment was another way to avoid developing a capital goods sector because foreign firms brought with them their own technology and products. When the new operations were financed by the parent company and not by local banks, foreign direct investment also represented an infusion of wealth with the parent firm assuming the entrepreneurial risk. Prebisch himself believed that foreign investment could be compatible with ISI. Corporations welcomed the opportunity to expand.[48]

All three options limit development. With low prices on capital goods and parts, with foreign firms bringing in their own technology, with attractive foreign products available under licence and with tariff-protected profits, producers saw no advantage in expanding into capital goods industries themselves. In fact, if they did begin producing capital goods, the price would likely be high, reducing the incentive of domestic industries to buy them.[49] Without capital goods development, industries were limited to producing consumer goods. That market in turn was limited by income gaps between the wealthy and the broader population—a major consideration in developing states. These factors restricted the amount of industrial expansion—and industrial-wage-earning consumers—that ISI could generate.[50] Internationally, these same factors discouraged attempts to export. Without a network of domestic suppliers—the payoff of diversified industrialization—producers would have to import their capital goods and supplies. For small firms just entering world markets, these costs and limitations did not promise success. Export markets themselves were not initially hospitable. Until trade liberalization under the GATT began lowering barriers in the developed world, protectionist pressures restricted export opportunities there, particularly for manufactures that compete with domestic products.[51]

Can dependency analysis explain ISI's problems? One explanation focuses on importing production technologies. Developed in advanced economies, they are highly mechanized and do not make use of the abundance of labour in developing economies and thereby fail to expand the income base that supports development. If anything, these technologies, by producing good jobs for a few, widen class divisions. Foreign corporations increase inequality by creating miniatures of their home states' industrial sectors and social conditions—islands of development and prosperity in poor societies. People who benefit from the prosperity acquire a stake in maintaining their position and become allies of the corporations and enemies of change. Their behaviour replicates domestically the unequal centre-periphery relationship that exists internationally. In that way, foreign investment makes income distribution in developing economies worse, hardens incentives against reform and retards development.

FIGURE 12.3 ISI and Dependency in Canada

ISI and dependency analysis are part of Canada's economic history. By fostering industrial development inside a tariff wall, the National Policy was a form of ISI. Its advocates believed they were achieving nationalist ends by developing a "balanced economy within the confines of a single country."[52] The basis for a consumer goods industry was provided by Canada's prosperous agricultural and resource economy, and production expanded quickly. By creating good industrial jobs, the new factories were helping to form a solid basis for the development of Canadian society by delivering stability and prosperity to ordinary people. Rapid industrialization made the National Policy popular particularly in central Canada where the factories were concentrated. ISI appeared to work.

Critics have argued that the National Policy was also subject to ISI's weaknesses. Importing technology discouraged development of industrial depth. The tariff made Canada an attractive site for foreign corporations, which could produce inside a protected market. ISI's limitation showed in a manufacturing sector that had no incentive to export and a domestic market that limited expansion.[53]

That limitation became increasingly apparent as world trade expanded under the General Agreement on Tariffs and Trade. The question was economies of scale. Those economies occur as the level of production increases. Firms that achieve economies of scale enjoy lower costs per unit of production and can charge lower prices, giving them an advantage over higher-cost producers. Those advantages show particularly in international markets. Firms selling in moderately sized domestic markets and not exporting may be unable to reach the levels of production where scale economies develop, leaving them saddled with high costs and high prices. The alternative is to specialize in efficiently produced items and export. The market volume gained allows economies of scale to be achieved. Failure to specialize risks becoming increasingly uncompetitive and isolated.

As world trade began its rapid growth in the 1960s and as export-oriented states began their impressive entry in world markets, critics of Canada's policy began to worry about the future. The concern grew that foreign investment had produced in Canada a branch-plant economy that was excessively dependent on foreign technology and limited to a moderately sized Canadian market.[54] By the 1980s, domestic and foreign-owned Canadian firms, like their counterparts elsewhere, began looking at global markets and restructuring, keeping some operations at home and relocating others. In the face of that change, ISI thinking not only limits firms to increasingly contested domestic markets but prevents them from becoming competitive enough to survive even there. In the words of one economist, "This is a dangerous situation for a small, open economy under any circumstances."[55] To the federal government, the deep recession of 1980, which did serious harm to Canada's manufacturing sector and which the government feared was beyond its ability to contain, showed that such dangers were quite real. The outcome was a shift of government and corporate opinion toward trading and exporting. ISI was over.

There was an alternative view. Dependency thinking, particularly its core/periphery perspective, attracted interest in Canada just when concern about foreign investment, export competitiveness and the role of the state had become keen. In the late 1960s, the Waffle Group, a faction of the New Democratic Party, called for an "independent socialist Canada." In a dependency perspective, Canada was a part of America's periphery, constrained in its autonomy by powerful economic links. For

Canadian Marxists, the core/periphery perspective showed that Canada, along with developing states, was a victim of imperialism although Canada's elites, benefiting from capitalist ties to the United States, fully cooperated.[56] For others, Canada's position is an ambiguous one of semi-periphery in which the state pursues policies to ascend to central status but remains "caught between core and periphery status, unable to reap the advantages of either, while lacking the capacity to become an independent semi-periphery."[57] For still others, Canada's increasing international involvement as a banking and industrial power qualify it as part of the centre.[58] In one scholar's view, Canada's historical association with Britain and the United States and its development of a high-wage economy make it so much a part of the centre that it is an economic region of the United States.[59] Dependency's themes of centre-periphery and hegemony shape all three interpretations.

Dependency's Estate

Neither of the state roles advocated by dependency, socialism and ISI, was very successful in promoting sound economic growth. Some economists believe they did only slightly better in reducing long-term poverty.[60] A serious challenge to socialism came from the operating costs of state-owned industries. In both the Soviet Union and China as well as in the developing world they tended to become bloated and inefficient and required ongoing government subsidies. The cost of those subsidies added to governments' debt levels. And with the exception of the military arms sector and some high-technology industries to which governments were willing to commit considerable resources, state-owned industries also showed little inclination to innovate, resulting in products that were often outclassed in world markets. The International Monetary Fund granted debt relief with conditions attached. A frequent condition was selling off state industries. The IMF's rationale was that subsidy-dependent industries consume too much state revenue, block financial recovery and hamper development. The most serious blow to socialism, however, was the Soviet Union's collapse and China's move toward economic liberalization. The size and impact of the Soviet and Chinese experiences, and particularly the economic malaise they revealed, discredited what had been a plausible alternative to capitalist development.

The most serious challenge to ISI came from the Asian Tigers.[61] They also had relied heavily on state intervention to industrialize, but by the 1970s their economies were booming. When the global debt crisis came in the 1980s, the Asian Tigers were much less severely affected than other developing states because their large export returns kept their debt burden small. A major point of comparison was South America. The Asian Tigers had no cost advantages over those economies in basic factors such as labour and transportation and received no special treatment in the large American market.[62] The difference between the two experiences directly challenges dependency's structural explanation of underdevelopment. In one scholar's words, "If the most important explanation for the economic prospects of a state is its peripheral position in the world capitalist system, it is impossible to explain this variation."[63] The variation can also not be explained by differing state objectives. The South Korean government decided to seek export-led growth precisely to become powerful and avoid dependency.[64]

Explanations have looked to domestic practices. One area of difference between Latin America and Asia was currency exchange rates. South Korea maintained a currency exchange rate low enough to make exports attractively priced but not low enough to make export prices unrealistically cheap and their producers complacent. Latin American governments kept their currency exchange rates artificially high to support ISI. High rates pleased consumers but inflated domestic production costs and raised the prices of exports.

Industrial practices are another difference. Dealing with the question of why Latin American garment producers did not export as successfully as their East Asian competitors, several studies have found that "it was the flexibility of East Asian producers with their readiness to adapt and innovate quickly and their emphasis on quality control and punctual delivery that gave these countries their initial edge."[65] It was not that Latin American states were "inherently uncompetitive" with the Asian Tigers. "Rather, they lacked an appropriate set of policies and political institutions that would capitalize on their strengths."[66] After a long and detailed comparison of the Asian and Latin American experiences, one scholar concluded that dependence was as much a *result* of developing states' policies as a *cause* of them, fostering and perpetuating the conditions they were seeking to overcome.[67]

Economic Liberalism

Economic liberalism emerged as a critique of mercantilism. For economic liberals, viewing state welfare in terms of cash and trade surpluses was a fundamental confusion between money and "productive material capital." It is not stores of money that make a state wealthy "but the accumulation and efficient utilization of productive resources."[68] British economist David Ricardo (1772-1823) contributed the supporting economic theory of comparative advantage. In an elegant demonstration, Ricardo showed that Britain and Portugal, which could produce both cloth and wine, would be better off specializing—England in cloth and Portugal in wine. Even though cloth sells for more than wine, Portugal would still do better by specializing than by producing its own cloth. That is so because each state maximizes its welfare by producing the goods in which it is most efficient. The benefits are reaped through trade with each selling what it produces best. Although some states may do better than others, all gain from the efficiency of specialization, and all are better off. The point to emphasize, in the liberal view, is not the higher gains of some (their relative gains) but the net gains of everyone (their absolute gains). Seeing the absolute gains was the genius of Ricardo's insight. When the theory of **comparative advantage** is properly specified, it is, in one Nobel laureate's words, "unassailable."

Amassing and hoarding state wealth, in the view of liberals, was a serious error leading not to power but to stagnation and decline. The better policy would be for all states to seek joint benefits by removing restrictions and allowing goods to be traded freely.[69] Productive capacity, in the liberal view, is a source not of unilateral power but of benefits to exchange with others. To realize the mutual gains of comparative advantage, trade must be unrestricted. There must be no artificial barriers to the exchange of goods. Such barriers create distortions that lead to sub-optimal allocations of productive resources and decreased efficiency. Instead, international trade must be a fully open market. States must withhold their sovereign power to intervene in the natural flow of goods. The most obvious intervention is **tariffs**, which discourage trade by taxing it.

If the compelling logic of comparative advantage were the sole determinant, the world by now would have had a long-established system of universal free trade. The General Agreement on Tariffs and Trade is only 50 years old. In successive rounds of negotiation, it reduced tariffs dramatically, with the Kennedy Round of the 1960s and the Tokyo Round of the 1970s achieving reductions among the major states from an average level of 30 percent to around five percent. Restrictions still exist, and further liberalization has become contentious. The Uruguay Round, the most recent effort, sought to extend the GATT into areas such as agricultural commodities and service industries and met almost intractable resistance from states determined to keep particular restrictions. Agriculture was especially difficult because of the maze of barriers and price supports worldwide, the domestic political power of farmers in many developed states, the farming sector's assumed ability to soak up unemployment and because of a desire, with origins going back to the age of siege warfare, to maintain food self-sufficiency regardless of cost. The Uruguay Round's eventual success owes much to the tireless persistence and diplomacy of the GATT's director-general, Arthur Dunkel.

Individual Selfishness and Collective Gain

Joint endeavours such as GATT negotiations pit the multilateral openness advocated by economic Liberalism against a "world of national-welfare—or income-maximizing—states."[70] Structurally, the problem is abandoning selfish advantages for collective gain. That problem is a focal concern of Liberal IR theory and Neorealism.

Liberal IR theory, as we saw in Chapter 3, treats the state as a mediator of group demands. Those demands may be affected by international as well as domestic factors. That makes trade a particularly important issue area because it transmits international price signals to domestic producers. Trade exposes domestic markets to international price signals and creates preferences for restrictive or open policies.[71] Industries threatened by foreign competition—signals that their prices are too high or their goods too unattractive—may demand protection, which the state can provide through tariffs and other measures.[72] The state may have its own preferences for protecting vulnerable industries. These include maintaining important bases of political support or shielding an industry or region from unemployment. Industries benefiting from trade—price signals that its costs are competitive and its goods attractive—may favour openness. There too the state may have its own preferences for expanding trade. These include stimulating important economic sectors and encouraging promising exporters.

Reconciling preferences is not simple because economies normally contain strong sectors as well as vulnerable ones, generating preferences for both openness and protection. The behaviour of trading partners—which is affected by *their* preferences—adds more factors to reconcile. The outcomes by no means produce universal support for open markets and unrestricted trade. What emerges instead is a blend that varies by state, by sector and by time.

There is also the question of non-democratic states and their insulation from domestic group pressures. What shapes those states' trade policy preferences? In the view of one scholar, their rulers are "positioned at the nexus of domestic and global political economies," enabling them to "skim off profits from the world economy." Their preferences depend not on the wisdom of liberal economic theory nor even on their state's welfare but on the way they can use trade relations for their own ends.[73] Interdependence transmits the effects of their behaviour to trading partners, affecting their preferences.

Neorealists, as we saw in Chapter 2, discount collective gains because of fear and mistrust. Their worry is that states will exploit opportunities and take more for themselves. For neorealists, the gains that matter are not the absolute ones produced by mutual benefits but the relative ones produced by one-sided advantages. Opportunities for relative gains are created by removing barriers and restrictions to achieve free trade. International anarchy tempts states to exploit any opportunities, even seemingly small ones, for relative gains. Neorealists worry most about the relative gains that affect security, as we saw in Chapter 10, but economic relations can still be a concern. A relative gain can provide the leverage to force partners to accept unfavourable deals. The problem multiplies if the leverage is used to capture more relative gains and extend advantages into other issue areas. For the disadvantaged side, the result may be a cumulative loss of bargaining power and independent action. Worse, relative economic gains can be converted to relative military ones. Worse still, states' objectives may change as their position and capabilities change.[74] Removing trade barriers does open the way to absolute gains for everyone, but it also provides new opportunities for relative gains. In the face of that prospect, neorealists recommend caution and vigilance, even among friends.

Greedy partners spoil collective enterprises. The French political philosopher Jean-Jacques Rousseau (1712-1778) captured the problem in his parable of the stag hunt. A group of hunters sets out to catch a stag. If they are successful they will all have plenty to eat. On the way, one of the hunters spots a rabbit and chases it, leaving the others too short-handed to continue. All end up worse off: the defector gets a meal, but only a small one, and the others get nothing.[75] What is needed is some way of making partners resist selfish temptations to defect. There are three possible measures: ones that make cooperation more attractive and lower the loss if others defect; ones that decrease the advantages of defecting; and ones that increase the participants' expectation that all will cooperate.[76] The task is to design a structure that provides these incentives and assurances.

Institutionalists, as we saw in Chapter 2, share the neorealist fear about cheating but believe that states prefer cooperation if protection against cheating can be provided. The answer is an enforceable set of rules that promotes cooperation and controls for cheating. With effective rules and controls, absolute gains are possible. Constructing an effective institution requires getting the participants to surrender enough of their protections to produce a collective benefit and providing the means to verify behaviour and penalize cheating. In trade, the motivating prospect is the absolute gains of comparative advantage.

The GATT and the WTO: Rules and Enforcement

At the end of World War II, the allied powers resolved to construct international institutions to avoid the repeating of mistakes that led to war. To deal with aggression, they founded the United Nations and gave it a powerful Security Council. To prevent the financial instability that exacerbated the Great Depression and to deal with the balance-of-payments problems that would come with postwar reconstruction, they created the International Monetary Fund. To finance that recovery, they created the International Bank for Reconstruction and Development, later to become the World Bank. To prevent the discriminatory trade practices that marked the 1930s and that were at the centre of Nazi economic diplomacy, they founded an International Trade Organization. To provide a temporary framework while the ITO's charter was being ratified, it included a set of trade principles. The ITO was never ratified, but the framework remained to become the General Agreement on Tariffs and Trade. The GATT is easiest to understand as a set of rules.

The main purpose of the GATT was to lower trade barriers, reduce discriminatory trade practices and provide a means of resolving trade disputes. It was not a blueprint for global free trade. Instead, it was an effort to formalize and centralize trade negotiations and to ensure that the liberalizations states might achieve between themselves would be extended to all states. The liberalizations themselves would have to emerge from negotiations, and the result would be whatever states could agree upon. The agreements that now constitute the rules of world trade were achieved in negotiations over almost 50 years.

The core principle of the GATT is non-discrimination. Its purpose is to prevent states from constructing privileged blocs. Before the war, Nazi Germany used bilateral trade agreements with other states to lock in sources of supply at concessionary prices and discourage their partners from trading with others. Such practices discriminate against third parties who may also want to trade with those states and against the partner states themselves who are denied the opportunity.

Non-discrimination is also intended to generalize the benefits of liberalization. The GATT allows states to negotiate trade agreements between themselves, but requires that they immediately grant any benefits or concessions to all other states. That provision, contained in the most-favoured-nation clause (MFN), proved to be a powerful tool of trade liberalization because a concession negotiated with one state would apply across the board. A state agreeing to a lower tariff on, say, textiles with one trading partner would be required to grant that same tariff to all other states selling it textiles. Non-discrimination also underpins the principle of national treatment, which requires member states to treat imported goods the same as domestically produced ones. Imports must be subject to no special taxes or restrictions, and domestic products must be given no special advantages.

States' obligations under the GATT and now under its successor institution, the World Trade Organization, are contained in the basic principles and in the agreements negotiated among the members. Provision for enforcement rests with a tribunal that hears complaints from members about unfair trade practices. Adjudication centres on determining whether the alleged practice is actually occurring and whether it violates the state's obligations. If a violation is found, the state is instructed on what it must do to come into compliance. If the state does not comply, the complaining side has recourse to punitive retaliation normally in the form of special tariffs. The prospect of such retaliation usually brings compliance. In an institutionalist perspective, the states' obligations constitute a set of rules. Individual members, who have an interest in their partners' behaviour, are responsible for monitoring compliance and can lodge complaints if they detect cheating. Enforcement is a matter of adjudication by the institution and action by the members.

The GATT recognizes that states may be subject to special circumstances that penalize them if they adhere to the rules. The preferred mechanism of adjustment is tariffs, and the GATT has provisions under which states can unilaterally raise them to compensate for an injury or serious disadvantage. **Non-tariff barriers** (NTBs) are not preferred. These are measures that are intended to discourage imports without taxing them. States seeking to increase trade surpluses can use NTBs to keep out imports. States with declining industries can use NTBs to provide protection. NTBs are a less desirable form of restriction than tariffs because they are often invisible, and their effects are much more difficult to factor into supply and pricing decisions. Tariffs, on the other hand, operate quite openly, and their effects are readily calculated. NTBs violate the principle of national treatment, but proving discrimination is often difficult because NTBs officially serve some other purpose.

One way of disguising NTBs is product standards, which specify particular design and performance requirements. They cover everything from the gauge of wiring in appliances to the dimensions of food containers and can be exact and unique. They become NTBs when they are set to exclude imported goods that do not meet them. Since the main purpose of product standards is to protect consumers, import exclusion may indeed be a secondary result. Even so, exporters facing different product standards have the choice of modifying their goods specifically to incorporate another state's standards or foregoing sales there. For that reason, the European Union is negotiating common standards among its members—product by product. Another NTB is packaging and labeling requirements. The packaging that is approved for domestic sales, for example, may not be available outside that state, forcing exporters to import and apply the packaging, which often requires special equipment or retooling, or to have the product packaged once it is landed. Another NTB is deliberately long and complex customs clearance and inspection procedures that delay or interrupt delivery of imports. Exporters facing complicated clearances, high foreign brokerage and warehousing fees, and unpredictable delays in delivery may decide that the prospective sales are not worth the trouble.

NTBs are often defended as part of a state's legitimate and established ways of doing business, making them very resistant to pressure even in direct bilateral negotiations. The United States, convinced that Japan was using customary business practices as an excuse to avoid opening its market, launched a long negotiation aimed at reducing "structural impediments" in Japan's economic system. There were some changes, but the process was slow and difficult. Some critics charged that Japan actually gave up very little. Others charged that pressuring another state to change its business practices goes too far.

Industrial policies are another tool. They can be used to promote successful industries and exports, as we saw with Japan and Korea, but they can also be used to protect vulnerable industries from imports through direct and indirect subsidies. Anti-dumping tariffs, which are legal if harm can be shown, can be used to remove the price advantage of imports that are priced artificially or unfairly low. Finally, exporters can be pressured directly to limit their level of sales. As tariffs began falling significantly in the 1970s, states began turning to these measures. They became so widespread in the 1970s and 1980s that they were termed the new protectionism (the companion of the new mercantilism). They continue to affect as much as half of world trade.[77] Negotiating adjustments "touch[es] the exposed nerve of sovereignty and the entire historical, cultural and institutional fabric of differing societies."[78]

Anti-dumping tariffs are also open to abuse. Under the WTO, a state may apply a tariff to an imported commodity that is priced either below the home market price or below the cost of production. Producers seeking relief file anti-dumping complaints with their governments. Although producers must show they are being harmed, critics argue that making a successful case is too easy. Selling at discounts, they add, is not necessarily evil. Anti-dumping measures had previously been used by industries in the developed states as a substitute for the protections being lost through general tariff cuts. The targets were generally cheaper imports from developing states. Now, developing states are taking up the practice themselves. The levels of duty that can be set are high. Twenty-nine percent was the average level of anti-dumping duties assessed by the European Union between 1991 and 1995.[79] What is worse is that most anti-dumping requests are granted.

Resisting anti-dumping actions requires exporters to spend time and money defending themselves in foreign tribunals. The prospect of long, expensive and unsuccessful litigation, like coping with NTBs, may tip the balance against exporting to a particular market. The hope of gaining exemption from American trade action, as we saw earlier, was one of Ottawa's incentives for negotiating a free trade agreement with the United States, but the problem is not just bilateral. Liberals lament restrictive trade practices because they distort the workings of comparative advantage and introduce non-price factors into the terms of exchange. Because anti-dumping actions are directed at particular states and commodities, they re-introduce discriminatory practices. Increasingly widespread use of anti-dumping action, liberals fear, will undercut the reforms achieved in decades of multilateral GATT negotiations. At the same time, it does provide a remedy for real abuses.

Problems with Liberalism

The implications of comparative advantage point to a single world market. Not everyone has welcomed this prospect. One criticism is that corporations shifting production to lower-wage states harm mature economies such as Canada's. That was a principal reason for the opposition of the Canadian Labour Congress and its American counterpart, the AFL-CIO, to NAFTA. There was a more general concern that states might lose whole industries as they migrate to places with cheaper costs.

Liberal economists argue that these views are misguided and base their argument on the effects of productivity gains. The basic principle is contained in the theory of comparative advantage: *all* states benefit from specialization and trade. Wages that fall in mature economies because of competition from developing states are offset by cheaper imports, and purchasing power remains the same. That is so because the imports' lower prices reflect their producers' higher productivity. The benefit is passed on to the buyer. Productivity is also reflected in hourly wages. As productivity rises in developing states, workers there will demand higher wages. "Economic history," in the words of one economist, "offers no example of a country that experienced long-term productivity growth without a roughly equal rise in real wages."[80] That in turn increases the workers' purchasing power and expands their demand for imports. These arguments leave many people unpersuaded, particularly those in traditional manufacturing industries, and trade liberalization remains politically contentious. One place where contention is highly visible is in the U.S. Senate when trade agreements must be ratified or when the president requests "fast-track" authority to bypass the Senate's power to amend draft treaties.

The Asian crisis of 1998 sparked a second criticism. Removal of monetary restrictions has produced a global financial market in which investors are free to shift massive amounts of money at once. Instant fluidity can produce two negative results. The first is over-confidence in rapidly expanding economies and over-investment. As investment surges in, asset values are inflated, pressure is put on exchange rates and banks and businesses overextend. But speculative bubbles burst, and when they do, the opposite result occurs: investors panic and pull out, prices and asset values collapse, currencies come under devaluation pressure and the affected economy suffers a drastic shock.[81] The problem is not **foreign direct investment**, which is tied up in physical plant and is not portable in the short run, nor even portfolio investment in foreign firms' securities.[82] The volatile factor is short-term loans to local banks. Indonesia illustrates what can happen when short-term financing is withdrawn. The human side of Indonesia's crisis shows a hard and unforgiving side of liberalism.

The second result is excessive currency speculation. Currencies are traded on world financial markets where speculators seek to profit from shifts in exchange rates. If a state's economic prospects look bright, investors expect its currency to gain value and buy it. That creates demand for the currency and raises its price. If a state's economic prospects look gloomy, the opposite happens. Investors expect the currency to lose value and sell it. That drops demand for the currency and lowers its price. Those results themselves are not necessarily bad. Economists regard exchange rates as an adjustment mechanism. Lower exchange rates enable states that are otherwise less competitive to continue trading because their exports are cheaper. Speculators, who watch for signs of weakening competitiveness, set the stage by selling the state's currency, lowering the price of its exports.

Trouble comes with panic selling of a currency. If a state appears headed for an economic crisis, investors holding that currency will hurry to unload it. Psychologically, the rush creates a sense of urgency and prompts even more vigorous selling. For a troubled state, a drop in its currency makes foreign debt loads harder to service and puts heavy burdens on its banks and government finances. Those developments herald worse trouble and undercut confidence even further. With more devaluation and devastated asset values in prospect, investors who have stayed to that point begin contemplating heavy losses. Since these investors are likely to be large institutions that are accustomed to financial give and take, their departure feeds the sense of panic.

In 1998, the world's major states and the IMF put together an emergency loan for Brazil to avert that process. The worry was that the Asian crisis had badly weakened confidence in all developing economies. There was great concern that speculators, shaken by the Asian crisis, would watch Brazil for any signs of weakness. As Latin America's largest economy, as a state making earnest efforts to reform its finances and as a major recipient of foreign investment, Brazil was a bellwether. If its currency dropped under speculative pressure, its financial reforms would be difficult to maintain, its debt would soar and its economic underpinnings might collapse. On the heels of the Asian crisis, that alone might be enough to send Europe and North America into recession. Worse, it might trigger subsequent crises in states such as Mexico. In prospect was potentially grave trouble for the world's financial system. All those considerations prompted the wealthy states and the IMF to attempt a rescue of Brazil.

What should be done to limit speculative binges? One approach looks to the regulatory protections that were developed in states such as Canada (many of those protections representing lessons learned from the Great Depression): regulations on borrowing and lending, on bank liquidity, on financial reporting for investors and on securities trading. Much of the fuel of the financial panics of 1998, according to this approach, was uncertainty. States that had received massive inflows of foreign investment lacked regulatory structures that could provide enough financial accountability to assure investors. Without those protections, investors decided not to take chances. In withdrawing from a state, investors are sending a powerful signal for reform. Just as lost sales are a price signal to uncompetitive producers, so are lost investments a signal to unreformed governments. The consequence of tolerating overextended banks, business cronyism and poor standards of accountability is absent investors. Remedy involves bringing the states' regulatory capabilities up to their level of industrial development.

Portfolio investment in developing economies, in one view, is worth encouraging. Investment tends to gravitate to established firms and industries, but the most promising prospects for growth in any economy are often new firms in emerging industries. Financing from speculative investors—international growth mutual funds, for example—provides a valuable service in economies with few venture capital sources of their own.[83] In that light, mutual funds are a quick and direct way of transferring savings from developed states to developing ones. The disadvantage is that international mutual fund managers need to stay competitive with other funds by delivering high earnings to their investors and avoiding losses. That objective makes many mutual fund managers too focused on short-run fluctuations to be dependable investors in any industry, particularly ones in developing states.

There is also recognition that international financial markets are prone to irrational enthusiasm and sudden panic—the twin forces of greed and fear. There have been proposals to tax international currency transactions. That would increase the cost of shifting money, curb speculation and reduce volatility.[84] Another proposal is to compel banks to share more fully the costs of IMF bailouts. In that view, the IMF is not a lender of last resort, its official role, but of first resort, shielding banks that over-lend from the full consequences of their actions. They should take a bigger share of the losses and bear more of the costs of remediation.[85]

Another approach holds more generally that a single global market is a myth and that it is an error to proceed by creating rules as though such a market existed. In the view of one political economist, states are too embedded in their societies to fit some universal standard. There will always be regulatory differences, various business cultures and unequal exposure to international market forces. Instead of seeking to press all states into a common mold by imposing uniform investment and business rules, a more prudent and realistic approach is to recognize that some diversity is inherent and seek to accommodate it through negotiations, case by case and state by state, within a general framework of principles. That, and not a universal trade formula, was the GATT's original design.[86]

Summary

We have seen that economic activity is rooted in individual and national welfare. Sovereignty gives the state potentially wide power to intervene in the domestic economy and in exchanges with other states. The purposes and effectiveness of state intervention underpin three doctrines and a diversity of practical experience and results. Mercantilism, the oldest rationale, equates state power with liquid wealth. The rise of popular nationalism joined mercantilist thought to democracy and industrialization. Mercantilism's modern variant equates state power with industries that earn hefty trade surpluses. Dependency, which emerged from the experience of Latin American states after World War II, blends Marxist views of imperialism and class oppression with nationalist views of economic independence. Liberalism, originally a reaction to mercantilism, emphasizes the rationality of markets. Liberalism is expressed internationally in the theory of comparative advantage, which holds that states are best off concentrating on their most efficient areas of production. Free trade allows producers to reap the benefits of one another's respective efficiencies. Mercantilism and dependency, in their separate ways, emphasize inequality. Liberalism emphasizes mutual advantages.

In practice, modern mercantilism and dependency both relied on the state to guide development. Both approaches enjoyed periods of success but also pivotal setbacks. Modern mercantilism's policy of export-led development produced rapid growth and apparently strong economies. The Asian crisis of 1998 called the state's role into question, and the resolution remains to be seen. Dependency's policy of ISI led first to rapid industrial growth but then to stagnation and debt. Again, the state's role was brought into question. Liberalism's policy of unrestricted trade and finance led to economic globalization. The advantage was rapid growth in a number of states as investors backed rising industries. The disadvantage appeared in the financial market's behaviour during the Asian crisis when large sums of investment were hurriedly withdrawn, leaving states in economic crisis.

At this point, the role of the state has become inescapably international. What balance will be struck between market latitude and state intervention remains to be seen. Also in question is the approach to that issue: seeking more uniformity of state practices or negotiating to accommodate existing diversity.

ENDNOTES

1   *Statistical Yearbook 1995,* New York, United Nations, 1997, pp. 93, 96.

2   *United Nations Human Development Report, 1998*, New York: Oxford University Press, 1998, p. 26.

3   Andrew Janos, "Paradigms Revisited: Productionism, Globality and Postmodernity in Comparative Politics," *World Politics* 50 (October 1997) 125.

4   Robert Jackson, *Quasi States: Sovereignty, International Relations, and the Third World*, Cambridge: Cambridge University Press, 1990, p. 110.

5   Andre Blais, *A Political Sociology of Public Aid to Industry*, Toronto: University of Toronto Press, 1985, pp. 65–80.

6   Robert Gilpin, "Economic Evolution of National Systems," *International Studies Quarterly* 40 (September 1996) 415.

7   Pier Carlo Padroan, "The International System and the Diversity of States and Markets," in Roger Benjamin, C. Richard Neu and Denise Quigley, eds., *Balancing State Intervention*, New York: St. Martin's Press, 1995, p. 28.

8   Robert Gilpin, *The Political Economy of International Relations*, Princeton: Princeton University Press, 1987, p. 31.

9   Harry Johnson, *The New Mercantilism: Some Problems in International Trade, Money and Investment*, Oxford: Basil Blackwell, 1974, p. 4.

10 Stephen Krasner, "The Accomplishments of International Political Economy," in Steve Smith, Ken Booth, Marysia Zalewski, eds., *International Theory: Beyond Positivism?* Cambridge: Cambridge University Press, 1996, p. 115.

11 Otto Hieronymi, "The New Economic Nationalism," in Otto Hieronymi, ed., *The New Economic Nationalism*, London: Macmillan, 1980, p. 12.

12 David Baldwin, *Economic Statecraft,* Princeton: Princeton University Press, 1985, p. 74.

13 Gilpin, *The Political Economy of International Relations*, p. 181.

14 *ibid.*, p. 33.

15 J.L. Granatstein, "Free Trade between Canada and the United States: The Issue That Will Not Go Away," in Denis Stairs and Gilbert Winham, eds., *The Politics of Canada's Economic Relationship with the United States,* Toronto: University of Toronto Press, 1985, p. 17.

16 *ibid.*

17 Richard Lipsey and Murray Smith, *Taking the Initiative: Canada's Trade Options in a Turbulent World,* Toronto: C.D. Howe Institute, 1985, p. 45.

18 Granatstein, "Free Trade between Canada and the United States," p. 17.

19   Paul Phillips, "National Policy, Continental Economics, and National Disintegration," in David Jay Bercuson, ed., *Canada and the Burden of Unity*, Toronto: Copp Clark Pitman, 1986, pp. 20-21.

20   Kim Richard Nossal, "Economic Nationalism and Continental Integration: Assumptions, Arguments and Advocacies," in Denis Stairs and Gilbert Winham, eds., *The Politics of Canada's Economic Relationship with the United States*, Toronto: University of Toronto Press, 1985, p. 67

21   *ibid.,* pp. 56, 69.

22   Kozo Yakamura, "Caveat Emptor: The Industrial Policy of Japan," in Paul Krugman, ed., *Strategic Trade Policy and the New International Economics*, Cambridge: MIT Press, 1986, p. 174.

23   Karl Fields, *Enterprise and the State in Korea and Taiwan*, Ithaca: Cornell University Press, 1995, p. 29.

24   *ibid.,* p. 26.

25   Stephan Haggard and Chung-in Moon, "The South Korean State in the International Economy: Liberal, Dependent, or Mercantile," in John Gerard Ruggie, ed., *The Antinomies of Interdependence: National Welfare and the International Division of Labor*, New York: Columbia University Press, 1983 p. 148.

26   Fields, *Enterprise and the State,* p. 34.

27   Kwang Suk Kim, "Lessons from South Korea's Experience with Industrialization," in Vittorio Corbo, Anne Krueger and Fernando Ossa, eds, *Export-Oriented Development Strategies*, Boulder: Westview Press, 1985, p. 60.

28   *ibid.,* pp. 61–62.

29   *World Economic Outlook, May 1998*, Washington, D.C.: International Monetary Fund, 1988, p. 3.

30   Paul Dibb, David D. Hale and Peter Prince, "The Strategic Implications of Asia's Economic Crisis," *Survival* 40 (Summer 1998) 13.

31   Peter van Bergeijk, *Economic Diplomacy, Trade and Commercial Policy*, London: Edward Elgar, 1994, p. 106.

32   Charles Oman and Ganeshan Wignaraja, *The Postwar Evolution of Development Thinking*, New York: St. Martin's Press, 1991, p. 161.

33   David Greenaway and Chris Milner, *Trade and Industrial Policy in Developing Countries*, London: Macmillan, 1993, p. 44.

34   Bjorn Hettne, *Development Theory and the Three Worlds*, Harlow, UK: Longman Scientific and Technical, 1990, pp. 86–87.

35   Stephen Neff, *Friends but No Allies: Economic Liberalism and the Law of Nations*, New York: Columbia University Press, 1990, p. 155.

36   Hettne, *Development Theory and the Three Worlds,* p. 85.

37   Christine Sylvester, "The Contributions of Feminist Theory," in Smith, Booth and Zalewski, eds., *International Theory: Positivism and Beyond,* p. 270.

38   Karl Deutsch, "Theories of Imperialism and Neo-Imperialism," in Steven Rosen and James Kurth, eds., *Testing Theories of Economic Imperialism*, Lexington, MA: Lexington Books, 1974, p. 26.

39   Hazel Smith, "Marxism and IR Theory," in Margot Light and A.J.R. Groom, eds., *Contemporary International Relations: A Guide to Theory*, London: Pinter, 1994, p. 148.

40   Neff, *Friends but No Allies,* p. 157.

41   *ibid* p. 155.

42   Glen Williams, *Not For Export: The International Competitiveness of Canadian Manufacturing* (3rd ed.), Toronto: McClelland and Stewart, 1994, p. 27.

43   Greenaway and Milner, *Trade and Industrial Policy in Developing Countries,* p. 10.

44   Bela Belassa, et. al., *The Structure of Protection in Developing Countries*, Baltimore: Johns Hopkins University Press, 1971, p. 179.

45   Albert O. Hirschman, "The Political Economy of Import-Substituting Industrialization in Latin America," *Quarterly Journal of Economics* 82 (February 1968), 2.

46   *ibid.,* pp. 7, 8.

47   Williams, *Not for Export*, pp. 30–32.

48   Sylvia Maxfield and James H. Nolt, "Protectionism and the Internationalization of Capital: U.S. Sponsorship of Import Substitution Industrialization in the Philippines, Turkey and Argentina," *International Studies Quarterly* 34 (March 1990) 52–53.

49   Hirschman, "The Political Economy of Import-Substituting Industrialization in Latin America," p. 18.

50   Klaus Esser, "Modification of the Industrialization Model in Latin America," *CEPAL Review 26* (August 1985) 101–102.

51   Maxfield and Nolt, "Protectionism and the Internationalization of Capital," p. 61.

52   Neff, *Friends But No Allies*, p. 156.

53   Robert Z. Lawrence, "A Depressed View of Policies for Depressed Industries," in Robert Stern, ed., *Trade and Investment Relations among the United States, Canada and Japan,* Chicago: University of Chicago Press, 1989, 203.

54   Nossal, "Economic Nationalism and Continental Integration: Assumptions, Arguments and Advocacies," p. 72.

55   A. Edward Safarian, "The FTA and NAFTA: One Canadian's Perspective," in Charles Doran and Alvin Paul Drischler, eds., *A New North America: Cooperation and Enhanced Interdependence,* Westport: Praeger, 1996, p. 35.

56   Daniel Drache, "The Canadian Bourgeoisie and Its National Consciousness," in Ian Lumsden, ed., *Close the 49th Parallel, Etc: The Americanization of Canada,* Toronto: University of Toronto Press, 1970; Daniel Drache, "Harold Innis and Canadian Capitalist Development," *Canadian Journal of Political and Social Theory 6* (Winter/Spring 1982) 35-60.

57   Robert W. Cox, "Employment, Labour, and Future Political Structures," in R.B. Byers and Robert Reford., eds., *Canada Challenged: The Viability of Confederation*, Toronto: Canadian Institute for International Affairs, 1979, pp. 266–267.

58   Philip Resnick, *Masks of Proteus: Canadian Reflections on the State*, Montreal and Kingston: McGill-Queen's University Press, 1990, pp. 179-204.

59   Glen Williams, "On Determining Canada's Location within the International Political Economy," *Studies in Political Economy 25* (Spring 1988) 130–133.

60   Jagdish Bhagwati, "Poverty and Reforms: Friends or Foes?" *Journal of International Affairs* 52 (Fall 1998) 33-45.

61   Greenaway and Milner, *Trade and Industrial Policy in Developing Countries,*

62   David Yoffie, *Power and Protectionism: Strategies of the Newly Industrializing Countries*, New York: Columbia University Press, 1983, p. 213.

63   Krasner, "The Accomplishments of International Political Economy," p. 123.

64   Haggard and Moon, "The South Korean State in the International Economy," pp. 154–160.

65   Yoffie, *Power and Protectionism*, p. 213.

66   *ibid.*

67   Stephan Haggard, *Pathways from the Periphery: The Politics of Growth in the Newly Industrializing Countries*, Ithaca: Cornell University Press, 1990, p. 193.

68   Johnson, "Mercantilism: Past, Present, Future," p. 5.

69   Baldwin, *Economic Statecraft*, p. 81.

70   John Conybeare, *Trade Wars: The Theory and Practice of International Commercial Rivalry*, New York: Columbia University Press, 1987, p. 21.

71   Andrew Moravcsik, "Taking Preferences Seriously: A Liberal Theory of International Politics," *International Organization* 51 (Fall 1997) 529.

72   Conybeare, *Trade Wars*, pp. 14–17.

73   Robert O. Keohane, "Problematic Lucidity: Stephen Krasner's 'State Power and the Structure of International Trade,'" *World Politics* 50 (October 1997) 170.

74   Joseph Grieco, "Understanding the Problem of International Cooperation: The Limits of Neoliberal Institutionalism and the Future of Realist Theory," in David Baldwin, ed., *Neorealism and Neoliberalism: The Contemporary Debate*, New York: Columbia University Press, 1993, pp. 314–315.

75   Robert Jervis, "Cooperation under the Security Dilemma," *World Politics* 30 (January 1978) 167.

76   *ibid.*, 171

77   Robert Baldwin, "Changes in the Global Trading System: A Response to Shifts in National Economic Power," in Dominick Salvatore, ed., *Protectionism and World Welfare*, New York: Cambridge University Press, 1993, p. 87.

78   Sylvia Ostry, *Governments and Corporations in a Shrinking World: Trade and Innovation Policies in the United States, Europe and Japan*, New York: Council on Foreign Relations Press, 1990, p. 77.

79   "Unfair Protection," *Economist* November 7, 1998, p. 75.

80   Paul Krugman, *Pop Internationalism*, Cambridge: MIT Press, 1996, p. 56.

81   Jagdish Bhagwati, "The Capital Myth: The Difference between Trade in Widgets and Dollars," *Foreign Affairs* 77 (May/June 1998) 8.

82   *Economist*, November 7, 1998, p. 79.

83   *ibid.*

84   Eric Helleiner, "Great Transformations: A Polanyian Perspective on the Contemporary Global Financial Order," *Studies in Political Economy* 48 (Fall 1995) 156–159.

85   Bhagwati, "The Capital Myth," p. 12.

86   Dani Rodrik, "The Global Fix," *The New Republic*, November 2, 1998, 17–19.

WEBLINKS

The World Bank's site is:
www.worldbank.org

The IMF's site is:
www.imf.org

The World Trade Organization's site is:
www.wto.org

A site devoted to APEC and Canada can be found at:
www.apfnet.org

Information about NAFTA can be found at:
www.nafta.net/naftagre.htm

Information about trade complaints and decisions in Canada can be found on the site of the Canadian International Trade Tribunal:
www.citt.gc.ca

Excellent analyses are produced by the Institute for International Economics:
www.iie.com

Tufts University Fletcher School of Law and Diplomacy maintains a site of international trade treaties and agreements:
www.tufts.edu/fletcher/multilaterals/html

The United Nations Human Development Report is found at:
www.igc.apc.org/undp/hdro

The Friends of the Earth's site has links to various studies of quality of life:
www.foe.co.uk/progress/contacts

The University of British Columbia Library has an online listing of resources on economic development:
www.library.ubc.ca/poli/international

Chapter (13)

Human Rights and the Environment

Norms: The Invisible Force

Norms are widely accepted standards of behaviour. Legal norms are established in law, and social norms are established in common practices. Law itself can be seen as a way of formalizing practices that are widely accepted. Indeed, law can lose legitimacy if it makes illegal something that is generally done and not treated with disapproval. Norms are followed because people accept them personally and because violating them brings unwelcome consequences. Legal norms are enforced by judicial systems and the formal penalties of fines and imprisonment. Social norms are enforced by interpersonal systems and the informal penalties of disfavour, retaliation and ostracism. Both formally and informally, norms direct behaviour into desired and approved modes and discourage deviation. They support coherence and order and account for patterns we see in human relations: forms of politeness, conduct with strangers, practices involving money. Norms are effective to the degree that they guide behaviour. Measuring effectiveness involves factoring out self-interest, which eliminates behaviour that would occur in any case. The remaining behaviour can be attributed to norms.[1]

Applied to IR, norms have intriguing possibilities for explaining order. As we saw in Chapter 2, neorealists explain order in light of anarchy and power. In the absence of any central authority, whatever order exists is due to the distribution of power. Some scholars acknowledge the effects of anarchy but see something more. Besides reflecting power, the actions of states often appear to follow common standards and expectations. To the late IR scholar Hedley Bull, that behaviour was evidence of an international society.[2]

The presence of common norms distinguishes a society from an anarchy. Behaviour that would otherwise be ungoverned follows particular conventions and avoids particular practices. Those conventions emerge from a consensus about proper forms of conduct. Among states as well as among people, that consensus is the basis of society. As consensus solidifies over time, it generates particular rules and expectations that govern behaviour, constraining the excesses and disorder that would be possible in an anarchy. In domestic societies, norms can be codified in law and enforced by the state, making compliance mandatory. In international societies, norms also can be codified in law, but there is no equivalent of a state, making compliance voluntary. The fact that there *are* areas of voluntary compliance in the international system, in Bull's view, is evidence that an international society is present among states. It is not as comprehensive as a civil society, but common rules and expectations do affect the actions of most states most of the time. Although that order does not include all states and all areas of interaction, it still provides sectors of stability and predictability, mitigating anarchy's stark potential.[3]

The notion of an international society and common norms underpins international law. The idea of law based in mutual understandings and practices among sovereign states was formalized in the writings of the Dutch legal philosopher Hugo Grotius (1583–1645) who sought ways of ensuring cooperation and order in the growing spheres of international trade and navigation. Grotius recognized sovereign statehood as the source of action but believed that a combination of a shared morality and common material interests formed the basis of "coexistence and cooperation in a society of states."[4]

Sovereignty itself owes much to reciprocal practice. As we saw in Chapter 6, states maintain sovereignty by recognizing it in their dealings with one another. The norm is that all states are sovereign and equal. From that norm, more particular rules and expectations derive: Agreements should be kept. Aggressive use of armed force is illegitimate.[5] Following them day to day upholds not only individual state sovereignty but also an international system with particular basic structures and forms.[6] They in turn support a "sense of community among like units that is the essential ingredient of any society."[7]

Like domestic law, **international law** reflects actual behaviour. Until recently, most international law was customary—a codification of rules and expectations that had evolved from practices and declarations among states and from adjudication in domestic and international courts. The other source of law is **treaties** and conventions between sovereign states. Their importance has expanded in recent years because of the number of international agreements and institutions. Both sources can be seen as reflections of an international society: custom as accumulated and established practices and treaties as specific undertakings. Treaty and customary law often converge. As we saw in the last chapter, the GATT and its successor organization, the WTO, are based on a set of common principles augmented by a set of agreements negotiated among the member states.

The Origin of Norms

How do norms arise? There are two basic perspectives. The first stresses mutual convenience and necessity. To see how these could generate common norms, it is useful to think back to the time of Grotius. States were beginning to develop international trade and ship on the high seas. Without common expectations and practices, trade and shipping would be problematic and risky: contracts to buy and sell goods would not be reliable, the status of ships in foreign ports and the obligations of their owners would not be certain and liability for losses would be hard to establish. These risks would be reduced by norms to keep contracts and to apply common provisions to foreign vessels, crews and cargoes.

The second perspective stresses common social values. These arise among states with similar cultures and historical experience. At the time of Grotius, there was a general understanding in Europe of natural law, which held that people living together in society required common rules. One view of natural law held its origins to be divine instruction to humankind. Another view held human reason to be the source. Grotius supported the latter. Both versions contained specific notions of justice and obligation. More recently, democratic rule has been seen as generating common practices and values. As we saw in Chapter 9, states that have evolved into liberal democracies expect their political processes to be transparent, legitimate in the eyes of the public and open to compromise. Among other democratic states, these values form expectations of moderation, conciliation and fair play.

Norms also arise from public opinion to which democratic states respond. In recent years public opinion has become an important source of norms that stress international humanitarian obligation. The news media transmit vivid images of conditions abroad, making the public immediately aware and confronting its social values. As IR scholar James Rosenau puts it, "Under the harsh gaze of the television camera, some situations are so appalling, so utterly gruesome, that it is unimaginable the world will not eventually develop control systems to prevent their persistence and re-occurrence."[8] Because many of the conditions involve the way other states treat their people, this expectation extends the reach of international norms from conditions *between* states to conditions *within* states.

The origins of norms affect how widely they will be shared internationally. The broadest consensus is possible for norms that originate in practical utility. Norms about navigation on the high seas are of interest to all states involved in commercial shipping whatever the nature of their government and whatever their political and social values. Agreement about use of the electromagnetic spectrum is possible among states that have widely divergent preferences about what political and social messages telecommunications should actually transmit. Beyond this kind of operational pragmatism, norms require some consensus on underlying values. The GATT and the WTO, for example, require a basic commitment to the principle of non-discrimination. That value is not compatible with mercantilist orientations, and states following mercantilist trading strategies under the GATT courted complaints from their trading partners. Much of the partners' sense of grievance was over basic values of openness, reciprocity and non-discrimination. The consequence was not only trade complaints but also a broader sense that states following mercantilist practices had placed themselves apart from others. As one defence, those states justified their practices, as we saw with NTBs in the last chapter, as expressions of differing but legitimate national values.

If convenience and common values can generate norms, the opposite is also true: the basis for consensus narrows as interaction decreases and values diverge. Low interaction supports less interest in common practices. States may engage selectively, embracing only the norms that are the most necessary and staying apart from the others. Divergent values widen the gap. History and culture account for some of the distance. Early international law derived from historical experience in Europe. Understandings of justice and obligation were based in natural law, and notions of jurisprudence and codification derived from Roman law. These legacies were not present elsewhere. Although international law has expanded common forms and understandings, divergent incentives and values remain, producing a variegated pattern of international consensus.

One scholar envisages international society as a set of concentric circles. At the centre are states that are closely joined by agreements and common values. Since these states are wealthy, they are highly interdependent economically and interact heavily. That activity provides the basis for a broad foundation of pragmatic consensus. Since these states are also democratic, they share a set of common values about procedures and objectives. If an international society can be said to exist, these states are its pillars. In the next circle are states that engage selectively, aligning with the core on some issues and remaining independent on others. China might be one example. Since these states may affiliate on some issues and stay apart on others, they account for varying consistencies in international society. In issues in which there is wide consensus and affiliation—international aviation law, for example—the result is an even expanse of agreement and common practice. In areas of non-affiliation—nuclear non-proliferation, for example—these states leave gaps. How large these gaps are depends on the number of non-affiliates. In the outer circle are states that refuse most areas of agreement and stay aloof from much interaction. Because of the disadvantages of such isolation, such states are few. North Korea is one.[9] The result is an incomplete world society with wide adherence in some sectors and partial or non-adherence in others.

FIGURE 13.1 Identities and Norms: The View from Constructivism

Constructivists, as we saw in Chapter 4, believe that states in the international system constitute themselves through interaction. The role identities states possess are formed not only from their own beliefs, expectations and experience but also from their dealings with other states. Ongoing interaction confirms their role identities. That kind of mutual reinforcement, in the constructivist perspective, sustained the superpowers' adversarial role identities during the cold war. Role identities can also change through interaction. Constructivists account for the end of the cold war as an interactive shifting of role identities from adversaries to cooperators. The pattern is circular. As one state modifies its behaviour, it alters the other's expectations. Those expectations produce modified behaviour in turn, which affects the first state's expectations. The cycle can be positive and engender more cooperation or be negative and engender more conflict. The important point is the interactive connection between behaviour and role identities.

Role identities can also be shaped by norms. Social norms, as we just saw, contain standards of expected behaviour. They are effective to the extent that people accept them as guides to their conduct. As we also saw, social norms are enforced by interpersonal sanctions. Few sanctions are required for strong norms because the influence of general consensus and common opinion is so pervasive in shaping people's social understandings. The stronger the consensus, the greater is its authority. Consensus and authority are formalized in law and constitutions.[10]

Constructivists go one step further. Society's rules and expectations affect not only behaviour but also identity. People bring their beliefs, expectations and experience to social interactions. They take away approval or disapproval. Norms affect the interactions by providing standards. Approval is a positive reflection of identity and tends to sustain it. Disapproval signifies a discrepant or deviant identity and tends to contradict it. Pressure to change is measured against norms and is prompted by people's assessments. How much a person feels the need to change or to justify behaviour is a good index of the norms' power. The degree of change depends on the importance attached to the interaction.

Constructivists have applied the same reasoning to states. International norms are contained formally in law and particular institutions. Joining an institution requires a particular role identity to begin with: nuclear non-proliferator, free-trade promoter, environmental conservator. Once states are members, institutional norms become obligatory. As important as learning how to comply is learning how to understand problems and define appropriate action. States with fully congruent role identities will find them amply reflected in the institution, but states with less congruent ones will find their behaviour under scrutiny and evaluation and will find that compliance—or good excuses—are expected. In the words of two scholars, "the rationales and justifications which are proffered, together with pleas for understanding or admissions of guilt as well as the responsiveness to such reasoning on the part of other states, all are absolutely critical component parts of any explanation involving the efficacy of norms."[11] As in social interaction, the process is one of "debate...persuasion, argument and discursive legitimation."[12]

Norms, in the constrictivist view, prescribe "proper behaviour for a given identity."[13] Members of the WTO, for example, who wish to be regarded as living up to its obligations desire the identity of fair traders. Again, norms are the gauge. States wishing to acquire positive identities must be seen to be in compliance. In one scholar's words, "If rules had no explicit or implicit existence, such behaviour would make no sense."[14] Since identities, in the constructivist view, are flexible, rules shape identities by fostering consistent behaviour.[15] Behaving as a fair trader *makes* a state a fair trader. Institutions marshall states under a set of norms, mandate proper understandings and behaviour and foster congruent identities. They affect not only members' behaviour but also their understanding of what kind of states they should *be*.

Identities can also be an assertive force. States may sponsor institutions to entrench their identities into collective structures. As we saw in Chapters 10 and 11, NATO was an alliance of democratic states. Its purpose was to protect its members' normative identities as much as their physical security. As we saw in the last chapter, NATO not only provided almost 50 years of security but also entrenched democratic practices at the heart of a major regional organization. For its European members, the result was a dramatically changed collective identity. The security community that underpins the European Union is possible because its members no longer are military adversaries and no longer include calculations of military force in their relationships. That is so because the "process of creating institutions is one of internalizing new understandings of self and other [and] of acquiring new role identities."[16] Peaceful community was the collective form.

Membership in an institution shapes identity because it involves participating in "new forms of social knowledge."[17] At the core of any institution is a group that strongly espouses its norms and likely includes the founding members. Their identities were clear enough to support the effort to begin the institution. If the institution is long-standing, their identities formed and evolved along with it. In either case, there is a strong congruence between the members' identities and the institution's norms. In intermediate circles are states that either espouse some of the institution's norms, but maintain their independence regarding others, or espouse the norms generally, but without strong commitment. In the outer circles are states that are either tangential members who share few norms or very weak commitments. Beyond the outer rings are states that share the institution's norms not at all and do not belong.[18] That same concentric pattern, as we saw, has been used to describe states' degrees of adherence to international norms. Constructivists add the ingredient of identity.

Norms and Action

How do norms actually affect state behaviour? Compliance is easy to explain when norms require states to act in ways that are already in their own interest. Such norms tend to be self-policing because states have a practical incentive to detect and punish violators. Because violations can be punished by individual or collective retaliation, such norms do not require a central authority. Interdependence raises the pressure to comply, and states protecting their own interests provide the means and vigilance. The more one state's actions affect others, the greater are the consequences of violating common norms and the less latitude there is to act with disregard. The more specific the norms, the more obvious are any violations.[19] Some scholars believe that self-interest explains why most international law, which governs activities such as navigation and commercial transactions, is followed most of the time.[20]

Beyond pragmatic self-interest, explaining the effectiveness of norms focuses on the way governments—and decision-makers within governments—define choices and weigh alternatives. Effectiveness enters the picture when following a norm conflicts with self-interest. What makes a state forego an advantage in favour of following a norm? Some of the reason depends on the international system as it affects the issue at hand. When the system's anarchic features seem predominant, normative claims on behaviour will weaken. When the system's features seem orderly, compliance becomes more expected.

Common practices set broad limits even when anarchy is strong. The norm of sovereignty, for example, defines the legitimate actors and the way they are to be treated. Commitments in more specific areas are represented by treaties, conventions and agreements. A common rubric of standards and jurisprudence is provided by international law itself. Altogether, in one scholar's words, international norms tell "who shall play the international game, what the playing board will look like and which moves are acceptable."[21]

Norms classify particular actions. If a decision to use armed force can be shown to fit the norm of lawful self-defence, it falls within a justifiable category. If armed force can be shown to violate the norm of peaceful resolution of disputes, it is illegitimate.[22] Acts must plausibly fit preferred classifications, of course, but even when the fit is not obvious there is often room for argument. The *need* to argue reflects the international consensus behind such classifications. Even states that do not share the consensus are affected. "When such states wish to portray their [actions] as legitimate, they are under significant compulsion to justify [them] in terms of the system's primary norms."[23]

How can norms be attributed to particular decisions? IR theory offers four possibilities. First, norms may reflect the values which decision-makers and their societies already hold. Second, being well-established and widely held may give norms such authority that decision makers instill them into their values and outlooks. Third, norms require day-to-day compliance. They may become part of the standard operating procedures of government agencies and are taken into account like any other rule or requirement. Fourth, officials in government, and interest groups in society, may use international norms to bolster their positions when they make their claims in the domestic political process. The norms provide legality, legitimacy and connection to a broader consensus.[24]

Still: norms may "guide, inspire, rationalize or justify behaviour," but it is difficult to prove that they *cause* behaviour.[25] We saw the same difficulty in Chapter 4 with critiques of Constructivism. Explanation requires inferring that a particular understanding shaped a particular decision. Since understandings are not observable, the evidence of their force is indirect. The same critique applies to norms. Because they operate by shaping preferences, they are difficult to establish as the basis of action.[26] The converse is also true: it is difficult to prove that norms have no effect. Violations might make that conclusion tempting, but they do not prove ineffectiveness any more than particular offences, such as acts of drunk driving, invalidate the law.[27]

What happens to violators? Their reputations as reliable partners suffer, and repeated offences destroy their honour. States regarded as rule-breakers risk being left out of beneficial arrangements because other states no longer trust them.[28] When violations are taken to signify a more basic divergence of important values and understandings, they set the state apart from the international community. Shame and disgrace are important sanctions, particularly if the norms are widely accepted. Even when there is little chance of material penalties, the possibility of exposure and international stigma may be a strong reason to comply.[29] A final consequence may be in the violator's own domestic politics. International conventions and treaties become part of the ratifying states' domestic law. In states that respect their own laws, violating an international agreement, particularly one that reflects strong public values, may provoke more censure at home than abroad.

Human Rights Norms: Early Antecedents

Human rights norms benefited from this century's expansion of international legal institutions although until the end of World War II, **human rights** themselves were not considered "an appropriate topic for international scrutiny and rule formation."[35] The limiting condition was the norm of sovereignty, which grants states

FIGURE 13.2 Norms and Power: The Views from Neorealism, Postmodernism and Critical Theory

It is easy to regard norms as a liberal and positive force. Norms can embody any consensus, and support may be based on something other than high-mindedness. Neorealists, postmodernists and critical theorists regard norms in this light.

To neorealists, norms simply reflect the prevailing arrangement of power and state interests. International drug trafficking and airliner hijackings have both been subject to international agreements to control them and have attracted vigorous enforcement. Why these? In the neorealist view, powerful states set the international agenda, and they illegitimize those activities that harm their interests. In drug trafficking, it is from the large and wealthy states where drugs are consumed that initiative for control arises. The same is not necessarily true of states where drugs are produced. Suppressing growing, refining and exporting causes economic dislocation and, in some, disturbs connections between drug lords and national governments. Those interests do not provide the same support for control. "Powerful states," in short, ban particular practices when they become "a threat to themselves."[30]

Neorealists see human rights policies as ancillary to concrete foreign policy objectives, particularly those involving security.[31] Advocating human rights can embarrass authoritarian adversaries and encourage opposition movements. Neorealists are also skeptical about the effect of any norms that depend on voluntary compliance particularly if compliance goes against material interests. Norms are effective only when they validate states' interests or can be enforced by power.

Postmodernists also see norms as reflecting a prevailing dominance. They agree that states can form an international society through commonly held rules and expectations but disagree that the consensus is benign. Norms enforce hierarchies and control people who are defined as other. "It is with the help of [norms] that the international community disciplines practices, tames resistances, imposes regions of silence, maintains secured practices and legitimates subjects."[32] Postmodernists are intensely skeptical of any values or identities that are claimed as universal. Such claims ignore discrepant practices in particular places. Universal norms contain silences as well as consensus, and the silences are from those who are ignored, subdued or estranged.

To critical theorists, international institutions are instruments of hegemony, which powerful states construct to enforce their ruling ideology. Since hegemony is based as much on accepted ideas as on material power, international norms are "the rules which facilitate the expansion of hegemonic world orders," and give it legitimacy. As ideological constructs, norms mold the views of elites on the periphery and induce behaviour that supports the hegemonic powers' interests. [33] The apparent consensus reflects the centre's ability to dominate behaviour and thought.

Such objections are not just theoretical. Leaders of developing states who question UN humanitarian intervention have sometimes depicted it as ideological dominance backed by force. In that view, the UN Security Council, which authorizes these operations, is directed by powerful states whose interests govern the decision. The justifications for intervening in some places and the rationales for staying out of others reflect not so much a set of consistent moral principles as situational interests and inclinations.[34] In either case, it is the hegemonic states that make the call.

exclusive jurisdiction over domestic matters. The advance of human rights into the arena of international law and conventions was helped by two developments: the advent of international conferences that adopted common principles and accords, and the founding of an international court. Two important conferences were the Hague conferences of 1899 and 1907. Although they did not deal specifically with human rights, they did establish the first international court, the Permanent Court of Arbitration. The two conferences also established the precedent of setting important international standards by joint declaration.

The tradition of standard-setting in international conferences continued with the Versailles Conference after World War I, which institutionalized the practice by forming the League of Nations Assembly and incorporated the Permanent Court of Arbitration as the Permanent Court of International Justice.[36] The Versailles conference incorporated several human rights principles in the Covenant of the League of Nations, the most important of which was Article 23, which required states to maintain "fair and humane labour conditions."[37] The most important human rights work under the League, in fact, was done by the International Labor Organization, which encouraged states to negotiate international conventions on labour standards. Even so, the ILO's work was not primarily human rights advocacy.

The major advance in human rights as an international concern came with World War II. The allied powers were horrified by the way national and minority populations were persecuted and in particular by the way Jews, along with gypsies, homosexuals and the mentally ill, were singled out and killed by the Nazis. A complementary development was the view, seen in Chapter 6, that colonialism was illegitimate and that independence was necessary for proper government of inhabitant peoples. Unlike the delegates at the Versailles conference and the League of Nations, the founders of the United Nations were resolved to include specific human rights guarantees in the Charter itself. In doing so, they were guided by understandings of rights and liberties of the time. A central influence was the concept of the dignity and inviolability of the person. Evolved as a basic right in liberal democratic societies, it was universalized in the Charter.[38] The key provisions are contained in the Charter's preamble, which espouses the rights of individuals and the equal rights of women and minorities (see Figure 13.3). Non-discrimination is stated in Article 1 (3). Articles 55 and 56 commit member states to work individually and with the UN to "promote...universal respect for, and observance of, human rights." In 1948, the United Nations adopted the Universal Declaration on Human Rights, which set forth a comprehensive set of political, social and economic rights.

The Declaration was adopted as a resolution of the General Assembly, communicating a consensus of the international community. That consensus was not regarded as a binding commitment. Early legal interpretation of the Charter held that it set out no specific rules about human rights, established no specific obligations for states and did not make individual people directly subject to rights under international law. A legal analysis in 1962 acknowledged that the Declaration represented a major advance, but it was not binding.[39]

FIGURE 13.3 Universal Declaration of Human Rights Adopted and Proclaimed by General Assembly Resolution 217 A (III), December 10, 1948

Preamble

Whereas recognition of the inherent dignity and of the equal and inalienable rights of all members of the human family is the foundation of freedom, justice and peace in the world,

Whereas disregard and contempt for human rights have resulted in barbarous acts which have outraged the conscience of mankind, and the advent of a world in which human beings shall enjoy freedom of speech and belief and freedom from fear and want has been proclaimed as the highest aspiration of the common people,

Whereas it is essential, if man is not to be compelled to have recourse, as a last resort, to rebellion against tyranny and oppression, that human rights should be protected by rule of law,

Whereas it is essential to promote the development of friendly relations between nations,

Whereas the peoples of the United Nations have in the Charter reaffirmed their faith in fundamental human rights, in the dignity and worth of the human person and in the equal rights of men and women and have determined to promote social progress and better standards of life in larger freedom,

Whereas Member States have pledged themselves to achieve, in-cooperation with the United Nations, the promotion of universal respect for and observance of human rights and fundamental freedoms,

Whereas a common understanding of these rights and freedoms is of the greatest importance for the full realization of this pledge,

Now, therefore, The General Assembly Proclaims this Universal Declaration of Human Rights as a common standard of achievement for all peoples and all nations, to the end that every individual and every organ of society, keeping this Declaration constantly in mind, shall strive by teaching and education to promote respect for these rights and freedoms and by progressive measures, national and international to secure their universal and effective recognition and observance, both among the peoples of Member States themselves and among the peoples of territories under their jurisdiction.

Two developments changed that situation. The United Nations Human Rights Commission, created in 1946, drafted the Universal Declaration but then proceeded to work on a set of international conventions. In contrast to the Declaration, which was a resolution of the General Assembly, conventions are ratified by states. When states ratify, conventions represent a legal obligation by the state and become part of its domestic law (see Figure 13.4). The second development has been the expansion of customary international law, which also obligates states. Both extend the influence of international law from behaviour between states to behaviour within states.

FIGURE 13.4 The Roster of Conventions and Covenants

1949	Genocide
1951	Status of Refugees
1965	Racial Discrimination
1966	Covenant on Civil and Political Rights
1966	Covenant on Economic, Social and Cultural Rights
1967	Discrimination against Women
1967	Territorial Asylum
1981	Discrimination because of Religion
1983	Inhumane Weapons
1984	Torture and Other Inhumane Treatment
1989	Rights of Children

International Human Rights and Canadian Law

The influence of both international conventions and customary law shows clearly in Canada's *Charter of Rights and Freedoms*. International conventional law exists in formal agreements among states. When a state signs a convention, it agrees to abide by its provisions. In Canada, an international convention normally requires an act of Parliament (or a provincial legislature if the matter falls under provincial jurisdiction) to become part of domestic law, but then Canadian courts acknowledge its authority. In Canada, the link between conventional international law and domestic human rights law is even more intimate. The *Charter of Rights and Freedoms* was drafted in view of Canada's adherence to the Universal Declaration as well as to the three international conventions that Canada had ratified by that time: on racial discrimination, on civil and political rights and on economic, social and cultural rights. The framers of the *Charter* wanted to harmonize Canada's constitution with the obligations assumed when the human rights conventions were ratified. Those conventions, in fact, were the source of some of the *Charter's* legal concepts and specific language.[40] Because of their influence, the *Charter* is "indissoluably" linked to conventional international human rights law.[41]

Canada's *Charter* is also linked to customary international human rights law. Unlike **conventional international law**, which is recorded in formal agreements between states, **customary international law** exists in recognized international practices and principles. International custom is established from evidence that a particular norm is a part of regular state practice and by evidence that states recognize particular obligations. That evidence is shown not only in treaties and the acts of international organizations such as the UN, but also in domestic and international court decisions. Further evidence is found in states' domestic legislation, advisory legal opinions and official diplomatic communication.[42] Together, these sources show the existence of norms in regular activities.

Customary international law affects Canada's domestic law when the courts, using the kinds of evidence just seen, determine that a particular norm or principle has achieved that stature. If a norm or principle is determined to be customary, it is incorporated into Canadian jurisprudence. Unlike the incorporation of law established in international conventions, this adoption needs no implementing legislation. It is simply recognized. Adoption of international customary law bolsters the *Charter's* authority. Courts can treat particular rights in customary international law as existing also in Canada.[43] Together, international human rights conventions and customary international human rights law obligate the Canadian government to enforce human rights law in the Canadian courts and to recognize other states' human rights obligations in its dealings with them. Both obligations extend the reach of international human rights law.

It is important for international law that its provisions be part of states' domestic law because its practical effect depends on sovereign states and their judicial systems. Without that incorporation, some scholars believe, international law would have far less influence.[44] A major expansion of human rights law and an important step in the end of the cold war was the Soviet Union's decision announced in a speech to the UN by Mikhail Gorbachev to recognize the International Court of Justice's jurisdiction in cases involving human rights conventions.[45]

For many other states, acknowledging legal obligations does not mean putting them into effect. One hundred forty states signed the 1966 Covenant on Civil and Political Rights, and 137 signed the Covenant on Economic, Social and Cultural Rights, but many states flout them in practice. It is here that the normative effectiveness of international law comes directly into question. How can states that do not follow their own laws be pressured to comply?

International Scrutiny: The United Nations Commission on Human Rights

For the first 20 years of its existence, the UN Commission on Human Rights was content to draft conventions, and there was no inclination to investigate actual compliance. The investigations that were conducted were done through agencies such as the International Labor Organization or through the General Assembly itself. To initiate such investigations, a bloc of supporting votes was needed. In 1959 and again in 1965, for example, the General Assembly called for the end of practices against Tibetans that violated their human rights under the Charter and called on all members to seek an end to the situation.[46] The General Assembly also authorized the Human Rights Commission to undertake particular investigations, but these also depended on blocs of votes. In 1967, the Human Rights Commission was given broad authorization to identify and investigate any situations that appeared to involve a regular and systematic violation of human rights.

What kind of power do investigations exercise? International norms, as we saw, reflect a consensus, and a strong consensus among a significant group of states can be seen as evidence of an international society. With norms providing the gauge, public scrutiny constitutes an evaluation, and the exposure of violations constitutes an indictment. The power of investigation is exposure and condemnation. The stronger and more widespread the consensus, the more violators will be set apart.

The covenant on civil and political rights and the covenant on economic, social and cultural rights were both adopted in 1966. They require states to report regularly on their progress in implementing the provisions. The General Assembly established a Human Rights Committee to receive and evaluate the reports. The Soviet bloc, joined by many developing states, opposed the whole idea of monitoring and wanted the Committee to have the power only to receive (and not evaluate) reports. The Western states wanted full monitoring and disclosure. The Committee ended up with the role of receiving official reports but had no power to investigate independently or to criticize states publicly.[47] Even with these restrictions, the Committee was fully subject to the political tensions of the cold war. The West was interested in violations in the Soviet bloc. Backed by allies in the Arab world, the Soviet bloc sought to target Israel.[48]

In more recent years, the Human Rights Committee has worked steadily on investigating compliance with the 1966 conventions, and its results have been credited with some effect.[49] The Committee has become more open and critical. Previously, in its summary report to the General Assembly, it had dealt only generally with the situations in particular states and tended to frame problems in terms of common findings among a number of state reports. The effect was more categorical than specific. Recently, the Committee members have established a practice of commenting personally on specific matters to the state delegations at the end of the proceedings. These comments form part of the Committee's official reports and state specific criticisms and evaluations. Some observers see the Committee's process and reports becoming much more frank.[50]

Under Resolution 1503 of the UN Economic and Social Council, the Human Rights Commission can investigate "situations which appear to reveal a consistent pattern of gross and reliably attested violations of human rights."[51] Information regarding systematic abuses is brought to the Commission by the Sub-Commission on the Prevention of Discrimination and the Protection of Minorities, and the Commission is responsible for the inquiry. Although the 1503 process requires that the inquiry and consideration be confidential, since 1978 the Commission has made public the names of states in question. Human rights NGOs have no official standing in the inquiries although they often provide the most specific and important information. More about NGOs will be seen later.

The confidentiality provision shields states from public opinion, but including it was necessary to get UN members to approve an investigative mandate for the Commission. Confidentiality does make it possible to persuade states to improve their practices without having to bow to pressure in public. The Commission can bring the situations in particular countries into public discussion under the Resolution 1235 process.[52] Publicity heightens the stakes, often producing heated debate in the Commission about findings and implications. Because member states vote and because violators avoid bad publicity, the process is fully subject to political jockeying and pressure. In fact, the 1235 process has had the perverse effect of inducing the worst violators to seek seats on the Commission to stifle disclosure.[53] The fact that states are so sensitive to bad reports demonstrates that human rights norms are powerful enough to cause public embarrassment. If common standards were not widely accepted, violators would be less concerned to conceal their behaviour.

Efforts to fashion more standards are underway. In recent years the Human Rights Commission has directed its attention to states that still use the death penalty. In 1997, it voted 27 to 11 (with 14 abstentions) on a resolution that requested states that apply the death penalty to begin reducing the number of offences for which it can be imposed and to look towards total abolition. The Commission has also continued work on a draft protocol that would include in the Convention on the Rights of the Child a provision setting a minimum age of 17 for military conscription. Also underway is a draft protocol that would institute regular visits to jails and prisons to ensure compliance with standards of humane treatment.[54]

Although most of the world's states have ratified the UN's main human rights conventions, human rights abuses continue around the world. Much of the problem rests with sovereign statehood, and it poses this dilemma: Human rights are "very largely rights to be exercised *against* state power; yet it is state power itself which is expected to *protect* those rights."[55] (my emphasis) International human rights law can serve as a public standard, and violations can be brought to light, but the practices can still continue. Some scholars believe that international standards and public exposure are enough to bring shame and embarrassment, but for determined states they are not enough to bring reform. At issue is the basic relationship between law and society. In the same scholar's words, "It is never law that creates order. [Instead] order has to exist before there can even be a soil for law to take root and grow in."[56] States can sign conventions, and the international community can identify and condemn violations, but the actual rule of human rights law depends on conditions within states themselves.

One difficulty is divergent national values. Some of the values contained in the international human rights conventions and covenants, particularly those predicated on the integrity and sanctity of the individual, reflect experience and understandings that have evolved in Western societies.[57] While states may endorse human rights conventions in the abstract, practical implementation may be another matter particularly if local cultures and beliefs are not hospitable. The 1979 Convention on the Elimination of All Forms of Discrimination against Women provides a good example. It was unanimously adopted, but many states attached reservations. As expressions of disagreement and reluctance, the reservations provided a discouragingly extensive display of "true feelings and practical intentions."[58] Added to cultural limitations is the political reality that respecting human rights, particularly those of free association, speech and assembly, would threaten most of the world's authoritarian regimes. For governments determined to stay in power, external pressure may be enough to cause embarrassment but not basic reform.

The Role of NGOs

An NGO is an organization that operates outside of government, is concerned with particular issues and works both through advocacy and direct action. In the role of advocacy, NGOs may seek to broaden public awareness about their particular issues and to influence the policies of governments and international bodies such as UN agencies. In the role of direct action, NGOs gather information,

operate programs and coordinate with other NGOs on common projects and political objectives. They normally have a permanent core staff but depend heavily on
volunteers and contributions. Many, such as Amnesty International and Greenpeace,
are large and have chapters in states around the world. NGOs are very numerous. One tally, which includes only NGOs large enough to operate in three or
more states and to get financial backing from more than one state, counts some
15,000.[59] Even more numerous but also smaller and more obscure are NGOs that
operate locally with small staffs and meagre funds. According to one count, there
are some 10,000 human rights NGOs in Bangladesh and 27,000 in Chile.

The hurdles facing NGOs can involve both advocacy and direct action. NGOs
that are backed by a broad public consensus and whose goals do not diverge from
those of their governments have the advantage of at least a sympathetic disposition
to their cause. That disposition may even allow tolerance for tactics that would
normally invite prosecution. Environmental advocacy and action are a good example. Anti-whaling groups benefit from international concern, and when they
interfere with a whaling ship, public sympathy is on their side. So also are most governments, which observe international regulations or have abandoned whaling
altogether. Against that alignment, governments that do not conform are in such
disfavour that direct action puts *them* on the defensive.

Conditions are less favourable when public opinion is divided and when governments regard demands as unfeasible. A good example was anti-nuclear weapons
advocacy during the cold war. On the one hand, the public was genuinely fearful,
and their apprehensions escalated during times of high East-West tension. During
the early 1980s, a time of high tension, a campaign for a freeze on the number of
nuclear weapons gained considerable public support in the United States and
Canada. At the same time, many people recognized that reduction and elimination
of nuclear weapons would have to be balanced and that controls would be required to ensure compliance with measures such as freezes. That view provided
broad public support for arms negotiations and agreements but much less for unilateral initiatives. The picture becomes less favourable when NGOs find no areas
of agreement with their governments, public indifference and little international support. Such groups may simply be ignored. In authoritarian states, apathy and lack
of support—or simply isolation—expose them to intimidation particularly at local
levels where members are individually vulnerable.

Human rights NGOs also face hurdles in the UN. They "pursue agendas in
which governments, intergovernmental organizations and NGOs [themselves] disagree profoundly about goals, ideas, the nature of violations and appropriate forms
of redress."[60] These divisions narrow the base of consensus, making it more difficult to advocate common approaches and pool resources. The intergovernmental organizations themselves are often ambivalent about NGOs. On the one hand,
they rely on NGOs for most information on human rights practices. The organizations also hope that by allowing an informal role for NGOs, they give them
"normative leverage" over governments that violate human rights.[61] On the other
hand, these organizations regard themselves as organizations of states and their
relationships with NGOs as arms-length. The NGOs' own governments, when

they have things to hide, find them nuisances and do their best to limit their influence. Within these constraints, NGOs take advantage of informal opportunities to exercise influence. NGO pressure played a role in the UN's adoption of Resolution 1503, which authorizes the Human Rights Commission to investigate allegations of systematic abuses and of Resolution 1235, which authorizes public consideration of findings. NGOs, in the view of some scholars, deserve much of the credit for the UN's human rights advances over the last half century.[62]

NGOs have gradually gained the latitude to bring facts directly to UN human rights bodies. One of best times for doing so is when the NGOs' own governments are under review. As we saw earlier, the Human Rights Committee is one body that hears such reports. Although NGOs have no official standing on the Committee and take no direct part in the review procedure, the committee has felt free to consult with NGOs for information about particular governments. The legal principle is that the Committee does not sit as a court and does not follow judicial procedure. Since the Committee's interest is in having the widest access to facts, NGOs can be treated as informed sources.[63] A particularly useful contribution is indicating to the Committee what questions it should ask state representatives during review of their reports. Committee members themselves are often unfamiliar with particular institutions, policies and conditions, but NGOs from the state know them well. The NGOs' interest in exposing their governments' shortcomings is to enlist international public opinion.

Authoritarian states are the most vulnerable to detailed factual scrutiny, but others are by no means immune. In the fall of 1998, it was Canada's turn to have its implementation of the Covenant on Economic, Social and Cultural Rights reviewed. Canadian NGOs had carefully prepared the members of the Committee on Economic, Social and Cultural Rights with specific questions regarding poverty and homelessness, conditions on native reserves and levels of literacy. The two days of questioning were punctuated by exasperated exchanges between the Committee and the Canadian representative over what the Committee regarded as sketchy and inadequate answers. In his summary comments, one of the Committee members lectured the Canadian representative about the humanitarian consequences of cutting back social programs.[64] The session was widely reported in Canada. Whistle-blowing NGOs face reprisals in some states. The threat became serious enough to prompt the Human Rights Commission to establish a procedure to help protect NGO members threatened by their governments. States named in a 1995 report about reprisals and intimidation against information-providing NGO members were: Guatemala, Colombia, Mexico, Argentina, Honduras, Peru, Rwanda, Burma, Zaire and Iran.[65]

NGOs are aided by human rights norms in two important ways. First, the norms provide a set of common values that make cooperation possible. Cooperation is important because NGOs, as voluntary, independent and often small organizations, depend for much of their effectiveness on informal networks among themselves. Common values and purposes support their work together with shared understandings and points of reference. The procedures of the international organizations themselves provide a political and institutional framework for coordinating strategies. For organizations that operate through widespread informal networks, these are important resources. Second, human rights norms provide a "common language to make arguments and procedures to advance claims."[66] In a constructivist perspective, common language represents an intersubjective understanding. It allows human rights NGOs to communicate within the same terms of reference, define themselves and their purposes by shared principles and frame their knowledge and experience in mutually useful and meaningful terms.

NGOs working at the local level, in the view of many scholars, represent the best promise for advancing human rights. Sovereignty and governmental determination limit the effectiveness of external pressure, but NGOs operate internally. Working within their own societies and drawing upon local people, NGOs press for government accountability, tolerance of political opposition and freer public expression. In doing so they push for change—in their governments' behaviour and in values and practices more generally. To the extent that these values are alien and new, NGOs serve as conduits from the international community. In some places, such as China, they face arrest. In other places, such as Argentina, they have helped their societies move from military dictatorship to democratically elected government. Some governments and societies may eventually accommodate the values of human rights, and others may successfully resist them. Where accommodation appears possible, human rights have a future. Where it does not appear possible, the prospects are compromised. In either case, international norms and opinion operate indirectly, providing legitimacy and support for the thousands of local efforts that ultimately shape the outcome. There is, however, a growing form of direct international action, and it operates judicially.

Outrage and International Tribunals

International outrage over war crimes in Bosnia and genocide in Rwanda prompted a rapid and dramatic expansion of **humanitarian law**. (Humanitarian law deals with crimes in wartime, and human rights law deals with crimes by governments against their citizens.) Key humanitarian law precedents were set by establishing a special Bosnia war crimes tribunal in The Hague. Its rulings represented the greatest expansion of humanitarian international law since adoption of the Geneva war crimes conventions in 1949.

Those developments, in turn, set the stage for a more recent but similarly far-reaching expansion of human rights law. A key precedent was established by Britain in 1998 and upheld in a second decision in 1999. The House of Lords, Britain's highest court, decided to allow Chile's former president Augusto Pinochet, who was visiting Britain for medical treatment, to be extradited to Spain to face prosecution for genocide and gross human rights violations committed against Spanish citizens under his rule. That decision recognized the authority of states to prosecute foreign nationals for human rights crimes committed elsewhere. In Pinochet's case, those crimes were committed in Chile. By this legal precedent, human rights violators now face prosecution in any state at any time. Supporters of human rights saw the decision as a crucial victory. For the legal antecedents, we turn first to humanitarian law.

The Nuremberg Tribunal, which tried Nazi war criminals after World War II, established the precedent that military officers and government leaders could be brought to justice for crimes against enemy soldiers and against civilians. The Geneva Conventions for the Protection of Victims of War, ratified in 1949, set out standards of humane treatment and obliged the signatory states to follow them. Until Bosnia, those standards applied to conflicts between states, not civil wars. In the face of the Bosnian war's continuing atrocities, public pressure mounted for a "rapid adjustment of law, process and institutions" to allow war criminals to be brought to justice.[67] The legal consequences affected both international and domestic jurisprudence.

Internationally, the means to prosecute war crimes were expanded. The Security Council, acting under Article 7 of the Charter, established the International Tribunal for Former Yugoslavia to try war criminals in The Hague. That was the first time a war crimes tribunal had been set up on behalf of the international community. The Nuremberg and Tokyo war crimes trials had been established by victorious powers. By constituting the Hague tribunal under Article 7, the Security Council acted under its authority to deal with threats to the peace. The Security Council's earlier sanctions against Serbia and its authorization of NATO enforcement dealt with the violation of the peace. By that rationale, the Hague tribunal would be part of restoring the peace. A more comprehensive justification would have required a special international treaty, and there was concern that ratification would take too long. Even so, the Security Council was within its powers in establishing the tribunal under Article 7.[68]

Actions by the Hague tribunal set important precedents in international humanitarian law. One result was to extend humanitarian law, which previously had applied to international wars, into civil wars. Doing that overrode the doctrine of sovereignty under which civil wars are domestic matters beyond the reach of international bodies. That extension had several important results. First, where international humanitarian law previously had applied to regular military forces, it now includes irregular forces, armed civilians and terrorists. Second, crimes against civilians can now be prosecuted when any "widespread or systematic" pattern of abuse can be established, expanding the Nuremberg standard to take account of localized atrocities that occur in civil wars. Third, acts do not need to be part of a state's policy to qualify as crimes against humanity. Acts by forces under local command can now be prosecuted. Finally, criminal liability extends to individuals who commit acts within a context of systematic abuse. Within that context, single acts are sufficient to be treated as crimes against humanity and subject to prosecution.[69]

The Reach of Domestic Courts

Domestic courts also set important precedents by extending their jurisdiction to foreign nationals for war crimes in foreign states. In 1997, the Bavarian Supreme Court convicted a former Yugoslav citizen for being an accessory to the murder of 14 Bosnians and sentenced him to five years. The German court was able to act because the Hague tribunal had not requested the person for trial. More importantly, the Bavarian court determined that it had not only jurisdiction under German law but an obligation. That obligation, the court held, originates in the Geneva Convention of 1949 on war crimes, which Germany ratified. On that basis, German courts have not only a domestic war crimes obligation but an international one. The Bavarian court's action established a precedent of universality in prosecuting crimes against humanity: domestic courts may try and sentence citizens of other states for war crimes committed elsewhere.[70] The implications are far-reaching. In one legal scholar's words, "Once internal atrocities are recognized as international crimes and thus as matters of major international concern, the right of third states to prosecute violators must be accepted."[71]

The same reasoning was applied in the Pinochet affair, but unlike the Bavarian case, this one involved international human rights law. (Remember the difference: humanitarian law deals with crimes in wartime, and human rights law deals with government crimes against their own populations.) The facts of the Pinochet affair are interesting to note. In the fall of 1998, a high court judge in Spain, knowing that Pinochet was temporarily in Britain, requested the British government to detain Pinochet and extradite him to Spain to be prosecuted for torture and genocide. The victims were Spanish nationals who were in Chile during Pinochet's rule. Three other European states were interested in extraditing Pinochet for prosecution in their courts. Switzerland was seeking him for the kidnap and murder of a Swiss student in Chile in 1977. Similar action was being considered by the French, Swedish and German governments. Belgium and Italy were preparing extradition requests on the basis of charges by expatriate Chileans of detainment and torture.

Pinochet appealed his arrest warrant in British court, and on October 28 the High Court ruled in his favour. Lord Bingham, Lord Chief Justice, based his decision on an interpretation of sovereignty. Pinochet, as a former head of state, enjoyed immunity from British jurisdiction. In favour of granting extradition, it was argued that Pinochet was responsible for some 4,000 deaths and amply deserved prosecution. In favour of denying extradition, it was argued that a far-reaching precedent could be set. On a visit to the United States, for example, Queen Elizabeth might be extradited to Argentina to answer charges for deaths caused by Britain in the Falklands War of 1982.[72]

The High Court decision was appealed to the House of Lords, which ruled in a dramatic 3-2 decision in favour of extradition. In a startling development, one of the Law Lords issuing the decision subsequently acknowledged an affiliation with Amnesty International and was excused from the case. Issuing a second decision in 1999, the Lords ruled 6-1 in favour of extradition. In reconciling the case to British law, they limited their judgment to crimes committed after 1988 (Pinochet came to power in 1973 and stepped down in 1990). In 1988, Britain had changed its legal code to make torture a crime that could be tried outside the state where it was committed. Lawyers arguing for Pinochet referred to a longer-standing legal doctrine restraining courts from ruling on official acts in other states. The Spanish government, arguing that prosecution for torture had become part of customary international law, advocated no restrictions on the terms of Pinochet's extradition. As a lifetime member of Chile's Senate, Pinochet is immune from prosecution there. The Lord's decision can be seen as seeking to reconcile expectations under customary international law with strictures under British domestic law. One interpretation is that the jurisdiction of domestic courts is still evolving.

A touchstone for the Bavarian and British courts are international conventions. By signing them, states make themselves subject to their provisions. The conservative interpretation is that states are obligated in their own conduct. The more expansive recent interpretation is that states are obligated to act when other states fail in their human rights responsibilities. Support for this broader view comes from customary international law. The difference is important to remember. Conventional law is found in specific international human rights conventions. Customary law is an accumulation of international and domestic court decisions, important declarations of principle by governments, provisions in states' laws and jurisprudence and acts by states that show an acknowledged obligation. The task of establishing the existence of customary law is demonstrating its recognition and effect in states' behaviour.

The accumulated moral authority and influence of the Universal Declaration on Human Rights along with the general acknowledgement of the major human rights conventions have been used to support the existence of human rights in customary international law. Some legal scholars believe that human rights have strong authority in customary law because the values and traditions are deeply rooted in the international community.[73] That view influenced the House of Lords' decision on Pinochet. Because international human rights law has become generally acknowledged, the majority side argued, domestic courts may act in cases involving foreign nationals and foreign jurisdictions. If these kinds of precedents accumulate, customary international law, applied by domestic courts, may become human rights' most active agent.

States gain no immunity by refusing to ratify human rights conventions. Instead, there is a strong legal precedent that holds states responsible regardless. The reasoning applies customary law: standards that become widely acknowledged assume legal force. The case was heard by the International Court of Justice. At issue was South Africa's occupation of Namibia and its installation of apartheid.[74] South Africa, the court ruled, occupied Namibia illegally, and one of the reasons for the ruling involved human rights. Because apartheid violated South Africa's obligations under the international conventions that prohibit discrimination, introducing it in Namibia made the occupation illegal. The fact that South Africa had not signed the convention on racial discrimination was no protection. Instead, the ICJ ruled, international human rights conventions "lay down the law which binds states which are members of the United Nations, *even though they have not signed the conventions themselves.*"[75] [my emphasis] The effect of the ruling was to apply human rights obligations to all states. In light of that principle, it can be argued that the obligations are indeed universal. That being so, human rights have a basis in customary international law.

Prosecution of humanitarian and human rights cases by the ICJ itself is limited by states' willingness to grant it compulsory jurisdiction—advance agreement to recognize ICJ decisions. Article 36 of the UN Charter provides that members may declare their recognition of the Court's compulsory jurisdiction whenever they wish, but many states, wary about sovereignty and adverse judgments, have never done that. Others have withdrawn or qualified their declarations. The United States refused to recognize the court's jurisdiction in a case between it and Nicaragua, and Canada terminated its declaration of unconditional jurisdiction in 1994 as part of a dispute with members of the North Atlantic Fishing Organization. As we saw in Chapter 3, Canada unilaterally declared jurisdiction beyond the internationally recognized 200-mile exclusive economic zone. Jurisdiction was at the heart of the Turbot War that followed, with Spain and the European Union claiming that Canada's seizure of vessels outside the zone violated international law. In terminating its declaration, Canada further claimed the right to "add, amend or withdraw" any reservations on the Court's jurisdiction.[76] Because of those kinds of limitations at the ICJ, international human rights law may find its most active venues in national courts.

The Environment

Global Warming: Local Sources, Global Results

Of all the environmental problems affecting the earth, global warming is the most universal. Emissions of carbon dioxide, methane gas and nitrous oxide anywhere in the world form a generalized and growing concentration in the atmosphere. Concentration in the earth's atmosphere prevents heat from the sun from reflecting from the earth back into space. The result is to trap more heat within the earth's atmosphere. Over time, the accumulated heat will cause a rise of the earth's average temperature. Unlike many environmental problems, this one is not local but global. There is a growing consensus among scientists that the problem is genuine and is related to human activity. Carbon dioxide is emitted from burning any fossil fuel, methane is produced by agriculture and from the oil, coal and gas industries and nitrous oxide from industry and motor vehicles.

That consensus comes from the Intergovernmental Panel on Climate Change (IPCC), established in 1988 in connection with the United Nations Environment Program and the World Meteorological Organization. Composed of 2,500 scientists from around the world and devoted to pooling scientific knowledge about global warming and its causes, its efforts over the last decade have been the most elaborate and complex scientific endeavour in the UN's history.[77] In its 1995 report, the IPCC linked the rise in atmospheric temperature to human activity and warned that the change will affect human health and well-being.

The increase in greenhouse gases (GHGs) is startling. Concentrations of carbon dioxide and methane were stable from the end of the last Ice Age 10,000 years ago until about 1800. Since then, carbon dioxide concentration has increased by 30 percent, methane by 145 percent and nitrous oxide by 15 percent. They are now higher than the levels measured in frozen glacier bubbles that provide air samples from the last 200,000 years.[78] At the present rates of accumulation, GHG concentrations may rise over the next century to levels not seen on earth in 50 million years. Compared to previous patterns, the present rate of change is rapid. The last major global temperature change began 15,000 years ago and ended the Ice Age. The temperature increase, enough to melt the glaciers that covered most of Canada, was only between four and five degrees celsius and stretched over 5,000 years. This time the same temperature increase may occur in only 100 years. As another index of the relatively small band of temperature and the historically large scale of change, the average temperature during the last Ice Age was only about five degrees celsius colder than now.[79]

What do these changes mean? Scientists are not sure. Forecasting the effects of temperature increases is uncertain and difficult because the earth's climate is interactive in complex ways. Atmospheric changes are related to changes in ocean temperatures and currents, dryness or humidity in local climates, the tracks of storms and violent weather and seasonal characteristics. It is also not known how GHGs interact in the atmosphere with ozone-depleting gases and smog. That complexity makes computer modeling difficult and uncertain, and projections even of basic factors such as average temperature cover a range of possible outcomes. What is projected for North America are more frequent and extreme summer heat waves, more frequent and severe summer thunderstorms and more extreme variation between heavy rainfalls and dry spells. Storm tracks may alter, and regions as a whole may become wetter or drier.[80]

For the world overall, the IPCC, in its second assessment report of 1995, put forward these possible consequences:

➤ a melting of the polar ice caps and a rise in sea levels, posing threats of inundation of low-lying islands and coastal areas and exposing larger areas to dangers of flooding from ocean storms

➤ more frequent and severe storms

➤ changes in rainfall patterns with the probability of an overall increase because of more moisture in the atmosphere

➤ alterations in the patterns of ocean currents

➤ expansion of the zones of tropical diseases

➤ large migrations of people abandoning desert or flood areas

➤ benefits to agriculture from more carbon dioxide and longer growing seasons balanced against larger zones of aridity and desertification

➤ the need for all organisms, plant and animal, to make unprecedentedly rapid adjustments to change[81]

The IPCC scientists warned of damage to human health through increased disease and loss of life through storms and floods. Scientists generally acknowledge that the GHG accumulation has now reached the point that stabilization at the current level would require reducing emissions by half. Since that would require enormous transformations in the way the world's societies use energy—from firewood to jet fuel—scientists recognize that there will be global warming. The question is how much warming there will be.

Following the IPCC's establishment in 1988, the UN Conference on the Environment and Development was held at Rio de Janeiro in 1992. Emerging from that conference was the Framework Convention on Climate Change (FCCC). Its purpose, as set out in Article 2 of the 1992 Climate Change Convention, was to "stabilize greenhouse gas concentrations in the atmosphere at a level that will prevent dangerous interference in the climate system."[82] It obligated signatory states to begin inventory systems to locate and measure sources of GHG emission and to cooperate in efforts to reduce them. For industrial states, a specific emission reduction target was set, requiring a return to the level of emission of 1990. No levels were set for developing states, which were held to the less stringent objective of "aiming" to reduce emissions, and the industrial states were intended to become the leaders in controlling GHGs.

By 1995, it was clear that most states were nowhere near close to meeting these targets. Canada, for example, had pledged that it would stabilize its GHG emissions at the 1990 level by the year 2000. Instead, between 1990 and 1995 Canadian GHG emissions increased by 9.4 percent and from that level to 11 percent between 1995 and 1996.[83] There was also realization that stabilizing emissions at the 1990 levels would not be enough to stop the growth of GHGs. These results persuaded the FCCC members, meeting in Berlin in 1995, that specific targets were necessary and had to be extended beyond 2000. There was also realization that voluntary targets would not be effective. Mandatory standards were needed instead. A meeting of the FCCC states in Geneva the next year confirmed this intention and set the stage for an FCCC conference in Kyoto in 1997 to draft a more effective agreement.

Of all the measures that must be taken to combat environmental problems, controlling GHG emissions is the most pervasive because the sources are at the centre of economic activity: energy for industry and transportation, heat for homes and buildings, by-products of large-scale activities such as oil refining and coal mining. Greater reliance on electricity is not a solution if it is generated by burning fossil fuels. The problem is worsened by any activity that reduces carbon dioxide-consuming plant life: timber cutting in states such as Canada and forest clearing in the developing world. Adequately addressing the GHG problem requires major changes—reducing fossil fuel use in all its applications.

Some argue that the adjustments are not a net loss because they tend to generate compensating efficiencies that actually lower costs. They also argue that many existing technologies can be made much cleaner and more efficient given the proper incentive. Regulation of car emissions, for example, has led to major improvements in internal combustion technology.

Another optimistic view is that states, even less wealthy ones, have remarkable abilities to substitute and adapt. We saw that reasoning in Chapter 11 with the ability of states to persevere through bruising economic sanctions. The same principle applies here: when faced with necessity, states are more resourceful than they may appear.

Others look to the investment needed in new technologies to achieve the significant reductions required. Design codes for everything from houses to pipelines will have to be changed. Any system in which operating parameters include climatic conditions will be affected. Equally large adjustments are needed in people's personal lives and habits—decreased use of automobiles, for example. In the developing world, adjustment means halting clearance of tropical forests. Changes will be widespread and felt at both aggregate and personal levels. The costs will not be marginal ones.

Who Pays?

It makes a big difference how each state's fair share of adjustment is calculated and apportioned. Using the same 1990 national emission levels as a baseline, setting an overall target of a 20-percent reduction and following the FCCC's principle of assigning reductions only to industrialized states, two alternative principles of apportioning each individual state's contribution produce very different results. One principle allocates reduction on a per capita basis so that people in all states bear the same burden and make the same absolute reduction. Reductions are also relative; some would have to cut much more than others. Who would be relatively worse off under a per capita formula? Both the efficient states and the least industrially developed ones would have to make big cuts (remember that the overall average target is 20 percent). France, for example would have to reduce by 35.7 percent, Japan by 27.4 percent and Portugal by a whopping 60 percent. The winners would be states that are less efficient. The United States would only have to cut by 12.2 percent, Canada by 14.5 percent and Australia by 15.2 percent.[84]

An alternative principle is to allocate reductions on the basis of carbon dioxide emissions per unit of Gross Domestic Product. As we saw in the last chapter, GDP measures individual shares of contribution to the total value of goods and services produced by a state's economy. High levels of GDP reflect advanced industrialization and large outputs per person. The states penalized under this formula are the less efficient (more units of carbon dioxide per unit of GDP): Australia would have to cut by 35 percent, the United States by 34.5 percent and Canada by 23.6 percent. In contrast, France and Japan would have to make no cuts and Portugal only 15 percent.[85] Given the adjustment costs we just saw, the differences between the two formulas translate to billions of dollars and to major differences in the burdens of adjustment.

A stable atmospheric temperature is a classic example of a **public good**. These are commodities or benefits that are available to anyone. In the last chapter we saw that governments provide some public goods, such as currencies and highways, to support economic activities. One of the characteristics that identify public goods from others is that they are non-excludable. Anyone can enjoy them. A city sidewalk, for example, is available for all to use; in fact, the only way of reserving sidewalk use to some people and denying it to others is to charge tolls. Environmental collective goods can be completely non-excludable—there is no way to grant breathing of air to some and deny it to others. *Clean* air is an excellent example of an environmental public good.

What if some people have to pay to produce or protect a particular good but are unable to keep others from enjoying it for free? People tuning into a listener-supported television or FM station during a fund-raising drive experience that situation. If viewers and listeners do not support the station, the announcers say, its programming will not be available to enjoy. People who believe they should contribute their fair share do so. Some, however, make the calculation that since other people are paying enough (the station is, in fact, broadcasting), *they* can bear the cost. Political economists call this behaviour free-riding. It takes advantage of a non-excludable public good (a television channel) without sharing the cost of providing it.

The same principle applies to improving public goods. Any state that reduces its air pollution will improve air quality for everyone. The principle applies as well to protecting public goods: any state that reduces its GHG emissions will prevent generalized climate warming. Under the two allocation formulas, the same public good will be produced (a 20-percent overall reduction), and its benefits will be available to everyone. Some states will have to pay heavily, and others will get off lightly. The choice of formula determines which states those will be. The **free-rider problem** appeared in the FCCC negotiations at Kyoto, as we will see next.

The Kyoto Protocol

The agreement negotiated as a protocol for the FCCC members at Kyoto, Japan in 1997 tightens the previous requirements. As we saw, there was concern that voluntary requirements would not be enough to get significant reductions. To close that gap, the Kyoto Protocol set legally binding limits over five years although these apply only to the developed states. The protocol also allows states to trade their emissions quotas amongst themselves, and it allows developed and developing states to join in cooperative reduction programs. Finally, the protocol establishes reporting procedures to monitor compliance.

Reaching these provisions required hard bargaining. One major split was between the developing and industrialized states. The developing states insisted that the greenhouse problem was not their fault. Since it had been generated over the years by the industrialized states' development, it is those states that should bear the cost of reductions. Adopting control technologies, the developing states argued, would impose a disadvantage that had not been present when the developed states industrialized. At the developing states' insistence, they were exempted from the mandatory reduction targets.

Among the industrialized states, the question was how much GHGs should be cut and by whom. The European Union and the United States argued for the same reduction for all industrialized states. Other states, including Australia, Japan, Norway and Iceland, argued for differential cuts because of the differences between their economies and the others. In the end, an overall reduction target for the developed states was set at 5.2 percent, with the EU agreeing to an eight percent reduction and the United States to a seven percent reduction..[86] Canada agreed to cut its emissions by six percent.

Trading emissions quotas also evoked sharp differences. The idea behind the proposal is that states that are efficient enough to bring their emissions below

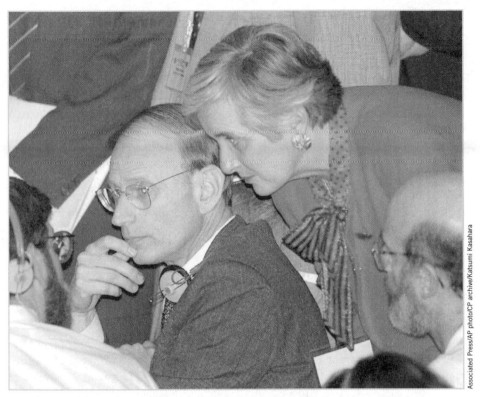

Associated Press/AP photo/CP archive/Katsumi Kasahara

Chief U.S. negotiator Stuart Eizenstat, left, listens to Canadian Environment Minister Christine Stewart during a meeting at the UN Conference on Climate Change in Kyoto, Japan in December 1997.

their assigned level can sell the surplus to another state, which can use it as a credit against its own assigned level. Many economists favour this approach to pollution abatement because it gives a cash reward for exceeding a reduction target. With GHGs, states that would have difficulty meeting their requirement can use the credit as a cheaper alternative. The overall result is the same because one state's surplus is simply exchanged for another's deficit. India, China and other developing states vehemently denounced the idea. Adopting the proposal would mean recognizing an obligation to meet set targets, which they opposed. There was also distaste for paying developed states for permission to pollute. Advocates of the proposal argued that it would greatly soften the developing states' cost of adjustment. The issue nearly caused the conference to collapse.[87] In the end, a compromise was reached that would allow trading of quotas but only among developed states and only then in connection with new emission-reduction projects.

Whether the Kyoto Protocol is ever implemented is problematic. A major hurdle is the U.S. Senate, which regards the developing states' exclusion as free riding. Until targets are set for them, the Protocol is unlikely to be ratified. American abstention may give other major states, which are also facing costly adjustments to stay on target, an excuse to drop out. Indeed, *The Economist* regards the inability to win commitment even in principle from the developing states as the Kyoto conference's biggest failure.[88] China, which already has heavily polluting industries, has the potential to become a fossil-fuel superburner as it develops and at present is covered only by aspirational obligations.

Some international legal specialists see aspirational, but not substantive, commitments as characteristic of international environmental agreements. Only two of the initiatives emerging from the Rio Conference in 1992 fall under the Vienna Convention on the Law of Treaties' provisions for mandatory compliance. The others are much less obligatory declarations. Without binding commitments, parties to agreements can decide how and when to comply. One interpretation of such behaviour is that it is a way of satisfying expectations from domestic audiences and other states without having to give up sovereign discretion or abide with onerous requirements. In that form, they remain more declarations of good intentions than solid commitments.[89]

On the positive side, the Kyoto conference was seen as a major step forward in environmental diplomacy and a valuable way of raising the awareness of governments and the public of the need for prompt and effective collective action. What becomes of the initiative—if not the Kyoto Protocol, then some other joint means for dealing with GHGs—is an important test of states' ability to cooperate in the face of a demonstrated peril.

Do norms and public values bear on states' actions on the environment? We saw considerable influence in human rights through the accumulation of a widespread consensus and its practical expression in customary international law. What about the environment? There are grounds for pessimistic and optimistic views. On the pessimistic side, the material costs of compliance can be formidable even at the relatively modest levels set at Kyoto. The industrial democratic states bear few of the adjustment costs when they advocate human rights because those rights are already practiced. Because their economies are well developed and complex, because their governments may be reluctant to court electoral unpopularity by imposing the stringent measures that will be required and because voluntary measures alone have not been enough, meeting the Kyoto protocol's targets is probably an unrealistic goal. The public, which espouses environmental values in principle, may be much less willing to make practical changes in its way of life. If the developing states' behaviour at Kyoto is any indicator, they regard GHGs as the wealthy states' responsibility.

On the optimistic side, one could argue that global warming is now widely understood and is regarded more seriously. That result is a credit to the influence of science on public affairs and on the ability of international bodies such as the UN to set collective agendas. There is also growing awareness that environmental problems are inherently collective ones and beyond the ability of any government to solve. That awareness is reflected in the number of existing international institutions devoted to particular areas of environmental regulation. There is already a sizeable number of international environmental institutions that work to coordinate state activities, and some do so effectively. At the same time, there is recognition that international legal commitments are not enough. Ways must be found to design effective international institutions that can use their own authority and expertise to tackle problems day to day and enlist the effective participation of states.[90] Awareness of this need, too, can be seen as encouraging.

Finally, at both the global and the grass-roots levels, are environmental NGOs. They focus much of their effort on the UN because of the number of its programs that have environmental dimensions and because the UN has shown itself attentive to environmental issues. Some environmental NGOs are well funded, operate in many states and are well skilled in generating public interest. Greenpeace, the largest, has offices in 30 states and a $100 million budget. At the local level in various states, the number of environmental NGOs is immense—200,000 is one estimate.[91] As with local human rights NGOs, environmental NGOs serve as conduits for information and expertise. Just as importantly, they work to channel funds from international organizations and donor states to local projects, and, by working with local governments, they can implement environmental concerns in practical policies and projects. And like human rights NGOs, they transmit values as well as information. On the developed- state side of the relationship, they can build environmental concerns into overall program design and priorities of loans and grants. One organization that has begun taking environmental NGO views into account is the World Bank. Like human rights NGOs, one of the environmental NGOs' assets is that their members care deeply about their purpose and are willing to work hard.

In tackling global warming, we took on the most difficult case—a problem with universal scope, significant adjustment costs, strikingly different perceptions of responsibility and incentives to procrastinate or take a free ride. Precisely because of these challenges, how the world's governments meet global warming in the coming years may be the ultimate test of abilities to cooperate in the face of common necessity.

Summary

We have seen that norms, while they embody no material force, can have significant influence on behaviour. The absence of international authority makes the effect of norms variable. Compliance is easiest to establish when following a norm accords with a state's pragmatic interests. It is more difficult when no practical interest is served. That is so because norms, unlike material factors, operate invisibly. Establishing their effect means inferring how they affected the preferences and calculations of the people who make state decisions. At the same time, regularities in state behaviour are apparent enough that some scholars discern an international society based on common values and understandings.

Human rights are based on values that dignify and protect the individual person. Over the last 50 years they have became established in UN human rights conventions and in the domestic law of states such as Canada. That acceptance has given human rights increasing stature in customary international law. The Hague tribunal has established new precedents in the prosecution of war crimes, and in late 1998, the British House of Lords decided to allow extradition of a foreign ex-head of state to face charges of torture and genocide. In both cases, views of jurisdiction and obligation were derived from conventional and customary international law.

The environment presents a different set of problems. Protection is based not only on normative values but also on practical self-interest. With GHGs, the problem is truly global because all states, regardless of their contribution to the problem, share the same consequences. Awareness of the problem prompted the Framework Convention on Climate Change (FCCC), and an effort to strengthen its provisions led to the Kyoto Protocol. The protocol marks the most comprehensive environmental diplomacy to date. Whether states meet the challenge of compliance remains to be seen.

ENDNOTES

1   Gary Goertz and Paul F. Diehl, "Toward a Theory of International Norms," *Journal of Conflict Resolution* 36 (December 1992) 644.

2   Hedley Bull, *The Anarchical Society: A Study of Order in World Politics*, London: Macmillan, 1977, pp. 23–24.

3   Barry Buzan, "From International System to International Society: Structural Realism and Regime Theory Meet the English School," *International Organization* 47 (Summer 1993) 330.

4   Bull, *The Anarchical Society*, pp. 26, 27.

5   *ibid.*, p. 42.

6   James A. Caporaso, "International Relations Theory and Multilateralism: The Search for Foundations," *International Organization* 46 (Summer 1992) 626.

7   Buzan, "From International System to International Society," p. 346.

8   James N. Rosenau, *Along the Domestic-Foreign Frontier: Exploring Governance in a Turbulent World*, Cambridge: Cambridge University Press, 1997, p. 177.

9   Buzan, "From International System to International Society," pp. 345, 349.

10   Christian Reuss-Smit, "The Constitutional Structure of International Society," *International Organization* 51 (Fall 1997) 569.

11   Friedrich Kratochwil and John Gerard Ruggie, "International Organization: A State of the Art on the Art of the State," *International Organization* 40 (Fall 1986) 768.

12   Caporaso, "International Relations Theory and Multilateralism," 626

13   Ronald Jepperson, Alexander Wendt, Peter Katzenstein, "Norms, Identity, and Culture in National Security," in Peter Katzenstein, ed., *The Culture of National Security: Norms and Identity in Wrold Politics*, New York: Columbia University Press, 1996, p. 54.

14   David Dessler, "What's At Stake in the Agent-Structure Debate?" *Internaitonal Organization* 43 (Summer 1989) 472.

15   Caporaso, "International Relations Theory and Multilateralism," p. 626.

16   Alexander Wendt, "Anarchy is What States Make of It: The Social Construction of Power Politics," *International Organization* 46 (Spring 1993) 417.

17   *ibid.*, p. 399.

18   Buzan, "From International System to International Society," p. 349.

19   Oran R. Young, "The Effectiveness of International Institutions: Hard Cases and Critical Variables," in James N. Rosenau and Ernst-Otto Czemipel, eds., *Governance without Government: Order and Change in World Politics*, Cambridge; Cambridge University Press, 1992, p. 188–89.

20   Goertz and Diehl, "Toward A Theory of International Norms," p. 640.

21   Gregory A. Raymond, "Problems and Prospects in the Study of International Norms," *Mershon International Studies Review* 41 (November 1997) 215.

22   Rey Koslowski and Friedrich Kratochwil, "Understanding Change in International Politics: The Soviet Empire's Demisse and the International System," *International Organization* 48 (Spring 1994) 225.

23   Reuss-Smit, "The Constitutional Structure of International Society," 570.

24   Andrew P. Cottrell and James W. Davis, Jr., "How Do International Institutions Matter? The Domestic Impact of International Norms," *International Studies Quarterly* 40 (December 1996) 452-53.

25   Friedrich Kratochwil and John Gerard Ruggie, "International Organization: A State of the Art on an Art of the State," *International Organization* 40 (Fall 1986) 767.

26   Koslowski and Kratochwil, "Understanding Change in International Politics," 225.

27   Kratochwil and Ruggie, "International Organization," 767.

28   Dessler, "What's At Stake," p. 472.

29   Young, "The Effectiveness of International Institutions," p. 177.

30   Janice E. Thomson, "Explaining the Regulation of Transnational Practices: A State-Building Approach," in James N. Rosenau and Ernst-Otto Czempiel, eds., *Governance without Government: Order and Change in World Politics*, Cambridge: Cambridge University Press, 1992, p. 198.

31   Kathryn Sikkink, "The Power of Principled Ideas: Human Rights Policies in the United States and Western Europe," in Judith Goldstein and Robert O. Keohane, eds., *Ideas and Foreign Policy: Beliefs, Institutions, and Political Change,* Ithaca: Cornell University Press, 1993, p. 157.

32   Ramashav Roy, "The Limits of the Genealogical Approach to International Politics," *Alternatives* 13 (January 1988) 79.

33   Robert W. Cox, "Gramsci, Hegemony, and International Relations: An Essay on Method," *Millenium* 12 (Summer 1983) 172.

34   Tom Keating and Nicholas Gammer, "The 'New Look' in Canada's Foreign Policy," *International Journal* 48 (Fall 1993) 743.

35   Kathryn Sikkink, "The Power of Principled Ideas: Human Rights Policies in the United States and Western Europe," in Judith Goldstein and Robert O. Keohane, eds., *Ideas and Foreign Policy: Beliefs, Institutions, and Political Change*, Ithaca: Cornell University Press, 1993, p. 146.

36   Reuss-Smit, "The Constitutional Structure of International Society," p. 582.

37   S.A. Williams and A.L.C. de Mestral, *An Introduction to International Law: Chiefly as Interpreted and Applied in Canada*, Toronto: Butterworth's, 1987, p. 305.

38   *ibid.*, p. 307.

39   Carl Aage Norgaard, *The Position of the Individual in International Law*, Copenhagen: Munksgaard, 1962, p. 98.

40   Anne E. Bayevsky, "International Human Rights Law in Canadian Courts," in Irwin Cotler and F. Pearl Eliadis, eds., *International Human Rights Law: Theory and Practice*, Montreal: The Canadian Human Rights Foundation, 1992, pp. 125, 127.

41   Daniela Bassan, "The Canadian *Charter* and Public International Law: Redefining the State's Power to Deport Aliens," *Osgoode Hall Law Journal* 34 (Fall 1996) 591.

42   *ibid.*, p. 588.

43   *ibid*, p. 590.

44   Cottrell and Davis, "How Do International Institutions Matter?" p. 453.

45   Robert Jennings, "The International Court of Justice after Fifty Years," *American Journal of International Law* 89 (July 1995) 495.

46   Egon Schwelb, "The International Court of Justice and the Human Rights Clauses of the Charter," *American Journal of International Law* 66 (April 1972) 341.

47   Cathal J. Nolan, "The Human Rights Committee," in Robert O. Matthews and Cranford Pratt, eds., *Human Rights in Canadian Foreign Policy*, Kingston and Montreal: McGill-Queen's University Press, 1988, p. 103.

48 John W. Foster, "The U.N. Commission on Human Rights," in Matthews and Pratt, eds, *Human Rights in Canadian Foreign Policy*, p. 88.

49 Geoffrey Best, "Justice, International Relations, and Human Rights," *International Affairs* 71 (October 1995) 792.

50 Fausto Pocar, "Current Developments and Approach in the Practice of the Human Rights Committee in Consideration of State Reports," in Asbjorn Eide and Jan Helgesen, eds., *The Future of Human Rights Protection in a Changing World*, Oslo: Norwegian University Press, 1991, pp. 55–56.

51 John Humphrey, *No Distant Millennium: The International Law of Human Rights,* Paris: United Nations Educational, Scientific and Cultural Organization, 1989, p. 105.

52 *ibid.,* p. 109.

53 Felice D. Gaer, "Reality Check: Human Rights NGOs Confront Governments at the UN," in Thomas G. Weiss and Leon Gordenker, eds., *NGOs, The UN, and Global Governance*, Boulder, CO: Rienner, 1996, p. 53.

54 Michael Dennis, "The Fifty-Third Session of the UN Commission on Human Rights," *American Journal of International Law* 92 (January 1998) 113, 117.

55 Best, "Justice, International Relations, and Human Rights," p. 788.

56 *ibid.,* p. 794.

57 Williams and de Mestral, *An Introduction to International Law*, p. 307.

58 Best, "Justice, International Relations, and Human Rights," p. 790.

59 Leon Gordenker and Thomas G. Weiss, "Pluralizing Global Governance: Analytical Approaches and Dimensions," in Weiss and Gordenker, eds., *NGOs, The UN, and Global Governance*, p. 17.

60 *ibid.,* p. 41.

61 Michael N. Barnett, "Bringing in the New World Order: Liberalism, Legitimacy, and the United Nations," *World Politics* 49 (July 1997) 539.

62 Gaer, "Reality Check," p. 51.

63 Pocar, "The Human Rights Committee" p. 57.

64 Southam Newspapers, November 27, 28, 1998.

65 Gaer, "Reality Check," p. 56.

66 Kathryn Sikkink, "Human Rights, Principled Issue-Networks, and Sovereignty in Latin America," *International Organization* 47 (Summer 1993) 416.

67 Theodor Meron, "International Criminalization of Internal Atrocities," *American Journal of International Law* 89 (July 1995) 555.

68 Christopher Greenwood, "The International Tribunal for Former Yugoslavia," *International Affairs* 69 (October 1993) 646.

69 Theodor Meron, "War Crimes Law Comes of Age," *American Journal of International Law* 92 (July 1998) 464–65.

70 Christoph J.M. Safferling, *Public Prosecutor v. Djajic*, No 20/96, *American Journal of International Law* 92 (July 1998) 528–30.

71 Meron, "International Criminalization," p. 576.

72 *Economist*, October 31, 1998, p. 62.

73 Theodor Meron, "The Geneva Conventions as Customary Law," *American Journal of International Law* 81 (April 1987) 350.

74 *Advisory Opinion on the Legal Consequences for States of the Continued Presence of South Africa in Namibia*, International Court of Justice, *Reports* 1971, p. 16.

75 Schwelb, "The International Court of Justice and the Human Rights Clauses," 351.

76 Robert Jennings, "The International Court of Justice after Fifty Years," *American Journal of International Law* 89 (July 1995) 495..

77 Clare Breidenich, Daniel Magraw, Ann Rowley and James W. Rubin, "The Kyoto Protocol to the United Nations Framework Convention on Climate Change," *American Journal of International Law* 92 (April 1998) 316.

78   Gordon A. McBean and Henry G. Hengeveld, "Climate Change," *Policy Options* 19 (May 1998) 4.

79   Stuart Eizenstat, "Stick with Kyoto: A Sound Start on Global Warming," *Foreign Affairs* 77 (May/June 1998) 120.

80   McBean and Hengeveld, "Climate Change," 4, 5.

81   Breidenich, Magraw, Rowley and Rubin, "The Kyoto Protocol" 316

82   Brendan McGivern, Introductory Note, Conference of the Parties to the Framework Convention on Climate Change: Kyoto Protocol, *International Legal Materials* 37 (January 1998) 22.

83   Robert Hornung, "The Voluntary Challenge Program Will Not Work," *Policy Options* 19 (May 1998) 11.

84   Ian H. Rowlands, "International Fairness and Justice in Addressing Global Climate Change," *Environmental Politics* 6 (Fall 1997) 10.

85   *ibid.* 12.

86   Breidenich, Magraw, Rowley and Rubin, "The Kyoto Protocol," 320.

87   McGivern, "Introductory Note," 26.

88   *Economist* December 13, 1997, 16.

89   Alberto Szekely, "A Commentary on the Softening of International Environmental Law," *Proceedings, American Society of International Law, 1997*, 238.

90   Michael Zurn, "The Rise of International Environmental Politics: A Review of Current Research," *World Politics* 50 (July 1998) 633–37.

91   Ken Conca, "Greening the UN: Environmental Organizations and the UN System," in Weiss and Gordenker, eds., *NGOs, the UN and Global Governance*, 106.

WEBLINKS

New Zealand's Justice Ministry has a database of international agreements. Related treaty Web sites are listed in Part V:
www.justice.govt.nz/pubs/reports/1966/agreements

Indiana University's law school has a directory of foreign and international law sites and resources:
www.inlaw.indy.indiana.edu/library/international

The International Humanitarian Law Review site contains a list of treaties, protocols, documents and related organizations:
www.icrc.org.unicc/ihl_eng.nsf

The United Nations Division for the Advancement of Women can be found at:
www.undp.org/fwcw/daw.htm

The Human Rights Internet maintains a directory of Web sites:
www.hri.ca/

The International Centre for Human Rights and Democratic Development can be found at:
www.ichrdd.ca

Amnesty International's site is:
www.amnesty.org

Human Rights Watch issues regular reports and updates:
www.hrw.org

The Canadian Institute of Environmental Law and Policy can be found at:
www.web.net/cielap/

Environmental NGO network links are maintained by the Earth Council:
www.ecouncil.ac.cr/cfbin/cfml

and by the National Councils for Sustainable Development:
www.ncsdnetwork.org

Greenpeace's site, with links to other NGOs, is:
www.greenpeaecanada.org

The Sierra Club's site is:
www.sierraclub.ca

Glossary

Absolute gains: Gains that yield a net increase in welfare. Institutionalists base their confidence in international cooperation on states' rational interests in securing these benefits in common. (See relative gains) Ch. 2 (p. 29)

Agency culture: Within government departments, a set of stable outlooks, ways of defining and addressing problems and policy rationales that are socially anchored and transmitted to new employees and that shape agency actions and self-justification. Ch. 9 (p. 199)

Alliance: An agreement among states to provide mutual assistance in time of military attack by another state or alliance. Ch. 11 (p. 240)

Anarchy: Absence of a central authority to impose order. The order that exists in anarchy is a result of the actions of individuals. In IR, those individuals most often are states. Ch. 1 (p. 3)

Autarky: Complete economic independence and detachment from trade. Ch. 12 (p. 301)

Bandwagoning: Joining a rising coalition in order to avoid being victimized by it or to share in its prospective benefits. Ch. 10 (p. 240)

Bipolarity: A concentration of military power and political influence in two predominant and opposed states. The international system during the cold war was regarded as bipolar. (See multipolarity) Ch. 9 (p. 188)

Boycott: A refusal to buy goods from designated states or suppliers. A tool of economic sanctions. (See embargo). Ch. 11 (p. 261)

Buck-passing: Abstaining from acting on a joint commitment in the hope that other members will act effectively on their own. Ch. 10 (p. 240)

City-state: A political unit possessing population and a sovereign government but limited territorially to a city and its environs. Ch. 6 (p. 103)

Collective security: An agreement among states to unite against any state that violates the peace, whoever that state may be. Ch. 11 (p. 269)

Common security: A term designating post-cold war proposals for European security in which emphasis shifts from military deterrence to preventive intervention in local and regional conflicts. Ch. 11 (p. 275)

Comparative advantage: The theory which holds that states do best when they concentrate on producing goods in which they enjoy the greatest efficiencies and trading them with other states for goods in which they enjoy the greatest efficiencies. Ch. 12 (p. 307)

Complex governance: A term coined to characterize a variegated pattern of political integration in which states pool their authority in a common institution in some policy areas, cooperate closely in other areas and retain individual control in still others. Ch. 8 (p. 173)

Constructivism: A recent theory of IR that emphasizes interaction and the mutual understandings arising from it, as the basis of state role identities and state behaviour. Ch. 4 (p. 56)

Conventional international law: Norms and obligations based on formal commitments made by states in adopting treaties and international conventions. (See customary international law) Ch. 13 (p. 330)

Critical Theory: A view of the international system that emphasizes a powerful centre and a subordinate periphery. Dominance is maintained not only by the centre's material position but also by its ability to shape people's understandings to accord with its interests. Ch. 5 (p. 71)

Customary international law: Norms and obligations based on commonly held values and understandings as expressed in international agreements and declarations, domestic legislation and court decisions, and official statements of policy. (See conventional international law). Ch. 13 (p. 330)

Dependency: A doctrine of international political economy that emphasizes centre-periphery relations and the permanent subordination of peripheral states. Ch. 12 (p. 299)

Deterrence: The ability to discourage attack. Ch. 11 (p. 265)

Economic sanctions: Use of embargoes and boycotts to coerce a target state by harming its economy. (see boycott, embargo) Ch. 11 (p. 283)

Embargo: A refusal to sell goods to designated states or buyers. A tool of economic sanctions. (See boycott) Ch. 11 (p. 261)

Empirical statehood: The doctrine that states, to be recognized as sovereign, must have practical political, administrative and economic viability. Ch. 6 (p. 113)

English School: A theoretical approach to IR which was stimulated by the work of the late Oxford scholar Hedley Bull. The English School accepts anarchy as the international system's basic structure but emphasizes order arising from international law and common norms. Ch. 1 (p. 10)

Epistemology: The branch of philosophy that deals with the way things are known. Ch. 5 (p. 73)

Export-led development: An economic strategy that focuses on using sales in foreign markets for earnings to be used for economic and industrial development. Ch. 12 (p. 295)

Feminism: An eclectic movement whose basic premise holds gender to be primary. To represent human experience fully, any theory or description must incorporate gender as a fundamental emphasis. Excluding gender is an act of political power that minimizes or ignores women's experience. Ch. 5 (p. 83)

Fordism: Named after Henry Ford, highly standardized industrial mass production that concentrates activity in large installations that either manufacture most of the necessary components on site or receive them from local suppliers. This form is being supplanted in many industries by widely dispersed component production and assembly. Ch. 8 (p. 173)

Foreign direct investment (FDI): Investment by corporations or entrepreneurs in productive facilities in another state. Ch. 12 (p. 313)

Free-rider problem: In political economy, use of a public good by individuals who do not share the costs of providing it. (See public good) Ch. 13 (p. 344)

Game theory: The calculation of optimal interactive behaviour on the basis of assumptions about information, utilities, gain-seeking motives and rationality. Ch. 2 (p. 27)

Harmonization: In political economy, a deliberate effort among states, or among jurisdictions within states, to remove differences in their public policies and regulations, particularly those that affect business and investment. Ch. 8 (p. 158)

Hegemony: A predominance of influence over others. Ch. 5 (p. 76)

Hierarchy: An ascending order of power and authority. Ch. 5 (p. 80)

Human rights: Rights enjoyed by individuals by virtue of their humanity and regardless of political or economic circumstance. Ch. 13 (p. 326)

Humanitarian law: International law governing the treatment of individuals in time of war. Ch. 13 (p. 336)

Import Substitution Industrialization: A policy of encouraging industrialization by providing domestic producers a protected national market. Ch. 12 (p. 301)

Institutionalism: One of IR's main theories emphasizing the anarchic nature of the international system, the primacy of states and state interests as the central phenomena. The possibilities of cooperation within common rules and organizations are its emphasis. Ch. 2 (p. 19)

Interdependence: In IR, the condition in which actions by one state affect others even when the result is not intentional. Ch. 3 (p. 40)

International law: The body of rules, norms, treaties and customs that apply to the obligations and conduct of states. Ch. 13 (p. 321)

International system: The totality of international actors together with the rules and institutions that exist among them. Ch. 1 (p. 3)

Intersubjective understanding: Knowledge and expectations that arise between individuals as they interact. Over time they can become powerful and mutually reinforcing guides to action. Constructivists seek intersubjective understandings in the interactions of states. (See Constructivism) Ch. 4 (p. 65)

Isolationism: A preference for detachment from the international system and particularly from agreements and commitments. Ch. 1 (p. 254)

Liberal IR Theory: In its most recent form, a view of IR that emphasizes that states are embedded in their societies and that group interests are the source of the preferences that shape political action. Reconciling the preferences arising from domestic politics with the behavior of other states is the role of governments. Ch. 3 (p. 37)

Liberal peace: A term denoting the pattern of war-avoidance among liberal democratic states. Ch. 9 (p. 213)

Marginalization: Relegation away from the centres of power, influence, authority, attention, and wealth. Ch. 5 (p. 77)

Mercantilism: A doctrine of political economy that subordinates all economic decisions to the interests of the state. Ch. 12 (p. 292)

Metatheory: Theory about the process of theorizing. Ch. 5 (p. 72)

Microeconomic reasoning: As applied by Neorealists, an emphasis on the situation of an individual actor among other actors all of which are assumed to be rational and to pursue gains and minimize losses in their dealings with one another. For microeconomics, the actors are firms in a market; for Neorealism, the actors are states in an international system. Ch. 2 (p. 18)

Middle Power: A term coined after World War II to designate states that had fewer economic and military capabilities than the two superpowers and less than major states such as Britain, but which were actively engaged in international diplomacy particularly through intergovernmental organizations such as the United Nations. Canada in those years was regarded as a quintessential example. Ch. 9 (p. 11)

Multipolarity: An arrangement of military power and political influence among four or more principal states. With the exception of the cold war, this has been the international system's characteristic organization. (See bipolarity) Ch. 8 (p. 172)

National self-determination: The principle that every people deserves its own state. Ch. 6 (p. 114)

National Treatment: A core principle of the General Agreement on Tariffs and Trade and its successor, the World Trade Organization, which holds that states must not subject foreign firms or products to special restrictions or taxes and must not favour their own firms or products with special benefits. Ch. 8 (p. 159)

Nationalism: A popular sentiment that emphasizes a particular people's distinctive qualities, distinguishing it from others and providing a rationale of purpose and virtue. Ch. 7 (p. 132)

Neo-medievalism: A term characterizing diffuse and overlapping patterns of political organization through analogies to medievel Europe. Ch. 8 (p. 180)

Neorealism: One of IR's main theories, emphasizing the anarchic nature of the international system and the primacy of states and state interests as the central phenomena. Insecurity and rivalry are its expected conditions. It was inspired by Realism's focus on power and conflict but saw it as unsystematic and used deductive method to achive universality and rigour. (See realism) Ch. 2 (p.17)

Non-falsifiability: Stating a theory in terms that prevent its ever being disproved. Non- falsifiable theories cannot be empirically tested and depend for acceptance on personal allegiance and belief. Ch. 1 (p. 7)

Non-governmental organization (NGO). Any organization whose purpose is political advocacy and which operates, domestically or internationally, free of governmental control and direct sponsorship. Ch. 9 (p. 195)

Non-tariff barrier: Government or commercial practices besides tariffs that exclude or hinder the entry of imported goods. Product standards, customs requirements and closed distribution channels are some of many possibilities. Ch. 12 (p. 311)

Norm: A standard of conduct that is contained both in formal and explicit expression, as in laws, and in informal and implicit understandings, as in social conventions. Ch. 4 (p. 58)

Ontology: The branch of philosophy that deals with the nature of being. Ch. 5 (p. 73)

Peacekeeping: Use of international military forces to enforce cease-fires. Recent use of peacekeeping has expanded to providing humanitarian protection in civil conflicts. Ch. 11 (p. 278)

Philadelphian system: A form of political integration resembling the American federal system in its initial decades, in which a central government provides vital common functions such as defence, but individual units maintain many areas of sovereign control themselves. Ch. 8 (p. 179)

Postmodernism: An eclectic movement whose main idea is denial of any authoritative basis for describing or organizing people, objects and relationships or for narrating ideas and events. Whatever authoritative statements or ideas are accepted are maintained by power and not by any inherent validity or accuracy. Ch. 5 (p. 79)

Power: The ability to alter others' preferences and actions. Ch 11. (p. 259)

Pre-emptive warfare: Acting on the belief that war is imminent or inevitable and that the other side has more advantages, attacking first to minimize those advantages. Ch. 10 (p. 236)

Prisoner's Dilemma: A two-person game in which each player's incentive to cooperate is tempered by the knowledge that the other side, by defecting, can score the largest winnings for itself. Mutual defection leaves both worse off but avoids the risk of cooperating while the other defects. Ch. 2 (p. 23)

Production offset: An arrangement in which a state purchasing large and expensive goods from another—generally military systems or large commercial items such as airliners—can produce some of the components itself, offsetting the purchase cost with technology transfer and local employment. Ch. 10 (p. 262)

Public good: A commodity or condition that is freely available to anyone. Ch. 13 (p. 343)

Rationality, assumptions of: Belief in the ability of reason to guide thought and action. Such thought accurately and dispassionately weighs and compares gains, and accommodates risk and uncertainty. Ch. 2 (p. 23)

Realism: A theory of IR which holds that struggle for power among states is the central fact and that prudent behaviour requires continuous assessment of other states' intentions and capabilities. The international system is stable when power is balanced. (See Neorealism) Ch. 2 (p. 16)

Reciprocity: The practice of responding in kind to favours or concessions. Ch. 2 (p. 23)

Relative gains: Gains that improve one side's position or advantage respective to others. Changes in the international system that are of most concern to neorealists are those that yield relative gains that adversaries can exploit. (See absolute gains) Ch. 2 (p. 20)

Right of establishment: A core principle of the General Agreement on Tariffs and Trade and its successor, the World Trade Organization, which holds that states may not arbitrarily exclude foreign firms. Ch. 8 (p. 159)

Second-strike capability: Protecting enough nuclear weapons from attack to have available a highly probable ability to retaliate. That ability deters attack. Ch. 10 (p. 247)

Security community: States that have ruled out the use of force in relations amongst themselves. Ch 2 (p. 21)

Security dilemma: A situation that exists in conditions of anarchy in which efforts to improve one's own security make others feel less secure. Ch. 10 (p. 230)

Soft power: A view of international influence that emphasizes a state's ability to assemble coalitions on important international issues and to exercise leadership through moral standing and example. Ch. 10 (p. 263)

Sovereign equality: The principle that all states have the same rights and obligations regardless of size and capability. Ch. 6 (p. 112)

Sovereignty: Effective rule within a state. The principle of sovereignty holds that the state is the highest political authority and exercises the right to conduct its domestic affairs without external interference. Ch. 6 (p. 97)

State: An international entity that possesses territory, population and a sovereign government and is recognized by other states. Ch. 6 (p. 97)

Statism: In IR, a view of political action and authority that emphasizes the role and influence of the state *vis-à-vis* civil society. Ch. 9 (p. 196)

Strategic behavior: The calculation of one's actions in light of others' purposes and likely actions. Ch. 1 (p. 2)

Structuration theory: In sociology, an analytical approach that treats individuals and society as mutually constitutive with each influencing and transforming the other. Ch. 4 (p. 57)

Superpower: A term coined by IR scholar William T.R. Fox to denote the predominant postwar positions occupied by the United States and the Soviet Union. Ch. 1 (p. 11)

Tariff: A tax on imports and exports. Ch. 12 (p. 308)

Terms of trade: A ratio of exchange that measures the units of one commodity that must be traded to obtain equivalent units of another commodity. Ch. 12 (p. 299)

Theory: An organized set of statements that seeks to order and explain the central structures and dynamics of a given set of phenomena. Ch. 1 (p. 1)

Tit-for-Tat: A strategy for serial-play Prisoner's Dilemma that assumes cooperation, punishes defections by retaliation and resumes cooperating when the other side does. (See Prisoner's Dilemma) Ch. 2 (p. 25)

Trade barrier: Any condition that hinders the flow of goods across national boundaries. The most common ones are tariffs and non-tariff barriers. (See non-tariff barriers) Ch. 8 (p. 158)

Treaty: A formal agreement between states possessing legal force and constituting one of the bases of international law. Ch. 13 (p. 321)

Index